The Military
Hardware
of
World War II

Tanks, aircraft and naval vessels

The Military
Hardware
of
World War II

Tanks, aircraft and naval vessels

Eric Grove, Christopher Chant,
David Lyon and Hugh Lyon

The Military Press
New York

Photographs
Associated Press, Bapty, Blitz Publications,
Charles E. Brown, Bundesarchiv, Fox
Photos, Holmes-Lebel, Imperial War
Museum, Keystone Press Agency, La Société
Jersiaise (Archives), Nicole Marchand, H. le
Masson, Novosti Press Agency, Popperfoto,
RAC Tank Museum, Signal, Staatsbibliothek
Berlin, Ufficiostorico Fototeca, Ferdinand
Urbahns, US Army, US National Archives,
US Navy.

This 1984 edition is published by
The Military Press, distributed
by Crown Publishers, Inc.

Printed in Italy

Library of Congress Cataloging in Publication Data
Main entry under title:

The Military hardware of World War II.

    1. Tanks (Military science)   2. Airplanes, Military.
3. Warships.   4. World War, 1939–1945––Equipment and
supplies.   I. Gilbert, Adrian.
UG446.5.M47 1984   623.74'09'044   84–16652

ISBN 0-517-45779-2 (Crown)

h g f e d c b a

Contents

Introduction

World War II saw more advances than ever before in the technology of weaponry. The impetus of that momentous struggle between the forces of Nazi Germany, Italy and Japan, and those of the Western Allies and the Soviet Union, created an unprecedented demand for munitions and machines, as highly developed industrial societies mobilised every ounce of their technological muscle for the war effort.

This book examines the way that the major nations involved in World War II developed the basic hardware of modern war – the aircraft, ships and tanks that were at the 'sharp end' of the conflict. It shows how the ideas and designs of the 1930s were modified as the terrible conflict grew in intensity, until by 1945 the modern age was heralded by the atomic bombs dropped on Hiroshima and Nagasaki.

The basic advances in weaponry that took place in World War II are with us still. Indeed, they have become the bedrock of modern military technology. Jet aircraft, guided missiles, automatic rifles, the snorkel that enabled submarines to remain submerged for long periods, all came into practical service during this conflict. The shape of the modern Main Battle Tank was defined by the Soviet T-34 and the German Panther; and the composition of the modern battle fleet, based around the aircraft carrier rather than the battleship, was first revealed.

Development was not only in technical excellence and performance, however. There was also a proliferation of types and designs, to undertake the enormously extended range of tasks necessary for modern armed forces. In aircraft, for example, there grew up a new generation of heavy bombers, capable of carrying huge loads; a specialist family of ground attack planes, such as the Shturmovik and the Tempest, was developed; long range fighters designed to establish air superiority over enemy air space, like the Mustang, came into service; and designs such as the Corsair took the development of specialist carrier aircraft still further. Tanks, too, displayed a new diversity – the 'Funnies' that were devised to sweep minefields and cross obstacles for the D-Day landings were perhaps the most extreme examples. At sea the different types of aircraft carrier and the wide range of escort vessels needed for convoy protection added new ships to the world's navies.

While there were many new types, however, some older weapons systems declined in importance. The battleship was downgraded to the role of fire support for amphibious landings, and the battlecruiser all but disappeared. The 'Cruiser' tanks that were a mainstay of Britain's armoured forces of the early 1940s had all been abandoned by 1945, and improved anti-aircraft fire rendered the torpedo bomber, long the main specialist carrier aircraft, obsolescent.

There were two final lessons that ultimately defined the development of all weapons. These were the need for greater hitting power, and for designs that were capable of easy mass production: for tanks with bigger guns that could be manufactured in great quantities; for aircraft that could pack in more and more armament while remaining the shortest possible time on the production line. In this respect, the victors of the war were very much the powers that learned how to combine adequate quality with enormous production runs. The American shipyards and steel plants and the Soviet tank factories were the keys to Allied success, providing irresistible hardware that even sophisticated German armoured vehicles and suicidal Japanese bravery could not match.

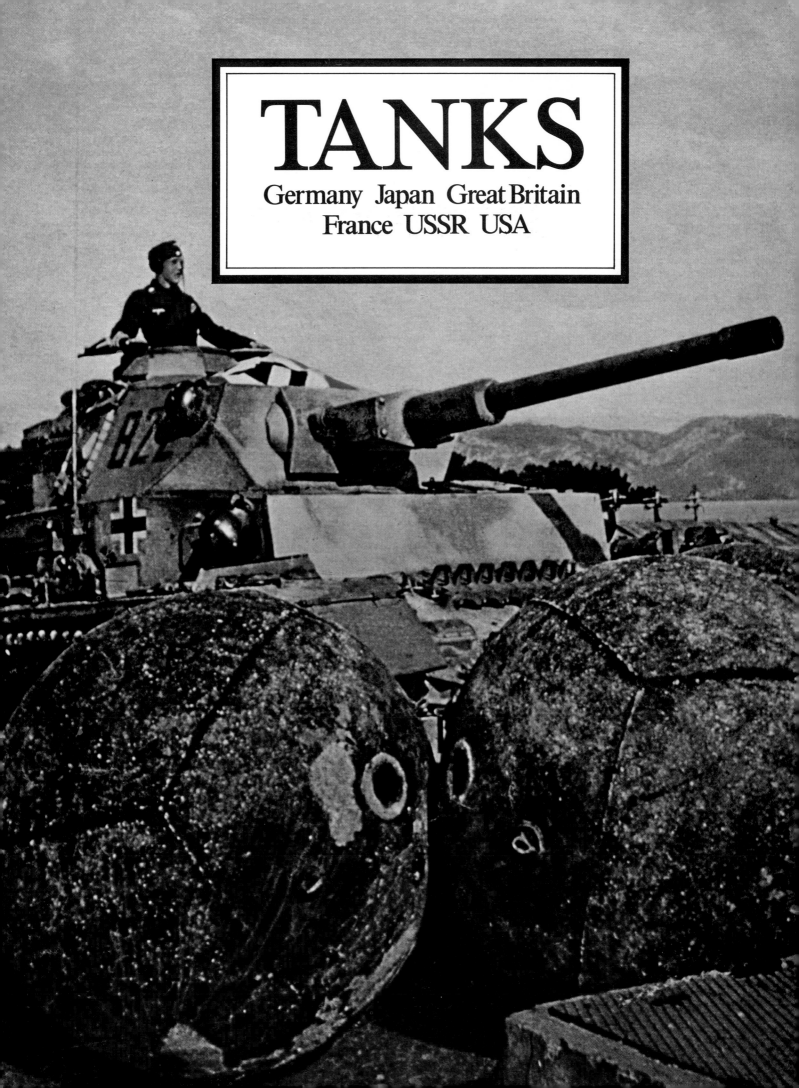

TANKS

Germany Japan Great Britain
France USSR USA

PzKpfw I and II

The *PzKpfw* I and II – originally designed as stop-gap, light, training tanks – formed the backbone of the German *Panzer* forces until well after the beginning of World War II. The *PzKpfw* I dated back to 1932 when a specification for a simple tank, to train the new armoured divisions, was issued to MAN, Krupp, Daimler Benz and Rheinmetall Borsig. Krupp were going ahead with a 'Kleintraktor' light tank and had already designed an *LKA* chassis with four coil-sprung road wheels each side and a trailing idler touching the ground. A rear-mounted, 57-hp, Krupp M305 petrol engine drove through the front sprockets. This two-man vehicle mounting two 7·9-mm MG 13 machine-guns in a small turret on the right-hand side was chosen for production, with Daimler Benz superstructure, under the pseudonym

Landwirtschaftschlepper (*LaS*) – agricultural tractor – to disguise its intended purpose.

Production began in 1934 by which time it had been fitted with smaller wheels and an external girder each side to carry the leaf-spring suspension of the rear three wheels and idler. Troop trials showed that the new tank was underpowered and the IB *LaS* May was developed with a new larger 100-bhp Maybach NL 38 TR engine. This improved the tank's power to weight ratio and ability to cover difficult ground but the already disappointing range of 91 miles (146 km) was reduced slightly to 87 miles (140 km). Weight was also increased and length from 13 feet 2 inches to 14 feet 7 inches (4·02 m to 4·42 m). Height remained 5 feet 8 inches (1·72 m), width 6 feet 10 inches (2·06 m) and armour was also unchanged at

13 mm maximum, enough to protect against small-arms fire only. The new engine necessitated a lengthened suspension with five wheels and a raised idler.

In 1935, with open rearmament, the need for subterfuge disappeared and the two tanks became *Panzerkampfwagen* I (MG) *Ausführung* A and B; about 500 and 1,300 respectively were built. Despite their lack of firepower and protection, due to delays in the development of the *PzKpfw* III and IV production continued until 1941; while at the outbreak of war they constituted over a third of Germany's tank force.

Many fought in Poland in 1939 and they also appeared in Norway and Denmark the next year. In the French campaign 523 were still on the strength of the *Panzer* divisions where good logistics made up for deficiencies in range. As late as the invasion of Russia and the campaign in the Western Desert *PzKpfw* I *Ausf* A and B were still in first-line service although by the end of 1941 most were relegated to their original training roles or had been converted.

The *PzKpfw* II dated back to 1934 when a specification was issued for an improved light tank to fill the gap caused by the delay in development of heavier vehicles. Krupp offered an *LKA* II prototype based on their previous tank but this time the MAN offering was chosen. This new *LaS* 100 chassis had six small road wheels each side, sprung in pairs between the sides of the tank and an outside girder. A 130-hp Maybach engine drove the seven-ton vehicle via the front sprocket. The driver steered using the normal clutch and brake system as on the earlier *LaS*. A turret mounting a 20-mm *KwK* 30 automatic gun, together with an *MG* 34 machine-gun was fitted and maximum armour thickness was 14·5 mm.

Limited production began in 1935 and the first 25 1/*LaS* 100s entered service as the *PzKpfw* II (2 cm) *Ausf* a1 (*SdKfz* 121). A further 25 a2 and 50 a3 followed with minor improvements to engine and suspension. A new larger (140-hp) engine was fitted to the next 100 *Ausf* bs with modified steering which upped weight to nearly eight tons. With the next limited pre-production series, *Ausf* c, a new suspension of five medium-sized, elliptically-sprung road wheels was adopted which became standard for the remainder of the series. With larger tanks still in short supply, full-scale production began in 1937 by MAN, Famo, MIAG and later Wegmann. The first production model was the *Ausf* A which was soon followed by the B and C. During this production run extra 14·5–20-mm armour was added to the hull and turret front and a new angular nose appeared.

In 1939 there were 1,226 *PzKpfw* IIs of all types in service, although by this time the deficiencies of the tank in armour and firepower had already become clear – the armour was not thick enough to withstand modern anti-tank guns and, perhaps more important, the 20-mm gun was becoming increasingly useless against more modern tanks. Nevertheless, the *PzKpfw* II proved adequate in Poland and even in France as the major single type (950 tanks) in the *Panzer* Divisions that struck on 10 May.

This initial success perhaps distorted the perspective of the High Command, which kept the *PzKpfw* II in production; although only 15 had been built in 1939 and 9 in 1940, 233 appeared in 1941. These were of a new version, *Ausf* F, with redesigned frontal plating up-armoured to 30·35 mm, but speed was reduced by 10 mph (16 km/h) due to the extra weight. A few had a new 20-mm gun, the lengthened *KwK* 38. Observation for the commander was improved by the addition of a turret cupola, a modification also added to older *PzKpfw* IIs on factory overhaul. Over 1,060 *PzKpfw* IIs were available for action during the opening weeks of the invasion of Russia but over such vast distances, and against a more heavily armed and armoured enemy, the weaknesses of the design were even more apparent. In order to make good the vehicle's deficiencies a few *PzKpfw* IIs received new armament, some being fitted with what appears from photographic evidence to be a French 37-mm *SA* 38. By April of the next year the number in action had slumped to 866 despite continued production, and increasingly they were relegated to reconnaissance duties.

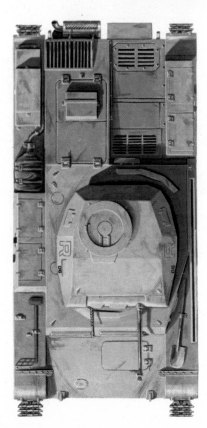

Above: *In the first winter on the Russian front PzKpfw II and III were still operating together as main battle tanks. The interesting PzKpfw II Ausf F on the right, appears to have had its puny 20-mm gun replaced with a more powerful weapon, possibly a captured French 37-mm SA-38. The cupola is also modified*

Opposite page, top: *A PzKpfw I Ausf B. Originally conceived as stop-gap, light training tanks, these little vehicles remained in first-line service until 1942. The earlier Ausf A had only four similar road wheels each side and return rollers trailing at ground level*

Opposite page, bottom: *A PzKpfw II Ausf B in action in Russia in 1941. Pre-production variants of PzKpfw II, which included A, B, and C models, saw operational service during the opening campaigns of the war. The Ausf B was fitted with 14·5-mm armour and weighed nearly eight tons; the early suspension with external girder can be clearly seen in the photograph*

PzKpfw II Ausf F
Weight 9.35 tons (9.5 tonnes)
Crew three
Armament one 20-mm KwK 30 gun with 180 rounds and one 7.92-mm MG 34 machine-gun with 2,550 rounds
Armour hull nose 35 mm, driver's plate 30 mm, sides 20 mm, decking 10 mm, belly 5 mm, tail 15 mm; turret front 30 mm, sides 20 mm, rear 15 mm, top 10 mm
Engine one Maybach HL 62 TR inline six-cylinder liquid-cooled petrol, 140-hp
Speed 25 mph (40 km/h)
Range 118 miles (190 km)
Trench crossing 5 feet 7 inches (1.7 m)
Vertical step 1 foot 4½ inches (42 cm)
Fording 3 feet (90 cm)
Length 15 feet 9 inches (4.81 m)
Width 7 feet 6 inches (2.28 m)
Height 6 feet 8 inches (2.02 m)

Left: *A PzKpfw Ausf F captured from 10th Panzer division in Tunisia. It is painted sand yellow and the turret markings are those of a headquarters vehicle of one of the division's Panzer regiments. A Panzer regiment HQ had up to five such reconnaissance tanks.*

PzKpfw III

In 1935, after experience gained with the design of smaller tanks had been consolidated, a specification was issued for the larger 15-ton 'light tank' which Guderian intended to be the major weapon of his armoured divisions. It was to have a high-velocity gun and have a five man crew – gunner, loader, driver, wireless operator and commander – to enable each member to concentrate on his own tasks. For maximum liaison, communications between driver, wireless operator and commander were connected to the external radio. There was considerable debate over the armament of the new vehicle. The Mechanized Troops Inspectorate wanted a 50-mm weapon but the Ordnance Department felt that the standard infantry 37-mm anti-tank gun would be sufficient. The latter view eventually prevailed and the smaller weapon was chosen but it was also decided that the turret ring would be made large enough for up-gunning should it become necessary.

In 1936 the first prototypes appeared designated *Zugführerwagen* (*ZW* – platoon commander's vehicle) from MAN, Krupp, Rheinmetall Borsig and Daimler Benz. The last-named version was chosen and the first ten production vehicles, designated 1/*ZW Ausf* A, built. The initial suspension consisted of five, large, coil-sprung road wheels each side, but the development of the tank was seriously delayed by a long search to find a better design. It was only just before the outbreak of war, after three years' time-consuming development that the definitive suspension was fitted to the *Ausf* E using torsion bars connected to six medium-sized road wheels each side. A completely new, advanced Maybach pre-selector transmission was also fitted with ten forward speeds and one

reverse; gear change and steering were both power-assisted. The design of the front plate was improved with new driver's visor and machine-gun mounting. The armour thickness was 30 mm; the engine, a 120 TR of 300 hp, gave a top speed of 25 mph (40 km/h). 41 *Ausf* E were built and after successful trials this design was standardized as the *PzKpfw* III (3·7 cm) (*SdKfz* 141); in September 1939, 98 of the above *Ausf* A to E pre-production tanks were available for service with the *Panzer Lehr* (Demonstration) Battalion and a few examples with the Panzer Divisions for the invasion of Poland.

To speed up production, manufacture of the *PzKpfw* III was spread out among several firms – Alkett, Wegmann, Daimler Benz, Henschel, Famo, MAN and MNH – and the hull of the *PzKpfw* III was divided into four prefabricated welded assemblies – hull, front superstructure, rear superstructure and turret. But output was slow as the concerns chosen for the programme were unused to the mass-production of motor vehicles and others such as Ford and Opel were not considered due to the fact that they were not nationally owned. The first major production

PzKpfw III Ausf E
Armament one 45-calibre 37-mm KwK gun with 120 rounds and three 7.92-mm MG 34 machine-guns with 3,750 rounds.
Other details as PzKpfw III Ausf F

Above: *A PzKpfw III Ausf E as used in the conquest of France in 1940. Note the 45-calibre 37-mm gun with internal mantlet and lack of turret stowage bin. The camouflage is based on the standard contemporary dark 'Panzer Grey' with green patches added for combat service. With this model and earlier types two 7.92-mm MG 34 machine-guns were usually mounted co-axially with the main armament; 120 rounds of 37-mm ammunition were carried. Only 41 of this type were built and they constituted the last of a long line of pre-production variants. The Ausf E introduced the standard PzKpfw III torsion bar suspension. PzKpfw III Ausf E tanks were later fitted with 50-mm guns*
Below: *A PzKpfw III Ausf E loaded down with extra stowage bins finds its wider tracks useful in the final unsuccessful push for Moscow in December 1941. A national flag is draped over the turret for identification*

PzKpfw III Ausf F
Weight 20 tons (20.3 tonnes)
Crew five
Armament one 50-mm KwK L/42 gun with 99
rounds and two 7.92-mm MG 34 machine-guns
with 3,750 rounds
Armour hull nose 30 mm, glacis 25 mm, driver's
plate 30 mm, sides 30 mm, decking 17 mm, belly
16 mm, tail 21 mm; turret front, sides and rear
30 mm, top 10 mm
Engine one Maybach HL 120 TRM V-12 water-
cooled petrol, 300-hp
Speed 25 mph (40 km/h)
Range 109 miles (175 km)
Trench crossing 7 feet 7 inches (2.3 m)
Vertical step 2 feet (60 cm)
Fording 2 feet 7 inches (80 cm)
Overall length 17 feet 9 inches (5.41 m)
Width 9 feet 7 inches (2.92 m)
Height 8 feet 3 inches (2.51 m)

Above: *The Ausf F was the first major production
variant of the PzKpfw III. Note the 42-calibre
50-mm gun in an external mantlet, turret ventilator and stowage box. Early Ausf Fs had similar
guns and mantlets to the Ausf E illustrated previously. This particular tank is one of those sent
to Africa to form Deutsche Afrika Korps: note the
palm tree and swastika marking on the left hull
front. Next to it is the divisional sign of the 15th
Panzer Division, sent to reinforce Rommel*

mark was the *Ausf* F, little changed from the E except for improved brake ventilation and a slightly modified 300-hp TRM engine.

By the end of 1939, 157 *PzKpfw* IIIs of all types had been built and by May 1940 there were 349 available to take part in the French invasion. Another 39 converted to armoured command vehicles enabled higher commanders of *Panzer* formations to stay up with their leading troops, a vital aid in blitzkrieg operations. On 10 May, 1940 the majority of *PzKpfw* IIIs were concentrated in Guderian's XIX *Panzer* Corps, whose task it was to make the decisive break-through in the Ardennes. Here their success was due more to the *PzKpfw* IIIs good crew layout, which assisted well co-ordinated mobile operations, than to its rather poor armament and protection. The L/45 37-mm gun with a muzzle velocity of 2,500 fps (762 m/s) could not penetrate any but the least protected enemy tanks and 30-mm armour was little protection from most Allied guns. The shortcomings of this gun had become apparent long before and in 1939 orders had been given to Krupp to develop a new 50-mm tank gun for the *PzKpfw* III. Forty *Ausf* Gs, with the new 50-mm *KwK* L/42, were rushed into action before the end of the French campaign but had little affect on the outcome.

After the lessons of France, Hitler ordered the up-gunning of the *PzKpfw* III with the longer L/60 50-mm anti-tank gun; but to save time the Army continued fitting the L/42. *Ausf* Es and Fs were retro-fitted with this gun which was in a new external mantlet. The 1940 model tanks, the *Ausf* Gs with slightly modified cupolas and driver's visors, were fitted as new – although the first Gs had 37-mm guns as the 50-mm remained in short supply. Some Gs were fitted with air filters and improved ventilation as *Ausf* G (*Tp*) (Tropical) and these served in the Western Desert. In this theatre, although the *PzKpfw* III was vulnerable to the British two-pounder (40-mm) gun (at least until later increases in protection) its armament proved effective against all British tanks except the Matilda. Although the 50-mm gun's AP performance was less good

in actual penetration, its projectile carried a high explosive charge, inflicting more permanent damage on enemy armour than that of the British two-pounder's (40-mm) solid shot. High explosive shells were also carried, useful for action against anti-tank guns; it was a particular weakness of British tanks that their two-pounder (40-mm) guns did not have this facility.

At the end of 1940 yet another new version appeared, the *Ausf* H which embodied the results of combat experience in improved armour protection. Extra 30-mm plates were bolted and welded to the hull front; wider tracks of 400 as against 360 mm were introduced to compensate for the extra weight and there was a new manual gear-box with only six forward speeds as the older one had been unnecessarily complex. Older models were retro-fitted to the new standards. There was also a command

version (*Panzerbefehlswagen* III *Ausf* C, later H) with a dummy gun. Used in North Africa from 1941 the up-armoured *PzKpfw* IIIs (both *Ausf* H and *Ausf* G modified in the field) proved unexpectedly difficult to defeat with the two-pounder (40-mm) gun, previously effective against the 30-mm plates.

When the Germans invaded Russia 1,440 *PzKpfw* IIIs were available for service. Initially, 965 were used and they were the backbone of the strongest *Panzer* divisions' tank regiments, equipping two out of the three companies of each of their tank battalions. In addition to the standard vehicles there were others fitted for deep wading which were used in the initial offensive across the River Bug and later across the Dnieper. The *PzKpfw* III was adequate for dealing with the older Soviet tanks but the KV and *T-34* tanks with their thick well-shaped

armour and powerful guns proved difficult to defeat. Up-gunning could no longer be postponed and as Hitler was furious that his orders had been ignored, plans for the development of a tank version of the longer L/60 50-mm weapon were at last put in hand.

The new *Ausf* J (*SdKfz* 141/1) was built with heavier armour of 50 mm all round, which was stronger than the 60-mm welded appliqué armour of its predecessors. The driver's visor was again changed and a new ball-mounting

Above: *All types of PzKpfw III from Ausf F onwards fought in North Africa. The protection of this early Ausf J with short 50-mm gun has been modified to Ausf L standard with extra 20-mm spaced armour on the driver's plate and mantlet. The tank was knocked out during the battles around Alamein in 1942*
Left: *One of the 75-mm armed PzKpfw III Ausf N gunfire support tanks attached to the 501st Heavy Tank Battalion of Tigers knocked out in Tunisia. This PzKpfw III model was sometimes known as the Sturmpanzer III and was designed to provide a suitable infantry support tank for the Panzergrenadier divisions*

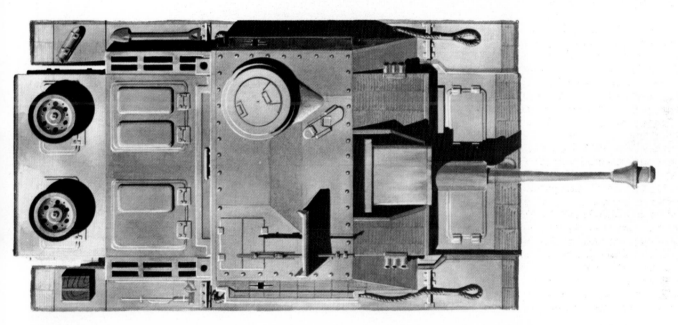

for the hull *MG* 34 adopted. Mechanical steering was fitted and other details changed to assist mass-production. From November the new L/60 50-mm gun began to be fitted and 40 *Ausf* Js were constructed by the end of the year with this weapon. The *KwK* 39 L/60 had a muzzle velocity with normal AP rounds of 2,700 fps (822 m/s), or 3,835 fps (1168 m/s) with *PzGr* 40, but even this was soon found to be insufficient. These first 'Mark III Specials' only reached the Western Desert in May 1942.

Only 862 *PzKpfw* IIIs had been built in 1940 and when the invasion of Russia boosted demand to 7,992 vehicles for 36 *Panzer* divisions (twice the total existing German armoured fighting vehicle strength) German industry, demobilized from a not very high level of war production after the fall of France, was hard pressed to meet its targets. Plans to develop a replacement 22 ton *VK* 2001 (DB) or *ZW* 40 tank were soon dropped and another factory MIAG was brought into the *PzKpfw* III programme. Still only 1,713 tanks of this type were built in 1941 and even by 1942 production targets of 190 vehicles a month were not being met. Some of these were of yet another model, the

Ausf L, also L/60 armed. To increase protection at low cost, a spaced 20-mm armour plate was added to the mantlet and hull front. A special *Ausf* L *(Trop)* was developed with improved ventilation, filters and hatches; these were widely used in North Africa from mid-1942.

Some 2,605 *PzKpfw* IIIs were built in 1942 (1,907 with the *KwK* 39) as German industry at last began to mobilize itself for total war. In order to simplify production the next *Ausf* M dispensed with the vision ports and escape hatches in the hull sides and it was also modified to wade up to five feet (1·52 m). By the end of the year the *PzKpfw* III was outmoded as a battle tank and the final variant appeared as the *Ausf* N (*SdKfz* 141/2) close support tank with low velocity L/24 75-mm guns taken from *PzKpfw* IVs. This gun had inferior AP performance to the 50-mm L/60 but it was a better weapon for HE support and the N was designed to provide the vehicles for the tank battalions of *Panzer-grenadier* divisions. Some were also allocated to *Tiger* heavy tank battalions. The first were *Ausf* L modified to N standard and saw action by the end of 1942; 660 were converted or built new up to August 1943.

Sturmgeschutz III Ausf G
Weight 23.5 tons (23.9 tonnes)
Crew four
Armament one 75-mm StuK 40 (L/48) gun with 54 rounds and one 7.92-mm MG 34 machine-gun with 600 rounds
Armour nose 80 mm, driver's plate 50 and 30 mm, sides 30 mm, decking 11–17 mm, belly 16 mm, tail 30 mm
Range 105 miles (169 km)
Overall length 22 feet 2½ inches (6.77 m)
Width 9 feet 8½ inches (2.96 m)
Height 7 feet 1¼ inches (2.15 m)
Other details as PzKpfw III Ausf F

Above: *These Sturmgeschutz III Ausf G assault guns, were widely produced from late 1942. Originally under the control of the artillery arm, they were first organized into 18-gun assault gun battalions each of 3 batteries of 6 vehicles. These were later enlarged into army assault artillery brigades of up to 45 assault guns (3 batteries of 14 with 3 HQ vehicles) and a small infantry component. Assault guns were the élite troops of the artillery with an impressive record against enemy armour – 20,000 enemy tanks claimed by early 1944 alone*

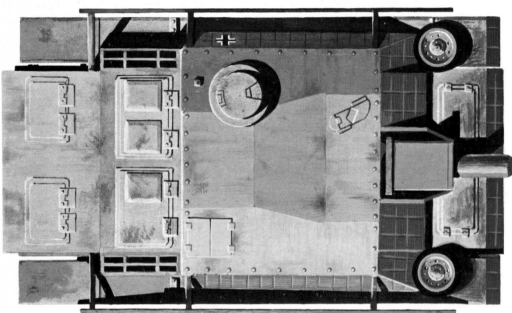

10.5-cm Sturmhaubitze 42 Ausf G
Armament one L/28 105-mm howitzer with
36 rounds and one 7.92-mm MG 34 machine-gun
with 600 rounds
Overall length 20 feet 1½ inches (6.13 m)
Other details as StuG III Ausf G

Above: *The 10.5-cm Sturmhaubitze 42 Ausf G is
basically the same as the StuG except for the
L/28 105-mm howitzer. This model has Schürtzen
protective plates fitted as was commonly done on
StuG vehicles and late model PzKpfw III tanks.
Early StuH 42s had muzzle brakes and later
StuG and StuH were fitted with better-shaped
rounded mantlets. Muzzle brakes of a new design
were adopted with some of these later StuH 42.
A 1944 type army assault artillery brigade would
contain one platoon of StuH 42 in each of its
three batteries, a total of 12 assault howitzers
per brigade. These, together with the 33 75-mm
armed StuG III, gave a powerful high velocity
armour piercing/low velocity high explosive mix
of capabilities to the unit*
Left: *A typical StuG III Ausf G fully fitted out
with protective Schürtzen abandoned to the
enemy. Note the extra armour fitted to the nose
and superstructure front*

Construction of *PzKpfw* III tanks ceased in order that production resources could be concentrated on the production of *Sturmgeschütze* (assault guns). These originated with infantry demands for an armoured close-support artillery vehicle, very necessary if all tanks were to be concentrated in the *Panzer* divisions. Daimler Benz developed a vehicle based on the *PzKpfw* III chassis with a low 50-mm armoured superstructure in which was mounted a limited traverse 75-mm L/24 tank gun. Thirty were ordered for troop trials and some took part in the invasion of France in May and June 1940 helping to clear the roads through the Ardennes. These operational tests were successful and the vehicle was ordered into production as the *Gepanzerte Selbstfahrlafette für Sturmgeschutz 7·5-cm Kanone* (*SdKfz* 142), normally shortened to *StuG* III. The *Ausf* A version was mounted on an *Ausf* F (5/*ZW*) tank chassis with no side escape hatches. Alkett, the major *PzKpfw* III contractor, had built 184 by the end of 1940. With the introduction of the new *Ausf* H tank chassis the model letter changed to B, – the C and D assault gun models were basically similar. An E version was developed as a commander's vehicle with extra radio facilities. Although production was concentrated on the *PzKpfw* III tank, 548 of these assault guns were produced in 1941.

In September, Hitler, to whom the concept appealed for its economy of resources, demanded that *StuG* vehicles should be up-armoured and up-gunned. As an interim measure some were fitted with a 33-calibre 75-mm gun but by February 1942 a version of the L/43 75-mm gun

of the contemporary *PzKpfw* IV had been fitted and demonstrated to the *Führer* as the 7·5-cm *Sturmgeschutz* 40 *Ausf* F (*SdKfz* 142/1). After 119 vehicles the weapon was changed to the L/48 gun and this changed the designation to *Ausf* F/8. At the end of 1942, again in accordance with Hitler's wishes, 80-mm armour was fitted by means of bolting on an extra 30-mm plate over the existing 50-mm base. This produced the *Ausf* G which also had a commander's cupola and, often, a shield-mounted machine-gun. Production of these continued until the end of the war. These assault guns were in reality turretless tanks and increasing numbers were produced by Alkett, MIAG and Krupp as Germany's need for large numbers of mobile, armoured high-velocity guns outstripped her tank building capabilities. In 1942, 791 *StuG* IIIs of all types were constructed, no less than 3,041 *Ausf* Gs in 1943 and 4,850 in 1944 – 123 were produced in 1945.

With such a large amount of German resources going into assault guns and given the German tendency for competing authorities it was natural that a struggle should break out over their control between the artillery to whom they were first allocated and Guderian who wished to utilize the *StuG* IIIs to spin out his limited armoured strength and provide better anti-tank protection for the infantry divisions. The artillery strongly resisted the Inspector General of Armoured Troops' claim and it was not until the end of 1943 that assault gun units came under full armoured control.

In addition to the 75-mm gun *StuG* there was

a version mounting a 105-mm howitzer with greater HE power though at the expense of armour penetration capability. These first used the *Ausf* F superstructure but the production vehicles were 10·5-cm *Sturmhaubitze* 42 *Ausf* G (*SdKfz* 142/2). Nine 105-mm *StuH* IIIs were constructed in 1942 (including prototype), 204 in 1943 and 904 in 1944. Another assault variant mounted the 150-mm sIG 33 infantry gun. In all 15,350 *PzKpfw* III chassis were built.

PzKpfw IIIs were supplied to Hungary and friendly neutrals such as Spain and Turkey also received them. Captured examples were used by the Free Polish forces for training in the Middle East while the Soviets converted others into assault guns with 76·2-mm guns (with or without muzzle brake) in a slightly higher superstructure than the *StuG* III. As the *SU 76I* this served against its former owners and some were recaptured by the Germans and used 'third hand'! The *PzKpfw* III survived the war in the armies of Eastern Europe.

The *StuG* III was also supplied to allies, Finland, Rumania and Bulgaria receiving examples from the Germans and some were even acquired by Syria after the war.

Below: *When captured by Soviet forces PzKpfw III and Sturmgeschütze were often pressed into service against their former owners. Some PzKpfw III tanks were re-armed with 76.2-mm guns and others were converted by the Russians into assault guns. This Ausf J, however, appears to be in its original condition, as are the StuG IIIs supporting it in the usual Soviet style*

PzKpfw IV

The *PzKpfw* IV was the only German battle tank to remain in production throughout the war years and it became the major such vehicle of the German army. This, however, had never been intended. Originally the IV was seen as an artillery support vehicle only to the lighter tanks in the *Panzer* Division, equipping one company in a battalion. Hence a low-velocity, relatively high-calibre gun was fitted in order to obtain a good high-explosive capability.

The first prototype appeared in 1934 from Rheinmetall-Borsig under the pseudonym *Bataillonsführerwagen* (battalion commander's vehicle) and used a version of that firm's standard tractor. Both Krupp and MAN also designed prototypes with advanced interleaved wheel suspensions but, in order to get the tank into production quickly, the various features were combined together with the leaf-spring coupled bogie suspension of the Krupp design for the *Zugführerwagen* specification, and the result was produced by the latter manufacturer as the *I/BW Ausf* A.

The specification had called for a tank of no more than 24 tons due to the limitations of the standard German bridge although the first vehicles only weighed just over 17 tons. The suspension, which remained standard for the whole series, was composed of four pairs of wheels and there were four return rollers; a standard 250-hp Maybach HL 108R petrol engine was fitted, driving through the front sprockets and producing a speed of 18·2 mph (30 km/h); and the five-man crew were dispersed in the same efficient way as in the *PzKpfw* III, with similar communication equipment. The L/24 75-mm gun was mounted in the turret with a co-axial MG 34 machine-gun; a second machine-gun was in the hull front, set back a little from the driver's position. The turret had electrical traverse. Again, as in the early III, hull armour was thin, a mere 14·5 mm on the hull and 20 mm on the turret. Production and troop trials were dilatory and only 35 were constructed in 1937–8. In the year of Munich 42 *Ausf* Bs were manufactured and 140 *Ausf* Cs in 1938–9. These introduced HL 120 engines and 30-mm armour on hull (B) and turret (C) fronts. Both had new straight superstructure fronts from which the machine-gun had been deleted. The old layout was restored in the *Ausf* D which appeared in September 1939. 248 of this new model were ordered.

Combat experience showed that although the type was basically sound and could finally be officially adopted for service as the *PzKpfw* IV (7·5-cm) (*SdKfz* 161) it needed further up-armouring if it was to act as a real back-up to the *PzKpfw* III. Hence the next model, the *Ausf* E, production of which began in late 1940, had a thicker nose and appliqué plates added to the front and sides to bring protection up to 50–60 mm; older models were retro-fitted. On the *Ausf* E a new type of visor and cupola was adopted and the latter was moved forward in the turret. In mid 1941 production of the definitive version began, the *Ausf* F. This reverted to a single, and therefore stronger, 50-mm front plate; a new ball machine-gun mount was fitted and the driver's visor was altered again; weight was up to over 22 tons and wider tracks were fitted (400 mm instead of 380 mm) which necessitated a widened front sprocket.

Below: A PzKpfw IV Ausf E knocked out and captured in December 1941 near Sidi Rezegh. Note the extra armour on the superstructure front (30 mm) and the sides (20 mm) and the new lower cupola. The Afrika Korps badge is on a patch of Panzer Grey left when the tank was roughly camouflaged in desert yellow

PzKpfw IV Ausf D
Weight 19.7 tons (20 tonnes)
Crew five
Armament one 75-mm KwK L/24 gun with 80 rounds and two 7.92-mm MG 34 machine-guns with 2,800 rounds
Armour basic: hull nose 30 mm, glacis 20 mm, driver's plate 30 mm, sides 20 mm, decking 11 mm, belly 10–20 mm, tail 20 mm; turret front 30 mm, sides and rear 20 mm, top 10 mm
Engine one Maybach HL 120 TRM V-12 water-cooled petrol, 300-hp
Speed 26 mph (42 km/h)
Range 125 miles (200 km)
Trench crossing 7 feet 7 inches (2.3 m)
Vertical step 2 feet (60 cm)
Fording 2 feet 7½ inches (80 cm)
Overall length 19 feet 4½ inches (5.91 m)
Width 9 feet 7 inches (2.92 m)
Height 8 feet 6 inches (2.59 m)

Above: *By 1943–4 most PzKpfw IVs in action were fully equipped with long 75-mm guns and Schürtzen plates, 8 mm around the turret and 5 mm on the sides. These new Ausf H vehicles (note the single cupola hatch) advancing through the outskirts of a Russian town have only the extra turret protection*
Right: *The PzKpfw IV Ausf D was introduced in 1939. Its external mantlet for the 75-mm gun and re-adoption of 7.92-mm hull machine-gun distinguished it externally from the preceding Ausf C. The driver's plate was 'stepped back' on the right side. Tanks of this type were progressively up-armoured and fitted with new long 75-mm guns to bring them up to the latest standards. After this model, a new type of cupola was adopted. This tank is in the condition in which it might have fought in the French campaign of 1940, or in the opening year of the campaign in Russia. The fitting under the gun is a deflector to protect the tank's aerials from the blast of the short weapon*

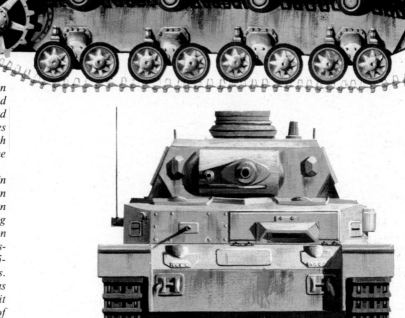

Altogether 278 *PzKpfw* IVs of various models were available with the medium companies of the ten *Panzer* divisions that attacked France in 1940. They provided some useful support being just able to defeat the armour of most Allied tanks. They were the only German tanks with powerful guns, and, despite their small numbers, their presence was often decisive.

Limited production continued at Krupp in 1941 and by the time Germany attacked Russia about 580 *PzKpfw* IVs were available. Demand was stepped up with the proposed expansion to 36 Armoured Divisions in July but by April 1942 the number of *PzKpfw* IVs in service had barely risen above the numbers available the year before; more factories were brought into the programme and numbers finally increased from 480 in 1941 to 964 in 1942. But this was still hardly enough as it was becoming apparent that the *PzKpfw* IV was the only German tank capable of up-gunning to penetrate the well-shaped armour of the *T-34s* and KV-1s. A long 75-mm gun, the *KsK* 40 L/43 tank gun was produced and fitted from March 1942 to the new *Ausf* F2 version of the *PzKpfw* IV – the earlier *Ausf* F now became F1. With a muzzle velocity with ordinary shot of 2,428 fps (740 m/s), and a penetration against 30-degree armour of 89 mm, this gun allowed *Panzer* units to face up to the Soviet tanks on equal terms.

A further model, the *Ausf* G, appeared in 1942 with slightly improved protection and an improved double-baffle muzzle brake on the gun. Older IVs were brought up to the latest standard as they returned to Germany for overhaul. In March 1943, in accordance with Hitler's orders of the previous year, the *Ausf* H, with 80-mm armour and an L/48 75-mm gun (2,461 fps) was introduced. To increase protection from infantry thin, 5-mm *Schürzen* (side plates) were fitted and with Guderian's encouragement production increased: 3,073 *PzKpfw* IVs were built in 1943 and 3,161 more in 1944 to 1945. From March 1944 these were the last model, the *Ausf* J, with the electrical turret traverse replaced by a purely manual arrangement. As well as simplyifying production this also allowed an extra fuel tank to be fitted, boosting the range to 200 miles (322 km). Wire mesh *Schürtzen* were fitted to lower weight and material demands, and a new idler was also fitted. *Ostkette* wide tracks also began to be adopted from the late summer of 1944 to improve mobility.

Below: 'Guderian's Duck'. This side view of an early L/48-armed Jagdpanzer IV illustrates the vehicle's low silhouette. The muzzle brake on the L/48 gun proved something of a problem – raising a great deal of dust from the deflected blast – and was later deleted

Bottom: Something of a rarity, this Bergepanzer IV recovery vehicle was knocked out in North Africa. Indeed, this may well have been the only PzKpfw IV chassis, an Ausf D, so modified. An extra weapon, possibly a flame-thrower, appears to have been added in the driver's visor, giving this specialized vehicle a useful combat capability

In June 1944 Hitler ordered that production of the *PzKpfw* IV should be abandoned to concentrate on its tank destroyer derivative, the *Jagdpanzer* IV, which had the 3,068 fps (935 m/s) L/70 gun of the *Panther* in a limited-traverse mounting. This vehicle dated from 1942 when a request had gone out for a new heavy assault gun with 100-mm armour. Guderian was against the project from the start; he was satisfied with the development capability of the *StuG* III and was loath to diversify production of the *PzKpfw* IV which he regarded as the mainstay of the armoured forces. Development of what was to be nicknamed 'Guderian's Duck' was slow and an interim assault gun on the IV chassis with a standard *StuG* III superstructure and an L/48 75-mm gun was designed. On some of these *Sturmgeschutz* IV assault guns (*SdKfz* 163) concrete armour was added, particularly over the driver's compartment where it could be up to 100 mm thick. About 1,000 were built in 1944, on *Ausf* H and *Ausf* J chassis, and issued to both tank battalions and artillery assault gun battalions.

The *Jagdpanzer* IV had meanwhile been developed with the same L/48 gun as it took time to develop a suitable L/70 weapon. Frontal protection was 60 mm with 30-mm armour fitted at the sides. Early vehicles carried a muzzle brake on the gun but as it was mounted so low – only four feet seven inches (1·40 m) above the ground – this led to a great deal of dust from the deflected blast and later vehicles had this deleted. The L/70 was eventually adapted and armour thickness was also increased to 80 mm (front) and 40 mm (sides).

Small numbers of *PzKpfw* IV/70, as the up-gunned *Jagdpanzer* IV was redesignated, were in action by August 1944. Its armament made it a formidable defensive weapon, particularly in the west against less well-protected British and American armour. However, despite ambitious production schedules only 1,531 *Jagdpanzer* IVs of all types were constructed. They usually served with the tank destroyer battalions of *Panzer* divisions.

Later examples were built with a slightly modified chassis incorporating features from the *PzKpfw* III tank, notably three return rollers instead of four. This reflected a final abortive attempt to rationalize the production of the two basic German tracked AFV chassis and

develop a common III/IV chassis on which various vehicles could be mounted. For example, Alkett designed a *Geschützwagen* (gun carriage) III/IV on a front-engined *PzKpfw* IV chassis with the sprockets and final drive of the III. There were four return rollers and the gun was carried in a lightly armoured superstructure at the rear. The most numerous vehicle on this chassis was the *Hummel* (Bumblebee) (*SdKfz* 165) which mounted a 150-mm FH 18/1 heavy field howitzer. The prototype vehicle had a muzzle brake and was mounted on a standard *PzKpfw* IV chassis but production vehicles had a clean barrel and the III/IV modifications. From 1942, 666 were built and they equipped the heavy batteries of the artillery battalions of favoured *Panzer* divisions.

From 1943 another version of the III/IV gun carriage appeared, mounting the 71-calibre 88-mm *PaK* 43/1 anti-tank gun. This heavy new weapon needed a self-propelled platform in the difficult conditions of the Eastern Front; the *Nashorn* (Rhinoceros) gave heavy tank destroyer brigades a new mobility, although for a direct fire weapon armour protection was poor. Some 150 chassis were completed as gunless ammunition carriers for both the anti-tank gun and also the howitzer variants.

Due to a mixture of conservatism and the tactical disadvantages of existing vehicles, with their high prominent superstructures and limited-traverse mounts, the artillery arm was not very happy with the concept of the self-propelled gun. Development, therefore, began on a series of *Waffenträger* (weapon carrier) vehicles which allowed the gun to be dismounted if necessary and also provided the lighter weapons with all round traverse. Two models mounting the 105-mm Le FH were produced, the *Heuschrecke* (Grasshopper) built on a slightly lengthened version of the *PzKpfw* IV chassis and a less specialized version using the III/IV gun carriage. Both proved difficult to operate and were never put into production.

The need for a heavy assault howitzer had become apparent during the severe street fighting in Russia in 1941–2 where existing tanks and armoured assault guns had insufficient high-explosive capability to deal with well-protected buildings and fortifications, and existing heavy howitzers were too lightly protected. Hitler felt the problem could be solved by a much more

Panzerjäger III/IV Nashorn (Rhinoceros)
Weight 23.6 tons (24 tonnes)
Crew four
Armament one 88-mm PaK 43/1 (L/71) gun with 40 rounds
Armour hull nose and driver's plate 30 mm, glacis 10 mm, sides 20 mm, decking and belly 15 mm, tail 22 mm, superstructure 10 mm
Fording 3 feet 3 inches (1 m)
Overall length 27 feet 8½ inches (8.44 m)
Width 9 feet 8 inches (2.95 m)
Height 9 feet 7½ inches (2.94 m)
Other details as Ausf D tank

Above: *A total of 473 of these heavy tank destroyers were constructed on the Geschützwagen III/IV, a front-engined PzKpfw IV chassis with the transmission and final drive of the PzKpfw III. The vehicle's earlier name was Hornisse (Hornet) but this was changed at Hitler's insistence to the more aggressive Nashorn (Rhinoceros)*

heavily armoured mounting for the 150-mm *sIG* 33 heavy infantry gun which would have to go on the *PzKpfw* IV chassis. The vehicles were ordered in October 1942 and in service by April of the next year as *Sturmpanzer* IV *Brummbär* (Grizzly Bear) *Sdkfz* 166. Early Grizzly Bears were on the *Ausf* F and *Ausf* G chassis with a relatively high armoured superstructure with 100-mm sloping plates at the front and 70-mm protection at the sides, with a new version of the infantry gun the *SturmHaubitze* 43 L/12 in a ball mounting in the frontal plate. Later models on the H and J chassis had several differences, notably a modified gun-mounting with longer 'collar', a new driver's compartment with periscopes and in the last production run a new roomier superstructure with a machine-gun, lack of which had proved a serious weakness. A total of 313 Grizzly Bears saw service with independent *Sturmpanzer* battalions and the artillery units of *Panzer* divisions in Russia, Italy and France. They were powerful, if specialized, vehicles in the infantry support role but reliability could be erratic due to the chassis being overloaded.

As the war progressed so the Germans began to lose air superiority and their armoured units became very vulnerable to Allied air attack. Suitable protection was urgently required and from 1943 *PzKpfw* IV chassis were diverted to become *Flakpanzer* IV anti-aircraft vehicles. Hitler demanded a *Flakpanzer* with twin 37-mm guns but as an interim measure either a single

Sturmpanzer IV Brummbär (Grizzly Bear)
Weight 27.7 tons (28.2 tonnes)
Crew five
Armament one 150-mm StuH 53 (L/12) howitzer
with 38 rounds
Armour hull nose 80 mm, sides 30 mm, decking
and tail 20 mm, belly 10 mm; superstructure
front 100 mm, sides 30–70 mm, top 20 mm,
rear 20–60 mm
Speed 24 mph (38 km/h)
Trench crossing 7 feet 3 inches (2.2 m)
Fording 3 feet 1½ inches (95 cm)
Height 8 feet (2.44 m)
Other details as Ausf D tank

Right: *A middle production Brummbär built in
1944 after the success of the first 60 built in late
Spring 1943. Note the long 'sleeve' on the howitzer
barrel and the heavily armoured driver's position
with periscopes, instead of direct vision as on the
earlier model. PzKpfw IV type Schürtzen were
usually carried by these vehicles. The last Brummbär produced had a new superstructure with more
vertical sides. Sturmpanzer battalions could de-
ploy up to 45 of these powerful assault howitzers*

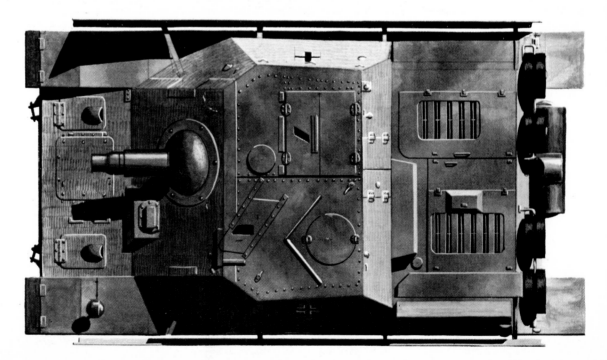

37-mm *FlaK* 43 or the quadruple 20-mm *Flakvierling* 38 was mounted in a high open 10-mm protected superstructure, the sides of which could drop to give all round traverse – if little protection to the gun crew who were behind a small open shield. However, they did provide some degree of extra mobility for the anti-aircraft platoons of tank regiments and 211 of these high, box-shaped *'Mobelwagen'* (furniture vans) were converted from *Ausf* H and J chassis.

A much better vehicle appeared in December 1943 which put the *Flakvierling* weapon in a 16-mm armoured revolving turret. This was known as *Wirbelwind* (Whirlwind) and was built by Ostbau using an *Ausf* J chassis. It was supplemented from March 1944 by the *Ostwind* (East Wind), built by Deutsche Eisenwerke, which put the 37-mm *FlaK* 43 in a slightly better protected 25-mm turret. The rates of fire of these weapons were respectively 800 to 1,800 rounds per minute and 80 to 160 rounds. Some 140 *Wirbelwind* and 40 *Ostwind* vehicles were built and some saw service but they could not do a great deal to mitigate the effects of Allied air power. However, even these vehicles were only considered as interim designs due to their open-topped turrets. A more permanent *leichte Flakpanzer* IV *Kugelblitz* (Fireball) was developed and built by Deutsche Eisenwerke with twin 30-mm *FlaK* 103/38 guns, developed from aircraft cannon, mounted in a fully rotating turret – together these could deliver up to 900 rounds per minute. Only five or six vehicles were completed and on troop trials when the war ended.

Over 10,500 vehicles were produced on the *PzKpfw* IV chassis and its derivatives including over 7,000 tanks. Except on the Eastern Front during 1941 and 1942, before up-gunning, the IV could usually perform adequately on the battlefield; although in the terms of 1944 and 1945 it was hardly up to the highest contemporary standards in protection or gun-power. Its capacity for constant improvement, however, bore witness to the foresight of its original designers. The IV enabled the Germans to keep a satisfactory vehicle coming off the production lines while developments of better tanks were completed, and Guderian was right to insist on its continued production. The 'Mark IV' was less famous than its later named compatriots but it was never replaced by the *Panther* and fought right up to the end of the war.

Flakpanzer IV Wirbelwind (Whirlwind)
Armament four 20-mm Flakvierling 38s with 3,200 rounds, one hull machine-gun with 1,350 rounds
Armour hull nose and driver's plate 80 mm, sides 30 mm; turret sides 16 mm.
Other details as the PzKpfw IV Ausf D

Left: *A total of three or four of these quadruple 20-mm anti-aircraft vehicles the Flakpanzer IV Wirbelwind (Whirlwind) were deployed with the HQ companies of individual Panzer battalions from 1944. In all 3,200 rounds of 20-mm ammunition were carried, enough for 40 minutes at minimum firing rate; 1,350 rounds were carried for the hull machine-gun. Problems were faced with the relatively slow speed of traverse of the turret which was armoured to 16 mm. Hull armour was as in the Ausf J with 80 mm on the nose and driver's plate and 30 mm on the sides*

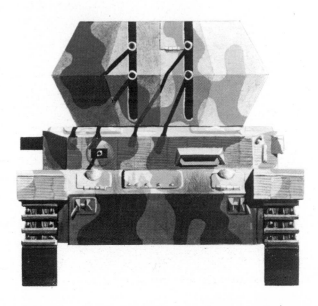

PzKpfw Tiger

Undoubtedly the most famous German tank of the war, the *Tiger,* became to the Allies the symbol of German technological superiority in armoured fighting vehicles. Although by no means invulnerable it was, at the time of its introduction, the most powerfully armed and well-protected tank in the world. To the Allied soldier every German tank became a Tiger, endowed with its offensive and defensive potency and a rather distorted view of German capabilities resulted, as Allied tactical and doctrinal shortcomings could be easily blamed on bigger enemy guns and thicker enemy armour.

The tank which fostered this legend dated back to a 1937 requirement for a 30-ton *Durchbruchswagen* or break-through vehicle. Various designs emerged as ideas changed and finally in May 1941, a month before the invasion of Russia, Hitler demanded a still more powerful tank superior to such heavily armoured vehicles as the French *Char* B and the British Matilda already encountered in the West. The existing plans were enlarged and a year later Henschel and Porsche demonstrated their prototypes.

Trials showed that the Henschel *VK 4501* design was superior and it was accepted into service as the *PzKpfw* VI *Tiger Ausf* H (*SdKfz* 181). The tank was renamed *PzKpfw Tiger Ausf* E in 1944. It was a relatively conventional vehicle with eight torsion bar suspended interleaved rubber-tyred road wheels each side. This suspension was designed to distribute the heavy weight of the tank as evenly as possible and it gave a very smooth and steady ride

to the tank. Reliability was, however, a problem and from early 1944 new all-steel resilient wheels were introduced which allowed the outside wheels to be deleted. The transmission was an advanced design to cope with the tank's 52-ton weight and a pre-selector gear box was fitted. As the Tiger was too heavy for the normal clutch and brake steering a hydraulic fully regenerative system operated by a driver's wheel was adopted which gave two turning radii in each gear. Control was very light but a price was paid in complexity of maintenance and construction.

The construction of the hull was relatively simple with a single unit welded superstructure in turn welded to the hull. As the tank had been designed before the full lessons of the *T-34* had been learnt, the superstructure armour was not sloped but it made up for this in thickness of protection. The turret, originally developed for the Porsche tank, was also simple and well protected, the sides and rear being formed from a single bent piece of 80-mm armour. It mounted in a heavy mantlet a 56-calibre *KwK* 36 88-mm gun which could penetrate 112 mm of 30 degree armour at 500 yards (457 m) using conventional armour-piercing shot. A machine-gun was fitted co-axially in the mantlet fired by a pedal operated by the gunner. There was another in the right hull-front operated by the radio operator/gunner. The other members of the crew were the driver in the left hull-front and the loader and commander who occupied the turret together with the gunner.

Given its weight the Tiger was a relatively

compact vehicle but its heaviness had disadvantages and both range and speed were very limited. The turret traverse was very low-geared and the gun could only be revolved slowly. Power tranverse was fitted but if this failed it took no less than 720 turns of the traversing wheel to get the gun round 360 degrees; this allowed well-handled Allied tanks to put shots into the more vulnerable sides and rear. Wide (725-mm) tracks were fitted to spread the weight although special narrow (520-mm) tracks had to be used for transport by rail to get the tank within the loading gauge. Even with its wide tracks the *Tiger* was too heavy for normal bridges and the first production vehicles were fitted to wade rivers.

Tiger tanks were intended for use in independent three company battalions of 30 tanks allocated to higher Army or Corps HQ for issue in the support role to stiffen various units. This remained the case despite Guderian's intention to make a *Tiger* battalion organic to each Panzer division. This occurred in few

Below: *One of the initial designs that led to the Tiger was the VK 3001(H) sometimes known as 'Leopard'. When made obsolete by changing requirements two of the four prototypes were lengthened and converted into tank destroyers mounting large 128-mm K 40 guns*
Opposite page, bottom: *This clear rear view of a 1942–3 production Tiger shows off the Feifel air pre-cleaners fitted for the dusty conditions in both Russia and North Africa*

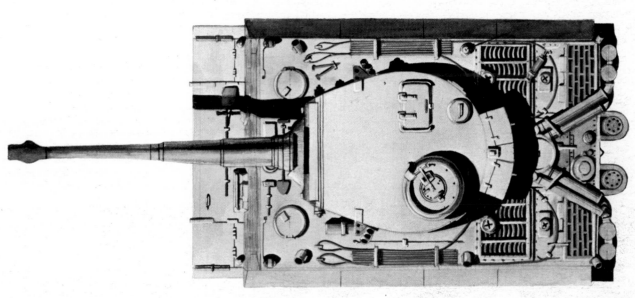

PzKpfw Tiger Ausf E
Weight 54.1 tons (55 tonnes)
Crew five
Armament one 88-mm KwK 36 (L/56) gun with
92 rounds and two 7.92-mm MG 34 machine-
guns with 5,700 rounds
Armour hull nose 100 mm, glacis 60 mm, driver's
plate 100 mm, sides 60–80 mm, decking and belly
26 mm, tail 82 mm; turret mantlet 110 mm,
front 100 mm, sides and rear 80 mm, top 26 mm
Engine one Maybach HL 230 P 45 water-cooled
petrol, 694-hp
Speed 23 mph (37 km/h)
Range 62 miles (100 km)
Trench crossing 7 feet 6 inches (2.29 m)
Vertical step 2 feet 7 inches (79 cm)
Fording 4 feet (1.22 m) or with special equipment
13 feet (3.96 m)
Overall length 27 feet 9 inches (8.46 m)
Width wide tracks: 12 feet 3 inches (3.73 m),
narrow tracks: 10 feet 4 inches (3.15 m)
Height 9 feet 6 inches (2.9 m)

Above: *A middle production PzKpfw VI Tiger
Ausf H, as the tank was originally designated.
Note the Feifel air cleaners and the cup-like
grenade dischargers*

23

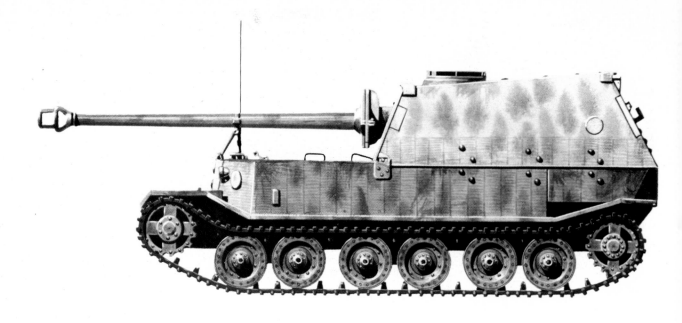

Panzerjager Tiger (P), Elefant
Weight 66.9 tons (68 tonnes)
Crew six
Armament one 88-mm StuK 43/2 (L/71) gun
with 50 rounds
Armour hull nose and driver's plate 100 + 100 mm,
sides 80 mm, decking 30 mm, belly 20 + 30 mm,
tail 80 mm; superstructure front 200 mm, sides
and rear 80 mm, top 30 mm
Engines two Maybach HL 120 TRM V-12 liquid
cooled petrol, 530-hp
Speed 12.5 mph (20 km/h)
Range 95 miles (153 km)
Trench crossing 10 feet 6 inches (3.20 m)
Vertical step 31 inches (78 cm)
Fording 4 feet (1.22 m)
Overall length 26 feet 8 inches (8.13 m)
Width 11 feet 1 inch (3.38 m)
Height 9 feet 10 inches (3.00 m)

Above: *The ill-fated Elefant tank destroyer. One
of the type's crucial weaknesses is clearly visible,
the lack of a hull machine-gun deleted in up-
armouring. As can be seen, vision to the rear and
sides was very limited and the 88-mm gun had a
traverse of only 14° in elevation, 8° in depression
and 14° either side. The extra protection was
added to the mantlet after the appearance of the
initial production vehicles*

Army units, the politically influential *Waffen SS* getting priority. *Tiger* tanks were also used with remote control demolition tanks in *Panzer Funklenk Abteilungen* (Radio Controlled Tank Battalions) in the assault role.

With a gun that could defeat the best Allied tank of its time, and frontal armour that could deflect any available Allied anti-tank projectile, the success of the *Tiger* seemed assured. Unfortunately Hitler's desire to see them in action as soon as possible led to fiasco: badly deployed in small quantities in unsuitable terrain, they were overwhelmed in their first offensive action near Leningrad in the autumn of 1942. Misused at Kursk, in July 1943, as a battering ram against mile upon mile of alerted *Pakfront* defences, defeat was on a larger scale. But in defence the *Tiger* showed its great strength and the real legend grew. When firing from camouflaged positions, using tracked mobility to move from one to the other and supported by other tanks or small groups of infantry the *Tiger* took a great deal of stalking and absorbed a disproportionate amount of Allied strength. On one famous occasion, in July 1944, a single *Tiger* of the 501 *Waffen SS* Heavy Tank Battalion held up the British Seventh Armoured Division, the Desert Rats, knocking out 25 armoured vehicles.

However, as time went on the *Tiger*'s superiority began to be eroded by new Allied tank

Above: *After the Kursk disaster several Elefant tank destroyers fell into Russian hands like this example here. The burnt superstructure is evidence of attack with flame-thrower or 'Molotov cocktail' petrol bombs. In action a wooden plank was wired to the rear on which German infantrymen could ride though at considerable risk*

Below: *The Tiger tanks of the 501st Heavy Tank Battalion were sent to Tunisia in January 1943 to reinforce the Axis position there. Although providing much useful support they did not prove completely invulnerable as shown by this example which has been blown on its side, probably by an Allied bomb or mine*

Sturmpanzer VI, Sturmtiger
Weight 66.9 tons (68 tonnes)
Crew five or six
Armament one 380-mm Raketenwerfer 61 with
12 rounds and one 7.92-mm MG 34 machine-gun
Armour superstructure front 150 mm, sides and
rear 84 mm, top 40 mm
Overall length 20 feet 8½ inches (6.30 m)
Height (with crane) 11 feet 4 inches (3.45 m)
Other details as PzKpfw IV Tiger Ausf E tank

Right: *This is one of the ten production Sturmtigers built on a 1944 production Ausf E tank chassis with the later type wheel arrangement. The prototype Sturmtiger had a similar suspension to that of the tank previously illustrated. The new arrangement placed a lower strain on the wheel bearings and was less prone to packing with mud or ice. The crane was to assist in loading the 761-lb (345-kg) 380-mm rocket projectiles. Their maximum range was over 6,000 yards (5,500 m) but accuracy was not very great and the Sturmtiger was meant to be used at closer distances*

guns which had sufficient performance to penetrate the *Tiger*'s armour at average combat ranges (500 to 1,000 yards or 457 m to 914 m). Production was gradually phased out, and finally ceased in August 1944. In all 1,355 had been built, surprisingly few considering their tremendous reputation.

Although not selected for quantity production the *Tiger* offered by Dr Ferdinand Porsche, the *VK 4501* (P), saw limited service as a heavy assault gun chassis with the long (70-calibre) 88-mm *PaK 43/2* – a more powerful gun than that of the Tiger tank. Eighty-five chassis were converted by Alkett and they emerged as the *Panzerjäger Tiger* (P) (*SdKfz* 184); originally called *Ferdinand* after their designer they later received the official name *Elefant*. To make it more suitable for its task the chassis was changed in layout. The driver and radio operator remained in the front, the former fighting compartment now contained the engines – two standard Maybach 120 TR units – and a large fighting compartment was rear-mounted to minimize the long gun's overhang. The suspension remained on the Porsche principle with six large, steel-rimmed road wheels each side, in pairs mounted on three horizontal torsion bars. Drive was transmitted to rear sprockets via a Siemens Schuckert electric generator and two electric drive motors; steering was hydro-pneumatically assisted. Armour was increased to an extraordinary level, an extra 100-

mm armour plate being bolted to the hull front, already armoured to this thickness. The superstructure received 200-mm armour at the front, the rest being armoured to 80 mm.

The *Elefant* was a formidable, if specialized, tank destroyer. Great things were expected of it and two army Tank Destroyer Battalions, 653 and 654 were re-equipped each with three companies of twelve *Elefants* with an HQ Company of two extra vehicles and a *PzKpfw* III. But its first major offensive role at Kursk was a disaster. Employed as an assault vehicle, to lead the infantry through the Soviet defences, its lack of flexibility or close-in defence capability was fatal. The *Elefant* is usually remembered for this failure but this was as much a product of misuse as intrinsic defects. As a long range tank killer it was supreme for its day, totally impervious frontally to enemy fire and capable of knocking out a *T-34* at three miles (4·83 km) in open country. The lessons of Kursk were learnt and those which were salvaged from the battlefield were fitted with machine-guns in the right hull-front. The two battalions served later in Russia and Italy, where they were used more prudently as mobile anti-tank pillboxes. Nevertheless, they remained awkward machines to operate, proving too heavy to be very mobile especially on Italian roads in bad weather; reliability and spare parts remained a problem and many had to be destroyed to escape capture.

The spectacular *Sturmtiger* assault howitzer

originated from a requirement for a 210-mm assault howitzer to destroy heavy buildings which the Russians had converted into fortresses; no suitable weapon was available and a 380-mm heavy rocket launcher, developed as an anti-submarine weapon for the German Navy, was mounted in a Henschel *Tiger* chassis. A prototype was built in October 1943 but production only began at Alkett in August 1944 when ten standard chassis could be spared for re-working.

Sturmtiger was a clumsy vehicle, almost as heavy and certainly as specialized as *Elefant* and by the time it came into service there was little real function for a mobile assault rocket launcher as Germany's armies were on the defensive, not storming through Russian cities. Its fuel consumption, two gallons per mile, was even higher than the *Tiger* tanks, not very suitable for a country short of fuel with its synthetic oil plants coming under increasing air attack. *Sturmtiger* assault howitzers were committed to battle individually but were soon knocked out or captured.

Not many *Tiger* tanks were exported but Italy received 36 which were repossessed when she changed sides. Spain also managed to acquire a few as part of arms deals with Germany.

Below: *A captured Sturmtiger with an example of its ammunition in front of it. The spin-stabilized 761-lb (345-kg) rocket came in two versions, a normal high explosive and a hollow charge*

PzKpfw Panther

In early October 1941 the Fourth *Panzer* Division, part of Guderian's recently renamed Second *Panzer* Army was severely mauled by the new Soviet *T*-34 tanks, encountered in significant numbers for the first time, near Mtsensk. Tank losses were heavy and Guderian asked for a commission of representatives from all sides of German tank development to be sent to the front to report on the situation. Ideas of building a simple copy of the *T*-34 were soon dismissed due to difficulties in copying the Soviet aluminium diesel engine and other problems with materials. Daimler Benz and MAN were therefore contracted to produce a new German *VK* 3002 design to regain technological superiority.

Detailed specifications were issued in January 1942 with the following parameters: weight 35 tons, armament a 75-mm gun and co-axial machine-gun, maximum hull armour 60 mm and turret armour 100 mm and speed 37 mph (60 km/h). The design was also to include all the features of the *T*-34 that made it such a formidable opponent: sloped armour which increased the effective thickness of any given plate, large road wheels to improve the ride and a long powerful gun overhanging the chassis, a feature which German designers had been wary of.

In April designs were submitted by Daimler Benz and MAN. Hitler preferred the former's but a special committee of the OKH's Army Weapons Department, set up to deal with the problem, came down in favour of the more conventional MAN design with a petrol engine, front drive sprockets. interleaved suspension and a turret set back to minimize the overhang problem. The hull was a single welded unit with strengthened edges and well-sloped 55 degree 60-mm glacis armour. It was hoped that 250 *PzKpfw* V *Panther* (*SdKfz* 171) would be in service by May 1943; in September, the month that the first two pilot models appeared, Hitler raised this target to 600.

Tests showed that the design was overweight and underpowered but the first 20 vehicles designated *Ausf* A (but not to be confused with the later *Ausf* A mass produced after the battle of Kursk) were built to the prototype design in order to get production under way. To increase power a new HL 230 engine was fitted to subsequent production vehicles (*Ausf* D) together with a specially designed AK7 200 synchromesh gearbox and regenerative steering system to cope with the extra weight. Armour thickness was increased, in accordance with Hitler's order of June 1942, to 80 mm and the turret cupola was moved over to the right to simplify production. A new double-baffle gun muzzle brake began to be fitted.

In January the first production *Panther* appeared from both MAN and Daimler Benz – the latter having been brought in to meet the ambitious production schedule. By February MNH were also in the programme and Henschel and Demag joined later. In early 1943 *Ausf* A vehicles were officially reclassified D1 and production vehicles D2 while from May *Schürtzen* began to be fitted to guard the gap between the track top and the superstructure side. By that month 324 *Panther* tanks were in service.

The modifications to the *Panther Ausf* D2 were far from sufficient to solve its mechanical difficulties: the HL 230 engine was prone to overheating and catching fire; the final drive was also a particular weakness, closely followed by the rest of the transmission and the steering. The increased weight (44 tons) also put extra stress on the rim bolts holding on the tyres which often necessitated much time consuming wheel removal to get at the offending failure. All this reflected insufficient development time but, despite Guderian's doubts, Hitler insisted that the *Panther* should be put into service as soon as possible, notably in time for the big armoured offensive at Kursk, Operation *Zitadelle*, which was delayed until July 1943 so that the new tanks could be used. Not surprisingly their *début* was inauspicious. Of the 200 *Panther* tanks in Hoth's Fourth *Panzer* Army, 160 were out of action by the end of the first day, and, nine days later, only 43 were in German hands. Many had broken down between the railheads and the front, others on the battlefield where, as they could not be easily towed, they had had to be left.

By the time the Kursk offensive was abandoned a new *Panther* model, rather confusingly called the *Ausf* A was in production, with a proper ball-mounted hull machine-gun and a better protected turret with new cupola. To ease production and in order to help mitigate the effects of the weight problem more tyre bolts were used in the wheels, 24 instead of 16.

Below: *The fate of many a Panther is exemplified by this burnt out Ausf A; neither its extra camouflage nor well-sloped armour has saved it from Allied firepower*
Opposite page, top: *A Panther Ausf G – note the new shape of the superstructure sides*

PzKpfw V Panther Ausf G
Weight 44.8 tons (45.5 tonnes)
Crew five
Armament one 75-mm KwK 42 (L/70) gun with 79 rounds and two 7.92-mm MG 34 machine-guns with 4,500 rounds
Armour hull front 80 mm, sides 50 mm, tail 40 mm, decking 15 mm, belly 20 + 13 mm; turret front 120–110 mm, sides and rear 45 mm, top 15 mm
Engine one Maybach HL 230 P 30 V-12 liquid-cooled petrol, 690-hp
Speed 34 mph (55 km/h)
Range 110 miles (177 km)
Trench crossing 6 feet 3 inches (1.9 m)
Vertical step 3 feet (90 cm)
Fording 4 feet 7 inches (1.4 m)
Overall length 29 feet 1 inch (8.86 m)
Width 10 feet 10 inches (3.30 m)
Height 9 feet 8 inches (2.95 m)

Below: *This Ausf G Panther is identified as such by its new-style upward hinging hatches and the deletion of the driver's vision visor. A brown camouflage scheme has been applied over the basic sand yellow which was the standard finish for tanks leaving the factories in 1943–4*

Jagdpanther
Weight 44.8 tons (45.5 tonnes)
Crew six
Armament one 88-mm PaK 43/3 (L/71) with
60 rounds and one 7.92-mm MG 34 machine-gun
with 600 rounds
Armour front 80 mm, mantlet 120 mm, sides
40–50 mm, decking 17 mm, belly 20 + 13 mm,
tail 40 mm
Speed 28.5 mph (46 km/h)
Range 100 miles (160 km)
Overall length 33 feet 3 inches (10.m)
Height 8 feet 11 inches (2.72 m)
Other details as PzKpfw V Panther Ausf G tank

Left: A late model Jagdpanther with two-piece gun barrel and simplified heavy bolted-on mantlet collar. Schürtzen are fitted and the excellent ballistic shape of the vehicle's armour can be seen. Grey camouflage schemes became increasingly common once more from late 1944. Jagdpanther was a formidable vehicle; on July 30th 1944 three from the 654 heavy AT battalion knocked out over half a squadron of 15 British Churchills in a little over a minute

Ausf Ds were modified with extra bolts put in between the existing 16, making 32 in all. Although the engine became a little more reliable with extra cooling fans, improved bearings and other modifications, transmission failures remained endemic. New *Ausf* A turrets were fitted to *Ausf* D hulls by Henschel who kept the older chassis in production until November 1943. Altogether 1,768 *Panthers* were produced in 1943. Further modifications were planned to produce the *Panther* II *Ausf* F to simplify production and improve reliability but production was not quite under way when the war ended.

The need in 1944 was for as many tanks as possible of existing design in the front-line and some of the innovations of the proposed *Panther* II were added to the standard *Panther* in early 1944 to produce the *PzKpfw Panther Ausf* G. (The term *PzKpfw* V was now dropped.) To simplify production further the design of the sides of the tank were modified to make the rear stowage areas integral with the hull. The hull sides were also increased to 50-mm armour and the driver acquired a rotating periscope. Late production vehicles had a modified mantlet with thicker bottom to prevent the deflection of enemy rounds into the thin deck armour. In the last vehicles constructed all-steel resilient wheels were fitted which finally solved one dimension of the weight problem and the improved AK7-400 gearbox was also adopted. A progressive

Below: *A knocked out Jagdpanther being inspected by an American soldier. This vehicle has the 'clean' gun barrel but the later style mantlet collar. Note the penetration made through the wheels. Jagdpanthers were vulnerable to such flanking shots and also to track damage caused by high-explosive fire*

feature introduced in action just before the end of the war was the use of infra-red night fighting equipment which enabled the crews to engage targets at night up to 547 yards (500 m) away.

During 1944 and 1945 over 3,740 *Panther* tanks were produced, more than any other single type of German tank in this period. It provided a numerous and powerful supplement to the *PzKpfw* IV as the major battle tank of the *Panzer* divisions. Each division was supposed to contain one battalion of *Panther* tanks together with one of *PzKpfw* IV but as usual the *élite Waffen SS* tended to get priority.

Ausf A and G vehicles played a prominent part in the large-scale defensive tank battles in Normandy. Here mobility was less important than their formidable frontal protection and 3,068 fps (935 m/s) gun that could penetrate over 120 mm of 30-degree plate at 1,000 yards (914 m). Only crushing Allied air and numerical superiority prevented this technological advantage becoming decisive strategically.

The *Panther* had a small number of special versions, the most famous was the *Jagdpanther* (Hunting Panther) tank destroyer. This was developed in 1943 as a well-protected mobile mount for the formidable *PaK* 43 88-mm gun with its 3,708 fps (1,130 m/s) muzzle velocity and which could penetrate 226 mm of 30 degree armour at 500 yards (457 m). *Nashorn* was too lightly protected and *Elefant* too expensive, complex and vulnerable for the task, so it was decided to use the *Panther* chassis with a low sloped front superstructure. The gun was fitted in the frontal plate with 11-degree traverse to each side, 8-degree elevation and 14-degree depression and a machine-gun was fitted in the right hull front to prevent a repetition of the Kursk débâcle. A crew of six was needed: commander,

gunner, wireless operator/machine-gunner, driver and two loaders for the heavy, clumsy ammunition. First called *Panzerjäger Panther* (*SfKfz* 173) it received from Hitler the designation *Jagdpanther* in 1944.

Production began in December 1943 and MIAG had it well under way by May using *Ausf* G chassis with an improved AK7-400 gearbox to take the extra weight. The vehicles were issued to special tank destroyer battalions composed of 30 *Jagdpanther* which were kept under central army control. It was intended to build 150 *Jagdpanther* a month but an increasingly bombed and starved German industry could not keep up and only 382 were eventually completed. Several other *Panther*-based vehicles saw service: the demand for heavy recovery vehicles after Kursk resulted in the *Bergepanzer Panther* or *Bergepanther* recovery vehicle (*SdKfz* 179); *Ausf* D, A and G vehicles were converted to *Befehlspanzer* (command tanks) and there was also an artillery observation post vehicle or *Beobachtungspanzer* (*SdKfz* 172).

Some 5,508 examples of the *Panther* tank were built in all. Although considered excessively large by the Ministry of Armaments and retaining mechanical problems which were never entirely ironed out, it was probably the best all round German tank of the war, not too heavy but well-armoured and armed. Its complexity hindered mass production but two could be built in as many man-hours as one *Tiger* and, in the 1944 rationalization plan, it was hoped to concentrate on it and the *Panther* II as the main battle tanks of the 1945 German Army. A total of 400 a month was planned but this was far beyond the capacity of German industry, even though 132 *Ausf* Gs were still produced as late as February 1945.

PzKpfw Tiger Ausf B

In August 1942 specifications were issued for a modified *Tiger* tank incorporating the latest sloped armour of the *T-34* and *Panther*, increased protection and the longer 71-calibre 88-mm gun. It was hoped that this would keep German tanks ahead of any future Soviet designs in the gun/armour race. Both Porsche and Henschel were again asked to tender and the former produced modified *VK* 4502 (P) versions of his earlier *Tiger* (P). Interest was shown in a version with electric drive and rear mounted 88-mm gun, and, with Porsche this time sure of a production order, construction of turrets was begun. But the need for copper, a scarce commodity in blockaded Germany, for the electric transmission resulted in the Henschel *VK* 4503 (H) design being chosen for service.

Ordered in January 1943 the first *PzKpfw VI Tiger* II or *Ausf* B (*SdKfz* 182) did not appear until the end of the year due to the need for close liaison with MAN in order to standardize as many components as possible with the proposed *Panther* II – the *Tiger* II, for example used the same engine as late model *Panther* tanks. Suspension was on the classic German principle with conventional torsion bars but the arrangement of wheels was slightly altered compared with the earlier *Tiger*; the interleaved system was abandoned due to the difficulty of access to the inner wheels and the tendency of these arrangements to freeze or jam and the nine sets of double bogie wheels were set merely to overlap. Resilient steel wheels were also employed to improve reliability. As with the older

Tiger two sets of tracks were provided: one for action and the other for transport to minimize the vehicle's width.

Production was under way by February 1944 when the first eight vehicles were produced by Henschel side by side with 95 standard *Tiger Ausf* Es. It was the intention to produce 145 *Tiger* II *Ausf* Bs per month by 1945 but this proved impossible and the total production run was only 480. The first 50 vehicles carried the turret designed for the Porsche tank, the others had the proper Henschel turret with its heavier armour and squared-off front which prevented shots being deflected down into the hull. Some Porsche turreted vehicles and all the Henschel turreted tanks had a two-piece gun barrel which allowed differential wear to be exploited in replacement of parts.

Tiger Ausf B, known to its own side as *Königstiger* and to the English-speaking world as Royal or King Tiger, was a formidable and huge vehicle. It was at once the heaviest, most thickly protected and most powerfully armed battle tank to see service in any numbers during the war. Its armour would do justice to a modern main battle tank and its gun had a muzzle velocity of 3,220 fps (981 m/s) and could penetrate 182 mm of 30-degree armour at 500 yards (457 m). This was more than enough to deal with the heaviest Soviet JS IIs. But a price had to be paid in size, weight and reliability. Hull length was 23 feet 8½ inches (7·22 m) and height was also greater. Most important, weight was also increased, by over ten tons. Although, sur-

prisingly, this did not affect performance 'on paper', speed and radius of action actually being slightly increased, power/weight ratio, manoeuvrability and ground pressure all suffered. Also, inevitably, reliability was a problem with a highly stressed engine and transmission.

These drawbacks did not matter too much in defensive battles but it was a significant drawback in, for example, the Ardennes offensive. Indeed, although *Tiger* IIs were available to Obersturmführer (Lieutenant-Colonel) Jochen Peiper he chose *PzKpfw* IVs and *Panther* tanks to lead his *Kampfgruppe* that spearheaded the advance of First *SS Panzer* Division. The *Tiger* II had made its combat *début* on the Eastern Front in May 1944 and was in service in France by August of the same year. It was allocated in the same way as the *Tiger* I being either kept in independent battalions or being formed into the tank regiments of privileged *Panzer* divisions. With such a small production run the *Tiger* II was never a common tank and, although the previously mentioned Ardennes offensive is usually associated with it, there were comparatively few in action.

Opposite page, right: *A Tiger Ausf B with standard Henschel turret. These vehicles were used, to a limited extent, in the closing months of the war only being employed in any numbers in the Ardennes and in the defence of Budapest in late 1944 and early 1945*
Below: *One of the first 50 Royal Tiger tanks with Porsche turret, knocked out in Normandy*

PzKpfw Tiger Ausf B
Weight 68.7 tons (69.4 tonnes)
Crew five
Armament one 88-mm KwK 43 (L/71) gun with 80 rounds and two 7.92-mm MG 34 machine-guns with 5,850 rounds
Armour hull nose 100 mm, glacis 150 mm, sides and tail 80 mm, decking 40 mm; turret front 185 mm, sides and rear 80 mm, top 44 mm
Engine one Maybach HL 230 P 30 V-12 liquid-cooled petrol, 600-hp
Speed 23.6 mph (38 km/h)
Range 68.4 miles (110 km)
Trench crossing 8 feet 2 inches (2.5 m)
Vertical step 2 feet 9½ inches (85 cm)
Fording 5 feet 3 inches (1.6 m)
Overall length 33 feet 8 inches (10.26 m)
Width wide tracks: 12 feet 3½ inches (4.72 m), narrow tracks: 10 feet 8¾ inches (3.27 m)
Height 10 feet 1½ inches (3.08 m)

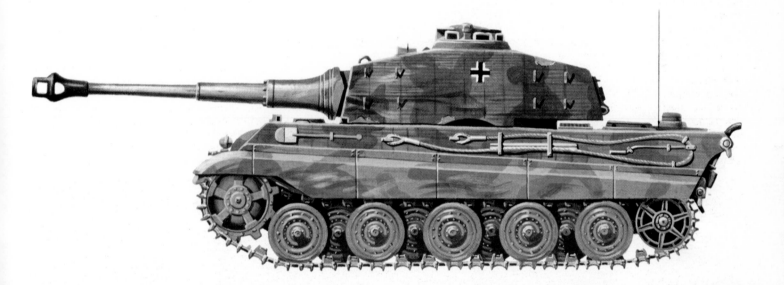

If the Royal Tiger was the most powerful tank of the war then its tank destroyer derivative *Jagdtiger* (*SdKfz* 186) was the most powerful armoured vehicle. It was German policy to build a limited-traverse mounting of the 'next size gun up' on any given tank chassis and the Royal Tiger was no exception. A lengthened hull was used with a large fixed central super-structure armoured to the extraordinary frontal thickness of 250 mm and mounting a 55-calibre 128-mm *PaK* 80 – a weapon which could out-range any other tank gun and pene-trate any other AFV. Earlier models mounted the shorter 128-mm *PaK* 44 and some had to make do with the *Jagdpanther*'s 88-mm *PaK* 43/3. The tank's machine-gun in the hull front was retained and a grenade launcher was also fitted, as in the tank, to deter stalkers.

The first mock-up appeared in October 1943; 150 were ordered but only 70 were completed by the end of the war. The close connection between the plant – Neibelüngenwerke – and the designer enabled Dr Porsche to tinker with the design. Two vehicles were fitted with a Porsche type sus-pension with eight overlapping wheels instead of nine; one of these may also have been the *Jagdtiger* experimentally fitted with a Porsche *SLa* 16 (Type 212) 700-hp diesel engine. Neither of these developments went further due to the need to concentrate on existing designs if any vehicles were to be built at all. A more powerful engine would at least have alleviated the *Jagdtiger*'s greatest drawback – its extra-

ordinary weight of over 70½ tons, more than any other AFV that has ever seen widespread service in any army. This created severe tactical prob-lems as the *Jagdtiger* was impossible to operate on anything but strong roads and the hardest ground and its practical maximum road speed was also very slow, no more than seven to nine mph (11 to 14 km/h).

The *Jagdtiger* equipped independent tank de-stroyer battalions, usually those of the *Waffen SS*. They were used as infantry support vehicles and as stiffeners in the *Panzer* forces used in the Ardennes offensive but their lack of mobility was a severe drawback and they were most suitable for the final last ditch stands against the Allied forces closing into Germany. Im-penetrable to Allied fire, the *Jagdtiger* provided a formidable static anti-tank defence.

There were two other versions of the *Tiger* II *Ausf* B. One, the *Panzerbefehlswagen* command vehicle, was a normal tank with extra radio equipment added and armament stowage de-creased in the usual manner; few were produced. The other, the largest of the family of weapons carriers, had *Tiger* II chassis with two extra bogie wheels fitted with a large protected rear superstructure to carry a dismountable 170-mm gun or a 210-mm howitzer. A prototype was almost completed when the war ended. After the war some *Tiger* II tanks served with the French army until being expended as targets.

The massive proportions of the *Tiger* II series reflected Hitler's enthusiasm for large

AFVs and there were plans for even larger vehicles. In 1942 he had given personal authoriz-ation to Porsche to develop a huge 185-ton *Maus* (Mouse) tank with 200-mm armour and an armament of one 128-mm gun with co-axial 75-mm. This led the Army Weapons Office to look for a slightly less impractical design of 'super tank'. At first it was hoped to build a bigger version of *Tiger* II developed by Krupp as the *VK* 7001 (K) called *Tiger-Maus* or *Löwe* (Lion). A model was built showing a redesigned hull with rear-mounted 128-mm armed turret and steeply-sloped armour. This was eventually cancelled and efforts concentrated on the de-velopment of the largest of a planned *E* (*Ent-wicklung* – development) series of standardized tanks. Adler developed the 140-ton *E-100* with a suspension based on the *Tiger* II but with helical springs instead of torsion bars, and its main armament was increased to 150-mm calibre. One prototype petrol-engined *Maus* was built and another with a diesel engine.

Although super-tank projects had soon to be downgraded much time and energy were wasted on what had been described by Porsche himself as mere mobile fortifications. Even less rational were plans for a 1,500-ton tank with one 800-mm gun, two 150-mm weapons and 250-mm armour powered by four U-Boat engines! Such a land monitor would have been the final monu-ment to the German failure to understand that practicality and serviceability were of greater importance than mere technological virtue.

Jagdtiger
Weight 70.6 tons (71.7 tonnes)
Crew six
Armament one 128-mm PaK 80 (L/55) gun
with 38 rounds and one MG 34 machine-gun
with 2,925 rounds
Armour superstructure front 250 mm, sides and
rear 80 mm, top 40 mm
Overall length 35 feet (10.66 m)
Height 9 feet 3 inches (2.82 m)
Other details as Tiger Ausf B tank

Opposite page: A battalion of normal production Royal Tigers parade late in 1944. Such pictures made good propaganda but belied Germany's true armoured strength at this time. The two piece gun barrel and 'Zimmerit' anti magnetic-mine paste are clearly visible. Despite its powerful main armament, the unwieldy Royal Tiger was not a great success as an AFV

Left: *Not even massive armour and firepower could hold out for ever. This Jagdtiger has been used as a dug in pill box before being overwhelmed by American firepower*

Below: *The spectacular Jagdtiger, the most powerful service AFV of the war, did not see a great deal of action, only being available in very limited quantities by the end of the war*

Type 97 Medium Series

The stimulus to develop a new medium tank came, as in the case of most other Japanese tanks, from the technical rather than the operational branch of the Japanese Army's command structure. Army Technical Headquarters saw that the Type 89 was increasingly inferior to European tanks being slow, under-gunned and under-armoured. It was also felt that a new, fast medium should be developed for the Independent Mixed Brigade rather than a light tank and two designs were initiated, a 13.5-ton First Plan from Mitsubishi and a 10-ton Second Plan from Osaka Arsenal. Both prototypes appeared in 1937 as the CHI-HA and CHI-NI respectively and, although the Operations Department preferred the latter, which only had a one-man turret and was therefore cheaper, the outbreak of the China incident downgraded considerations of economy, and led to the adoption of the larger design for service use.

Two prototype CHI-HAs appeared, one with interleaved wheels, and the other employing a version of the standard suspension of the Type 94 tankette and Type 95 Light with three pairs of large, double bogie wheels each side connected by middle-mounted bell cranks horizontally sprung against each other. To improve cross-country performance the production vehicles adopted a modification of this suspension for the centre pairs only, the front and back wheels being independently sprung. Construction was by welding and riveting and the armour was well shaped. A small turret was mounted to the right of the hull. Its firepower was disappointing, being a new Type 97 version of the old short 57-mm gun. This did fire an armour-piercing round, but only at 1,378 fps (420 m/s) – half the velocity of the later British six-pounder (57-mm) of similar calibre. Unlike that of the CHI-NI the turret was two-man so the tank commander did not have to double as gunner, and the ring was large enough to allow later up-gunning. Machine-guns in armoured sleeves were in the hull front and turret rear with a third sometimes fitted for AA use. A powerful new engine of standard pattern drove through the front sprockets and steering was by normal clutch and brake.

The CHI-HA compared favourably with its contemporaries in all except gun power and this deficiency became apparent when the Soviet Army showed the Japanese the nature of modern armoured opposition in 1938–9. Development, therefore, began of a larger turret, mounting a high-velocity armament based on the standard 47-mm anti-tank weapon. The new 48-calibre Type 1 tank gun had a muzzle velocity of 2,625 fps (800 m/s) which compared satisfactorily with foreign weapons such as the contemporary *PzKpfw* III's 2,240 fps (684 m/s) 42-calibre 50-mm. The programme was delayed, however, by renewed complacency and the new SHINHOTO (New Turret) CHI-HA only began to enter service in 1942. By this time it was already becoming obsolete particularly in terms of its armour protection which was only slightly improved on the hull sides. Again, the new turret was set towards the right and had a machine-gun in the rear.

By this time the standard CHI-HA had equipped some independent tank regiments and those

in the armoured divisions. It had seen service in China and Malaya where individual tank companies were handled daringly in co-operation with infantry and engineers to break the British defences at Jitra and on the Slim River. They then spearheaded the swift advance down the peninsula which followed.

In a Japanese tank regiment the Type 97 provided the three or four medium companies, each of three platoons of three with a company commander. More were attached to Regimental HQ, one or more of these sometimes being the SHI-KI command vehicle with extra communications and vision equipment and an additional 37-mm or 57-mm gun in place of the machine-gun in the hull front. There was also a commander's SHINHOTO CHI-HA with a dummy gun. Most CHI-HAs had radio fitted to help tactical co-ordination with a prominent curved aerial in the original tanks being mounted around the top of the turret front. There were various specialized variants. In 1942 three self-propelled guns (gun tanks) appeared on the Type 97 chassis, perhaps stimulated by the successful assault gun designs of Japan's Axis allies. The HO-NI I mounted a modern 75-mm high-velocity gun, the HO-NI II, a shorter 105-mm weapon and the HO-RO, an old 150-mm howitzer. These were mounted in open shields, armoured frontally to the same thickness as the tank, and they proved useful in providing extra firepower in the final defensive battles. A few original CHI-HAs were converted to flail mine-

clearers, flamethrower tanks and bridgelayers while some SHINHOTO CHI-HAs became bull-dozer tanks. There was also a SE-RI recovery vehicle on the Type 97 chassis with rear crane jib and small machine-gun turret.

The SHINHOTO CHI-HA, to which standard many older vehicles were converted, was the only new tank to see large-scale service in the period after 1942. A 17-ton Type 1 CHI-HE with the 47-mm gun in a revised turret, a slightly better-shaped welded hull armoured to 50-mm, and a 240-hp engine was put into limited production in 1941. A Type 2 HO-I gun tank with a short 75-mm gun in a revolving turret was adopted for its support the next year, but, although some of both these types saw action, few were produced.

The appearance of larger Allied tanks with 75-mm guns led to experiments with the Type 95 75-mm field gun to improve the Japanese medium tank's firepower. Eventually a version of the higher-velocity Type 90 weapon was adopted and fitted in an enlarged turret on the CHI-HE chassis as the Type 3 CHI-NU. The gun was a 38-calibre weapon and had a muzzle velocity of 2,231 fps (680 m/s) which put it in terms of performance between that of the British and American tank guns of similar calibre. The 18.5-ton tank, if something of an improvization, was almost of American Sherman standard, but it suffered from production problems and only saw service in limited numbers from 1944. The same gun was also mounted in an enclosed

Type 97 SHINHOTO CHI-HA

Weight 15.6 tons
Crew five
Armament one 47-mm Type 1 (L/48) gun with 104 rounds and two 7.7-mm Type 97 machine-guns with 2,575 rounds
Armour hull nose 15 mm, glacis 17 mm, driver's plate 25 mm, sides 20–35 mm, decking 10 mm, belly 8 mm, tail 20 mm; turret front 25 mm, mantlet 30 mm, sides and rear 25 mm, top 10 mm
Engine one Mitsubishi V-12 air-cooled diesel, 170-hp
Speed 24 mph (38 km/h)
Range 130.5 miles (210 km)
Trench crossing 8 feet 1½ inches (2.5 m)
Vertical step 3 feet (91 cm)
Fording 3 feet 3 inches (1 m)
Overall length 18 feet 1 inch (5.5 m)
Width 7 feet 8 inches (2.33 m)
Height 7 feet 11 inches (2.38 m)

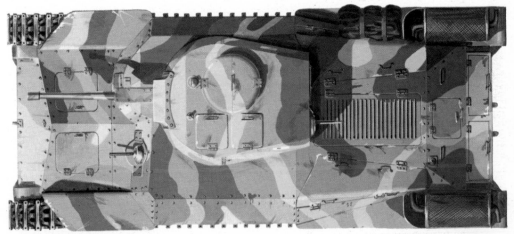

Right: The SHINHOTO CHI-HA was the most important Japanese medium tank of the war. Known as the 'Type 97 Special' to the Americans it could barely hold its own against the Sherman, and was totally outclassed by Soviet armour in 1945. Note the machine-gun mounted in the turret rear, and also the lengthened version of the standard Japanese suspension with centre-mounted bell cranks on the middle wheel pairs. The novel camouflage scheme was a Japanese standard
Below: An original CHI-HA of the Third Company, Seventh Tank Regiment advances in Bataan during the conquest of the Philippines – the Japanese were adept at using tanks in difficult conditions

central superstructure on the Type 97 chassis as the HO-NI III gun tank.

A scaled-up 30-ton Type 4 CHI-TO with 75-mm armour retained the same suspension principles as its predecessors but had seven wheels each side as opposed to six and a 400 bhp engine. A new 38-calibre 75-mm gun, based this time on the Type 88 AA weapon, was fitted but its muzzle velocity was little improved at 2,362 fps (703 m/s), less than the German 43-calibre 75-mm tank gun. The six tanks of this type that were produced were left in Japan for home defence.

All these tanks were diesel-powered but the final Japanese design was fitted with a German-designed 550-hp BMW petrol engine in an attempt to bypass shortages of the standard diesel engines and speed production. This 37-ton Type 5 CHI-RI was the final extrapolation of the

Type 97. It had eight bogie wheels each side and the Type 4 gun in a large turret with a Type 1 37-mm in the hull. Armour was the same as the Type 4. However, it appeared only as a prototype.

As with the Type 98, such a plethora of new designs was hardly necessary and only complicated a production system that was already grinding to a halt. Once the Type 3 had been developed, a vehicle of moderate size and adequate firepower, it might well have been standardized without going on to the larger tanks of 30 tons or more that unnecessarily confused the situation.

Experiments went on in other fields too, although few results saw service. Prototype KA-TO and HO-RI heavy self-propelled guns, on the CHI-RI chassis, were produced just before the war's end. Earlier, an amphibious tank had been produced on the CHI-HE chassis and some were used in action. This 26-ton Type 3 KA-CHI (which weighed almost 29 tons with pontoons) had a large box-type superstructure on which was mounted a turret with a Type 1 47-mm gun. A later Type 5 TO-KU was lower and mounted the 47-mm in the hull. A 25-mm automatic cannon was in the turret.

Despite all this activity it was still the SHINHOTO CHI-HA which met the Americans from Saipan to the Philippines and had to fight Soviet armoured forces when they mounted their offensive in August 1945. Its gun could just defeat the American Sherman but 25-mm armour was no protection from even the smallest enemy anti-tank gun. It stood no chance at all against a Soviet T-34/85. After the war the SHINHOTO CHI-HA saw considerable service with the People's Republic of China.

Infantry Tanks Marks I and II Matilda

In 1934 the requirement was drawn up for a tank whose task would be to give direct support to infantry. Speed was unimportant and the emphasis was to be on protection. Major General Sir Hugh Elles, Master General of the Ordnance, was a strong supporter of this concept and accepted an offer from Sir John Carden to design a small, cheap infantry tank for around £5,000 to £6,000. The first prototype A11 appeared in September 1936.

Soon dubbed 'Matilda', the new tank was simple to an extreme. It was small, 15 feet 11 inches (4.85 m) long and 6 feet 1½ inches (1.86 m) high, had a narrow, 7 feet 6 inch (2.28 m), riveted hull with small cast turret, and was armoured to 60 mm, more than enough protection from contemporary anti-tank guns. A standard Ford V8 car engine and transmission drove through the rear sprockets; steering was a version of the system used in the Vickers light tank series. Suspension was again of standard Vickers type with two leaf-sprung four wheel bogie assemblies each side to which, in the prototype, the two return rollers were attached.

In the 60 vehicles ordered for production in 1937 as Infantry Tank Mark I the return rollers were repositioned on the hull sides. Another 89 vehicles were ordered before production ceased in August, 1940. This first Matilda weighed 11 tons, was extremely slow (8 mph or 13 km/h), and lightly armed with either a 0.303-inch (7.7-mm) or 0.5-inch (12.7-mm) Vickers machine-gun in an armoured sleeve. These weapons could shoot up enemy infantry and light defences and the 0.5-inch (12.7-mm) had some capability against lightly armoured vehicles.

Several shortcomings were soon apparent, and as early as 1936 a successor was being developed which would be faster (15 mph or 24 km/h), have heavier armament and a much better crew lay-out with a three-man turret. This new tank had very thick 78-mm armour fitted to the hull front and a turret of the same standard of protection. Unlike the A11, the new A12's hull was formed of steel castings, and plates bolted together. The turret was also cast. A new suspension, protected by armoured skirting, was based on that of the Vickers Medium, with five twin bogie assemblies each side mounted on bell cranks coil-sprung against each other with a larger jockey roller at the front. The form of construction and the suspension proved complex to construct and did not lend itself to mass production.

Two rear-mounted AEC diesel engines connected at the front and drove through a Wilson epicyclic pre-selector gearbox via the rear sprockets. Steering was by clutch and brake, and the driver sat in the centre of the hull front. The armament of a standard two-pounder (40-mm) gun and 0.303 inch (7.7-mm) Vickers machine-gun mounted co-axially was concentrated in the hydraulically traversed turret. With its greater protection and firepower the 'Matilda Senior', as it was soon dubbed, was far superior to its predecessor.

In May 1938 orders totalled 165. More soon followed, but only two Infantry Tanks Mark II were in service in September 1939. When First Army Tank Brigade joined the BEF later the same month only one battalion – Fourth Battalion Royal Tank Regiment – of 50 Mark Is was available.

Not until May 1940, days before the German offensive, was Seventh RTR sent over to France with 27 Matildas and 23 new Matilda Seniors. They played a crucial role in the campaign. With the Mark II tanks redistributed among the two battalions and supporting two reinforced infantry battalions the tank brigades struck at the advancing *Panzer* corridor south of Arras. Rommel's Seventh *Panzer* Division and the *Totenkopf SS* Motorized Infantry Division were severely shaken by the sudden onslaught of British armour which proved impervious to the standard German anti-tank weapon, the 37-mm gun. Only hastily deployed 105-mm and 150-mm field howitzers which proved effective against the Matilda Is' unprotected suspension, and 88-mm anti-aircraft guns which were able to penetrate the tanks' armour, saved the day for the Germans. The British attack, delivered with little support, soon ran out of steam, but the

Below: *Matilda II. Note the thick well-shaped armour, the Matilda's main strength. In some tanks from Mark III onwards the two-pounder (40-mm) gun was replaced by a three-inch (76.2-mm) howitzer*

report sent back to German high command confirmed them in their fears that the advanced *Panzer* units were dangerously exposed. Hitler, therefore, stopped short of Dunkirk and the BEF was given time to prepare a strong evacuation bridgehead before the offensive reopened.

After Dunkirk the remaining Infantry Tanks Mark I were relegated to training and the term Matilda became the official designation of the Infantry Tank Mark II. The first vehicles became known as Matilda I; a Matilda II soon appeared (Infantry Tank Mark IIA) with co-axial Besa machine-gun instead of the Vickers. Leyland joined the production programme and produced their own engines for the Matilda III. The Matilda IV had improved E170/1 Leyland diesel engines and the Matilda V an improved gear shift system. In all, some 2,987 A12 Matildas were produced by August 1943.

These later Matildas were modified for desert conditions and in North Africa the type scored its greatest successes. Re-equipped with the latest Matildas, Seventh RTR was sent out to join the Western Desert Force in September 1940. With the Fourth Indian and the Sixth Australian Infantry Divisions, they played a vital part in the Italian defeats at Nibeiwa, Tummar, Bardia and Tobruk. The Matilda's reputation as the 'Queen of the Battlefield' was soon established and their morale value enormous. The Commander of Sixth Australian Division compared the value of each tank to a whole battalion of infantry. The Matilda's

reliability was also demonstrated in East Africa where a squadron of Fourth RTR were sent at the end of 1940 to support Fourth Infantry Division against the Italians in Eritrea. In the absence of proper support facilities, they were able to keep going after suffering such major mechanical defects as damaged suspensions.

With the coming of the Germans to North Africa in 1941 the Matilda met its old opponent of the previous year. Seventh RTR, now joined by the Fourth helped to hold Tobruk, but victory was more elusive. In Operation Battleaxe of June 1941, when the two regiments were joined as the Fourth Armoured Brigade of Seventh Armoured Division, the Matilda was more vulnerable. Matildas could take three 88-mm hits and survive but the operation ended in failure with the loss of 64 tanks. In tank versus tank combat, however, Matildas had proved superior to the German armour: more than 60 per cent of 15th *Panzer* Division's tanks were knocked out in one clash with Seventh RTR at Capuzzo. Back in the infantry support role Matildas also did well during the Crusader offensive.

Yet the era of the Matilda was steadily passing. It lacked the long-range, high-explosive potential that would have enabled it to engage the German anti-tank guns on equal terms. Its two-pounder (40-mm) required a direct hit to destroy the enemy weapon while the Besa machine-gun had a maximum range of 800 yards (731 m), less than the effective range of the German 88-mm or

captured Russian 76.2-mm gun against the Matilda's armour.

First and 32nd Army Tank Brigades had Matildas on strength for the Gazala battle at the end of March 1942, but their counter-attacks were broken up, with heavy losses, by German anti-tank guns. Seventh RTR still had Matildas in the 32nd Brigade at Tobruk and these were lost in the final stand there. Such losses hastened the disappearance of the tank and its replacement by the more easily produced Valentine. Matilda Scorpion mine-sweeping tanks saw service in North Africa while later Baron vehicles were used for training. Matilda CDL (Canal Defence Light) vehicles were produced but never used in action.

As well as fighting in North Africa, standard Matildas served in Malta, Crete, Russia and the Far East. The tank's reliability and mobility made it well suited to the difficult conditions of the Pacific theatre where its armament and firepower were more than able to deal with the Japanese. The Australians turned to the Matilda for infantry support in New Guinea, Bougainville and Borneo. They also produced flame-thrower and bulldozer versions of the Matilda – undoubtedly the finest British tank of the early war years.

Below: *Infantry Tank Mark I Matilda. This first tank series gained its nickname from its appearance in profile which was said to resemble that of a contemporary cartoon duck*

Infantry Tank Mark III Valentine

When they were approached in 1938 with a view to constructing the Infantry Tank Mark II, Vickers decided to produce a comparable vehicle based on their previous A9 and A10 cruiser tanks. The design had certain drawbacks compared with the Matilda Senior, however, and when first offered to the War Office just before St Valentine's Day 1938, it did not gain immediate acceptance. But the deteriorating international situation led to a change in policy and 275 were ordered in 1939. The first tanks, designated Infantry Tank Mark III, were in service by the end of 1940. Soon known as 'Valentine', the designation became official in June 1941.

Construction of the new tank was simple, the hull comprising plates bolted and riveted together. Some castings were used in the construction of the turret. Suspension was on the same simple lines as the A9 and A10, with two three-wheel bogie assemblies each side, each with a single coil spring damped by shock absorbers. The 135-hp AEC A189 petrol engine drove through the rear sprockets. Steering was by clutch and brake. The power-traversed turret mounted a two-pounder (40-mm) gun and co-axial Besa machine-gun. Armour was thick, although not as strong as the Matilda's. Maximum speed was the same, 15 mph (24 km/h), but range disappointing at 70 miles (113 km). This could be extended to 105 miles (169 km) with auxiliary fuel tanks.

Valentine had one significant advantage over Matilda however – ease of construction. It took one-third less man hours to produce and soon other firms were producing the vehicles in addition to Vickers. Arrangements were also made for the construction of Valentines in Canada. Canadian Valentines were to be fitted with GMC diesel engines and it was soon decided to convert the British version to diesel power to increase range, reduce the fire risk and economize on crude oil. After 350 tanks, therefore, the

Valentine I was replaced by the Valentine II (Infantry Mark III Star) which adopted the A190 diesel version of the original AEC engine with slightly reduced power. Some 700 of this version were built before the end of 1941; it was the first type to see combat service, being sent out with Eighth RTR to take part in Operation Crusader as part of First Army Tank Brigade. Valentines were also used by other infantry tank regiments in the Western Desert, Seventh, 42nd and 44th RTR steadily replacing the Matilda tank with them as losses mounted during 1942.

Valentines did not go only to the infantry tank formations for which they had been intended. From the middle of 1941, as readily available and well-protected tanks, they were allocated to the armoured divisions as cruisers: Sixth, Eighth, Eleventh and First Polish Armoured Divisions were so equipped. In the Alamein fighting the Eighth's 23rd Armoured Brigade was thrown into action as an infantry support formation. Despite heavy losses charging anti-tank guns at Ruweisat Ridge unsupported, the Brigade played a vital part in assisting the initial infantry assaults during Second Alamein – the task for which the tank had been designed. Following the break-through, the 23rd's Valentines demonstrated their great mechanical reliability, travelling 3,000 miles (4,828 km) on a set of tracks. Sixth Armoured Division, which landed in North Africa with First Army in November 1942, had mixed squadrons of Crusaders and Valentines in its 26th Armoured Brigade.

By this time, design improvements had been made. Firstly, a three-man turret had been adopted with the gun moved forward and the turret sides extended backwards so that a fourth crew member could be incorporated. Not many of these Valentine IIIs, saw service. More common was the Valentine IV which adopted the General Motors engine of the

Canadian vehicle in a standard Valentine II. Although range was decreased to 90 miles (145 km) or 165 miles (266 km) with auxiliary fuel tanks compared to the AEC engined version, the twin stroke GM 6-71 Model 604 diesel of 138 hp was quieter and more reliable. The new engine was also fitted to the Valentine III to produce the Valentine V.

Before the end of 1941 development had begun of a Valentine mounting a new six-pounder (57-mm) gun. The three-man turret was used, with its crew reduced to two once more due to the size of the gun. The commander now doubled as loader and the gunner as wireless operator. Side armour was reduced to keep weight within limits at 17.2 tons and the machine-gun was deleted from the turret. The six-pounder (57-mm) had a disappointing high explosive capability, and the first tanks tended to be issued together with two-pounder (40-mm) vehicles (which at least had a machine-gun) as anti-tank support tanks. The AEC engined vehicles were designated Valentine Mark VIII and those with General Motors engines became Valentine Mark IX, some with uprated engines of 165 hp. Some of both marks had the 45-calibre Mark III six-pounder (57-mm) replaced by the longer 52-calibre Mark V. The Valentine X which came into production in 1943 reintroduced the turret machine-gun with the Mark V six-pounder (57-mm). By now the up-rated General Motors engine was standard. Finally came the Mark XI which had the six-pounder (57-mm) replaced by a 75-mm weapon with dual anti-tank/high explosive capability. The XI was the last Valentine mark to appear, as production of the tank ceased in early 1944.

Below: *Valentine IVs on manoeuvre in Britain. Valentines were widely used from 1941–3 for training new British armoured divisions as well as the infantry tank battalions for which they had been originally intended*

Valentine tanks remained in first line British Army service as battle tanks until their replacement by Shermans at the end of the North African campaign. A Special Service tank squadron took Valentines to fight the Vichy French in Madagascar, while Free French forces were allocated ex-British vehicles in North Africa in 1942–3. The Valentine also saw service against the Japanese with Indian and New Zealand forces. The Soviet Union were sent 2,690 of the tanks – 1,300 British and almost the entire Canadian production run. The tank proved very popular with the Russians who were the major operational user of up-gunned models. Britain used Valentine XIs as battery commander's tanks for tank destroyer battalions in the North-West Europe campaign of 1944–5. Valentines were also used as artillery observation post tanks.

Two types of self-propelled gun saw service on the Valentine chassis. The first of these mounted the standard 25-pounder (88-mm) field gun. An order for 100 was placed in November, 1941. The Carrier Valentine 25-pounder (88-mm) Gun Mark I placed the gun in a simple box-type, thinly protected superstructure on a normal Valentine II chassis. The weapon, intended primarily as a tank destroyer, had only limited traverse, 15° in elevation and 4° to each side. Only 32 rounds were carried and the vehicle normally towed a normal gun limber, in order to double ammunition capacity. The crew numbered four. By the time the vehicle entered service with the Royal Artillery in 1942 the six-pounder (57-mm) anti-tank gun had become available. The new SP became, therefore, a general purpose self-propelled gun, a role which emphasized its several shortcomings.

With the advent of the 'Priest' self-propelled 105-mm howitzer, the Valentine Carrier became known as the 'Bishop'. The superior American weapon eventually replaced the British gun but not until after Bishops had fought through North Africa into Tunisia, Sicily and the early part of the Italian campaign.

As the Bishop was being phased out of service, a much more successful Valentine-based SP was being put into production mounting the 17-pounder (76.2-mm) anti-tank gun. The gun faced towards the rear of the Valentine chassis; the welded front superstructure (later vehicles had a light steel roof) was armoured to 20 mm and the gun had a wide traverse of 45° to either side with 15½° of elevation and 7½° of depression. Together with the American M10, the SP 17-pounder (76.2-mm) Valentine or 'Archer' as it was usually known, served with the Royal Artillery in Northern Europe and Italy in 1944–5.

Valentines were used in the development of flame weapons and for mine-clearing purposes. Most important were the Valentine Scorpion flails – Valentine IIs and IIIs modified with fixed flail equipment powered by two Ford V8 engines in a protected superstructure (14 mm). Some 150 were built and used for training. The most novel means of dealing with minefields was a Valentine fitted with rockets to jump over the mine-laden area. Unfortunately, the tank usually landed upside down so the idea was abandoned.

Rather more practical were the amphibious Valentines. These were Marks V, IX and XI tanks fitted with Straussler duplex drive system with a propeller and collapsible canvas screen; 625 were produced and used mainly for training. The Valentine saw more extensive service as a bridge-layer. The standard 30-foot (9.14-m) 'scissors bridge', placed on the Valentine chassis, was laid by a hydraulic system without the crew needing to leave the tank. The Valentine bridge-layer was used in Italy, North-West Europe and Burma. There were also Valentine bulldozer and CDL variants.

More Valentine tank chassis were constructed than any other individual British type during the war years, 6,855 being built until production ceased in early 1944. Canadian production boosts the figure to 8,275. Ease of construction coupled with reliability were the Valentine's basic assets, but they could not completely overcome the disadvantages of low speed and poor crew layout and, as time went on, deficient armour and firepower. By 1944 the Valentine was patently inadequate as a battle tank and production plans for a later version, the 'Valiant', were abandoned.

Below: A Valentine X produced in 1943 which reintroduced the turret machine-gun combined with the six-pounder (57-mm) gun. Earlier six-pounder Valentines had dispensed with secondary armament to simplify production
Bottom: The reliable Valentine chassis was used for a variety of specialized purposes such as carrier for the 'scissors bridge'. Each armoured brigade had six of these vehicles and they were used in Italy, North-West Europe and Burma

Infantry Tank Mark IV Churchill

The last and best of the line of British infantry tanks had its origins in the first month of war when a larger and more heavily armed, armoured and mobile infantry tank was called for to replace the Matilda. Armour was to be 80 mm, the tank would be capable of climbing a five-foot (3.7-metre) obstacle and the engine was to be either a Harland and Wolff diesel or Meadows petrol engine giving a maximum speed of 15 mph (24 km/h). It was decided to mount a Matilda turret and armament with another two-pounder (40-mm) in the hull front and extra Besa machine-guns in the hull sides. Prototypes of this project, designated A20, were ordered, but when the first vehicles appeared the design was shown to be inadequate. The Meadows engine did not give enough power, the new Merritt Brown gearbox gave problems and the extra armament had to be deleted to keep weight down to the specified 37½ tons. In June 1940, Vauxhall were asked to redesign the vehicle as a new A22, a scaled down design that would be produced in large quantities from 1941.

The suspension was based on that of the French *Char* B with the tracks carried around the hull to aid mobility across rough ground. The A20's suspension of 14 small bogie wheels each side was shortened to 11, each independently coil sprung. Drive was through the rear sprockets and the new Merritt Brown gearbox steered the tank by means of the controlled differential principle. This system was similar in effect to that of the later German tanks, but simpler and more serviceable. Armament consisted of a standard two-pounder (40-mm) in the turret with co-axial Besa machine-gun; a three-inch (76.2-mm) howitzer was located in the hull. The tank therefore possessed three capabilities – anti-tank, high-explosive and anti-personnel. Armoured protection was 101 mm maximum and weight 38½ tons. The 350-hp Bedford twin six-cylinder had a maximum speed of 17 mph (27 km/h) which was adequate for the infantry support role. Although the turret was cast, hull construction was of riveted steel plates to which armour was bolted.

The first 14 production models of the Infantry Tank Mark I were completed in June 1941 and the name 'Churchill' was soon adopted. Some 303 were completed before the Mark II appeared, substituting a machine-gun for the three-inch (76.2-mm) hull howitzer. A few Mark II close support vehicles were completed with the howitzer in the turret and two-pounder (40-mm) guns in the hull. These were 1,127 Mark IIs completed while some Mark Is were converted to II standard.

These early Churchills had many mechanical defects due to the speed of development. Transmission, clutch, steering, suspension and even hull construction all needed modification. Older tanks were modified in a systematic reworking programme that began in May 1942. From then on, tanks were regularly brought up to the latest specifications.

Mechanical refinements were incorporated in the Churchill III, which had the new 43-calibre, six-pounder (57-mm) gun. This increased theoretical armour penetration to 81 mm of 30° plate at 500 yards (457 m) although high explosive capability was disappointing. A welded turret was adopted for the gun. The first IIIs appeared in March 1942; by the middle of the year 40 tanks per week were coming off the production lines. A total of 675 new Churchill IIIs were built. In the middle of 1942 a further type appeared, the Mark IV, which had a better-shaped cast turret. Some 1,622 were built, a number with the improved 50-calibre Mark V six-pounder (57-mm) and slightly improved muzzle velocity and armour penetration.

The first Churchills to see action were the Mark Is and IIIs of the Canadian Calgary Regiment in the Dieppe raid in August 1942. They were specially fitted for deep wading with extended intakes and exhausts. The operation ran into opposition and, without assault engineer or infantry support, the Churchills could do little to save a doomed operation.

The type's mechanical problems prevented immediate deployment in Africa, but six Mark IIIs were sent out to Egypt in time for the Second Battle of Alamein. The Churchills proved to be tough, with armour able to deflect 50-mm and

Below: *A Churchill III (note the angular welded turret) crosses a trench by means of fascines. This tank lacks the track guards fitted from the middle of 1942 and has non-standard extensions to its later model intakes*

even 75-mm anti-tank rounds – one tank was hit no fewer than 31 times by 50-mm anti-tank shells and still remained intact. In the entire battle the six tanks were hit 105 times but only one was knocked out.

With this experience to go on, two Brigades of Churchills, the 21st and 25th, were sent to North Africa to fight with First Army in Tunisia. The brigades were intended for allocation to infantry divisions in order to provide direct support, but each brigade was attached instead to two infantry brigades to form two of the short-lived 'new model' divisions. At Steamroller Farm, Hunt's Gap, Longstop Hill and elsewhere the techniques of 'all arms' warfare were developed anew. In tank versus tank combat the six-pounder (57-mm) proved extremely effective and the vehicle showed its remarkable mobility. Churchills could go where no German thought possible; at Steamroller Farm the German commander ascribed his defeat to the 'mad tank battalion' that had scaled 'impossible heights'.

A plan to replace the Churchill by the Cromwell, as the main battle tank, was soon shelved and it was decided to improve the Churchill's firepower – its major weakness being high explosive capability. A new close support Mark V appeared, therefore, which substituted a 95-mm howitzer for the six-pounder (57-mm) of the Mark IV. This weapon fired a 25-pounder

(95-mm) shell, almost double the weight of the three-inch (76.2-mm) howitzer's projectile. One tenth of all Churchills completed were to mount this new weapon to support more conventionally armed vehicles. Other close support firepower was provided by older Churchills kept in service in the Mediterranean theatre with two 3-inch (76.2-mm) howitzers as armament.

The real need, however, was for a genuine dual purpose armament and in North Africa 120 Churchill IVs and one Churchill III had their six-pounders (57-mm) replaced by the salvaged 75-mm guns and mountings of knocked out Sherman tanks. Known as Churchill NA75s, the tanks served throughout Sicily and the Italian campaign. A co-axial 0.30 inch (7.62-mm) Browning machine-gun was fitted in place of the 7.92-mm Besa.

When it became available the British 75-mm was fitted to new Churchills. The first major 75-mm model was the Churchill VI, production of which began in November 1943. It was only considered an interim type until the appearance of a new, drastically redesigned Churchill with improved protection and gun power.

The new vehicle, which appeared at the end of 1943, had armour increased to a formidable 152-mm maximum and 25-mm minimum. This thicker plate was now used as the basic constructional medium of the hull which became of

welded integral construction. The turret had cast sides and a welded roof; a cupola was fitted as standard, a modification made to some earlier marks also. Weight was increased to 40 tons with speed reduced to 13 mph (21 km/h). Adopted as the Churchill VII, those built with the 95-mm howitzer became Mark VIIIs.

Older tanks were brought up to the new standards, with appliqué armour and sometimes new turrets. Modified Mark IIIs and IVs were fitted with new turrets but retained the six-pounder (57-mm) to become Churchill Mark IXs. Those that kept the original turret, became Mark IX LTs (light turret). Older tanks with 75-mm guns, Mark VIs, became Mark Xs or X LTs and similarly reworked Mark Vs became Mark XIs or Mark XI LTs.

Three brigades of Churchills, Mark IIIs onwards, were deployed in North-Western Europe with Sixth Guards and 31st and 34th Tank Brigades. Two brigades, 21st and 25th, fought in Italy (still with proportions of older Churchills Is and IIIs), playing a vital part in breaching German lines. At 200 yards (182 m) even dug-in *Panther* turrets used as pillboxes could not withstand the Churchill's six-pounder (57-mm) and 75-mm guns.

In these campaigns of 1944–5 a whole range of specialized armour was unveiled that played a crucial part in operations. The stimulus to

Infantry Tank Mark IV Churchill IV
Weight 39 tons (39.6 tonnes)
Crew five
Armament one six-pounder (57-mm) Mark III (L/43) gun with 84 rounds and two 7.92-mm Besa machine-guns with 4,950 rounds
Armour hull nose 89 mm, glacis 38 mm, driver's plate 101 mm, sides 76 mm, decking 15–19 mm, belly 19 mm, tail 64 mm; turret front and sides 89 mm
Engine one Bedford 'Twin-Six' horizontally opposed 12-cylinder liquid-cooled petrol, 350-hp
Speed 17 mph (27 km/h)
Range 90 miles (144 km)
Trench crossing 12 feet (3.66 m)
Vertical step 4 feet (1.22 m)
Fording 3 feet (91 cm)
Overall length 25 feet 2 inches (7.65 m)
Width 10 feet 8 inches (3.25 m)
Height 8 feet 0.5 inches (2.45 m)

Left: *A Churchill IV as used in Tunisia where two brigades proved very successful*

develop what was in effect a modern mechanized siege train resulted from the Dieppe fiasco. This had shown that armoured protection was imperative for the vast majority of engineer tasks if the invading armies were to gain the beaches of North-West Europe. Major General Sir Percy Hobart of 79th Armoured Division cooperated with research organizations to produce 'funnies', as they were called, in profusion. The Churchill proved the best unit for conversion, being tough, highly mobile and with ample room for extra crew members and equipment.

The most significant 'funny' based on the Churchill was the AVRE, Assault Vehicle Royal Engineers. Some 734 conversion kits were produced for Churchills III and IV and slightly more than 700 tanks were factory converted. The AVRE's main armament was a 290-mm Petard mortar which could fire a 40-lb (88-kg) demolition charge over 80 yards (73 m). A wide range of fittings was designed for use with the vehicle. For example, fascines could be jettisoned into or against an obstacle and a Standard Box Girder Bridge or a large Bailey Bridge could be laid.

The development of the carpet-laying technique, to assist the crossing of soft terrain or barbed wire, acquired impetus when it was learned that the Normandy beaches contained soft patches of clay. An early type of carpet-layer had been used on a Churchill III at Dieppe

and four types were later produced for the AVRE. Carpet-layers (Types C and D) Marks II and III were the most important. Sometimes referred to as Bobbins Marks I and II, the first had a movable bobbin while the Type D consisted of a larger, fixed reel. After laying at two mph (3.3 km/h), both could be jettisoned.

The Petard was intended to clear mines as well as blow up obstacles although other sorts of gear were developed for the former role,

Below: Tank brigades equipped with Churchills were also given the 'Jumbo' Churchill Bridge-layers to assist in crossing small streams
Bottom: The Carpet-layer Type D Mark III (Bobbin Mark II). The large fixed reel unrolled a hessian carpet, reinforced with steel tubes, over soft ground or barbed wire. The AVRE here is a converted Churchill III, note the welded turret. It is fitted for deep-wading with long extensions to the air intakes and exhausts

such as the 'Snake' and two ploughs, the 'Bullshorn' and the 'Jeffries'. The Canadian Indestructable Roller Device was issued for use with 79th Armoured Division's AVREs. Another piece of mine-clearing equipment used in conjunction with the AVRE was the 'Conger', a long piece of hose projected by rocket across a minefield. It was then filled with nitro-glycerine and exploded to clear a narrow path.

Another vital contribution to assault operations was the Churchill Crocodile flame-thrower. The first flame-thrower versions of the Churchill were the Churchill Okes – three early Churchills modified for Dieppe to carry the Canadian Ronson flame-thrower system. Later, a Wasp II was adopted for fitting to the Churchill VII as the Churchill Crocodile. A flame projector was fitted to the hull front, fuelled by a 400 gallon (1,818 l) armoured trailer towed behind the tank. The maximum range of the flame-thrower was about 100 yards (91 m), and 80 one-second bursts were available. Conversion kits totalled 800, and all late production Churchill VIIs were built with conversion in mind.

While the AVRE was often used in a bridging role, other types of bridging vehicles were built on the Churchill chassis. A Bridge-layer (sometimes called Jumbo) was developed which put a hydraulically laid 60-ton capacity bridge on a Churchill III or IV chassis. It was usually used to cross small streams and craters. In order to provide a quick means of crossing such obstacles as sea walls or larger craters a Churchill ARK (Armoured Ramp Carrier) was developed by 79th Armoured Division in late 1943. A turretless tank with ramps that hinged down at either end and trackways across the top, it went into

an obstacle and was then driven over by following vehicles.

Soon after the D-Day landings 79th Armoured Division developed an improved Mark II. Extended ramps were fitted at the front; gaps of 47 feet 6 inches (14.47 m) could now be crossed against the 28 foot (8.53 m) span of the original. In Italy a different version was developed which could cross spans of up to 54 feet 4 inches (16.56 m). Armoured recovery versions of the Churchill included an ARV Mark I based on turretless Churchill Is and IIs and an ARV Mark II used the Churchill III or IV chassis with a fixed dummy gun and turret.

Once its initial problems had been overcome, the Churchill tank was arguably the best British tank available in quantity in the war years, being versatile, mobile, reliable and immensely tough. Its infantry support specification may have reflected limited strategic insight, but from 1942 onwards it was ideally suited to a war of mechanized attrition – particularly in difficult terrain where the sophisticated concepts of armoured warfare and blitzkrieg were irrelevant. The only major drawback was the limited armament due to the narrow turret ring dictated by the need to make the tank transportable within the British railway loading gauge. A wider 'Super Churchill', later renamed 'Black Prince' was developed mounting a 17-pounder (76.2-mm) gun but it was produced too late to take part in the war, and, with the decision to concentrate on one 'universal' tank, was abandoned as the requirement was better met by the new heavily armoured cruiser, Centurion. Nevertheless Churchills remained in service for long after the war and served in Korea where Crocodiles were also used.

Churchill VII
Weight 40 tons (40.6 tonnes)
Armament one L/36.5 75-mm Mark V or VA gun with 84 rounds, one 7.92-mm Besa machine-gun with 4,950 rounds
Armour hull front 140–152 mm, sides 95 mm, tail 50 mm; turret front 152 mm, sides 95 mm
Speed 13 mph (21 km/h)
Range 125 miles (201 km)
Width 11 feet 4 inches (3.45 m)
Other details as Churchill IV

Below: *A Churchill VII Crocodile flame-thrower. Note the new turret, redesigned side hatch and replacement of the hull-machine gun by a flame projector. The flame-thrower system was powered by high pressure nitrogen carried in the armoured fuel trailer; the trailer could be jettisoned if hit. Three regiments in 31st Armoured Brigade, part of 79th Armoured Division, were equipped with Crocodiles in North-West Europe. Seventh RTR had nine, three troops of three, one troop in each squadron. The Crocodile needed skill and experience to operate but when used properly it was a formidable weapon against enemy positions*

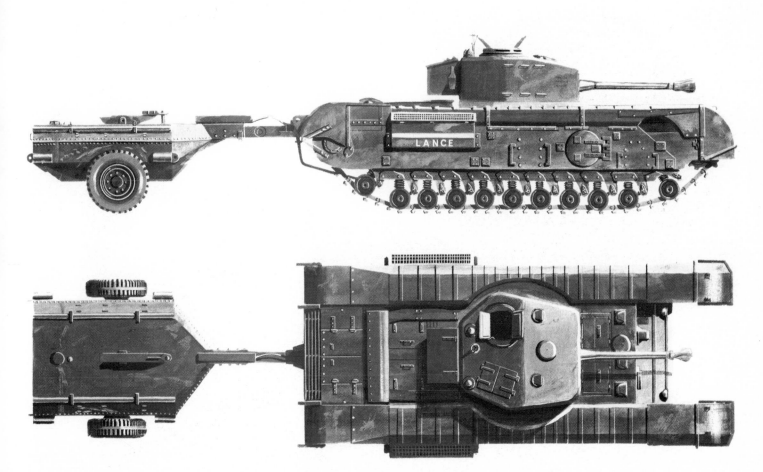

Char B Series

The *Char B* was the most powerfully armed and armoured tank available in quantity to any army in 1939. Instigated by General Estienne, the 'father of the French tank', work had begun in 1921 on a *char de bataille* to provide heavy support for the *chars d'accompagnement* of the infantry and to deal with difficult enemy defences including tanks. The new tank was to be heavily armed and armoured and equipped with radio to achieve some tactical co-ordination in its semi-independent operations, though its role was still basically one of infantry support and not independent attack.

After the construction of mock-ups, authorization was given at the beginning of 1926 for three prototypes to be built. It was decided to use the suspension of the design from FCM (Forges et Chantiers de la Méditerranée), the engine from Renault and the transmission from Schneider. In 1927 orders were placed with FCM, Renault and FAMH (Forges et Aciéries de la Marine et d'Homécourt). The Rueil Arsenal (ARL) co-ordinated the project and eventually the vehicles were completed between 1929 and 1931, two at ARL and one at FCM.

These tanks carried a short 75-mm gun in the hull front with two machine-guns, and two further machine-guns in a small turret. Armour protection was 25-mm and the tank weighed 25 tons. A 180-hp engine gave it a very limited speed of 12.5 mph (20 km/h), though its range was 160 miles (257 km). Trials during 1930 and 1931 were successful and development of what was now the *Char B* continued. Spurred by German rearmament and the occupation of the Rhineland in 1935, a modified version went into immediate production. A new cast turret carrying a short 47-mm gun was added, armour was increased to 40-mm, and a 250-hp engine was fitted to move the 30-ton vehicle at over 17 mph (27 km/h), which reduced the range of this slow, heavy tank to 125 miles (200 km).

The first 35 tanks, usually known as *Char B*1s, were followed by a further modified B1 *bis* with a more heavily-armoured APX4 turret with 34-calibre 47-mm gun, hull armour increased to 60 mm and weight to 32 tons. But a more power-

ful, and thirsty, engine of 307 hp reduced endurance to a mere 87 miles (140 km), which although not too important for infantry operations was a vital strategic drawback in long-ranging mobile war. Late production vehicles had auxiliary fuel tanks fitted to help solve this problem.

The B series had a frame of two girders and cross members upon which were bolted armoured plates and castings. The suspension was a modification of the Holt tractor type with three four-wheel bogie assemblies each side controlled by combined coil and compressed leaf springs. Three independently sprung wheels at the front and one at the back helped control each track, the tension of which could be adjusted from inside the vehicle using the spring-mounted front idlers. The rear-mounted engine worked via a synchromesh, double-differential transmission. The auxiliary differential was controlled from the steering wheel by a Naeder hydrostatic system, developed by Batignolles, for precision aiming of the fixed hull-mounted main armament. This concept is reminiscent of the principle of the modern Swedish turretless S Tank, which uses a sophisticated control system to aim the whole tank at the target.

The duties of the four-man crew were complex and even with a skilled and highly trained team the distribution of jobs did not lend itself to tactical efficiency in action. The driver of the tank also doubled as main gunner, elevating the 17.1-calibre 75-mm using a hand crank, while also usually controlling the single-hull machine-gun. A separate loader fused the 75-mm ammunition and passed 47-mm shells to the electrically-traversed turret, where an overworked commander/gunner attempted to direct the tank and/or formation and also work the high-velocity armament. The four-man crew was completed by a wireless operator.

In 1936 the four-year rearmament plan had aimed at 12 battalions of *Char B*s (about 400 tanks) to equip two *DCR*. The mechanical complexity of the B1 *bis* delayed mass production, however, and only 365 had been constructed by the French collapse, despite the use of five

manufacturers: Renault, Schneider, FCM, FAMH, and from 1939, AMX (Atelier de Construction d'Issy-les-Moulineaux). In the early months of the war a maximum of only 15 B1s *bis* per month were being produced. About 300 B1s and B1s *bis* were available to meet the Germans when the struck on 10 May 1940: 66 were on the strength of each of the three *DCR*, and 57 were scattered in various small *compagnies autonomes*. Up to 30 more formed the nucleus of De Gaulle's Fourth *DCR*.

The B1 *bis* had overwhelming strength in armament and armour. With its 47-mm it could out-gun the *PzKpfw* III and IV and could only be disabled by shooting off its tracks, putting a shot through the vulnerable engine grille on the left-hand side or bringing up an 88-mm AA gun. Yet the tank was largely a failure in action. Badly-trained crews found the complexities of the B too much for them, and, more importantly, the shortness of the tank's range coupled with stopping and starting on refugee-clogged roads, led to anxiety about fuel and numerous refuelling stops. First *DCR* never recovered from being surprised by German armour with its tanks refuelling. It is true that many *Char B*s were dispersed by ignorant higher commanders and never had a chance to be employed *en masse* in the general confusion, but these crucial design weaknesses, which also reflected French limited strategic concepts, did not help matters.

After June 1940 *Char B*s were used by the Germans for occupation duties (for example in the Channel Islands) as the *PzKpfw* B1 *bis* 740 (*f*). Some lost their turrets and armament to become *PzKpfw* B1 (*f*) driver training tanks, 24 had the 75-mm gun replaced by a flame-thrower to become *PzKpfw* B1 *bis* (*f*) *Flamm* and a small number were used as the chassis for a 105-mm SP field howitzer mounting, the

Opposite page: *A Char B painted in the standard 1939 camouflage of 'ochre, marron et vert-gris', although much of the brown on the side is mud carried by the tracks*
Below: *Three PzKpfw B1 bis tanks and a B1 bis Flamm on occupation duty in Jersey*

10.5-cm *le FH* 18 *Ausf Gw* B2 (*f*), used after conversion by Rheinmetall-Borsig with the occupation troops in France. A number of *Char* Bs back in native hands saw action during the Liberation.

A further modification of the B1 had appeared in 1937, the B1 *ter* with improved armour (75-mm), a five-man crew and a 75-mm gun with 5° lateral traverse. Only five were made, the first a prototype B reworked. The need to concentrate on the production B1 *bis* effectively killed the project although further theoretical development took place. It continued secretly during the occupation to form the basis of a new design, begun in earnest after the Liberation in 1944. This ARL-44 had a turret-mounted long 90-mm gun and 60 of these tanks saw service in the postwar French Army.

Char B1 bis
Weight 31.5 tons (32 tonnes)
Crew four
Armament one 75-mm SA-35 (L/17.1) gun with 74 rounds, one 47-mm SA-35 (L/34) gun with 50 rounds, and two 7.5-mm Model 1931 machine-guns with 5,100 rounds
Armour hull front and sides 60 mm, tail 55 m, decking 25 mm, belly 20 mm; turret front 55 mm, sides and rear 45 mm, top 30 mm
Engine one Renault inline six-cylinder liquid-cooled petrol, 307-hp
Speed 17½ mph (28 km/h)
Range 87 miles (150 km)
Trench crossing 9 feet (2.75 m)
Vertical step 3 feet 0.5 inches (93 cm)
Fording 4 feet 10 inches (1.47 m)
Overall length 21 feet 9 inches (6.52 m)
Width 8 feet 3 inches (2.5 m)
Height 9 feet 4 inches (2.79 m)

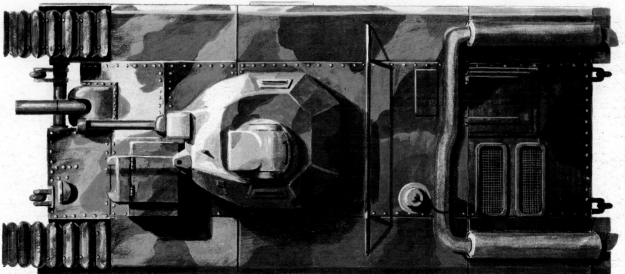

T-34 Series

Few armoured fighting vehicles have had a greater historical impact than the *T-34*. The finest tank in the world at the time of its introduction, it provided the central instrument of Soviet survival and final victory in World War II. It also set the pace of armoured development on a world scale, spurring advances in German tanks which called for similar moves among the Western Allies. Its descendants equip the Soviet Army to this day.

The *T-34* was developed from the BT series of fast tanks which were based on the designs of J Walter Christie. M I Koshkin, of the design bureau at the Komintern Factory in Kharkov, modified the original fast tank to improve protection and increase firepower. This resulted eventually in the *T-32*, which with its modified suspension of five large road wheels each side, well-sloped welded hull and turret and powerful 30.5-calibre 76.2-mm gun was the immediate predecessor of the *T-34*.

Trials in 1939 soon showed the qualities of the new design to be much greater than those of any comparable machine in the size range, and it was accepted as the model for future medium/cruiser tank construction. With armour thickness increased to 45 mm and modified transmission the resultant *T-34* weighed over 25.6 tons. Speed was slightly reduced from 35 to 32 mph (55 to 52 km/h), although this was still high, and tracks widened from 10.25 to 19.1

inches (26 cm to 48.5 cm) kept ground pressure at a very low level, so retaining the remarkable mobility of the *T-32* over soft ground. When these characteristics were combined with a relatively low profile, the heaviest protection of any tank in its speed range and firepower as great as any contemporary tank, the result was formidable.

Despite the drawbacks of a badly laid out interior, an overworked commander and an unreliable transmission, the *T-34* was the finest tank in the world; and with a deteriorating international situation was ordered off the drawing board in December 1939. However, due to the disorganization of the Soviet Army's armoured affairs, only 1,100 had been built by the time the Germans struck, and few had been issued to combat units.

The *T-34*, soon encountered in all sectors of the Eastern Front, came as a most unpleasant surprise for the advancing *Panzer* forces. But used in ones and twos the *T-34* proved little more than a nuisance, though more importantly the new tank shattered German illusions of technical superiority, causing some problem with morale. As the German advance weakened and slowed in the vastness of Western Russia so it became more vulnerable to armoured counter-attacks, operations in which the *T-34*'s technical superiority gave a crucial added edge.

As the Germans advanced so the Russians moved their tank production facilities east to join

those already set up in the Urals. The Kharkov plant joined the Nizhny Tagil industrial complex, so forming the Ural Tank Building Establishment which was to be the major single source of *T-34*s. By the end of 1941, various improvements had been made in the design of the *T-34*. A new, mainly cast, turret was developed with maximum protection improved to 60 mm and this gradually superseded the welded version in production at those plants with the facilities. More importantly, half the 2,810 *T-34*s produced in 1941 had the new M-40 41.2-calibre, 76.2-mm gun with penetration capacity of about 65-mm of 30° plate at 500 yards (457 m), more than enough to deal with the latest *PzKpfw* IV.

In 1942 two major operational shortcomings of the tank were overcome by further redesign. The original turret was so constructed that when the single hatch was lifted up the commander had to peer round it to get forward view, thus making an excellent target for German snipers.

Below: An early T34/76A put out of action during the German advance in 1941. This exceptional tank was the first to really shake the confidence of German tank crews, but the strategic mistakes made by the Soviets during the first year of the war meant that T-34s were often thrown into battle in isolation and were overcome by the inferior but more numerous German tanks

T-34/76B
Weight 27.6 tons (28 tonnes)
Crew four
Armament one 76.2-mm M-40 (L/41.2) gun with
77 rounds and two 7.62-mm DT machine-guns
with 2,394 rounds
Armour hull nose, glacis, sides and tail 45–47 mm,
decking and belly 20 mm; turret front, sides and
rear 45 mm, mantlet 20–46 mm, top 16 mm
Engine one V-2 V-12 liquid-cooled diesel, 500-hp
Speed 32 mph (52 km/h)
Range 188 miles (302.5 km)
Trench crossing 9 feet 8 inches (2.95 m)
Vertical step 2 feet 4 inches (71 cm)
Fording 4 feet 6 inches (1.37 m)
Overall length 21 feet 7 inches (6.58 m)
Width 9 feet 10 inches (3 m)
Height 8 feet (2.44 m)

*The tank illustrated is typical of those T-34/76Bs
produced in 1941–2. Note the long 76.2-mm gun,
the earlier hull machine-gun mount and early
rubber-tyred wheels*

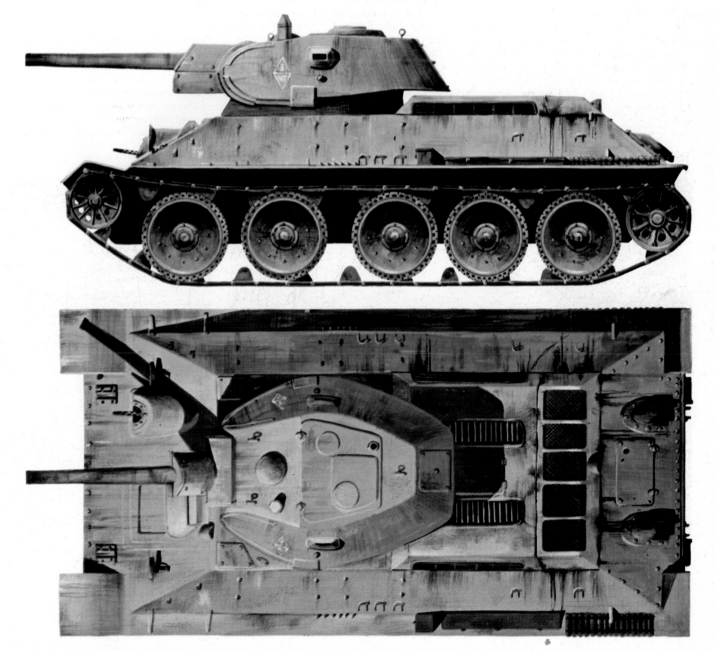

In order to cure the problem, therefore, a new turret was designed with twin hatches and this was also reshaped to delete the troublesome rear overhang – German infantrymen had often taken advantage of the preoccupation of the over-worked crew to climb on the T-34 and wedge a mine between the over-hanging turret rear and the hull. The first version of this turret was of composite welded/cast construction, although by 1943 a fully cast version of improved ballistic shape had appeared. Both types could be fitted with turret cupolas to improve the observation of the commander when 'closed down'. Maximum armour thickness of the new turret was 75 mm on the front, with 52 mm on the sides.

Other modifications to the design of the T-34 were numerous, although with 42 different plants engaged in production these were often introduced on a rather haphazard basis. Extra appliqué armour was sometimes added, new style mantlets and wheels appeared, a more protected machine-gun mount was developed, an improved five-speed gearbox, more reliable than the older four-speed type, was fitted and external fuel tanks began to be carried which increased the T-34's maximum range to 270 miles (435 kilometres). Various designation systems, none of which were employed by the Russians, have been used to help identify the various sub-versions of the tank. Perhaps the least misleading is that which divides all early model T-34s or T-34/76s into three broad sub-types. Those with the short gun are called T-34/76A, those with the earlier turrets and the long gun T-34/76B and those with the later style 'hexagonal' turret, either composite or fully cast, T-34/76C.

By 1943, newer German tanks had emerged to challenge their technological position. First the Tiger and then the Panther asserted their superiority of firepower and protection, but quantity could now make up for quality and the massed use of T-34/76s proved very effective in halting the German offensive at Kursk in 1943. Even the Tiger could still be penetrated by the 41.2-calibre 76.2-mm gun at close range. Like the Sherman the T-34/76 provided an adequate vehicle with which to assert numerical advantage. However, the Russians were not satisfied and by the end of 1943 the design had been revised.

A more heavily protected T-34 with 110-mm frontal armour had been developed at the end of 1942 and produced in small quantities as the T-43, but the Soviet Army wanted an increase in firepower rather than protection. The M-39 85-mm anti-aircraft gun, developed as a tank gun for the KV-85 heavy tank, was fitted in a new, three-man cast/welded turret to the latest standard T-34 chassis to produce the T-34/85. This was a much improved vehicle: the 51.5-calibre D-5T85 (M-43) 85-mm gun had a muzzle velocity of 2,600 fps (792 m/s) and could penetrate 95 mm of 30° armour at 1,000 yards (914 m) with conventional armour piercing rounds. This was sufficient to deal with both Tiger and Panther tanks. More sophisticated armour piercing rounds improved performance further. Later tanks had the improved ZIS-S53 (M-44) gun of similar length. The addition of an extra crewman and the separation of the commander's and gunner's functions also greatly increased the tank's combat efficiency. Turret armour was increased to 75 mm on the front and sides, though hull armour remained 45 mm to keep the weight down to 31 tons. The result of these changes was a vehicle that retained all the mobility of its predecessors coupled with excellent firepower. What it lost in protection to the Panther the T-34/85 more than made up in mobility, and eventually, quantity. The tank had entered service by the end of 1943 and in 1945 most of the 11,758 T-34s built were of the improved type.

As a simpler solution to the problem of putting powerful guns on tracks the T-34 chassis was also utilized as the basis for a series of turretless assault guns. The first such vehicle was the SU-122. This mounted the 122-mm M-38 field howitzer in a limited-traverse mount in the sloping front of a fixed super-structure mounted forward in the chassis. Eight SU-122s were initially allocated with 17 SU-76s in each SU regiment to provide heavier fire support. They were later concentrated in medium SU regiments of 16 vehicles each. But the anti-tank potential of the 122-mm howitzer was limited and the advent of heavier German tanks led to the need

Left: T-34/85 tanks in the East Prussian town of Heiligenbeil in January 1945. This tank was the Soviet answer to the introduction of the German Panther, retaining the mobility of the other T-34s but with added firepower. Note the extra track used to improve protection on the relatively thin hull plating

50

to increase armour piercing capability. In 1943, production therefore began of a similar *SU*-85 mounting the same weapon as the *T*-34/85 tank. These were produced concurrently with early *T*-34/85s and were used to provide readily available additional firepower for the armoured formations which retained the earlier *T*-34/76. There were 21 *SU*-85s per regiment, together with a *T*-34 command tank, and they were allocated on this basis to tank and mechanized corps. In late 1944 an improved *SU*-100 appeared with 54-calibre D-10S 100-mm weapons. This could give valuable support to *T*-34/85 formations. The 100-mm gun could penetrate 160 mm of vertical armour at 1,000 yards (914 m). Low and inconspicuous, both *SU* assault guns were excellent for defensive fire from cover. In the attack, they were used for dealing with difficult targets, such as Tiger tanks, bypassed by the leading battle tanks.

Between 1940 and 1945 almost 40,000 *T*-34 tanks of all types were constructed, a record for a single type equalled only by the American Sherman. Development of both the *T*-34/85 and specialized types continued after 1945 but even before the war's end the tank had been radically redesigned with thicker 90-mm armour, modified suspension, new transmission and transverse engine layout. Some of these *T*-44 tanks armed with 85-mm guns may have seen action before the end of the war. Rushed into service the type had serious deficiencies and was soon replaced by the modified *T*-54, which, together with its later *T*-55 variant, has been the major Eastern Bloc battle tank of the post-war era. Like later *T*-44s, the *T*-54/55 had the 100-mm weapon. Gun size has been increased still further to 115-mm in the contemporary *T*-62; this tank continues in current production and still bears a distinct family resemblance to its ancestor, the most significant tank of World War II, the *T*-34.

T-34/85
Weight 31.4 tons (32 tonnes)
Crew five
Armament one 85-mm M-43 or M-44 (L/51.5) gun with 55 rounds and two 7.62-mm DT machine-guns with 2,394 rounds
Armour turret front, sides and rear 75 mm; top 20 mm
Range 220 miles (354 km) with auxiliary fuel tanks as fitted in the illustration below
Other details as T-34/76B

The T-34/85 tank illustrated is in post-war condition, in the colours of the Egyptian army, who used these vehicles against the Israelis in 1956, 1967 and 1973. Note the rear-mounted turret ventilator, a feature of early as well as post-war models of this type

Medium Tank M3 Lee/Grant

Medium Tank M3 Lee I
Weight 26.8 tons (27.2 tonnes)
Crew six
Armament one 75-mm (L/28.5) M2 gun with 41 rounds, one 37-mm M5 gun with 179 rounds and three or four 0.30-inch (7.62-mm) Browning M1919A4 machine-guns with 8,000 rounds
Armour hull nose, glacis and driver's plate 50 mm, sides 38 mm, decking 13 mm, belly 13–25 mm, tail 13–50 mm; turret front, sides and rear 50 mm, roof 25 mm
Engine one Wright Continental R-975-EC2 radial nine-cylinder air-cooled petrol, 340-hp
Speed 26 mph (42 km/h)
Range 120 miles (193 km)
Trench crossing 7 feet 6 inches (2.29 m)
Vertical step 2 feet (61 cm)
Fording 3 feet 4 inches (1.02 m)
Overall length 18 feet 6 inches (5.64 m)
Width 8 feet 11 inches (2.72 m)
Height 10 feet 4 inches (3.15 m)

The tank illustrated is a British Lee I – note the distinctive high turret and hull-mounted radio

When the German offensive against the Low Countries began in May 1940, the United States Army possessed only 18 modern medium tanks. These were of the M2 type developed in 1937–38 by Rock Island Arsenal for infantry support. The M2 weighed 19 US tons (17.2 tonnes), had 25-mm armour and was armed with eight machine-guns. A 37-mm gun was mounted in a high turret to engage enemy armour and the engine was a nine-cylinder 350-hp Continental R-975 radial. An improved M2A1 was also developed with 400-hp engine, 32-mm armour and other small modifications.

The German victory in France transformed American armoured policy on medium tanks. Some 1,741 mediums were immediately called for and plans were soon approved for a new $21 million Tank Arsenal established by Chrysler at Detroit.

The success of the *PzKpfw* IV in the campaigns of 1939–40 led to demands for a 75-mm main armament for US mediums and an interim

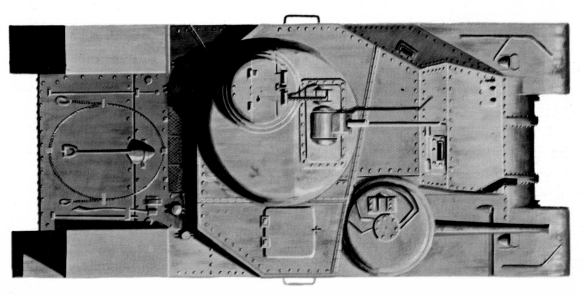

solution to this problem was offered by a T5E2 prototype SP gun built on the M2 chassis in 1939. This mounted a 75-mm pack howitzer in a limited traverse mount in the right hull front and it was used as the basis of the design of the new M3 Medium Tank. Three manufacturers – Chrysler, American Locomotive Company (Alco) and Baldwin Locomotive Company – had produced prototypes by April 1941, and by August production was in full swing.

The M3 kept the M2A1 layout with similar suspension and engine, derated to 340 hp. The hull was of riveted construction and maximum armour thickness was 56 mm. A cast hydraulically traversed turret, mounted to the left, retained the 50-calibre 37-mm gun, but a new M2 75-mm gun was mounted in the right hull front. This weapon had been designed from the standard American 75-mm field gun and was 28.5-calibres long with muzzle velocity of 1,860 fps (567 m/s). This was higher than that of the contemporary PzKpfw IV's 24-calibre 75-mm weapon and had

a similar armour penetration capacity to the later long L/60 50-mm gun of late model PzKpfw IIIs. The M2 could penetrate 60 mm of 30°-plate at 500 yards (457 m) and, just as importantly, had an adequate high-explosive capability also. The gun was mounted with limited traverse of 15° to each side, 20° in elevation and 9° in depression. This system had obvious tactical drawbacks, but a major leap in firepower had been achieved. In addition to the heavy weapons, a 0.30-inch (7.62-mm) machine-gun was mounted co-axially with the 37-mm, with a second weapon in the tank cupola and one or two machine-guns in the left-hand hull front. The M3's crew was six, a loader and a gunner for each weapon plus a commander and driver. A radio was mounted in the hull.

A major improvement with the M3 was gun stabilization and both larger weapons were fitted with gyroscopic systems to keep the gun at a given elevation. This allowed the tank to fire more accurately on the move and, more im-

portantly perhaps, to get its weapons into accurate action as soon as it had stopped.

Modified M3s, with lower turrets and turret-mounted radios, obtained by Britain were the first of the type to go into action. The new Grants (as they were dubbed by the British) were sent to the Western Desert in 1942: 167 were allocated to the Fourth Armoured Brigade of Seventh Armoured Division and to First Armoured Division's Second and 22nd Armoured Brigades. The Grants first saw action in the battle of Gazala in May, the firepower of their 75-mm guns holding off 21st Panzer Division in a long range fire fight. The Grants' merits were not enough to prevent eventual defeat, but in the retreat to Alamein the tank had a significant role in slowing the German advance. Heavy losses were incurred and by July First Armoured Division had all the Grants available to Eighth Army, a mere 38, to supplement about twice that number of Crusaders. Relief was on the way, however. With the passing of the Lend Lease Act in March, 250 standard M3s had been made available to the British and as the 'Lee' some were sent to Egypt. At the Battle of Alam Halfa the Eighth and 22nd Armoured Brigades fielded 164 Lee/Grants; with their heavy firepower, these played an important role in this defensive battle. By the Second Battle of Alamein there were some 210 M3s available to the Eighth Army; they were able to provide one of the most powerful elements in Montgomery's forces.

Production of the American M3 went on at Chrysler, Alco, Baldwin, Pressed Steel and Pullman until late 1942 when some 4,924 M3s had been built. Most were of the standard M3 type (Lee I to the British) some of which had Guiberson diesel engines. Alco produced about 300 M3A1s (Lee II) with a cast hull, some of which also had diesel engines. Twelve M3A2s were produced by Baldwin with welded hulls, and these were followed by 322 M3A3s, similar except for their General Motors 6-71 twin diesel engines of 375 combined hp. Some of these were later re-engined with Wright Continental units. The British called the M3A2 the Lee III, the Continental engined M3A3 Lee IV and the diesel-engined version Lee V. One hundred and nine M3A4s (Lee VI) built at Detroit had the 370-hp Chrysler A-57 multibank engine made up by putting five six-cylinder car engines on a common shaft. This necessitated a slight lengthening of the hull to 19 feet 8 inches (6 metres). Baldwin produced 591 M3A5s in 1942 which combined riveted hulls with the General Motors 6-71 engines. Although they retained their American turrets, these tanks received the British designation Grant II.

The various models were produced concurrently. Later tanks of all models had the longer

Top left: An M2 – the M3 was an up-gunned version of this pre-war medium tank
Bottom left: A well-camouflaged British Grant converted for armoured searchlight (CDL) work. The searchlight was mounted behind a slit in the heavily protected turret which was fitted with a dummy gun to disguise the tank's specialized role

53

M3 37.5-calibre 75-mm gun with 2,200 fps (671 m/s) muzzle velocity and a penetration capability against 30° armour at 500 yards (457 metres) increased by 10 mm.

United States Army M3s were used for training armoured forces, both in the United States and Britain, and they finally went into action with the landings in North Africa in November 1942. By then they were already only a 'substitute standard', following the adoption of the M4. Others were sent to the Pacific, but the newer tank quickly replaced the M3 in combat service with American forces in 1943. The older medium was finally declared obsolete in April 1944. M3s were also used for training British and Canadian troops but the type continued in first-line service until the end of the war with Commonwealth forces. As Lees and Grants were phased out of service with Eighth Army at the end of the North African campaign they were sent to the Far East. They formed a major part of Australian armoured strength while others fought with the 14th Army in Burma until the war's end. Unarmed Grant command tanks were also used by the Sherman-equipped Sixth South African Armoured Division in Italy until 1945. Other M3s were exported to Russia.

A number of other specialized types were developed on the M3 chassis. The Americans developed a T2 TRV (Tank Recovery Vehicle), later standardized as the M31. The M31B1 and B2 were similar vehicles based on the M3A3 and M3A5 respectively. M31s were supplied to the Free French armoured divisions and also to the British, who designated them 'Lee ARV'. The British and Australians also converted Grants into recovery vehicles. The Americans converted some of their M31s into M33 Full Tracked Prime Movers, which were used as tractors for heavy artillery, together with a similar M44.

The Lee/Grant's layout also lent itself to the CDL (Canal Defence Light) armoured search-light role. Following the advent of the Sherman, M3s were so converted by the British as Grant CDLs. First Tank Brigade took them to Europe with 79th Armoured Division and a few were used to illuminate the night crossings of the Rhine and Elbe rivers in 1945. Their guns proved useful in destroying mines floated downstream by the Germans.

The M3 saw use as a mine-sweeping tank, the British converting some Grant Mark Is into Scorpion flails for use in Tunisia, Sicily and Italy. The Americans produced a less satisfactory system of heavy rollers, with one set being pushed and the other being pulled by the M3, known as the Mine Exploder Device T1.

The M3 chassis played a vital part in the development of American self-propelled artillery, although an attempt to produce a tank destroyer on the chassis was abortive.

The M7 self-propelled 105-mm howitzer project began in 1941. The standard M1A2 American field howitzer was placed to right of centre in an open M3 chassis. Two T32 prototypes were built by Baldwin, and after certain modifications, including the addition of a pulpit-type cupola with 0.5-inch (12.7-mm) anti-aircraft machine-gun, the type was ordered into mass production. Alco built some 3,314 M7s until 1944, being joined by the Pressed Steel Car Company that year. After the latter had built 200 vehicles, however, production shifted to the M7B1 based on the Sherman chassis. Standard M7s which had the normal Continental R-975 engine of the M3, were issued to the artillery battalions of American armoured divisions. M7 battalions were also deployed separately and the gun was issued to the assault gun platoons of armoured infantry battalions.

British troops also received the M7, the first 90 arriving in Egypt in 1942 in time for the Second Battle of Alamein. Dubbed Priest by the British forces, due to the pulpit like superstruc-tures, M7s served with Eighth Army in North Africa and Italy. The British ordered a version mounting their own 25-pounder (88-mm) field gun and this led to the development of the Sexton which replaced the Priest in North West Europe after the initial fighting in Normandy. Free French forces also operated M7 self-propelled guns.

The largest of the M3 based SPs was the 155-mm Gun Motor Carriage M12. This originated as an experimental T6 carriage using M3 parts. In order to accommodate the heavy 155-mm gun the Continental R-975 engine was moved to the front and the standard M1917A1 gun was mounted in an open superstructure at the rear. A total of 100 were built during 1942–3 but due to mechanical problems and, doubts as to the general utility and reliability of such a weapon, it was not until 1944 that Baldwin was ordered to modify 75 M12s for service use. M12s then equipped six battalions, and they were used in North-West Europe from July 1944. A similar M30 cargo carrier without gun but with built up rear superstructure was also developed. Forty 155-mm shells could be carried by the M30, a useful supplement to the M12's stowage of only 10 shells.

The M3 medium tank was a stopgap weapon. It had severe tactical disadvantages but it did provide the first tank available to the western allies with an adequate dual purpose armament. Called 'the tank that surprised Rommel' and 'Egypt's last hope' it provided a vital boost to flagging Allied morale in the dismal summer of 1942 when it seemed that no Allied tank could approach a German in terms of quality.

Below: *The widely used M7 self-propelled 105-mm howitzer was based on the M3 chassis. Note the M3-type suspension of the leading vehicle in this American battery advancing through the snows of winter 1944*

Light Tank M3/M5 Stuart

The M3/M5 light tanks were the culmination of a series that dated from 1931. In that year General MacArthur, as Army Chief of Staff, had called for a new light tank armoured against small arms fire, relying on speed against larger weapons and suitable for service both as an infantry support tank and as a cavalry combat car for reconnaissance and exploitation. The existing T1 light tank series was too slow so a new T2 prototype was completed at Rock Island Arsenal in 1934. Its design owed a great deal to that of the Vickers 'Six Ton' light tank. The distinctive leaf-spring suspension and sloping hull front of the British tank were adopted; 0.30-inch (7.62-mm) and 0.50-inch (12.7-mm) machine-guns were mounted in the fixed turret with a further 0.30-inch (7.62-mm) gun in the hull. Armour was 16 mm maximum and the weight 6½ US tons (5.9 tonnes). A Continental radial aircraft engine of 250 hp, driving through the front sprockets, gave the required speed of 35 mph (56 km/h); steering was on the 'Cletrac' controlled differential principle. The Vickers suspension was ill suited to high speeds and the contemporary T5 Combat Car had a new

arrangement of two vertical volute springs each side, each supporting a double bogie. Trials proved this layout superior with maximum speed being increased to 45 mph (72 km/h), and despite flirtation with more complex Christie suspensions the simpler system was adopted for almost all future light tanks and combat cars.

Limited production began of 19 M2A1 light tanks in 1936, and these were followed by Light Tank M2A2 with a twin-turret arrangement. The cavalry had produced a prototype Combat Car T5E2 with a small hand traversed revolving turret which was standardized as the Combat Car M1. Some 170 M1 combat cars and M2A2 tanks were completed by the end of 1937.

In 1938 an improved M2A3 light tank appeared with a longer wheelbase to improve the ride. The cavalry combat car was similarly improved and also given a new transmission, offset turret and radio as the M1A1. An alternative approach was tried with the diesel-engined Combat Car M2 which had a trailing idler to help improve the ride, a system also experimented with on M2A2E3 and M2A3E3 light tanks. The infantry, however, persevered with

the raised idler in their next M2A4 tank of 1939, which was a major improvement over its predecessors with a single fully rotating turret mounting a 37-mm gun. With 25-mm armour weight was up to 12 US tons (10.5 tonnes) and speed was reduced to 37 mph (60 km/h). A 0.30-inch (7.62-mm) machine-gun was mounted co-axially with the 37-mm and another machine-gun was fitted in the nose and in each hull sponson. A fifth machine-gun could be mounted for anti-aircraft purposes. Most M2A4s had the 250-hp Continental W-670-9A seven-cylinder radial petrol engine but some later tanks had Guiberson (General Motors) diesel units.

Although only 50 M2A3 tanks and M2 combat cars had been built, the outbreak of war in Europe led to quantity production of the M2A4 light tank, 329 being ordered from the

Below: *A US Army M3A1 of Seventh Armoured Division on exercise in the United States in 1942. Note the lack of turret cupola on the power-traversed cast turret. This particular tank has a welded hull but retains the side-mounted machine-guns usually deleted on this model*

Light Tank M3 Stuart I
Weight 12.2 tons (12.4 tonnes)
Crew four
Armament one 37-mm M5 (L/50) gun with 103 rounds and three 0.30-inch (7.62-mm) Browning M1919A4 machine-guns with 8,270 rounds
Armour hull nose 51 mm, glacis 13 mm, driver's plate 38 mm, sides 25 mm, decking 10 mm, belly 10–12 mm, tail 19–25 mm; turret front 38 mm, sides and rear 30 mm, top 13 mm
Engine one Wright Continental W-970-9A radial seven-cylinder air-cooled petrol, 250-hp
Speed 36 mph (58 km/h)
Range 70 miles (113 km)
Trench crossing 6 feet (1.83 m)
Vertical step 2 feet (61 cm)
Fording 3 feet (91 cm)
Overall length 14 feet 10 inches (4.52 m)
Width 7 feet 6 inches (2.29 m)
Height 8 feet 3 inches (2.51 m)

The tank illustrated is a Stuart I of British Seventh Armoured Division, typical of the tanks which fought in North Africa in 1941–2. Note the deletion of the side-mounted hull machine-guns

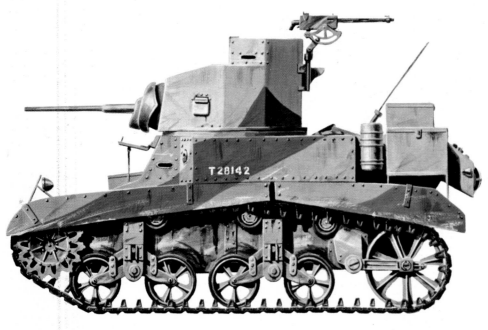

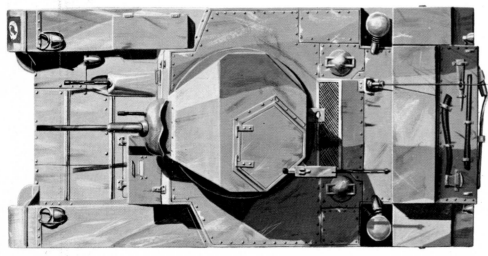

American Car and Foundry Company. The first tanks were delivered in April 1940. The production order was later increased to 365 with 10 to be built by the Baldwin Locomotive Company.

With the creation of the Armoured Force in June 1940, the M1 and M2 Combat Cars were redesignated Light Tanks M1A2 and M1A1, respectively. The lessons of the French campaign led to a major redesign of the M2A4 with thicker 51-mm armour and better distributed protection to guard against air attack. The hull was also lengthened to cover the exhausts, weight was increased by two US tons (1.8 tonnes) and trailing idler suspension decided upon. The new vehicle was designated Light Tank M3 and had a crew of four, like the M2A4.

Like its predecessors, the original M3 was of all riveted construction. A welded turret was soon adopted to reduce weight and this was later replaced with a partly cast turret. Gyro gun stabilizers were also fitted. Later M3s were fitted with Guiberson diesel power units and had welded hulls. In all some 5,811 M3s were produced from mid-1941 until August 1942.

With the passing of the Lend Lease Act in March 1941, M3s began to enter service with the British Army, in whose service the M3 became the Stuart I, diesel-engined versions being designated Stuart II. Combat experience led to various modifications, a new version entering production in June 1942 as the M3A1. This had power traverse for the turret, from which the prominent cupola was deleted. The two hull machine-guns were often removed, as they took up valuable stowage space for very little offensive return. Some 4,600 M3A1s, designated Stuart III by the British, were built by American Car and Foundry, the majority with welded hulls; 211 with Guiberson diesel engines became Stuart IVs.

The use of the Guiberson diesel reflected a shortage of Continental aero engines because of the demands of aircraft production, and this led to the development of a new version of the tank, the M5. The Cadillac division of General Motors had claimed that twin V-8 Cadillac car engines could replace the M3's standard Continental engine. An M3E2 prototype was so fitted in October 1941 together with the manufacturer's Hydra-Matic automatic transmission, and after a 500-mile (805-km) test trip the vehicle was ordered into production as M5.

The new version retained the turret, chassis and suspension of the M3A1, but the hull was redesigned with a raised rear section and the front maximum armour thickness was increased to 67 mm which gave a weight of $16\frac{1}{2}$ US tons (15 tonnes). The two engines with a combined output of 220 hp kept the maximum speed at 36 mph (58 km/h). Cadillac had the M5 in production by March 1942, and Massey Harris followed suit later.

In August a prototype M3A3 appeared, with a similar front hull shape to the M5. The radio was moved to the turret which was extended at the rear to accommodate it, while stowage and fuel capacity were increased and sand shields fitted. The following month an M5A1 prototype appeared to bring that type up to the new standard. Both M3A3 and M5A1 went into production in December. In Britain the M3A3 became Stuart V; M5 and M5A1 were both designated Stuart VI.

Despite an unfortunate tendency to catch fire

on starting, the Cadillac-engined tank was a generally superior vehicle to the Continental-engined version, with a more flexible power plant and automatic transmission. In August 1943, therefore, after 3,427 M3A3s had been built, the vehicle was replaced in production at American Car and Foundry by the M5A1. Production continued until June 1944, by which time some 6,810 M5A1 tanks had been completed. Total production figures for all versions of the M3 were 13,859 and for the M5 8,884.

The M1 to M5 light tank series played an important role in the United States Army. In the 1930s the early models provided virtually the only modern equipment of the infantry and cavalry armoured units. The old tanks continued in the early war years in a training role. The M2A4 was the only tank available in quantity in the early days of the Armoured Force. It was again employed mainly as a training tank. Some were used in action against Japan, still being deployed, together with the M3A1, by Marine Corps units at Guadalcanal in late 1942.

Although increasingly replaced by medium tanks in a major fighting role, M3 and M5 light tanks served throughout the war in the fighting, reconnaissance and headquarters echelons of the United States armoured forces and in USMC tank units. They saw action from the South Pacific and the Aleutians to North Africa and North-West Europe. The M3 was officially declared obsolete in the United States Army in July 1943, and the M5 was the major type in American service in 1944–5.

The Stuart saw action with British forces even before the United States was at war. With its 37-mm gun and 51-mm armour, the M3 was the equal of the British cruiser tanks in firepower and superior to them in protection. Although the American 50-calibre 37-mm gun was a little inferior to the British two-pounder (40-mm) it was still able to deal with Rommel's earlier model *PzKpfw* III and IV. Adopted as a cruiser tank before the later Grant M3 became available, the first 84 M3 lights arrived in North Africa in July 1941 and were soon nicknamed 'Honey' because of their reliability. Some 280 Stuart Is, more than half the 538 tanks produced in the initial three months of production, were sent to Africa and issued to the Fourth Armoured Brigade, Seventh Armoured Division which had 163 Stuarts on hand for the Crusader offensive of November 1941. The Stuarts proved ineffective when thrown against strong anti-tank defences but their manoeuvrability, speed and stabilized armament enabled them to outmanoeuvre more heavily armed and protected German tanks. Stuarts also served with British First Armoured Division and Australian and New Zealand units in North Africa. They saw further imperial service in Iraq, Europe and the Far East.

Left: An M2A4, the immediate predecessor of the M3 light tank. These vehicles were mainly used for training by American and British forces though some saw combat service against the Japanese
Below: M3A3 light tanks of the Chinese Army advance against the Japanese. Note the redesigned hull of this Continental-engined model, based on that of the M5

Medium Tank M4 Sherman

The M3 medium was always seen as an interim vehicle and in March 1941 a new project was begun at the Rock Island Arsenal for a tank with a turret-mounted 75-mm gun. The existing M3 was chosen as the basis for the new tank and by September a prototype had been constructed.

This T6 had a cast hull and turret which mounted an M2 75-mm gun and also contained a radio. The 28.5-calibre 75-mm gun was a provisional fitting until the longer 37.5-calibre M3 gun was available. There was a co-axial 0.30-inch (7.62-mm) machine-gun in the turret and three similar weapons in the hull front, two fixed and one in a ball mount (the twin guns were soon deleted in production tanks). Mechanically the new T6 was the same as the M3 with front sprocket drive, Cletrac steering, and a Wright Continental R-975 engine.

The tank was standardized as the M4, with a more easily produced welded hull, and the M4A1 with a cast unit. Initial targets were 2,000 vehicles per month and the first production M4A1 was produced in February 1942 by the

Sherman II (M4A1)
Weight 29.7 tons (30.2 tonnes)
Crew five
Armament one 75-mm M3 (37.5-calibre) gun, two 0.30-inch (7.62-mm) M1919A4 machine-guns with 4,750 rounds and one 0.50-inch (12.7-mm) M2 machine-gun with 500 rounds
Engine one Wright Continental R-975-C1 radial, nine-cylinder air-cooled petrol, 400-hp
Speed 25 mph (40 km/h)
Range 115 miles (185 km)
Trench crossing 7 feet 5 inches (2.26 m)
Vertical step 2 feet (60 cm)
Fording 3 feet (90 cm)
Overall length 19 feet 2 inches (5.84 m)
Width 8 feet 9 inches (2.66 m)
Height 9 feet (2.74 m)
Other details as Sherman VC Firefly

The tank illustrated is a Sherman II as used by the British Eighth Army in North Africa. Note the distinctive rounded cast hull, the M4-type trailing return rollers and the original style narrow mantlet and three-piece nose plate. Earlier British Shermans had M3-type return rollers

Sherman VC Firefly
Weight 34.75 tons (35.3 tonnes)
Crew four
Armament one 17-pounder (76.2-mm) Mk IV
(L/55) gun with 78 rounds and one 0.30-inch
(7.62-mm) Browning M1919A4 machine-gun
with 5,000 rounds
Armour hull nose and glacis 51 mm, sides and tail
38 mm, decking 19 mm, belly 13–25 mm; turret
front 76 mm, sides and rear 51 mm, top 25 mm
Engine one Chrysler A-57 Multibank 30-cylinder
liquid-cooled petrol, 425-hp
Speed 22.25 mph (36 km/h)
Range 125 miles (201 km)
Trench crossing 8 feet (2.44 m)
Vertical step 2 feet (61 cm)
Fording 3 feet 6 inches (1.07 m)
Overall length 25 feet 6 inches (7.77 m)
Width 9 feet 6 inches (2.9 m)
Height 9 feet 4 inches (2.85 m)

*The tank illustrated is the Sherman VC Firefly,
the British conversion of the Sherman V and one
of the most powerful tanks available to the
Allies during the war. Note the extension of the
turret caused by the 17-pounder (76.2-mm)*

Lima Locomotive Company. All the firms which
had produced the M3 – Detroit Tank Arsenal,
Baldwin, Alco, Pressed Steel and Pullman –
switched to the production of M4s and were soon
joined by Federal Machine and Welder, Pacific
Car and Foundry and the Fisher Body Division
of General Motors, which built another tank
arsenal at Grand Blanc, Michigan, based on
Chrysler's Detroit plant. Production of M4s was
on a massive scale, more M4s being produced
than any other single type in World War II. In
order to keep output high, different power
installations had to be fitted.

The different engine units produced the following major variants in addition to M4 and M4A1:
M4A2 with twin General Motors 6-71 diesels of
410 combined hp; M4A3 with purpose built
500-hp V-8 Ford GAA engine; M4A4 with 30-
cylinder Chrysler Multibank engine of 425 hp;
and M4A6 with Caterpillar RD-1820 nine-
cylinder radial diesel (an unsuccessful type
produced in very limited quantities). Both the
M4A4 and M4A6 had hulls lengthened by 6
inches (15 cm) to accommodate the larger

engines with lengthened suspensions and tracks. (The term M4A5 was applied to the Canadian Ram tank.)

All types, except M4A1, had welded hulls, although M4A6 had an interesting composite hull with a cast front to improve the ballistic shape. These hulls were also applied to late M4s produced at Detroit at the beginning of 1944. All except the earliest M4A1s had the M3 75-mm gun, mounted in later tanks in a new wider mantlet to improve protection. Very early tanks also had the idler arrangement of the M3, but most M4s had the improved trailing idlers.

M4 tanks with 51-mm frontal armour, sloped at 56° from the vertical and with 75-mm guns, which could penetrate 60 mm of 30° armour at 500 yards (457 m), were the equal of most existing German tanks at their time of introduction. The appearance of more powerful German tanks and guns later created problems, however, and various improvements were called for in both firepower and protection as the tank had a reputation for combustibility when hit.

By 1944 improved versions of the M4 were coming into service. The new 76-mm gun developed for the T20 series of medium tanks was tested in a standard M4A1 but the turret was found to be unsuitable. Luckily, the entire turret of the experimental T23 medium tank was found to fit the M4's turret ring and belatedly began to be fitted to the M4A1, M4A2 and M4A3 production chassis. Up-gunned tanks all had (76 mm) added to their designations. At first the M1A1 gun was used, but later M1A1C and M1A2 weapons, both of which had muzzle brakes, were fitted.

Up-gunned M4A1, 2 and 3 tanks began to be produced in early 1944 and arrived in Europe from the middle of the year. Their improved armour penetration capability (the 2,600 fps – 693 m/s – gun could penetrate 94 mm of 30° armour at 500 yards or 457 metres) proved useful against the heavily armoured German tanks they encountered.

Up-gunning went with the introduction of 'wet stowage' ammunition racks which had

M4A3E8
Weight 31.8 tons (32.2 tonnes)
Crew five
Armament one 76-mm M1A1C or M1A2 (L/52) gun with 71 rounds, two 0.30-inch (7.62 m) M1919A4 machine-gun with 6,250 rounds and one 0.50-inch (12.7-mm) M2 machine-gun with 600 rounds
Armour hull front 63.5 mm, sides and rear 38 mm, decking 19 mm, belly 25 mm; turret front and sides 63.5 mm, top 25 mm
Engine one Ford GAA-III V-8 liquid-cooled petrol, 450-hp
Speed 30 mph (48 km/h)
Length 24 feet 8 inches (7.51 m)
Width 8 feet 9 inches (2.66 m)
Height 11 feet 3 inches (3.42 m)
Other details as M4A1

The tank illustrated is a late model M4A3E8 (76-mm). Note the new turret and armament, stronger one-piece nose, 'clean' hull front, horizontal volute spring suspension and distinctive new decking design. Such tanks were in service for the Ardennes fighting in late 1944

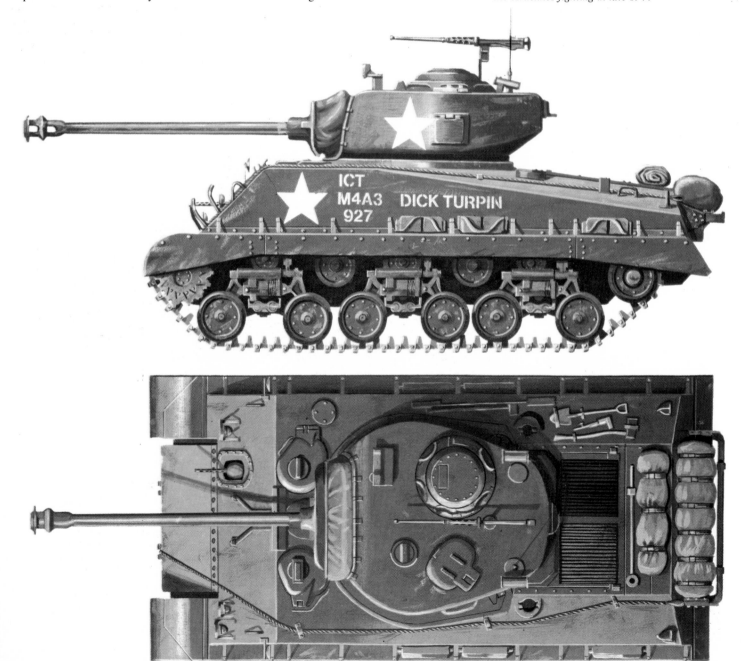

Below: *A British Sherman Crab Mark II mine-clearing flail. Earlier British mine-clearing attempts had used chain flails powered by auxiliary engines but in the Crab they were driven directly from the engine of the tank, a Sherman V, the most common British model. The drive was taken via chains and a drive shaft in the right hand boom. Once the mine-clearing was completed the vehicle could operate as a conventional gun tank. The arms could be raised and lowered to help stowage in the landing craft and the Mark II had a contour-following device to improve effectiveness over rough ground. The 'antennae' on the tank's rear are dim lights to guide following vehicles and the angled containers hold powdered chalk to mark the cleared path. The 30th Armoured Brigade used Crab Mark Is in Normandy and the rest of the North-West Europe campaign; the US Army also adopted and used the system*

hollow walls containing a mixture of water and glycerine that mitigated the fire risk when hit. The hull front was also redesigned to ease production with a new, slightly less sloping (47°) 'clean' front plate. The new hull and stowage system was also used on late 75-mm armed M4A3s built until March 1945. Earlier 75-mm gun tanks of all models except M4A6 were systematically reworked as part of a programme that began in 1944. Appliqué armour was added to the hull and new guns fitted in some cases. Spare track shoes, sandbags, wood and even concrete were often resorted to for improved protection in the field.

In late 1944 the final modification to the M4 took place with the fitting of improved, horizontal volute spring suspension (HVSS), together with wider tracks of 24 inches (61 cm). Instead of single road wheels with the track guide horns at the sides, the new track had centre horns and the road wheels were now double with return rollers being moved to the hull sides. The first prototype vehicle with this suspension was designated M4E8 and the E8 suffix was given to all the production prototypes of the HVSS M4A1, M4A2 and M4A3.

There were two other versions of the M4 tank which saw service. A special assault tank, the

M4A3E2, was designed quickly in 1944 as a heavily armoured, infantry support vehicle for use in North West Europe. The nose armour was increased to 140 mm and the frontal plating to 102 mm, while the side armour was increased to 76 mm. A new turret was fitted with an 178-mm mantlet and 152-mm sides. Although all M4A3E2s mounted the standard 75-mm gun, the new turret allowed the fitting of the 76-mm weapon by field workshops in Europe. The new armour increased weight to 42 US tons (37.4 tonnes), reduced maximum speed to 22 mph (35 km/h) and range to 100 miles (161 km). The extra weight also put greater strain on the suspension so the tracks were widened. M4A3E2s were first used during Operation Cobra, the breakout from Normandy in 1944, and became known as 'Cobra Kings' but later their more general name was 'Jumbo'. A total of 254 were produced.

In order to provide heavy fire support for the normal M4s in armoured units, two M4A4E1 prototypes were fitted in 1942 with 105-mm howitzers in place of the 75-mm guns. Two further M4E5 prototypes helped refine the concept and production of the M4 (105 mm) and M4A3 (105 mm) began in 1944; 800 and 500 of each type were built respectively before HVSS was adopted for the final production runs of 841

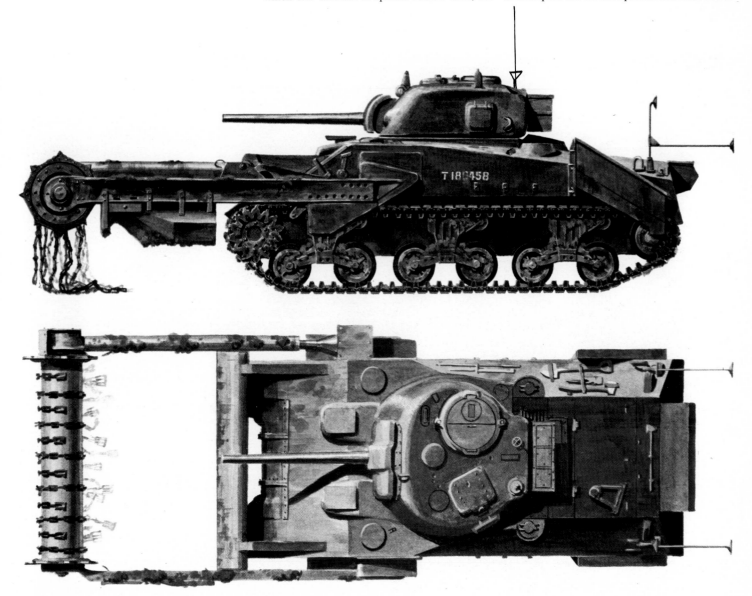

and 2,529. The howitzer was the 25-calibre M4 weapon, having the ability to fire a 33-pound (14.97-kg) shell over 6.9 miles (11.2 km).

Production figures for normal M4 battle tanks were as follows: M4 6,748; M4A1 6,281; M4A1 (76 mm) 3,396; M4A2 8,053; M4A2 (76 mm) 1,615; M4A3 3,071; M4A3 (76 mm) 3,370; M4A4 7,499; M4A6 75. When the M4A3E2, M4 (105 mm) and M4A3 (105 mm) tanks are taken into account this makes a total of 45,032 M4s produced, about twice Germany's production of all types of tank. With the M4 the United States became the tank arsenal of the Allies, large numbers of vehicles being supplied to Britain, Russia, the Free French and China.

The M4 became the standard battle tank of the British Army, who gave it its name, Sherman. Early Shermans, mainly M4A1s were rushed to the Western Desert to fight in the Alamein battles in September–October 1942 and they provided the Commonwealth armoured forces with a general superiority not known since the heyday of the Matilda. The turret-mounted 75-mm gun with its capacity to fire hull-down against a wide range of targets was a special advantage. Some 270 Shermans were used in the

Second Battle of Alamein and the tank soon became the most numerous in service with Eighth Army. The British, New Zealand and South African armoured forces in Italy in 1943–5 were almost entirely Sherman equipped, even Churchill units receiving the American tank.

The North-West Europe campaign began with 1,900 Shermans out of a total tank strength of 2,740 in 21st Army Group and Shermans continued to outnumber British tanks in the Group's British, Canadian and Polish armoured brigades by two to one. Indian and British troops also used the Sherman in Burma, while 4,000 of the vehicles went to the Soviet Union.

In February 1944 conversion began of Sherman Fireflies, equipped with the most powerful British high velocity gun, the 17-pounder (76.2 mm), which had an excellent performance (120 mm of 30° plate at 500 yards (457 m)) and made the vehicle the virtual equal of any German tank in firepower terms. About 600 were converted.

British designations for the various types of Sherman were: M4 – Sherman I; late production M4 with composite hull – Sherman Hybrid I; M4A1 – Sherman II; M4A2 – Sherman III; M4A3 – Sherman IV; M4A4 – Sherman V;

M4A6 – Sherman VII. If the tank carried a 76-mm gun the suffix A was used, B signifying 105-mm howitzer versions and C Fireflies. Y as a further suffix denoted HVSS. Most British Shermans were Sherman Vs.

The Americans carried out considerable work on specialized equipment for the M4, although with a standardization conscious United States Army, few saw service. An M19 swimming device was developed for use with standard wading gear which allowed the tank to fire whilst floating ashore: such vehicles were used by the USMC in the Pacific.

Two major types of American flame-thrower

Below: *The Sherman Duplex Drive amphibious tank. This vehicle was a basic Sherman III or V made watertight and fitted with a collapsible canvas screen which although it took 15 minutes to erect could be dropped immediately on landing. Two propellers gave a maximum speed through the water of about four knots and these could also be swivelled for steering, either by a hydraulic system or by means of a tiller operated by a crew member standing on the rear of the turret.*

M4 were developed. The standard E4 series flame-gun could be fitted in place of the hull machine-gun while the Marines also had a version that used a long-range United States Navy POA Mark I flame-gun inside the normal 75-mm barrel of a standard tank or in an old 105-mm howitzer tube mounted in the turret. A version also existed with the tube mounted beside the barrel so that the gun capability was retained.

Another sort of firepower deployed with US Shermans was the rocket. The major type used in Europe was the T34 Calliope, which used a jettisonable 60-round projector for 4.2-inch (107-mm) rockets mounted on a frame above the turret. The projector was connected to the gun for elevation and trained by using the turret. There were variants on this standard theme – the T34E1 with extra tubes, and the 7.2-inch (183 mm) T34E2. Another 7.2-inch (183-mm) system was the T40 'Whizz Bang', a box-like launcher mounted similarly to the Calliope. The T99, which put a box launcher with 22 4.5-inch (114-mm) rockets on each side of an M4 turret, was used in the Pacific.

Some M4s were fitted in the field with bull-dozer blades and this conversion was so successful that a standard M1 bulldozer attachment was developed. A few United States mine-sweeping equipment variants also saw service with the Sherman. Most spectacular was the Mine Exploder M1 'Aunt Jemima', two large 10-feet (3-m) roller wheels pushed in front of the M4. Flails and ploughs were also used and a wide range of other equipment developed experimentally. The M32 Tank Recovery Vehicle was also sometimes used for mine-sweeping. This was a turretless M4 with a fixed superstructure containing a winch. Its large front-mounted jib could be used to support T1E1 Earthworm mine-sweeping rollers.

The M4 chassis also lent itself for use as a self-propelled gun. In 1944 M7 Priests began to be built by Pressed Steel on the Ford-engined M4A3 chassis. These were designated M7B1 and over 500 were constructed in 1944–5; 127 M7B2s with higher mounted howitzers were produced by Federal Machine and Welder in 1945. Pressure from Armoured Centre led to a successor for the M12 heavy self-propelled gun being developed using a widened version of the M4A3 chassis. Before the war ended, 311 were

built and designated M40 Gun Motor Carriage, carrying the M2 155-mm gun; 48 were produced as the M43 with 8-inch (204-mm) howitzers. All were constructed in 1945 and fitted with HVSS.

The Sherman chassis was also used to provide mobile anti-tank weapons for the tank destroyer battalions. The M10 Tank Destroyer used the M7 76-mm gun which could penetrate over 100 mm of 30° plate at 500 yards (457 m). Production began in June 1942 and 4,993 were produced, along with 1,413 M10A1s which had the V-8 Ford petrol engine of the M4A3. Both types weighed 33 US tons (30 tonnes), had 57-mm turret and 38-mm hull armour and a maximum speed of 30 mph (48 km/h).

The balance of the M10's turret was never entirely satisfactory and a new turret was developed which could take the M3 90-mm gun. The 90-mm turret was fitted to the M10A1 chassis, and the combination was standardized in June 1944 as the M36. Vehicles with the M10 chassis became M36B2, and with the normal M4A3 tank chassis M36B1. From late 1944 they increasingly supplemented and replaced the M10 in American tank destroyer battalions, and together with the 76-mm armed M18 'Hellcat' formed their basic equipment by the end of the war. The M10/M36 series proved a useful source of mobile anti-tank firepower, speed and concealment making up for deficiencies in protection.

M10s and M10A1s were also issued to British and Free French forces. In British service the M10 became the 'Wolverine' self-propelled gun. From late 1944 Wolverines began to be up-gunned with 17-pounder (76.2-mm) guns as the 17-pounder SP Achilles, Mark IA if an M10 and Mark IIA if an M10A1.

The British used the Sherman as the basis for a number of special purpose vehicles of their own. One of the most important of these were the Duplex Drive (DD) amphibious tanks fitted with the flotation gear designed by Nicholas Straussler. In 1943, after experiments with Tetrarch and Valentine, the Sherman was chosen for use in the Normandy landings. The DD equipment consisted of collapsible canvas screen carried around the tank, erected by rubber tubing which could be filled with compressed air. The vehicle was waterproofed and with the screens

Top left: M4 series tanks of the 40th Tank Battalion, part of US Seventh Armoured Division, during the Ardennes fighting. Note the 75-mm guns and the effectiveness of the vehicle's winter camouflage. On its introduction the Sherman was soon called by its respectful opponents the 'T-34 of the West'. Speer, the German armaments minister always used these manoeuvrable all-round vehicles as an example for the size-conscious Wehrmacht with its passion for clumsy, unreliable monsters

Bottom left: One of the flame-thrower versions of Sherman fitted with the American E4 series flame-gun in place of the hull machine-gun mount. There were three variants E4R2, 3 and 4. Fuel was carried within the vehicle. Another similar device was the E6 which could be fitted above the co-driver's hatch. Both E4 and E6 flame-throwers were issued in kit form for fitting in the field. An E7 could be mounted in the turret. In addition to the POA some USMC M4s (and M3 light tanks) were fitted with turret-mounted Canadian Ronson flame-guns

erected could float, being propelled through the water by two propellers powered by the tank's engines via the tracks and rear idler wheels.

A total of 573 Sherman III and V tanks were initially chosen for conversion as Sherman III DD and V DD. Others were converted for American use. The various DD units were used on 6 June 1944 with general success. The only major failure was on Omaha where 27 of the 29 tanks launched at 6,000 yards (5,486 m) sank in the heavy swell. Those that got ashore played a vital part in breaking down the initial German defences and supporting the first Allied troops inland. British DD Shermans were later used in the crossing of the Scheldt, Rhine and Elbe and also in Italy.

Another important British conversion used by the Americans was the Sherman 'Crab' flail mine-clearing tank. Sherman Crabs, best of the British mine-sweeping tanks, were such a success that the Americans procured the system also as the Mine Exploder T2 Flail.

Right: *An early M4A1, still in service with US First Armoured Division, moves up to attack the Gothic Line in Italy during the late summer of 1944. Note the early 'narrow' mantlet and three-piece bolted nose plate as well as the improvised frontal 'protection'. First Armoured Division was the only such US Army formation to fight in Italy*
Below: *Two British 'Achilles' tank destroyers – M10 series vehicles up-gunned with British 17-pounder (76.2-mm) guns. Note the different shape of the M10 hull compared to the basic M4 tank, and the open-top turrets*

Two British flame-thrower systems were developed for the Sherman but neither was used in action. Four Shermans fitted with British Crocodile equipment were used by the United States Second Armoured Division, however, and the United States Marine Corps fitted some M4s with Canadian-designed Ronson flame-guns as with the 'Satan' based on the M3 light tank.

Various types of armoured recovery vehicles were modified by the British – the Sherman III and V ARV Mark I without turret and with simple recovery equipment, and the more sophisticated Sherman V ARV Mark II with dummy turret and gun, two jibs and a 60 ton winch fitted. A beach armoured recovery vehicle (BARV) was also built, and used successfully in the Normandy landings and Rhine crossings in rescuing 'drowned' vehicles.

The British converted Shermans into OP tanks, some with dummy guns; during 1945 First (Armoured) Battalion the Coldstream Guards converted a number of their Sherman Vs and V Cs with an improvised rocket-launcher mounting, a 60-pound (27.2 kg) rocket and aircraft rack on each side of the tank. These gave remarkably effective additional firepower in the final battles in Germany. Other tanks were converted into fascine carriers while Commonwealth Shermans were used in Italy as bridging vehicles, gun tractors and armoured personnel carriers.

Sherman production ceased in June 1945 but development went on after the war in both the United States and Britain and a new M74 recovery vehicle was developed on the chassis. Shermans were widely distributed after World War II and they fought again in various major post-war conflicts, notably with the US Army in Korea, on both sides in the Indo-Pakistani War of 1965 and with both Israeli and Egyptian forces in the Arab Israeli Wars since 1948. The Israelis still keep the Sherman in service as the Super Sherman and Isherman with new engines and guns. The Sherman also remains in service with Latin American countries (some Fireflies still exist in the Argentinian Army), and in Portugal, South Korea, Uganda and Yugoslavia.

Below: *A standard British Sherman festooned with extra front 'protection' in Normandy. The Sherman, mostly of the Sherman V type, provided the standard British medium tank from 1943 to the end of the war. The white star was used by all Allied forces in North-West Europe and Italy. Note the Sherman-based M10 Wolverine tank destroyers in the background*

Bottom: *The M1 Aunt Jemima, one of the most spectacular mine-clearance devices of the war, was used in conjunction with the M4 series. Note the chain drive from the sprockets to the 10-foot (3.1 m) 'indestructible' wheels. A total of 75 of these devices were built and the system was used in action by American forces, an extra M4 sometimes being necessary to push the heavy equipment along*

Focke-Wulf 190

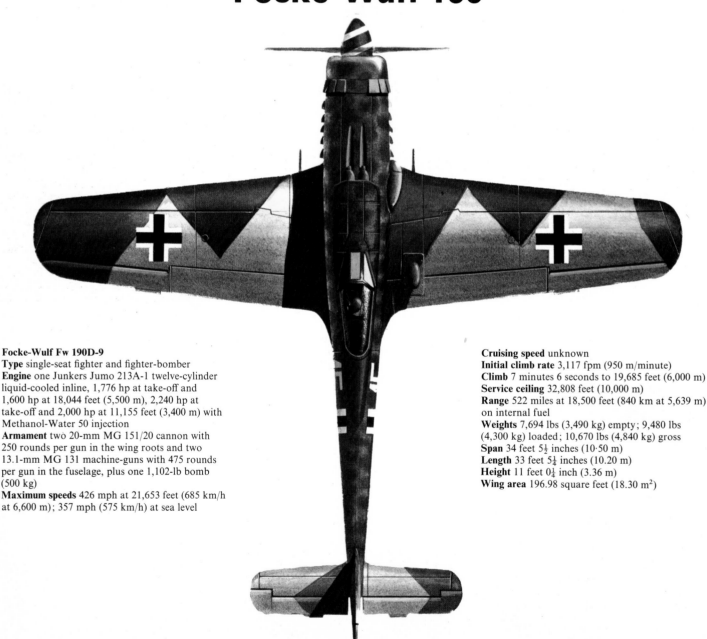

Focke-Wulf Fw 190D-9
Type single-seat fighter and fighter-bomber
Engine one Junkers Jumo 213A-1 twelve-cylinder liquid-cooled inline, 1,776 hp at take-off and 1,600 hp at 18,044 feet (5,500 m), 2,240 hp at take-off and 2,000 hp at 11,155 feet (3,400 m) with Methanol-Water 50 injection
Armament two 20-mm MG 151/20 cannon with 250 rounds per gun in the wing roots and two 13.1-mm MG 131 machine-guns with 475 rounds per gun in the fuselage, plus one 1,102-lb bomb (500 kg)
Maximum speeds 426 mph at 21,653 feet (685 km/h at 6,600 m); 357 mph (575 km/h) at sea level

Cruising speed unknown
Initial climb rate 3,117 fpm (950 m/minute)
Climb 7 minutes 6 seconds to 19,685 feet (6,000 m)
Service ceiling 32,808 feet (10,000 m)
Range 522 miles at 18,500 feet (840 km at 5,639 m) on internal fuel
Weights 7,694 lbs (3,490 kg) empty; 9,480 lbs (4,300 kg) loaded; 10,670 lbs (4,840 kg) gross
Span 34 feet 5½ inches (10·50 m)
Length 33 feet 5¼ inches (10.20 m)
Height 11 feet 0¼ inch (3.36 m)
Wing area 196.98 square feet (18.30 m^2)

The Focke-Wulf Fw 190 was Germany's second great fighter of World War II, and was in most respects superior to its front-line companion and rival for the title of the Third Reich's best fighter, the Bf 109.

Although opinion in the *RLM* was divided about the need for a successor to the Messerschmitt Bf 109, in 1938 the firm of Focke-Wulf received permission to proceed with the detailed design of a new fighter. Although inline engines, with their low frontal area, were in vogue with European fighter designers, Kurt Tank, in charge of the new project, had persuaded the *RLM* to allow him to use the BMW 139 radial, as this was already offering more power than any inline engine then in production and its use would not further strain inline engine production.

As work on the Fw 190 *V1* proceeded the BMW 139 engine was found to overheat and Focke-Wulf substituted the newer, and more promising, BMW 801 for the older engine in their plans for production aircraft. The first prototypes were too advanced to be changed, however. The 190 *V1* was flown for the first time on 1 June 1939, and immediately proved itself to be an admirable aircraft, with excellent speed and sensitive, but well-balanced, controls. The earlier fears about the BMW 139 were quickly realized, however, although the trouble was partially attributable to the fact that the engine-cooling fan had not yet been installed. The cooling fan was fitted on the 190 *V2*, but the engine still overheated. On production models a 12-blade fan replaced the 10-blade one.

The 190 *V5*, which flew in April 1940, was the first version of the *Würger* (Shrike), as Focke-Wulf had dubbed their fighter, to be powered by the BMW 801. This engine was considerably heavier than its predecessor, and Focke-Wulf had designed a larger wing for production aircraft to keep weight loadings down. After an accident, this larger wing was fitted to the *V5*. This resulted in a slight reduction in speed, although rate of climb was greatly improved and

handling characteristics restored to the precision of the first prototypes. The *V5* was in most respects similar to the first production models, and differed principally from the *V1* and *V2* in having a slightly larger wing and tailplane, with a fuselage four inches longer. To compensate for the greater weight of the new engine, the cockpit was moved further back. Nevertheless, the Fw 190 remained a very pleasing aircraft visually, beautifully streamlined, with as narrow a fuselage as it was possible to design around the bulky radial. One of the new fighter's most distinct advantages over the Bf 109 was its inward-retracting undercarriage, giving it greater stability on the ground compared with the 109's outward-retracting landing gear.

JG 26, the *Luftwaffe* unit detailed to develop the type operationally, had a very difficult time early in 1941: there was constant trouble with the engine, its cooling and the propeller. These problems were eventually resolved and the *Geschwader* went into action in September 1941. The new fighter proved very successful, outclassing the RAF's Spitfire Vs in almost every respect. The Fw 190A series went through many models, with increased power, better armament and provision for underslung bombs. With this last modification, Fw 190s made a large number of hit-and-run raids on British targets. These caused little real damage, but meant that the RAF had to resort to standing patrols, with their attendant strain on fuel stocks and aircraft serviceability.

The two definitive A-series models were the 190A-3 and 190A-8. The first was a pure fighter with four 20-mm cannon and a speed of 418 mph (673 km/h); the second was a fighter-bomber which could carry a 551-lb (250-kg) bomb and had a speed of 408 mph (657 km/h). The 190F series was derived from the A, and was intended as a close-support series, with up to 1,102 lbs (500 kg) of bombs or underwing armament of two 30-mm MK 108 cannon in addition to the standard fuselage- and wing-mounted machine-

gun and cannon armament. The 190G series was also derived from the A, and was designed as a long-range fighter-bomber series.

The 190B and 190C series never materialized except as prototypes, although these were very important in the overall development of the 190: the major combat disadvantage of the early production series had been inadequate performance at altitude as a result of the BMW radial engine, and the B and C were designed around the Daimler-Benz DB 603 inline. Tests with this engine, specially boosted with methanol-water (MW-50) or nitrous oxide (GM-1) injection, proved generally satisfactory, and the lessons were incorporated in the 190D series, the only inline-engined 190 series to enter widespread service. The major distinguishing feature of the *Dora*, as it was dubbed by the *Luftwaffe*, was its stretched fuselage compared with earlier models. The inline engine was very neatly cowled in a nose that kept the radial-engined shape of its predecessors by having an annular radiator instead of the more usual bath type. To compensate for the longer nose (the D series is generally known as the 'long-nosed' series), the rear fuselage also had to be lengthened. The definitive model of the D series was the 190D-9, a fighter-bomber with a medium cannon and machine-gun armament but a maximum speed of 426 mph (686 km/h) and range of 520 miles (837 km) on internal fuel. All the D series had Junkers Jumo engines.

Throughout its career the Fw 190 proved a remarkably successful machine, capable of adaptation to the most difficult missions (such as torpedo-bombing). It was fast, possessed a good range, was very manoeuvrable and very sturdy. Production amounted to 20,001 aircraft.

The final versions of the basic Fw 190 philosophy were the D series-derived Ta 152C and 152H (the Ta for Kurt Tank), respectively medium- and high-altitude fighters. The 152H-1 was capable of 472 mph (760 km/h) and an altitude of 48,550 feet (14,800 m).

Heinkel 111

Although several other German bombers of the World War II period first made their appearance in a civilian guise, the Heinkel 111 was notable for being designed from the outset both as a bomber and as a passenger aircraft. Designed by the brothers Siegfried and Walter Günter in 1934 to a *Deutsche Lufthansa* specification for a passenger transport to supplement the He 70, which was too small for certain routes, the He 111 had allowances for military uses built into it from the outset. In fact the first three prototypes, delivered in 1935, were basically military models, with provision for both offensive and defensive armament. These three prototypes differed from each other principally in the shape of their basically elliptical wing planforms. The first civilian prototype, the He 111 *V*4, first flew late in 1935, and was intended as the forerunner of the He 111C airliner series. In common with the early military models, the *V*4 had a long, finely-streamlined nose, quite unlike the fully-glazed nose of later military series. The chief external differences between the military and civilian models were the glazed bombardier's position in the extreme nose and the open dorsal position in the former models.

The first military series was the He 111A, of which only 10 were built in 1935. Performance with full military equipment was disappointing, especially with the retractable ventral 'dustbin' gun position, and the low-powered BMW VI 6, OZ inline engines. The shortage of power was rectified in the next model, the He 111B, which had two Daimler-Benz DB 600 engines. Service deliveries of this much-improved aircraft began in the winter of 1936. The He 111B was one of the first German types to see action in Spain, where its high speed (230 mph or 370 km/h) made it almost invulnerable to Republican fighters. Its bomb-load of over 3,000 lbs (1,361 kg) was also quite heavy for the time. At the same time, Heinkel was delivering civilian machines of the He 111C and G series to *Deutsche Lufthansa*, which decided that the type was uneconomical to run.

Early in 1937, Heinkel decided that with the latest DB 600 engine mark, the He 111's performance could be enhanced greatly, and a redesign of the cooling system, to reduce drag, was put in hand. This resulted in the He 111D series which replaced the surface radiators with deeper ones under the engines and which also had improved exhausts and better streamlining. Performance was radically improved (speed by 25 mph or 40 km/h), but no series production was undertaken as DB 600 engines were in short supply and Messerschmitt Bf 109 and 110 fighters had priority. Heinkel had foreseen this shortage, however, and had initiated design studies for a series to be powered by the Junkers Jumo 210 or 211 engine. The former engine proved to be insufficiently powerful, and production He 111E aircraft, which began to appear in 1938, were powered by a pair of Jumo 211 engines.

E series aircraft were soon sent to Spain, where they enjoyed the same success as the earlier B models. One of the major disadvantages of these early models was the elliptical wing, which was difficult, and therefore expensive, to build. A new wing, with straight leading and trailing edges, was thus introduced on the He 111F series, and was retained on all later series. The He 111J was designed in the second half of 1938 as a torpedo-bomber, without internal bomb-bays, but lack of *Luftwaffe* interest meant that the few examples produced were retrofitted with bomb-bays.

Another disadvantage of the He 111 discovered by service crews was lack of visibility. In an attempt to rectify this, Heinkel redesigned the nose in 1937, eliminating the previous finely-tapered one for a shorter, fully-glazed one, faired into the fuselage contours without any breaks. To improve the pilot's visibility yet further, the nose-gunner's position was offset to starboard, giving the He 111's later series their distinctive lop-sided appearance in plan-view. The first series to feature the new nose was the He 111P, which began to enter service early in 1939. The series, which was powered by DB 601 engines, also introduced a permanent ventral gondola with a single machine-gun in place of the earlier retractable 'dustbin', which had produced too much drag. By the time production of the He 111P series ended in the middle of 1940, combat experience with the British and French had shown that the defensive armament of three 7.92-mm machine-guns was totally inadequate, and a further three or four guns of the same calibre were added from the He 111P-4 model onwards. Some armour protection for the pilot was also added.

The most numerous He 111 series was the H model, which reverted to Junkers Jumo engines, and was built in a bewildering number of marks and sub-marks before He 111 production finally ended in 1944. Defensive armament was increased very considerably over the war years, and models to carry paratroops, torpedoes, guided bombs and even to launch *V*-1 flying bombs from the air were built. It was also intended to develop the basic He 111 as a high-altitude bomber, but the prototype of this He 111R was unsuccessful. Also built in limited numbers was the He 111Z glider tug, which consisted of two He 111H-6 fuselages, complete with empennage and one port and one starboard wing, joined by a new parallel-chord wing with a fifth engine. Remarkably, the type proved quite useful.

Throughout its life the He 111 remained a tractable, easy plane to fly, but it suffered several severe disadvantages: principal amongst these was the fact that as a suitable successor was slow to make its appearance, the He 111 was kept in service far too long. Although its range and bomb-load were adequate for the tactical tasks it was required to fulfil, the type was always underdefended, and therefore suffered heavy losses where air defence was good. Nevertheless, the He 111 was a tractable aircraft to fly, and found great favour as a torpedo-bomber. At the end of its career, the He 111 was also used as a paratroop aircraft. In all 5,656 He 111 were built.

Left: Groundcrew prepare to load a second Lufttorpedo F5b practice airborne-dropped torpedo onto the starboard PVC rack, under the wing root of an He 111H-6 bomber. The aircraft was probably one of the machines of I/KG 26, the Löwen Geschwader, which inflicted great losses on the Allied arctic convoys during the second half of 1942, operating from bases in northern Norway. The H-6 sub-mark of the He 111 was the most widely used variant of the basic type, and proved an excellent torpedo-bomber in addition to its designed task of level bombing

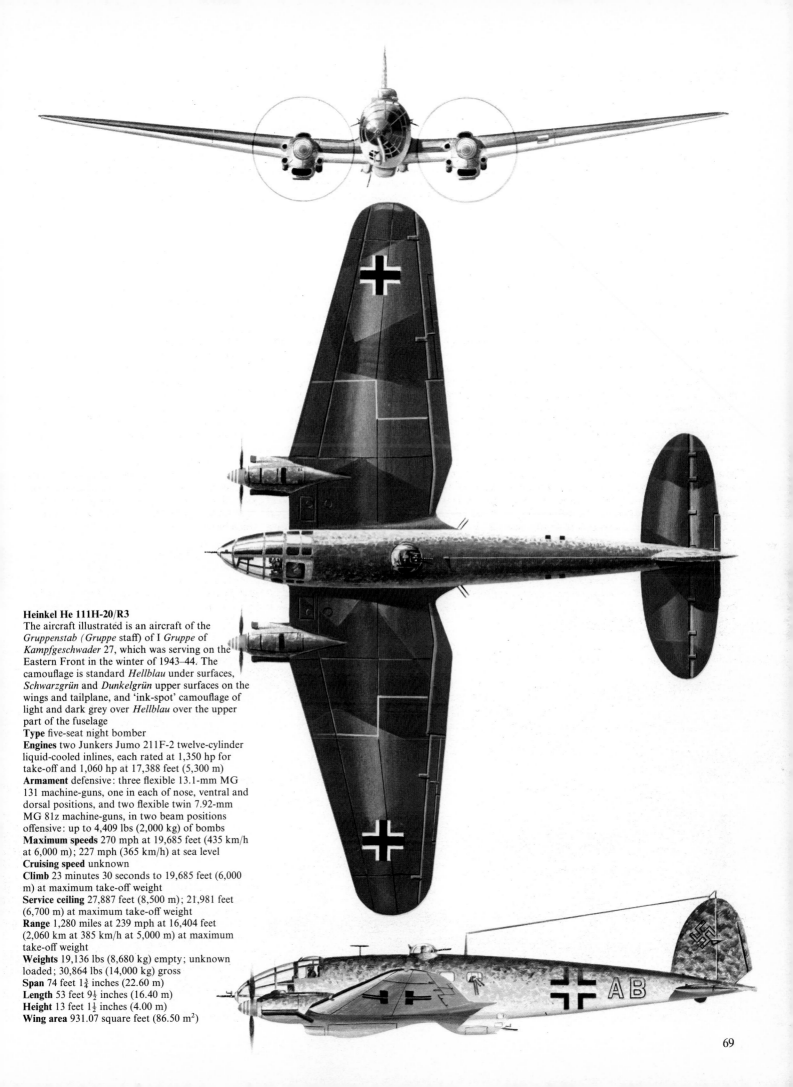

Heinkel He 111H-20/R3

The aircraft illustrated is an aircraft of the
Gruppenstab (Gruppe staff) of I *Gruppe* of
Kampfgeschwader 27, which was serving on the
Eastern Front in the winter of 1943–44. The
camouflage is standard *Hellblau* under surfaces,
Schwarzgrün and *Dunkelgrün* upper surfaces on the
wings and tailplane, and 'ink-spot' camouflage of
light and dark grey over *Hellblau* over the upper
part of the fuselage

Type five-seat night bomber
Engines two Junkers Jumo 211F-2 twelve-cylinder
liquid-cooled inlines, each rated at 1,350 hp for
take-off and 1,060 hp at 17,388 feet (5,300 m)
Armament defensive: three flexible 13.1-mm MG
131 machine-guns, one in each of nose, ventral and
dorsal positions, and two flexible twin 7.92-mm
MG 81z machine-guns, in two beam positions
offensive: up to 4,409 lbs (2,000 kg) of bombs
Maximum speeds 270 mph at 19,685 feet (435 km/h
at 6,000 m); 227 mph (365 km/h) at sea level
Cruising speed unknown
Climb 23 minutes 30 seconds to 19,685 feet (6,000
m) at maximum take-off weight
Service ceiling 27,887 feet (8,500 m); 21,981 feet
(6,700 m) at maximum take-off weight
Range 1,280 miles at 239 mph at 16,404 feet
(2,060 km at 385 km/h at 5,000 m) at maximum
take-off weight
Weights 19,136 lbs (8,680 kg) empty; unknown
loaded; 30,864 lbs (14,000 kg) gross
Span 74 feet 1¾ inches (22.60 m)
Length 53 feet 9½ inches (16.40 m)
Height 13 feet 1½ inches (4.00 m)
Wing area 931.07 square feet (86.50 m²)

Junkers 52/3m

For all its angular ugliness, the trimotor Junkers Ju 52/3 series of bomber and transport aircraft was one of the best-loved and most useful types to serve with the *Luftwaffe*, whose personnel knew the Ju 52/3 as *Tante Ju* or Auntie Ju. The Ju 52/3, or more properly Ju 52/3m, was designed by Ernst Zindel in 1932 as a more powerful version of the single-engined Ju 52 of 1930, which was in service as a cargo aircraft with *Deutsche Lufthansa*. From the outset the new aircraft proved very successful, and Junkers terminated production of the Ju 52 in favour of this three-motor (3m) version. Intended at first only for civil transport, the Ju 52/3m was soon pressed into service by the clandestine *Luftwaffe* as an interim heavy bomber, pending deliveries of the Dornier Do 11. This was the Ju 52/3m ge model, but when problems with the Do 11 prevented that type's widespread service use, the Ju 52/3m was pressed into extended service, as the Ju 52/3m g3e with improved bomb-release gear and radio. Up to 3,307 lbs (1,500 kg) of bombs could be carried. Defensive armament consisted of only two 7.92-mm machine-guns, one in an open dorsal position and one in a retractable ventral 'dustbin'.

The Ju 52/3m went to war in August 1936, first ferrying Franco's troops from Morocco to metropolitan Spain, and then performing a variety of bombing missions. In Spain the Ju 52/3m g3e was soon joined by the Ju 52/3m g4e, which was basically similar apart from having a

tailwheel rather than a skid. With the arrival of more modern bombers, the Ju 52/3m aircraft were relegated to their original transport role. In Germany they were finished as proper transport or operational training aircraft for multi-engined aircraft pilots and navigators. The next model to appear was the Ju 52/3m g5e, with superior flying equipment and provision for an interchangeable float, ski, or wheel undercarriage. Basically similar was the Ju 52/3m g6e, which was intended only for land operations, with simplified radio equipment.

The Ju 52/3m was also intended for use by airborne forces, and the type was used operationally in this role, and as a glider tug, over Denmark, Norway, Holland and Belgium. Losses were quite heavy, but production was at full tempo, and all losses had been made good by the end of 1940. Another task undertaken by the Ju 52/3m was that of minesweeping. For this the aircraft was fitted with a great dural hoop under the fuselage and wings, energized by an auxiliary motor in the fuselage, to set off magnetic mines.

The Ju 52/3m g5e and g6e had dispensed with the ventral 'dustbin' for two lateral 7.92-mm machine-guns, and this armament was supplemented in the Ju 52/3m g7e with a further 7.92-mm machine-gun (optional) in a forward dorsal position. The starboard loading door was also enlarged. A loading hatch in the fuselage roof was added on the Ju 52/3m g8e, which also had a 13.1-mm rear dorsal machine-gun in place

of the earlier models' 7.92-mm weapon. The next model of the Ju 52/3m was the g9e, which appeared in 1942. This had a glider-towing attachment fitted as standard, and an improved undercarriage for heavier take-off weights. The last model, the Ju 52/3m g14e, appeared in 1943 with armour protection and improved defensive armament. Production ceased in mid-1944 after 3,225 examples of the Ju 52/3m had been built, 2,804 during the war.

The utility of the Ju 52/3m to the German cause can never be overestimated. The type served as a bomber in Spain, transport and airborne troops aircraft in Denmark, Norway, Holland, Belgium, France, Greece, Crete and Russia, and in a multitude of transport, training and liaison tasks in Germany herself. Unfortunately for Germany, whenever a special need for such aircraft arose, as for the invasion of Crete or the Demyansk and Stalingrad airlifts, the necessary *Tante Ju* aircraft, together with their experienced crews, were taken from their training duties and used in combat. Their destruction not only meant the loss of the aircraft and men, but also affected the training of future crews.

Below: Apparent confusion on a German airfield in North Africa as Ju 52/3m transports are unloaded of their cargoes of fuel after the flight from Italy. In the foreground are a pair of Messerschmitt Bf 110 fighters

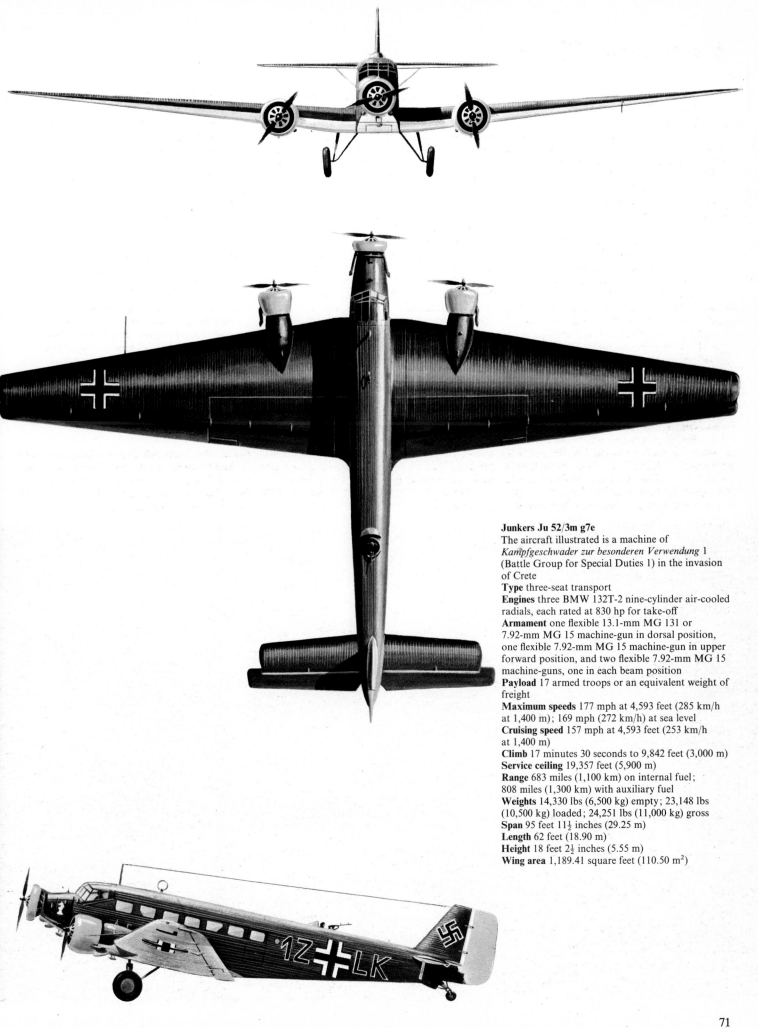

Junkers Ju 52/3m g7e
The aircraft illustrated is a machine of
Kampfgeschwader zur besonderen Verwendung 1
(Battle Group for Special Duties 1) in the invasion
of Crete
Type three-seat transport
Engines three BMW 132T-2 nine-cylinder air-cooled
radials, each rated at 830 hp for take-off
Armament one flexible 13.1-mm MG 131 or
7.92-mm MG 15 machine-gun in dorsal position,
one flexible 7.92-mm MG 15 machine-gun in upper
forward position, and two flexible 7.92-mm MG 15
machine-guns, one in each beam position
Payload 17 armed troops or an equivalent weight of
freight
Maximum speeds 177 mph at 4,593 feet (285 km/h
at 1,400 m); 169 mph (272 km/h) at sea level
Cruising speed 157 mph at 4,593 feet (253 km/h
at 1,400 m)
Climb 17 minutes 30 seconds to 9,842 feet (3,000 m)
Service ceiling 19,357 feet (5,900 m)
Range 683 miles (1,100 km) on internal fuel;
808 miles (1,300 km) with auxiliary fuel
Weights 14,330 lbs (6,500 kg) empty; 23,148 lbs
(10,500 kg) loaded; 24,251 lbs (11,000 kg) gross
Span 95 feet 11½ inches (29.25 m)
Length 62 feet (18.90 m)
Height 18 feet 2½ inches (5.55 m)
Wing area 1,189.41 square feet (110.50 m²)

Junkers 87

Rightly or wrongly, the Junkers Ju 87 has become synonymous with German blitzkrieg warfare under its nickname of *Stuka*. (This is an abbreviation of the German word for dive-bomber – *Sturzkampfflugzeug*.) And such has been the *Stuka*'s notoriety that a great body of legend has grown up around the aircraft itself, at times making it difficult to assess the *Stuka* correctly. For example, the aircraft has been described as 'cumbersome', because it was relatively simple for Allied fighters to shoot it down; however this is scarcely surprising as the *Stuka* was built not as a fighter but as a large, single-engined bomber. The fault implicit in the epithet 'cumbersome' belongs not to the aircraft, which was light and positive to handle and fully aerobatic, but to the false tactical doctrines of German commanders who sent in these dive-bombers against targets well-defended by good fighters, without an adequate escort of their own.

The Ju 87 stemmed directly from a visit made by Ernst Udet to the United States, where he had seen remarkable results in dive-bombing demonstrations. Designed by Hermann Pohlmann, the Ju 87 *V*1 flew for the first time in 1935. This initial prototype differed quite radically from most of its successors in several respects, having a Rolls-Royce Kestrel engine, twin vertical tail surfaces mounted at the ends of the tailplane, and a 'trousered' rather than 'spatted' undercarriage. The *V*2 had a single vertical tail surface.

The Ju 87 nearly came to a premature end in June 1936, when the head of the *Reichsluftfahrt-ministerium*'s technical department decided that development work should be discontinued. The history of World War II might well have been radically different had not Ernst Udet taken over the office the day after the order was issued and rescinded it. Thereafter development work went ahead swiftly. The Ju *V*3, which was flying by this time, was engined with the Junkers Jumo

that was to power the whole series. By the middle of 1936 the basic design of the Ju 87 had been fixed, only the later 'spatting' of the undercarriage altering the basic outline.

The first production Ju 87A series aircraft entered service in the early months of 1937, a few of the new dive-bombers being sent to Spain to test the aircraft operationally.

When the more powerful Jumo 211 engine appeared in 1937, Junkers took the chance to improve the Ju 87 by fitting the new engine in place of the previous Jumo 210. This necessitated a major redesign of the fuselage and vertical tail surfaces, with the result that the nose, cockpit enclosure and rear fuselage took on an appearance less streamlined than on the Ju 87A series. The undercarriage was also redesigned, the 'trousers' braced to the fuselage being replaced by cantilever 'spatted' units, which were far easier to maintain. By October 1938, some early Ju 87B-1 models had been sent to Spain, where they enjoyed considerable success. Maximum bomb-load was 2,205 lbs (1,000 kg), twice that of the Ju 87A. The Ju 87B-2 had several equipment refinements.

In the years before the war, Germany had started to build an aircraft-carrier, the *Graf Zeppelin*, and as part of its complement it was intended that it should have some navalized Ju 87 dive-bombers. The Ju 87C was derived from the 87B for this purpose, with catapult spools, flotation gear, folding wings and a jettisonable undercarriage. Only a few pre-production aircraft were built before the abandonment of the *Graf Zeppelin* project. Another contemporary of the Ju 87B series was the R series, which was basically similar, but had a reduced offensive load and increased fuel tankage for long-range anti-shipping strikes.

The next series to appear was the Ju 87D, intended to make use of the latest model of the

Jumo 211, the 211J. The nose contours were cleaned up considerably, and the cockpit canopy was streamlined more efficiently. Fixed armament was left at two 7.92-mm machine-guns, but the gunner was now given two weapons of the same calibre instead of the previous one. Bomb-load was raised to a maximum of nearly 4,000 lbs (1,814 kg). The Ju 87D-1 began to enter service in the spring of 1942. The Ju 87D series was built in large numbers and in a number of sub-marks.

The Ju 87F and Ju 187 were projected versions of the basic design to bring it up to date, but no examples of either design were built. In parallel with the Ju 87D series, Junkers built the Ju 87H, which was a dual-control trainer to enable fighter and bomber pilots to be taught to fly the *Stuka*. The final version of the *Stuka* was the Ju 87G series, of which only the Ju 87G-1 was built. This was a specialized 'tank-busting' aircraft, with a pair of 3.7-cm BK 3.7 cannon slung under the wings in pods with their ammunition. The weapon proved very successful, especially in the hands of *Stuka* aces such as Hans-Ulrich Rudel. Production of the Ju 87 ended in the summer of 1944 after 5,700 had been built, 4,881 during the war.

The *Stuka* was a very potent weapon when used against raw troops in circumstances of little air opposition; these conditions were to be found in the German campaigns against Poland, Belgium, Holland and France in 1939–40, and against Russia in 1941–43. But against competent fighter opposition, however, the *Stuka* was a death trap. All in all, though, the *Stuka* served the German cause very well.

Below: A Kette (flight) of Ju 87B Stukas in flight. Each aircraft appears to be carrying only four 110-lb (50-kg) bombs, two under each outer wing panel. A 1,102-lb (500-kg) bomb could also be carried on the crutch under the fuselage

Junkers Ju 87B-1

The aircraft illustrated is aircraft C of 1 *Staffel*,
I *Gruppe, Stukageschwader* 77. The *Staffel* emblem
was an orange pig, diving down to the left, on a
yellow shield with a white serrated top. Camouflage
is standard *Hellblau* under surfaces and
Schwarzgrün upper surfaces

Type two-seat dive-bomber
Engine one Junkers Jumo 211Da twelve-cylinder
liquid-cooled inline, 1,200 hp at take-off and
1,000 hp at 4,921 feet (1,500 m)
Armament defensive: two fixed 7.92-mm MG 17
machine-guns in the wings and one flexible 7.92-mm
MG 17 in the rear cockpit
offensive: up to one 1,102-lb (500-kg) and four
110-lb (50-kg) bombs
Maximum speeds 239 mph at 13,410 feet (385 km/h
at 4,087 m); 211 mph (340 km/h) at sea level
Cruising speed 209 mph at 12,140 feet (332 km/h
at 3,700 m)
Climb 12 minutes to 12,190 feet (3,700 m)
Service ceiling 26,246 feet (8,000 m)
Range 490 miles (790 km) without bomb-load;
370 miles (595 km) with 1,102 lbs (500 kg) of
bombs
Weights 6,090 lbs (2,762 kg) empty; 9,336 lbs
(4,235 kg) loaded; 9,560 lbs (4,336 kg) gross
Span 45 feet 3⅓ inches (13.80 m)
Length 36 feet 5 inches (11.10 m)
Height 13 feet 2 inches (4.00 m)
Wing area 343.368 square feet (31.90 m²)

Junkers 88

The Junkers Ju 88 was Germany's most versatile aircraft of World War II, serving the *Luftwaffe* as a level bomber, dive-bomber, reconnaissance machine, ground-attack aircraft, trainer, day and night fighter, minelayer and torpedo-bomber.

Despite the fact that the Ju 88 was employed operationally in a multitude of tasks, it was designed to a specification calling for a *Schnellbomber* or fast bomber, as was the de Havilland Mosquito, Britain's equivalent of the remarkable Ju 88. The specification was issued in the spring of 1935, and the Ju 88 flew for the first time in December 1936. The first two prototypes could not meet the requirements of the specification with their DB 600 engines, but the Ju 88 *V3*, with two DB 601 motors, exceeded them handsomely. The authorities were delighted, but then informed Junkers that the design would have to be modified to enable the machine to undertake dive-bombing missions. This led to the Ju 88 *V5* which had a strengthened airframe, a fully-glazed nose in place of the previous prototypes' conventional nose, and a ventral gondola with an additional machine-gun to double the type's defensive armament. Several world records were established by the Ju 88 *V5*, and by now the *Reichsluftfahrtministerium* had decided that the Ju 88 was to be the *Luftwaffe*'s next medium bomber.

Production got under way early in 1939, and the type entered service in August of the same year. The Ju 88A was destined to become the main bomber variant, and the series went through a long list of marks. In common with other combat aircraft, there was a constant growth in weight, the result of increased bomb-loads and enhanced offensive armament, with the need for more powerful engines and greater fuel capacity. The basic engine had been changed in the Ju 88 *V5* to the Junkers Jumo 211, which powered subsequent bomber marks up to the Ju 88S, which had BMW 801 radials. The chief Ju 88A series marks were the A-4, with a wing span increased by 5 feet 4¼ inches (1.63 m), a mixed cannon/machine-gun defensive armament, and nearly twice the offensive load at 4,410 lbs (2,000

kg); the A-13, which was a ground-attack variant with a forward-firing armament of 16 7.92-mm machine-guns; the A-14, an updated version of the A-4 with better protection and balloon-cable cutters; and the A-17 torpedo-bomber with two underslung torpedoes.

The Ju 88B and 88E were planned in parallel with the Ju 88A series, with Jumo 213 engines and a larger, but better streamlined, fully-glazed nose. These did not enter widespread production. Right from the beginning of the Ju 88 programme, the *RLM* had seen the type's possibilities as a heavy fighter, and a specific fighter version, the Ju 88C, was developed to meet this need. However, as bomber production took priority over that of fighters, it was not until 1943 that Ju 88 fighters began to reach the front in any number.

The first of these models, the Ju 88C-1, was powered by two BMW 801 radials, but as this engine had a priority allocation to Focke-Wulf for the Fw 190, the Ju 88C-1 was abandoned in favour of the Jumo 211-powered Ju 88C-2. The first fighter model to go into production on a large scale was the Ju 88C-6, from mid-1942 onwards. Like all C models, this had a solid nose, with an armament of three fixed 20-mm cannon and three fixed 7.92-mm machine-guns. The Ju 88C-6b was the first Ju 88 model to be fitted with radar for night fighting, and this entered production late in 1942. The next model, the Ju 88C-6c, had the extraordinary, but very successful, *schräge Musik* (Jazz music) installation: two 20-mm cannon in the fuselage, arranged to fire obliquely forward and upwards, to hit the bellies of bombers above. The Ju 88R series was the BMW 801-powered version of the night-fighting Ju 88C series aircraft. The next model to appear was the Ju 88D, a highly successful, long-range, reconnaissance machine.

The aircraft of the Ju 88G night-fighter series, derived from the interim Ju 88R, were more numerous. The first of the new series, the Ju 88G-1 appeared in the spring of 1944, and was soon followed by improved versions, the best being the Ju 88G-7b with four 20-mm cannon in the nose, two 20-mm cannon in the *schräge Musik*

installation, and a maximum speed of over 400 mph (644 km/h). The Ju 88H series was introduced in 1942 as a very long-range reconnaissance series, with a lengthened fuselage to hold extra fuel. Maximum range was 3,200 miles (5,150 km).

The Ju 88P series, also dating from 1942, was designed to counter the enormous Russian superiority in tanks with a powerful 'tank-busting' aircraft. Models in this series were fitted with a large ventral gondola housing one or more anti-tank gun: two 3.7-cm weapons in the Ju 88P-2 and P-3, a 5-cm weapon in the P-4 and a 7.5-cm weapon in the P-1. The final bomber variant of the basic design was the Ju 88S, which was powered by BMW 801 radials, had a top speed of 379 mph (610 km/h) and an offensive load of 4,410 lbs (2,000 kg). The Ju 88T series bore the same relation to the S series as the D to the A.

The most remarkable Ju 88 aircraft were those involved in the *Mistel* operations. In these, a Ju 88 loaded with explosives was flown to its target by the pilot of a fighter mounted above the fuselage on struts. When the explosive-laden Ju 88 was diving straight at the target, the pilot broke away in his fighter leaving the Ju 88 to plunge into the target. Only a few operations had been carried out by the end of the war, but these proved quite successful.

The Ju 88 was a quite extraordinary plane, very versatile, but also very good at its many tasks. The basic design was very sound, and proved itself to have enormous development potential, as was shown by the success of the Ju 188 and 288, which were built only in limited numbers compared with the Ju 88's 15,000.

Below: A Mistel (Mistletoe) Schulung 1 (Training 1) combination of a Ju 88A-4 and Bf 109F. The operational version of this remarkable weapon, named Beethoven, featured a 8,377-lb (3,800-kg) hollow-charge warhead in place of the crew compartment of the Ju 88, which was directed onto its target by the pick-a-back fighter, which in turn released itself at the last moment

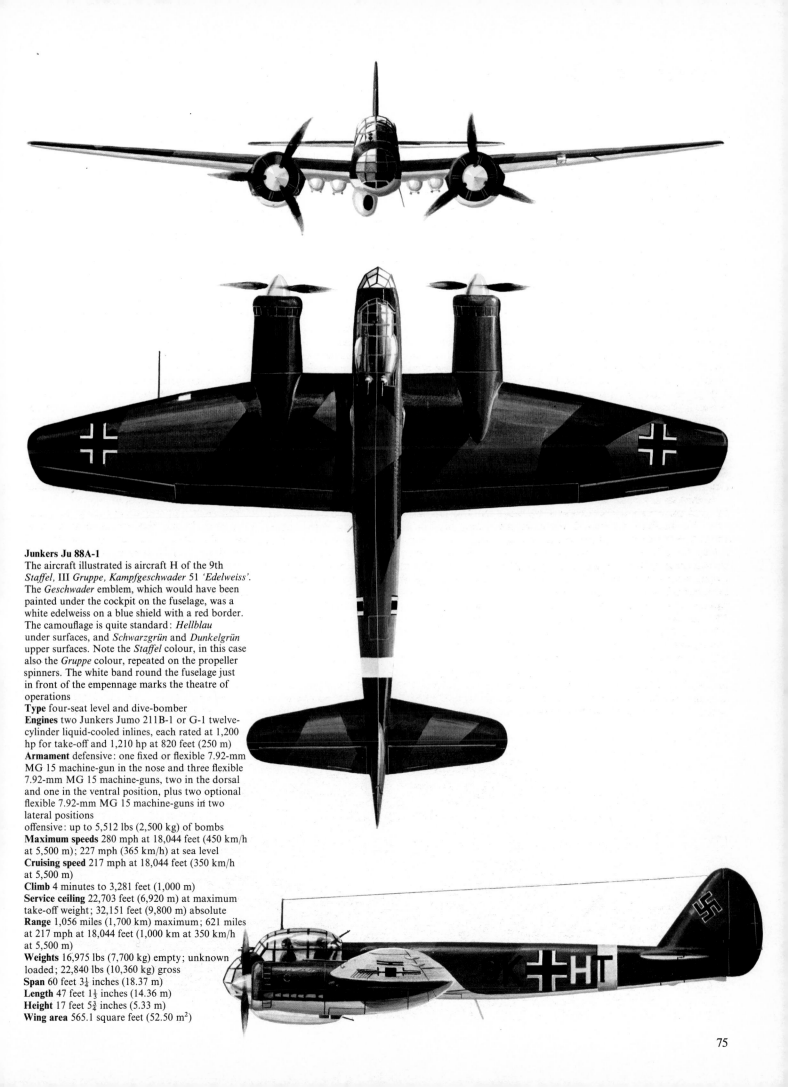

Junkers Ju 88A-1

The aircraft illustrated is aircraft H of the 9th *Staffel*, III *Gruppe*, *Kampfgeschwader* 51 *'Edelweiss'*. The *Geschwader* emblem, which would have been painted under the cockpit on the fuselage, was a white edelweiss on a blue shield with a red border. The camouflage is quite standard: *Hellblau* under surfaces, and *Schwarzgrün* and *Dunkelgrün* upper surfaces. Note the *Staffel* colour, in this case also the *Gruppe* colour, repeated on the propeller spinners. The white band round the fuselage just in front of the empennage marks the theatre of operations

Type four-seat level and dive-bomber

Engines two Junkers Jumo 211B-1 or G-1 twelve-cylinder liquid-cooled inlines, each rated at 1,200 hp for take-off and 1,210 hp at 820 feet (250 m)

Armament defensive: one fixed or flexible 7.92-mm MG 15 machine-gun in the nose and three flexible 7.92-mm MG 15 machine-guns, two in the dorsal and one in the ventral position, plus two optional flexible 7.92-mm MG 15 machine-guns in two lateral positions
offensive: up to 5,512 lbs (2,500 kg) of bombs

Maximum speeds 280 mph at 18,044 feet (450 km/h at 5,500 m); 227 mph (365 km/h) at sea level

Cruising speed 217 mph at 18,044 feet (350 km/h at 5,500 m)

Climb 4 minutes to 3,281 feet (1,000 m)

Service ceiling 22,703 feet (6,920 m) at maximum take-off weight; 32,151 feet (9,800 m) absolute

Range 1,056 miles (1,700 km) maximum; 621 miles at 217 mph at 18,044 feet (1,000 km at 350 km/h at 5,500 m)

Weights 16,975 lbs (7,700 kg) empty; unknown loaded; 22,840 lbs (10,360 kg) gross

Span 60 feet 3¼ inches (18.37 m)

Length 47 feet 1⅓ inches (14.36 m)

Height 17 feet 5¾ inches (5.33 m)

Wing area 565.1 square feet (52.50 m²)

Messerschmitt 109

The Messerschmitt Bf 109 was Germany's most celebrated fighter of World War II, and served in ever more advanced forms with the *Luftwaffe* from early in 1937 to the end of hostilities. At the time of its introduction it marked the absolute in single-seat fighter design, but yet was not derived, as were so many other equivalent aircraft, from a long line of other machines. It is worth noting here that although the fighter is usually designated Me 109, this is incorrect. Although Willi Messerschmitt bought the bankrupt Bayerische Flugzeugwerke (Bf) or Bavarian Aircraft Works in 1932, two years before design work on the Bf 109 started, the designation Bf was used up to design number 162.

The *Luftwaffe* in 1934 issued a specification and contracts for prototype construction for a new single-engined fighter to several companies, but not to Messerschmitt. This was partially the result of the personal enmity between Messerschmitt and Erhard Milch, the German Secretary of Aviation. However, the encouraging results obtained with the Bf 108 late in 1934 meant that the authorities could no longer ignore the Messerschmitt works in contracts concerning high-speed aircraft, and the Bavarian concern was added to the list of constructors for the new design competition.

The first prototype was unveiled in August of the following year. The new fighter was quite remarkable for the time, with all-metal construction, an enclosed cockpit, a retractable undercarriage, and low-set cantilever monoplane wings. A series of prototypes was produced before the *Luftwaffe* decided to accept the superlative Bf 109 as its next fighter after the competitive trials with Heinkel's contender, the He 112, late in 1936.

The first production version was the Bf 109B series, powered by a Junkers Jumo 210 engine. The first Bf 109B-1 fighters came off the production line in February 1937, and were soon sent to Spain for operational testing against the Polikarpov I-15 and I-16 fighters being flown by the Republicans. The Messerschmitt fighter soon showed itself to be superior to both. The Bf 109B-1 was soon replaced in production by the B-2, which had a variable-pitch metal propeller. These early types were quickly joined by the Bf 109C series, which had an improved engine and cooling installation, and better armament. Production models of the C series began to reach the *Luftwaffe* in the spring of 1938.

The next model to appear was the Bf 109D series, which featured a DB 600 engine and a 20-mm cannon. The new engine lifted top speed by nearly 70 mph (113 km/h), and the cannon, mounted between the cylinder banks to fire through the propeller hub, increased firepower very considerably. Deliveries of the new model began early in 1938, but trouble was soon experienced with the poor reliability of the engines. Thus few were built before the type was superseded by the Bf 109E series, which utilized the more reliable and more powerful DB 601. The new type started to reach the *Luftwaffe* in early 1938; it was destined to become the German air force's fighter mainstay until the advent of the Bf 109F in late 1940. Thus the

Bf 109E was the main German fighter encountered by RAF fighters in the Battle of Britain. Compared with the Bf 109D, the E series had an armament of two or three 20-mm cannon, which gave it a distinct advantage in certain respects over current RAF fighters, which had only a machine-gun armament.

The Bf 109F series, which entered service in 1941, was the best of the whole Bf 109 family from the aerodynamic point of view, the nose contours being cleaned up considerably and the tail being redesigned to eliminate the two bracing struts that had been so much a feature of the earlier marks. It is worth noting here that the last of the types with a braced tailplane had been the Bf 109T (T for *Träger* or Carrier), a navalized version of the Bf 109E. This type had been produced in very limited quantities for Germany's projected aircraft-carrier. The armament of the Bf 109F series was, remarkably for a warplane, lighter than that of its predecessor, at one 15- or 20-mm cannon and two 7.92-mm machine-guns. Handling characteristics were superb, however, and speed was nearly 380 mph (612 km/h).

Luftwaffe pilots were unhappy about the reduction in armament on the new series, however, and the next model to appear, the Bf 109G, had a much increased firepower. The engine was also changed, the latest Daimler-Benz power unit, the DB 605, being installed. Although the weight of fire and speed had thereby been improved, it was only at the expense of the fighter's handling qualities, which declined from the beginning of the G series. This decline was further helped by the need for yet heavier armament, which resulted in the replacement of the two fuselage-mounted 7.92-mm machine-guns by a pair of 13.1-mm weapons from the Bf 109G-5 onwards. To accommodate these bulkier guns, bulged humps had to be fitted over the

breeches, on each side of the fuselage in front of the cockpit. In the G series, provision was also made for the carriage of numerous different types of underwing and under-fuselage stores. These included drop-tanks, bombs, rockets, gun-packs etc.

The Bf 109H series was intended as a high-altitude fighter development of the F series, with an increased wing span and a DB 601 engine modified for high-altitude performance. In fact the Bf 109H-1 used a G-5 airframe with a DB 605 engine. No quantity production was undertaken. The last production variant of the Bf 109 was the Bf 109K, which began to appear in September 1944. This was intended to become the definitive model eliminating the need for the bewildering number of sub-marks that was bedevilling the *Luftwaffe* administrative and supply departments. A DB 605 engine boosted to over 2,000 hp was used, with this the Bf 109K-4 reached a speed of over 450 mph (724 km/h). Armament was one 30- and two 15-mm cannon. Chief distinguishing features of the K series were the revised cockpit canopy with fewer panels to improve vision, and the narrower, taller vertical tail surfaces. Not many of this last mark were built. Wartime Bf 109 production reached the vast total of 30,480 aircraft.

The Bf 109 is justly one of the most famous aircraft of World War II. Its importance was considerable, and although flying qualities had to take second place behind speed and armament from 1942 onwards, even the last marks of this redoubtable fighter had their staunch supporters. The Bf 109, despite its high wing-loading, was always manoeuvrable, capable of absorbing considerable battle damage, and always able to carry yet more in the way of weapons. The type's one real weakness lay in the outward-retracting undercarriage, which was prone to breakage, and which made taxiing difficult.

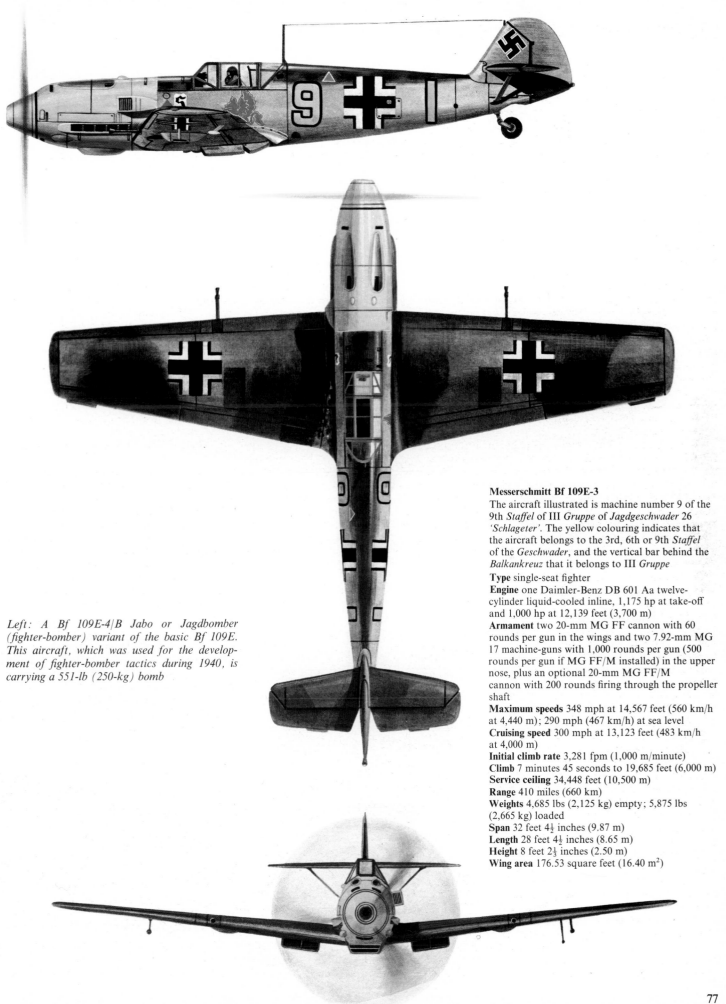

Left: A Bf 109E-4/B Jabo or Jagdbomber (fighter-bomber) variant of the basic Bf 109E. This aircraft, which was used for the development of fighter-bomber tactics during 1940, is carrying a 551-lb (250-kg) bomb

Messerschmitt Bf 109E-3
The aircraft illustrated is machine number 9 of the 9th *Staffel* of III *Gruppe* of *Jagdgeschwader* 26 *'Schlageter'*. The yellow colouring indicates that the aircraft belongs to the 3rd, 6th or 9th *Staffel* of the *Geschwader*, and the vertical bar behind the *Balkankreuz* that it belongs to III *Gruppe*

Type single-seat fighter
Engine one Daimler-Benz DB 601 Aa twelve-cylinder liquid-cooled inline, 1,175 hp at take-off and 1,000 hp at 12,139 feet (3,700 m)
Armament two 20-mm MG FF cannon with 60 rounds per gun in the wings and two 7.92-mm MG 17 machine-guns with 1,000 rounds per gun (500 rounds per gun if MG FF/M installed) in the upper nose, plus an optional 20-mm MG FF/M cannon with 200 rounds firing through the propeller shaft
Maximum speeds 348 mph at 14,567 feet (560 km/h at 4,440 m); 290 mph (467 km/h) at sea level
Cruising speed 300 mph at 13,123 feet (483 km/h at 4,000 m)
Initial climb rate 3,281 fpm (1,000 m/minute)
Climb 7 minutes 45 seconds to 19,685 feet (6,000 m)
Service ceiling 34,448 feet (10,500 m)
Range 410 miles (660 km)
Weights 4,685 lbs (2,125 kg) empty; 5,875 lbs (2,665 kg) loaded
Span 32 feet 4½ inches (9.87 m)
Length 28 feet 4½ inches (8.65 m)
Height 8 feet 2⅓ inches (2.50 m)
Wing area 176.53 square feet (16.40 m²)

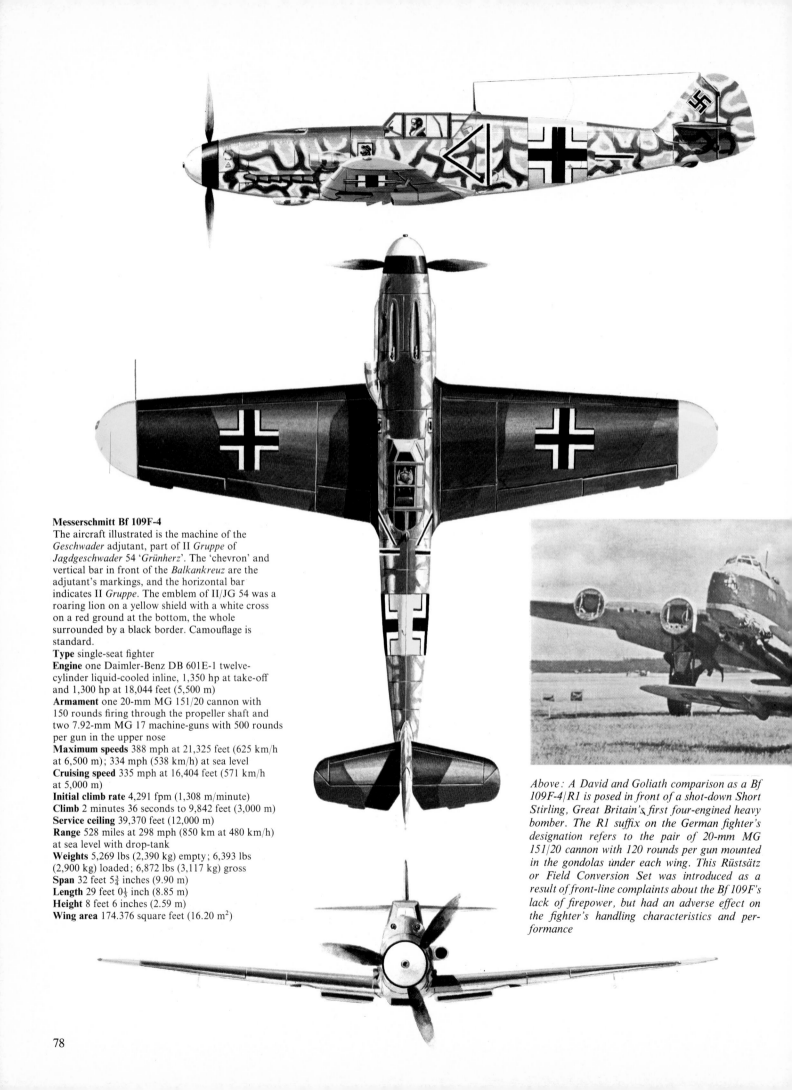

Messerschmitt Bf 109F-4

The aircraft illustrated is the machine of the
Geschwader adjutant, part of II *Gruppe* of
Jagdgeschwader 54 '*Grünherz*'. The 'chevron' and
vertical bar in front of the *Balkankreuz* are the
adjutant's markings, and the horizontal bar
indicates II *Gruppe*. The emblem of II/JG 54 was a
roaring lion on a yellow shield with a white cross
on a red ground at the bottom, the whole
surrounded by a black border. Camouflage is
standard.

Type single-seat fighter

Engine one Daimler-Benz DB 601E-1 twelve-
cylinder liquid-cooled inline, 1,350 hp at take-off
and 1,300 hp at 18,044 feet (5,500 m)

Armament one 20-mm MG 151/20 cannon with
150 rounds firing through the propeller shaft and
two 7.92-mm MG 17 machine-guns with 500 rounds
per gun in the upper nose

Maximum speeds 388 mph at 21,325 feet (625 km/h
at 6,500 m); 334 mph (538 km/h) at sea level

Cruising speed 335 mph at 16,404 feet (571 km/h
at 5,000 m)

Initial climb rate 4,291 fpm (1,308 m/minute)

Climb 2 minutes 36 seconds to 9,842 feet (3,000 m)

Service ceiling 39,370 feet (12,000 m)

Range 528 miles at 298 mph (850 km at 480 km/h)
at sea level with drop-tank

Weights 5,269 lbs (2,390 kg) empty; 6,393 lbs
(2,900 kg) loaded; 6,872 lbs (3,117 kg) gross

Span 32 feet 5¾ inches (9.90 m)

Length 29 feet 0⅓ inch (8.85 m)

Height 8 feet 6 inches (2.59 m)

Wing area 174.376 square feet (16.20 m²)

*Above: A David and Goliath comparison as a Bf
109F-4/R1 is posed in front of a shot-down Short
Stirling, Great Britain's first four-engined heavy
bomber. The R1 suffix on the German fighter's
designation refers to the pair of 20-mm MG
151/20 cannon with 120 rounds per gun mounted
in the gondolas under each wing. This Rüstsätz
or Field Conversion Set was introduced as a
result of front-line complaints about the Bf 109F's
lack of firepower, but had an adverse effect on
the fighter's handling characteristics and performance*

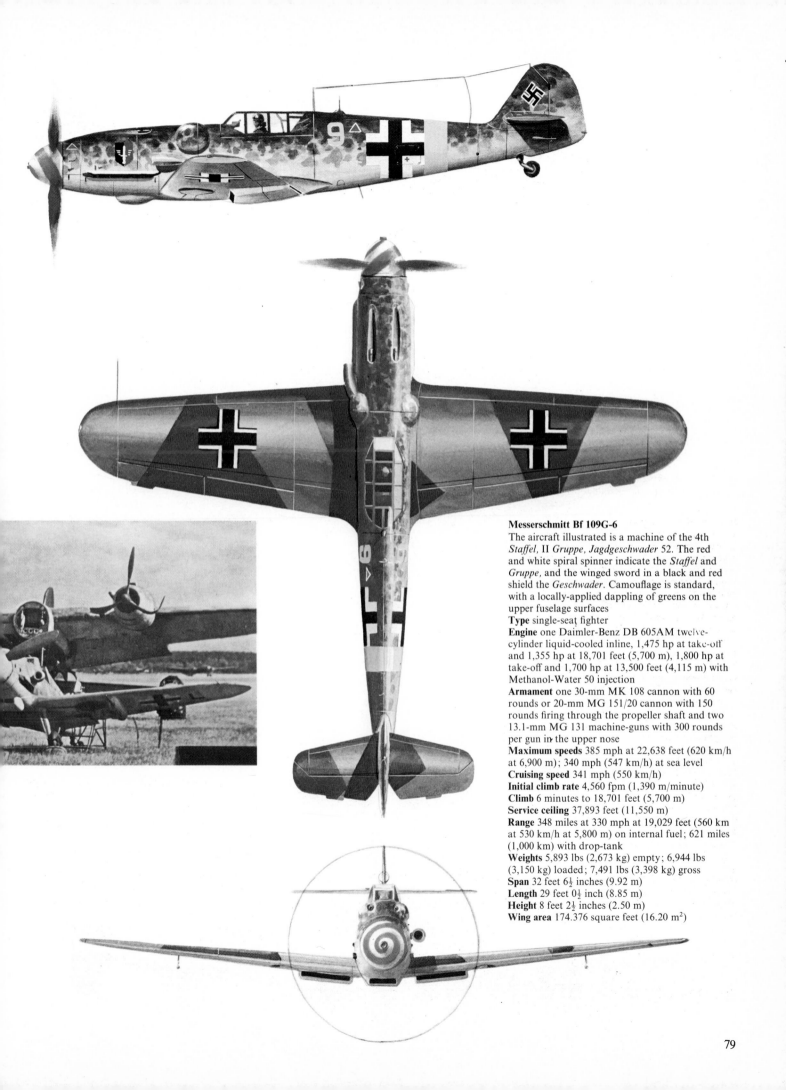

Messerschmitt Bf 109G-6

The aircraft illustrated is a machine of the 4th *Staffel, II Gruppe, Jagdgeschwader* 52. The red and white spiral spinner indicate the *Staffel* and *Gruppe*, and the winged sword in a black and red shield the *Geschwader*. Camouflage is standard, with a locally-applied dappling of greens on the upper fuselage surfaces

Type single-seat fighter
Engine one Daimler-Benz DB 605AM twelve-cylinder liquid-cooled inline, 1,475 hp at take-off and 1,355 hp at 18,701 feet (5,700 m), 1,800 hp at take-off and 1,700 hp at 13,500 feet (4,115 m) with Methanol-Water 50 injection
Armament one 30-mm MK 108 cannon with 60 rounds or 20-mm MG 151/20 cannon with 150 rounds firing through the propeller shaft and two 13.1-mm MG 131 machine-guns with 300 rounds per gun in the upper nose
Maximum speeds 385 mph at 22,638 feet (620 km/h at 6,900 m); 340 mph (547 km/h) at sea level
Cruising speed 341 mph (550 km/h)
Initial climb rate 4,560 fpm (1,390 m/minute)
Climb 6 minutes to 18,701 feet (5,700 m)
Service ceiling 37,893 feet (11,550 m)
Range 348 miles at 330 mph at 19,029 feet (560 km at 530 km/h at 5,800 m) on internal fuel; 621 miles (1,000 km) with drop-tank
Weights 5,893 lbs (2,673 kg) empty; 6,944 lbs (3,150 kg) loaded; 7,491 lbs (3,398 kg) gross
Span 32 feet 6½ inches (9.92 m)
Length 29 feet 0½ inch (8.85 m)
Height 8 feet 2½ inches (2.50 m)
Wing area 174.376 square feet (16.20 m²)

Messerschmitt 110

Like the Ju 87, the Bf 110 has had a considerable corpus of legend built up around it to the detriment of a true assessment of the real aircraft and its capabilities. Because the Bf 110 was basically a fighter, it has been compared with single-engined Allied fighters and so the assessment of the series has always been unfavourable.

The origins of the Bf 110 lay in a 1934 requirement for a twin-engined *Kampfzerstörer* or battle-destroyer, which would fulfil a basic role of clearing the way through enemy fighters for bombers, whilst still being able to undertake a variety of other tasks. After a considerable amount of political and personal wrangling within the *Luftwaffe* high command, Messerschmitt was given the order for prototype construction. Powered by two DB 600 engines, the first prototype flew in May 1936, being joined late in the year by the next two prototypes. Plans were laid for the production of a definitive Bf 110A series, but trouble with the DB 600 engine led to the abandonment of the idea. Instead the Bf 110 received two of the newer and less troublesome DB 601 engines. With these powerplants a new model, the Bf 110B series, was introduced.

The major visual differences between the A and B models were the better streamlined nose and fully enclosed retracted undercarriage of the latter. But there were production delays with the DB 601 engine, however, and the B series had to be powered by Junkers Jumo 210 motors. The first machine with the revised powerplant arrangement flew in April 1938. Thus problems with the engines had robbed the *Luftwaffe* of a chance to test their new fighter operationally in Spain. In fact performance with the Jumos was so low that machines of the B series were never considered as first-line fighters, and by the beginning of World War II had been relegated to a training role.

By the end of 1938 the troubles with production of the DB 601 had been ended, and a new series, the Bf 110C, had been introduced to take advantage of the superior power offered by the Daimler-Benz engines. Deliveries of the new model, which was over 50 mph (80 km/h) faster than its predecessor, began in January 1939. The Bf 110

saw action for the first time in the Polish campaign, in which it acquitted itself well against the inferior aircraft of the Polish air force. It also performed creditably in daylight actions against British bombers over the North Sea.

Luftwaffe confidence in the Bf 110 was by now great, and, in the spring of 1940, Messerschmitt was asked to develop the ability to perform light bombing duties to the 110's repertoire. As a result further C series aircraft were adapted for reconnaissance missions. After their severe handling by RAF fighters in the Battle of Britain, most of the C series aircraft were converted to bomber-interception and glider-towing models. The Bf 110D series was intended as a long-range model, fuel capacity being increased by either droppable or non-droppable extra tanks under the fuselage, but the model was not a success and was soon phased out of service.

Interest in the Bf 110 as a bomber had already been shown by the *Luftwaffe*, as evidenced by the Bf 110C-4/B, but now there emerged the Bf 110E series, which was intended to meet the need for a heavy fighter-bomber. The series entered service in the summer of 1941, and in the E-1/R2 variant the Bf 110 was able to deliver a bomb-load to 4,410 lbs (2,000 kg). A long-range reconnaissance model was also developed.

At the same time the Bf 110F series was introduced. This differed principally from the E series in having more powerful engines and increased protection for the crew. Apart from these differences, the Bf 110F-1 to F-3 were similar to the E-1 to E-3. However, later F series models had increased armament for the night-fighter role. The first Bf 110 model to feature radar equipment for the night-fighter role was the Bf 110F-4a. Production of the Bf 110 had been tapered off from the late summer of 1941 in expectation of the arrival of large quantities of the newer Me 210 series, but with the failure of this fighter, large-scale production of the Bf 110 was restarted early in 1942 with the Bf 110G series. This had the more powerful DB 605 engines, and the first models were intended as heavy fighter-bombers and bomber-destroyers. For this latter role a variety of weapons was

tested, ranging from massed underwing rocket batteries to heavy cannon mounted in packs under the fuselage. From the Bf 110G-4 onwards, however, it was decided to concentrate on the Bf 110 as a night fighter. Numerous models were introduced, with various radar and armament installations. Bf 110 wartime production totalled 5,762 aircraft.

The fault of the Bf 110 series lay not with the aircraft itself, but with the roles for which it was designed. Needless to say, it proved impossible to produce a fighter that could undertake several tasks, including combat with first-rate single-engined fighters, with any degree of competence. After the fallacy of this idea had been more than amply demonstrated by RAF fighters in the Battle of Britain, the multi-destroyer role of the Bf 110 series was abandoned and it then emerged as a highly successful bomber destroyer. With its good load-carrying capacity, heavy armament and more than adequate performance, Bf 110 night fighters and heavy day-fighting bomber-destroyers proved to be the single greatest scourge of the Allied bombers which tore Germany apart in the closing stages of the war. If for nothing else, the Bf 110 should be remembered for this. Compared with other twin-engined fighters designed to the voguish interest in such aircraft during the late 1930s, the Bf 110 was remarkably successful. The Dutch Fokker G-1 was a good aircraft, but built only in limited numbers; the British Westland Whirlwind was plagued by engine difficulties; the Italian Industrie Meccaniche e Aeronautiche Meridonali Ro 57 failed for lack of suitably powerful indigenous engines; and the French Hanriot NC 600 was flown only in prototype form. Only the French Potez 63 series of general purpose aircraft attained great success.

Left: A Bf 110 heavy fighter on a typical North African airfield. Aircraft movements on such airfields could be detected from considerable distances as a result of the large clouds of dust thrown up. This dust also proved a great problem for engine life: unless special filters against the dust were provided, engine life could be as short as 30 hours

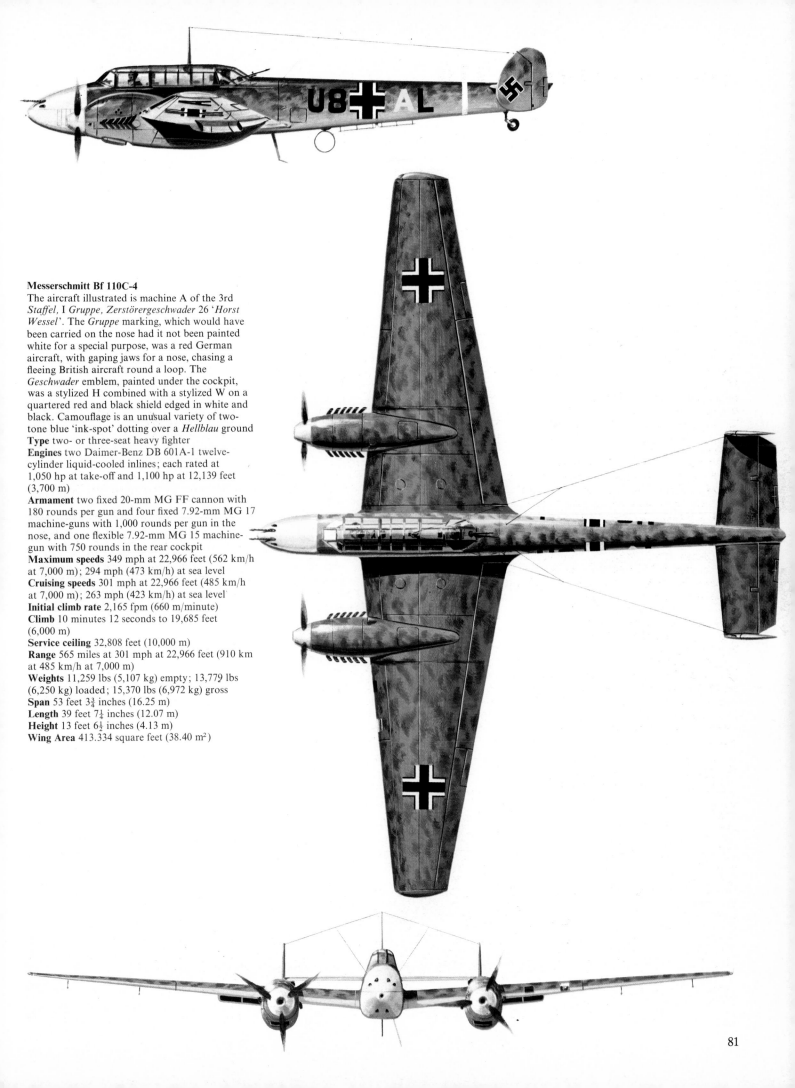

Messerschmitt Bf 110C-4

The aircraft illustrated is machine A of the 3rd *Staffel, I Gruppe, Zerstörergeschwader* 26 '*Horst Wessel*'. The *Gruppe* marking, which would have been carried on the nose had it not been painted white for a special purpose, was a red German aircraft, with gaping jaws for a nose, chasing a fleeing British aircraft round a loop. The *Geschwader* emblem, painted under the cockpit, was a stylized H combined with a stylized W on a quartered red and black shield edged in white and black. Camouflage is an unusual variety of two-tone blue 'ink-spot' dotting over a *Hellblau* ground

Type two- or three-seat heavy fighter

Engines two Daimer-Benz DB 601A-1 twelve-cylinder liquid-cooled inlines; each rated at 1,050 hp at take-off and 1,100 hp at 12,139 feet (3,700 m)

Armament two fixed 20-mm MG FF cannon with 180 rounds per gun and four fixed 7.92-mm MG 17 machine-guns with 1,000 rounds per gun in the nose, and one flexible 7.92-mm MG 15 machine-gun with 750 rounds in the rear cockpit

Maximum speeds 349 mph at 22,966 feet (562 km/h at 7,000 m); 294 mph (473 km/h) at sea level

Cruising speeds 301 mph at 22,966 feet (485 km/h at 7,000 m); 263 mph (423 km/h) at sea level

Initial climb rate 2,165 fpm (660 m/minute)

Climb 10 minutes 12 seconds to 19,685 feet (6,000 m)

Service ceiling 32,808 feet (10,000 m)

Range 565 miles at 301 mph at 22,966 feet (910 km at 485 km/h at 7,000 m)

Weights 11,259 lbs (5,107 kg) empty; 13,779 lbs (6,250 kg) loaded; 15,370 lbs (6,972 kg) gross

Span 53 feet 3¾ inches (16.25 m)

Length 39 feet 7¼ inches (12.07 m)

Height 13 feet 6½ inches (4.13 m)

Wing Area 413.334 square feet (38.40 m²)

Messerschmitt 262 Schwalbe

The Messerschmitt Me 262 was the first turbojet-powered aircraft in the world to see combat. Although the Allies had jet aircraft of their own by the end of World War II, none of those constructed or designed were as advanced aerodynamically as the superlative Messerschmitt fighter with its revolutionary 'swept' wings. This is all the more remarkable for the fact that design work on Messerschmitt's first jet aircraft started before the outbreak of war years before any comparable Allied development.

By the autumn of 1938, progress with the revolutionary new jet engines, being developed by BMW, was sufficiently encouraging to warrant the construction of an aircraft to use them. Accordingly the Messerschmitt concern was asked to develop an aircraft powered by two of the new engines, which it was hoped would be ready by the end of 1939. Messerschmitt realized that the engines would be ideal for an advanced fighter, and set to work to take advantage of all the latest developments in the field of aerodynamics.

Design work progressed smoothly, but trouble with the BMW motors meant firstly that plans to place the engines in the wing roots had to be amended to locate them actually in the wings, and finally to install a pair of Junkers Jumo 004 engines, the BMW 003s proving very slow in development. But by the time the first prototype of the Me 262 was ready for flight, the Jumo 004 programme had also run into trouble, and no engines were available. The type was first flown, therefore, with a Junkers Jumo 210 piston engine mounted in the nose. Basic flying trials were carried out satisfactorily with this engine. In November 1941, the first BMW engines were finally delivered, and were mounted under the wings; the piston engine was retained initially to provide extra power. The BMW engines proved a total failure on their first flight in March 1942 as the compressor blades in both engines sheared off. The BMW 003 had to be completely redesigned. Soon after the failure of the BMW 003 units, the first Jumo 004 engines were delivered. These were larger than the BMW motors,

and were accommodated under the wings in bigger nacelles. By this time the piston engine had also been removed. The Me 262 V3 thus became the first 262 prototype to fly on jet power alone in July 1942. After further testing of this and other prototypes, not all successful for a variety of aerodynamic and engine problems, the decision to produce the type in quantity as a fighter was taken in June 1943.

One of the chief difficulties with the prototypes had been the difficulty in getting the tail off the ground during the take-off run, but this problem was solved by the V5, which featured a fixed tricycle undercarriage, and the V6, which had a retractable unit of the same configuration. Hitler's insistence on bomb-carrying capability, and further problems with the jets, delayed the delivery of pre-production machines to the *Luftwaffe* until April 1944; production aircraft arrived in July 1944. These were Me 262A series aircraft, whose sub-types included night-fighter and fighter-bomber versions, as well as a number of fighter versions with different armament, including one with a 5-cm cannon.

The Me 262B series were two-seater aircraft, the principal variants being trainer and night-fighter models. The Me 262C series was designed as a fast-climbing interceptor, the rate of climb being boosted by rockets. For example the Me 262C-1a, with a liquid-fuelled Walter rocket in the tail, could reach an altitude of over 38,000 feet (11,583 m) in 4 minutes 30 seconds. However, none of the Me 262C series entered quantity production.

Although it was an excellent and very advanced type, the Me 262 did not have a significant impact on the course of the war. By the time of its service *début* the defeat of Germany was inevitable. The Me 262 did, however, perform very creditably, its high speed, good rate of climb and heavy firepower making it a formidable opponent for Allied bombers. Much has been made of Hitler's insistence that the aircraft should be able to carry a 2,205-lb (1,000-kg) bomb-load; but work to enable the machine to carry bombs had already been done, and any delay resulting from Hitler's

order occurred because the manufacturers and the users were reluctant to implement the order, not because of any difficulty in the work involved. The main reason for the Me 262's slow arrival in service was the trouble with production of the Jumo 004 turbojet. These troubles were never fully solved, and bedevilled service aircraft in combat. Total Me 263 production amounted to 1,294 aircraft.

The type's one major failing, as far as operations were concerned, was the low rate of acceleration bestowed by the jet engines. Most of the Me 262 aircraft shot down by Allied fighters were caught during their landing run, during which they had to approach the runway slowly, with the engines throttled down. In this landing mode they could be 'bounced' by patrolling Allied fighters: all the Me 262 pilot could do was to try to outdistance the enemy. And in this he had two problems: if he opened the throttles too swiftly, the engines would stall, and if he opened them slowly, the rate of acceleration was so slow that he was a sitting target for the Allied fighter for some time. Overall, however, the Me 262 was a superb aircraft, one that came as a very rude shock to the Allies, and one which showed how far ahead the Germans were of the Allies in overcoming the problems associated with high-speed flight.

Perhaps more interesting than the Me 262's war career, important as this was, is the very considerable effect the type (and the research into aerodynamics that made it so successful an aircraft) had on postwar thinking by the Russians and the Americans. The Me 262 was so clearly more advanced in concept than aircraft such as the Gloster Meteor and Bell P-59 Airacomet that great efforts were made to seize, assimilate and further expand on German work into high-speed aerodynamics, thus paving the way for the modern type of jet aircraft.

Below: An Me 262A captured and tested by the Allies at the end of the war. The fine, stream-lined appearance of the aircraft, in particular the fuselage, is well displayed

Messerschmitt Me 262A-1a Schwalbe (Swallow)
The aircraft illustrated is machine number 8 of the
3rd *Staffel, Jagdgeschwader* 7 *'Nowotny'*. The
emblem of JG 7 was a black fox on a diagonal
dark blue band on a light blue shield edged in
white. Camouflage is standard. The yellow band
round the fuselage was a theatre marking, this one
being used at various times to indicate central and
northern Russia, Scandinavia, the nothern French
coast and Reich defence. The Me 262 is using it in
the last capacity

Type single-seat fighter
Engines two Junkers Jumo 004B-1, 2, or 3 turbojets,
each rated at 1,980 lbs (898 kg) static thrust
Armament four 30-mm MK 108 cannon with 100
rounds per gun for the upper pair and 80 rounds
per gun for the lower pair, mounted in the fuselage
nose
Maximum speeds 540 mph at 19,685 feet (870 km/h
at 6,000 m); 514 mph (827 km/h) at sea level
Cruising speed unknown
Initial climb rate 3,937 fpm (1,200 m/minute)
Climb 6 minutes 48 seconds to 19,685 feet (6,000 m)
Service ceiling 36,089 feet (11,000 m)
Range 652 miles at 29,527 feet (1,050 km at
9,000 m)
Weights 9,742 lbs (4,420 kg) empty; 14,110 lbs
(6,400 kg) loaded; 15,720 lbs (7,130 kg) gross
Span 40 feet 11½ inches (12.50 m)
Length 34 feet 9½ inches (10.60 m)
Height 12 feet 7 inches (3.84 m)
Wing area 234 square feet (21.74 m²)

Savoia-Marchetti SM 79

The Savoia-Marchetti SM 79 was Italy's best medium bomber of the World War II period, and is considered by most authorities to have been unbeaten as a land-based torpedo-bomber during the whole of its service. Although it appeared superficially ungainly, the aircraft was in fact quite clean, adequately defended and well-powered.

The SM 79 could trace its origins back to the SM 73 commercial airliner and transport of the early 1930s. From this was developed the SM 81 *Pipistrello* (Bat), a trimotor monoplane bomber with a fixed undercarriage. For its time the *Pipistrello* was a good aircraft, and served with success in Abyssinia and Spain. A few were still in use as bombers when Italy entered the war in June 1940, but these were soon relegated to transport and paratroop-dropping roles as they were no match for Allied fighters. Despite its earlier sequence number, the SM 79 was in fact

derived from the SM 81, and appeared in 1934 as a civilian transport aircraft. It had nearly half as much power again as the SM 81, and, with its retractable undercarriage, a very respectable performance. The *Regia Aeronautica* soon developed an interest in the new type as a bomber.

The first production version for military use was the SM 79-I, which was intended only as a medium bomber. Power was provided by three Alfa Romeo 126 radials of 780 hp each, and a bomb-load of 2,756 lbs (1,250 kg) could be carried 1,180 miles (1,899 km). The new bomber was tested operationally in the Spanish Civil War, and proved to be very successful. With a top speed of nearly 270 mph (435 km), it was difficult for many Republican fighters to catch. Indeed, Fiat CR 32 fighters could not keep up with it, and Fiat G 50 fighters were only a little faster.

The Italian air force had always been interested

in the use of air-launched torpedoes against shipping in the Mediterranean, and led the world in the development of such weapons, aircraft to launch them, and tactical theories of employment in the period from the end of World War I to the end of World War II. Trials were carried out with the SM 79 as a launching aircraft in 1937, and by the summer of 1939 a new model, the SM 79-II, was in production as a torpedo-bomber. This could deliver two torpedoes, and proved an extremely efficient weapon in World War II.

After the capitulation of Italy, a few SM 79-IIIs were built for use by the *Aviazione della Repubblica Sociale Italiana*. This model was a cleaned-up version of the SM 79-II, with the ventral gondola removed and the forward-firing machine-gun replaced by a 20-mm cannon. Another version, the SM 79B, was produced before the war for export. This model had only two engines, the place of the fuselage-mounted engine being taken by a well-streamlined and glazed nose section. The fin and rudder were also modified. This variant achieved some commercial success with sales to countries in the Balkans. Production totalled 1,330 aircraft.

Left: US personnel inspect an SM 79 which had been flown to Sicily by an Italian instructor with six pupils on board after the Italian surrender in September 1943. Note the 12.7-mm machine-gun for rear defence mounted just to the rear of the cockpit

Below: Two SM 79 bombers (for obvious reasons the type was nicknamed il Gobbo or the hunchback) of the 10th Squadriglia in flight

Savoia-Marchetti SM 79-II Sparviero (Hawk)
The aircraft illustrated is a machine of the 192nd
Squadriglia. Note the triple *fasces* on the wing
markings, and the white cross on the rudder. The
marking at the top of the cross is a representation
of the arms of the House of Savoy, the Italian
royal family. Note also the *fasces* on a blue circle
on the fuselage engine's cowling. This was standard
fuselage marking for the *Regia Aeronautica*.
Camouflage is that for semi-desert conditions

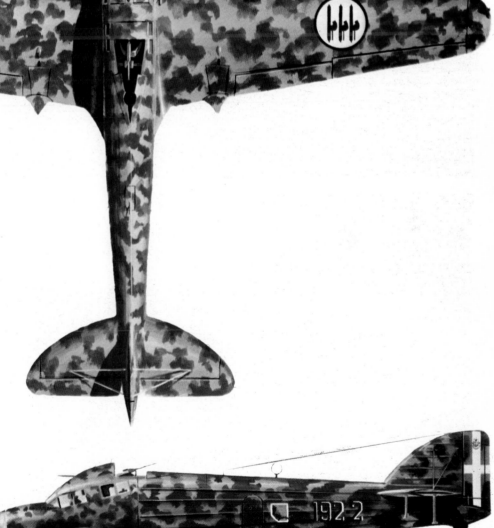

Type four-seat medium and torpedo-bomber
Engines three Piaggio P XI RC 40 nine-cylinder air-
cooled radials, each rated at 1,000 hp at take-off
Armament defensive: one fixed 12.7-mm Breda-
SAFAT machine-gun with 350 rounds in the
forward fuselage, one flexible 12.7-mm Breda-
SAFAT machine-gun with 500 rounds in the dorsal
position, one flexible 12.7-mm Breda-SAFAT
machine-gun with 500 rounds in the ventral
position, and one 7.7-mm Lewis machine-gun for
beam defence
offensive: up to 2,756 lbs (1,250 kg) of bombs
or two 17.7-inch (45-cm) torpedoes
Maximum speeds 267 mph at 13,123 feet (430 km/h
at 4,000 m); 224 mph (360 km/h) at sea level
Cruising speed 230 mph at 19,685 feet (370 km/h
at 6,000 m)
Climb 19 minutes 45 seconds to 16,404 feet
(5,000 m)
Service ceiling 22,966 feet (7,000 m)
Range 1,243 miles (2,000 km)
Weights 16,755 lbs (7,600 kg) empty; 24,912 lbs
(11,300 kg) loaded
Span 69 feet 6¾ inches (21.20 m)
Length 53 feet 1¾ inches (16.20 m)
Height 13 feet 5½ inches (4.10 m)
Wing area 656.6 square feet (61.00 m²)

Aichi D3A 'Val'

The Aichi D3A series was Japan's most celebrated naval dive-bomber of the war, and was the most successful Axis aircraft against Allied warships in the whole of World War II. The type was the last Japanese carrier aircraft to be fitted with a fixed undercarriage, but despite its apparent obsolescence, it performed with stunning success in the first year of the war. To a certain extent the D3A can be considered the Japanese navy's equivalent of the British navy's Fairey Swordfish.

The requirement for a monoplane dive-bomber to replace the biplane Aichi D1A was issued in 1936, and Aichi, Mitsubishi and Nakajima all tendered designs. Only the Aichi and Nakajima designs received prototype contracts, however. The Aichi aircraft, designed by Tokuhishiro Goake, drew many of its features, including the elliptical wing, from contemporary designs by Heinkel, especially the He 70 high-speed monoplane. A fixed undercarriage was used as it was felt that its simplicity and lightness would compensate for the increased drag. The initial prototype, powered by a Nakajima Hikari of 710 hp, was ready by the end of 1937, and trials began early in 1938. Although the aircraft proved to be very strong, it was also underpowered, and difficult to steer. The dive brakes, moreover, proved particularly troublesome. These problems were largely overcome in the second prototype, which had an 840-hp Mitsubishi Kinsei radial, a larger fin and rudder, and strengthened dive brakes. The wings were also enlarged by 21½ square feet (2 m²) to help in tight turns. The D3A was generally superior to the Nakajima D3N, and was ordered into production as the Navy Type 99 Carrier Bomber Model 11, with the company designation D3A1, in December 1939.

As the type went into production, further improvements were made, thereby increasing the weight and necessitating the instalment of the 1,000-hp Kinsei 43 engine. The wings were slightly smaller than those of the second prototype, and the last vestiges of the directional problems encountered with the first prototype were solved by the provision of a dorsal extension to the fin. Although the D3A1 performed satisfactory carrier trials on board the *Akagi* and *Kaga* in 1940, the type saw its first action operating from land bases against the Chinese later that year.

At Pearl Harbor, 126 D3A1 aircraft were involved, and thereafter the type had a spectacular career in the Pacific and Indian oceans. Losses in the Solomons campaign of late 1942 and early 1943 were very heavy, however, and the D3A1 was increasingly relegated to land-based units of the Imperial Japanese Naval Air Force. Realizing that its type was becoming obsolete, Aichi introduced the more powerful D3A2 in June 1942. This had a 1,300-hp Kinsei 54 radial engine, which boosted top speed by nearly 30 mph (48 km/h) to 267 mph (430 km/h). The new model was accepted for service as the Navy Type 99 Carrier Bomber Model 22. Externally, the later model could be distinguished by its revised cockpit canopy and the provision of a small propeller spinner. The D3A was by now obsolete, however, and was increasingly

replaced by the Yokosuka D4Y *Suisei* on the aircraft-carrier. Land-based units continued to use the D3A, but losses were very heavy, despite the type's remarkable agility, which enabled it to dogfight with American fighters. The D3A's service career ended as a *kamikaze* aircraft. In this role its losses were appallingly heavy, out of all proportion to any tasks it could have fulfilled. Production reached a total of 1,495 aircraft.

Above: An Aichi D3A1 'Val' carrier dive-bomber of the type that proved so successful in the Japanese surprise attack on Pearl Harbor
Below: The improved D3A2 model, which could be told from the D3A1 by its spinner, appeared in June 1942. Note the 551-lb (250-kg) bomb on the crutch under the fuselage. The crutch was used to swing the bomb out clear of the propeller as the aircraft dived on its target

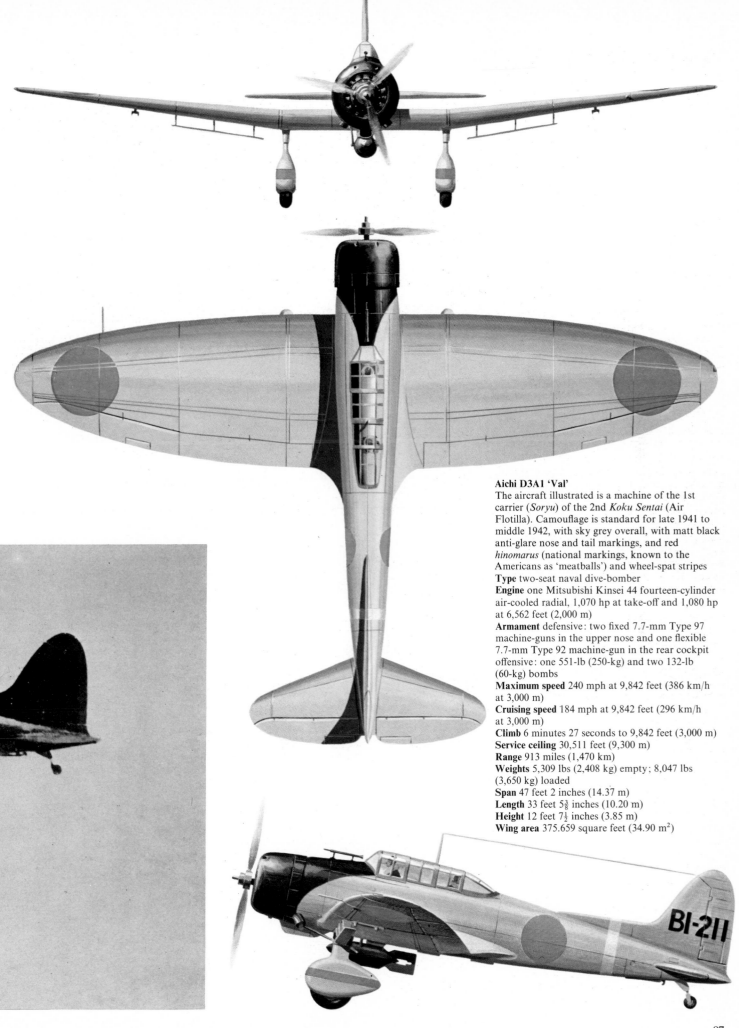

Aichi D3A1 'Val'
The aircraft illustrated is a machine of the 1st
carrier (*Soryu*) of the 2nd *Koku Sentai* (Air
Flotilla). Camouflage is standard for late 1941 to
middle 1942, with sky grey overall, with matt black
anti-glare nose and tail markings, and red
hinomarus (national markings, known to the
Americans as 'meatballs') and wheel-spat stripes
Type two-seat naval dive-bomber
Engine one Mitsubishi Kinsei 44 fourteen-cylinder
air-cooled radial, 1,070 hp at take-off and 1,080 hp
at 6,562 feet (2,000 m)
Armament defensive: two fixed 7.7-mm Type 97
machine-guns in the upper nose and one flexible
7.7-mm Type 92 machine-gun in the rear cockpit
offensive: one 551-lb (250-kg) and two 132-lb
(60-kg) bombs
Maximum speed 240 mph at 9,842 feet (386 km/h
at 3,000 m)
Cruising speed 184 mph at 9,842 feet (296 km/h
at 3,000 m)
Climb 6 minutes 27 seconds to 9,842 feet (3,000 m)
Service ceiling 30,511 feet (9,300 m)
Range 913 miles (1,470 km)
Weights 5,309 lbs (2,408 kg) empty; 8,047 lbs
(3,650 kg) loaded
Span 47 feet 2 inches (14.37 m)
Length 33 feet 5⅜ inches (10.20 m)
Height 12 feet 7½ inches (3.85 m)
Wing area 375.659 square feet (34.90 m²)

Mitsubishi A6M Reisen

The Mitsubishi A6M series of fighters is deservedly the most celebrated aircraft used by the Japanese armed forces in World War II. At a time when other naval fighters were slow, clumsy machines, in every way inferior to their land-based counterparts, the A6M could outfly almost all land-based fighters, had an enormous range, and was possessed of a heavy armament. The type operated from land bases as well as from aircraft-carriers, and was used in almost every major action in which the Imperial Japanese Navy was involved.

The origins of the A6M lay in a 1937 requirement for a fighter to replace the Mitsubishi A5M, which had just entered service. The A5M was a monoplane, but had an open cockpit and a fixed, 'spatted' undercarriage. The revised requirement issued by the navy later in 1937, which reflected the lessons of combat gained over China, meant that the new fighter would have to be a very advanced design. The Mitsubishi team, led by Jiro Horikoshi, produced an excellent all-metal machine, carefully streamlined and with a fully glazed, all-round vision cockpit canopy. This last was quite remarkable for 1938. The first prototype, powered by a 780-hp Mitsubishi Zuisei radial, first flew in April 1939, and proved to be a delightful aircraft, fulfilling or exceeding all the specifications except that of speed. To rectify this failing, Mitsubishi was instructed to replace the Zuisei engine with the 940-hp Nakajima Sakae. The third prototype was fitted with the new engine, and with it the type's designation was changed from A6M1 to A6M2. The new powerplant also raised speed to well over the specified minimum. The Mitsubishi A6M2 was ordered into production as the Navy Type 0 (Zero) Carrier Fighter Model 11 in July 1940. Pre-production models were already in service in China, where their record was extremely impressive.

Several minor modifications were incorporated in production aircraft but only the provision of folding wingtips for carrier use resulted in a different designation, the Model 21. The Japanese navy had 328 operational A6M2 fighters in December 1941, and these spearheaded the incredible run of Japanese successes in the Pacific and South-east Asia up to the middle of 1942. By this time the latest A6M model, the A6M3, was beginning to reach service units as the Model 32. This new model had a 1,130-hp Sakae 21 engine, greater cannon ammunition capacity, and, in later aircraft, wings shortened by the removal of the folding tips. The span now became 36 feet 1 inch (11 m). With these modifications speed was improved by 7 mph (11 km/h) at altitude although handling characteristics were very slightly impaired.

The A6M3 was the first of the A6M series to suffer severe losses at the hands of the Americans. This occurred in the fighting over Guadalcanal. The Sakae 21 was larger than the Sakae 12, which resulted in a reduced fuselage tankage capacity, and also had a higher fuel consumption, with the result that maximum range was reduced to 1,477 miles (2,377 km). As the A6M3s had to operate from airfields over 550 miles (885 km) from Guadalcanal, combat endurance was very

limited, damaged machines had a long haul back home, and casualties rose sharply. In an effort to restore the earlier range, Mitsubishi introduced the Model 22 or 22A, depending on the cannon fitted. This had provision for under-wing drop-tanks, and the longer wings of the Model 21. Range was restored to 1,930 miles (3,106 km), however, the A6M was now beginning to be equalled by the latest Allied fighters, and as a newer model was on its way, production of the Model 22 was very limited.

The next model to appear was designed to be able to hold its own with American fighters at medium and high altitudes. This was A6M4, with a turbo-supercharged Sakae, but it proved a failure as a result of problems with the supercharger. Thus the navy had to make do with the next model, the A6M5, pending the introduction of an A6M replacement.

The A6M5, or Model 52, had shorter wings again, with rounded tips, and individual exhausts, the thrust augmentation lifting speed to 351 mph (565 km/h). The wings were also covered with thicker skinning, which permitted higher diving speeds. Previously, Allied types had been able to escape the A6M by using their superior dive characteristics. This was now largely halted. The weakness of the A6M5 lay not in performance, however, but in protection, for even a short burst from six 0.50-inch (12.7-mm) machine-guns could cause the A6M5 to break up. Thus in March deliveries of the A6M5a began. This had thicker skinning again on the wings, and belt-fed instead of drum-fed cannon in the wings. This Model 52A was quickly superseded, however, by the Model 52B, or A6M5b, which had an armoured glass windscreen and fire extinguishers for the fuel tanks. One of the fuselage 7.7-mm machine-guns was also replaced by a 13.2-mm weapon. But the A6M series was now obsolete, and even the latest A6M5 fighters suffered almost total annihilation in the 'Great Marianas Turkey Shoot' in the Battle of the Philippine Sea in June 1944.

Production of an A6M replacement had still not made any headway, and so further development of the A6M had to be undertaken. Although the designers wished to replace the Sakae engine with the Mitsubishi Kinsei, the navy forbade this. Pending the arrival of the Sakae 31 with methanol-water fuel injection, the

Sakae 21 was retained in the A6M5c (Model 520). This had additional fuel tankage, armour protection for the pilot, and an additional pair of 13.2-mm Type 3 machine-guns in the wings, which had yet thicker skinning. Combat units often extemporized a rack to carry a 551-lb (250-kg) bomb instead of the drop-tank under the fuselage. Further official development of the idea to produce a dive-bomber for light carriers resulted in the A6M7 or Model 63.

The navy finally realized that the only way in which the necessary performance could be achieved was to allow the A6M to use the Kinsei engine. The need was borne home by the failure of the A6M6c (Model 53C), which had a top speed of only 346 mph (557 km/h) despite the methanol-water boosted Sakae 31. To accommodate the 1,560-hp Kinsei 62 the fuselage of the A6M had to be revised, and the first of the new type, designated A6M8, appeared in April 1945. Performance was promising, but no production Model 64 fighters were built before the end of the war.

Although the A6M had been pre-eminent amongst naval fighters in 1941, it was obsolete by 1943. Although its performance was still only a little inferior to that of the latest Allied fighters, it lacked protection for the pilot and fuel. The structure, moreover, was too light to take the combat damage caused by the firepower of Allied fighters in the closing stages of the war. But failure of the navy to develop a replacement in time meant that production of the A6M had to continue to the end of the war and in all 11,291 were built. Many of the earlier models were expended as *kamikaze* aircraft in the Philippines, Iwo Jima and Okinawa campaigns.

The importance of the A6M early in the war was as much psychological as physical: the 'Zero' shocked the Allies, who expected only second-rate *matériel*, copied from the West, to be used by the Japanese.

Below: One of a series of American recognition photographs of the Mitsubishi A6M5 Reisen Zero Fighter), known to the Imperial Japanese Navy as the Navy Type 0 Carrier Fighter Model 52 and to the Allies as the Zeke 52. Note the individual ejector exhaust stubs, which provided some thrust, boosting top speed by 13 mph (21 km/h) compared with the A6M3

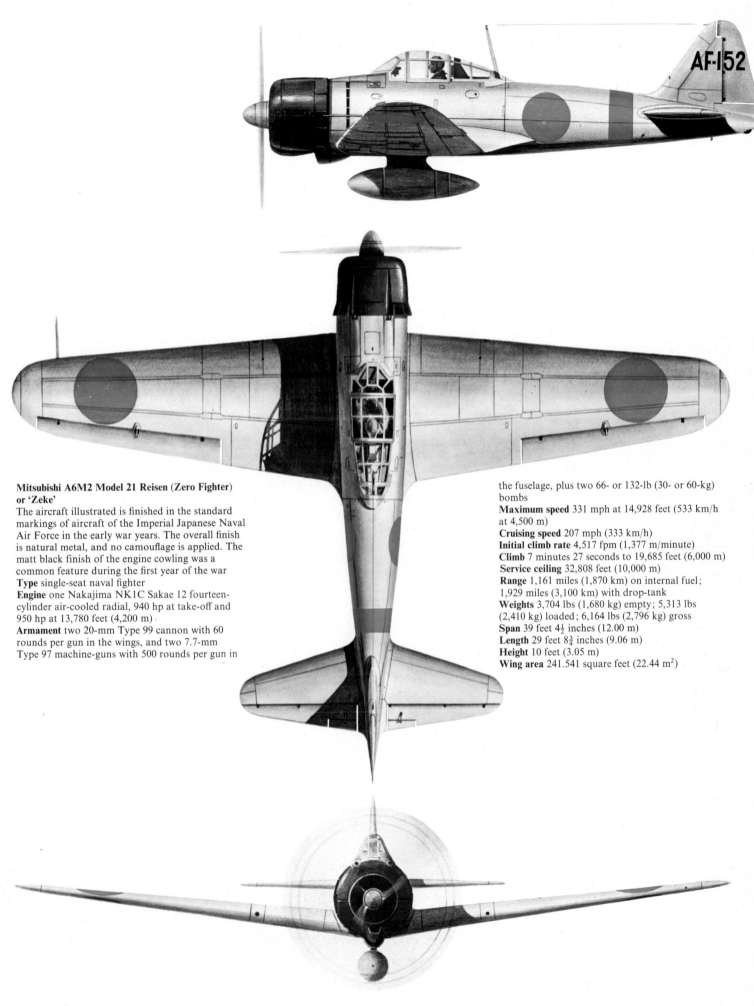

Mitsubishi A6M2 Model 21 Reisen (Zero Fighter) or 'Zeke'
The aircraft illustrated is finished in the standard markings of aircraft of the Imperial Japanese Naval Air Force in the early war years. The overall finish is natural metal, and no camouflage is applied. The matt black finish of the engine cowling was a common feature during the first year of the war
Type single-seat naval fighter
Engine one Nakajima NK1C Sakae 12 fourteen-cylinder air-cooled radial, 940 hp at take-off and 950 hp at 13,780 feet (4,200 m)
Armament two 20-mm Type 99 cannon with 60 rounds per gun in the wings, and two 7.7-mm Type 97 machine-guns with 500 rounds per gun in

the fuselage, plus two 66- or 132-lb (30- or 60-kg) bombs
Maximum speed 331 mph at 14,928 feet (533 km/h at 4,500 m)
Cruising speed 207 mph (333 km/h)
Initial climb rate 4,517 fpm (1,377 m/minute)
Climb 7 minutes 27 seconds to 19,685 feet (6,000 m)
Service ceiling 32,808 feet (10,000 m)
Range 1,161 miles (1,870 km) on internal fuel; 1,929 miles (3,100 km) with drop-tank
Weights 3,704 lbs (1,680 kg) empty; 5,313 lbs (2,410 kg) loaded; 6,164 lbs (2,796 kg) gross
Span 39 feet 4½ inches (12.00 m)
Length 29 feet 8¾ inches (9.06 m)
Height 10 feet (3.05 m)
Wing area 241.541 square feet (22.44 m²)

Nakajima B5N 'Kate'

Although it was produced only in relatively limited numbers, the Nakajima B5N had an enormous impact on the course of World War II, especially for its part in the surprise Japanese air strike on Pearl Harbor, the attack that finally brought the United States into the war. In other ways, too, the B5N was representative of the strengths and weaknesses of Japanese air power in World War II.

The origins of the B5N lay in a 1932 requirement for a high performance torpedo-bomber to replace the ageing Yokosuka B3Y. No suitable aircraft were forthcoming, and two years later the navy issued another specification. The Yokosuka B4Y was put into limited production to meet this, but the type was intended only as an interim torpedo-bomber.

In 1935 the navy again issued a requirement for an attack bomber, as torpedo-bombers were designated by the Imperial Japanese Navy, with a very high performance. Nakajima responded to the requirement with an advanced monoplane designed by a team led by Katsuji Nakamura. The prototype, designated B5N1, flew for the first time in January 1937, and soon proved to have excellent performance. The navy, however, was worried about certain advanced aspects of the design, which they feared might make maintenance too difficult, and Nakajima removed these. At the same time the Nakajima Hikari 2 radial was replaced by a Hikari 3, and with the new powerplant the B5N1 was judged superior to the rival Mitsubishi B5M1. The type was ordered into production as the Navy Type 97 Carrier Attack Bomber Model 1 in November 1937.

The type entered service in 1938, and was immediately issued to units on board Japanese aircraft-carriers and to units operating in support of the ground forces in China. In this latter capacity the B5N1 was used as a light, level bomber, and proved generally successful when escorted by fighters. During 1938 the designation of the Model 1 was changed to Model 11. The only modifications effected at this time were internal equipment changes to take advantage of the lessons learned in China. Combat experience in China led the Japanese navy to realize, however, that the B5N would have to be updated considerably to enable it to operate with any success in areas where strong fighter opposition might be met. Thus a new model appeared in 1939.

This was the B5N2 or Model 12, powered by a 1,000-hp Nakajima Sakae radial in place of the earlier 770-hp Hikari. The new engine was also more closely cowled than its predecessor, and a small spinner was provided over the propeller hub. Despite the increased power available, however, top speed was raised by only 6 mph (10 km/h). The navy nevertheless decided to place the latest model in production as the Sakae was a far more reliable engine than the Hikari. By the end of 1941 the B5N2 had replaced the B5N1 in all front-line units, the older model being relegated to training and liaison duties. The B5N2 was the most advanced carrier-borne torpedo-bomber in service anywhere in the world in 1941, as can be gauged from the success of the 144 such aircraft that took part in the raid on Pearl Harbor, and those that subsequently took part in the sinking of the three American aircraft-carriers *Lexington, Yorktown* and *Hornet* in 1942. B5N2 aircraft also operated as bombers in support of the Japanese amphibious assaults throughout the Pacific and South-east Asia during the early part of 1942.

By 1944 the B5N2 was obsolete, and the type suffered appalling casualties in the Philippines campaign. With the arrival of the Nakajima B6N1 *Tenzan* torpedo-bomber replacement that year, the B5N2 was relegated to second-line duties, the most important of which was the escort of Japanese convoys. In this capacity its long endurance and good visibility for the crew proved very useful in detecting Allied submarines. Visual sightings were quickly supplemented by radar ones when the type was equipped with air-sea search radar. This model could be distinguished by the antennae along the fuselage sides and wing leading-edges. Finally, the B5N2 replaced the B5N1-K, a modification of the standard B5N1, as a training, target-towing, and glider-tug aircraft. Total production was 1,149 aircraft.

Below: A Nakajima B5N accelerates down the flight-deck of a Japanese aircraft-carrier for an operational sortie. In the early months of the war the 'Kate' proved an excellent torpedo-bomber, capable of dropping its offensive load steadily and surely.

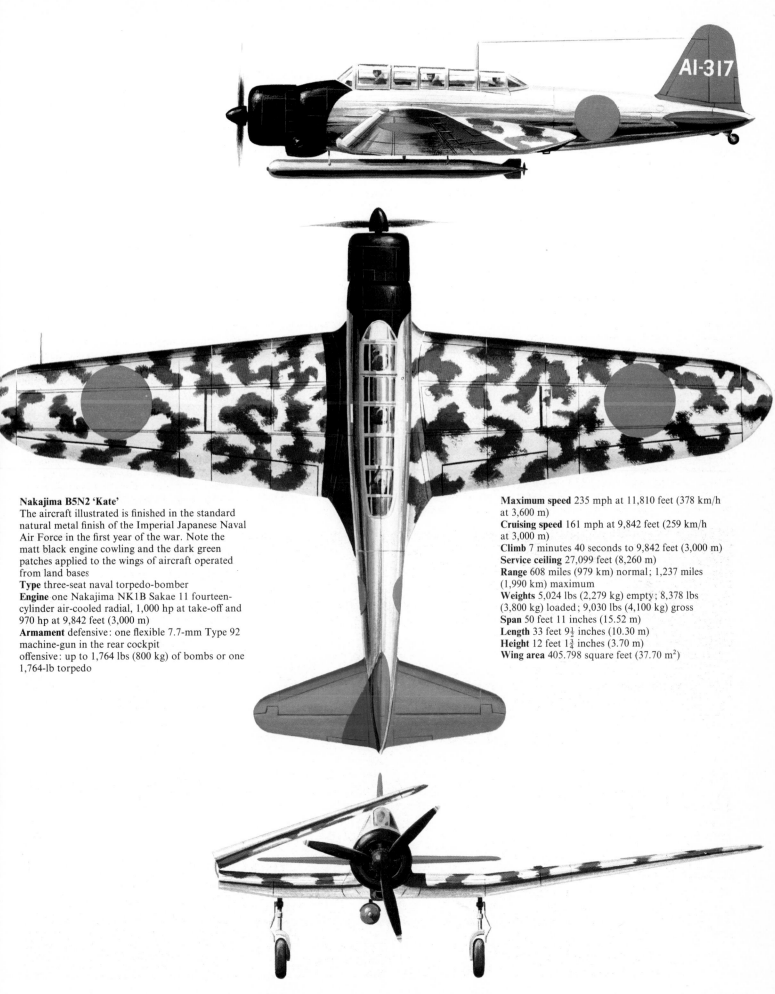

Nakajima B5N2 'Kate'
The aircraft illustrated is finished in the standard
natural metal finish of the Imperial Japanese Naval
Air Force in the first year of the war. Note the
matt black engine cowling and the dark green
patches applied to the wings of aircraft operated
from land bases
Type three-seat naval torpedo-bomber
Engine one Nakajima NK1B Sakae 11 fourteen-
cylinder air-cooled radial, 1,000 hp at take-off and
970 hp at 9,842 feet (3,000 m)
Armament defensive: one flexible 7.7-mm Type 92
machine-gun in the rear cockpit
offensive: up to 1,764 lbs (800 kg) of bombs or one
1,764-lb torpedo

Maximum speed 235 mph at 11,810 feet (378 km/h
at 3,600 m)
Cruising speed 161 mph at 9,842 feet (259 km/h
at 3,000 m)
Climb 7 minutes 40 seconds to 9,842 feet (3,000 m)
Service ceiling 27,099 feet (8,260 m)
Range 608 miles (979 km) normal; 1,237 miles
(1,990 km) maximum
Weights 5,024 lbs (2,279 kg) empty; 8,378 lbs
(3,800 kg) loaded; 9,030 lbs (4,100 kg) gross
Span 50 feet 11 inches (15.52 m)
Length 33 feet 9½ inches (10.30 m)
Height 12 feet 1¾ inches (3.70 m)
Wing area 405.798 square feet (37.70 m²)

Avro Lancaster

The Avro Lancaster was Great Britain's most successful bomber of World War II; indeed so effective was the initial version of the bomber that later marks and models differed from it significantly only in armament and equipment while the basic aircraft remained virtually unchanged. It was capable of lifting a heavier offensive load than any other comparable aircraft and hence bore the brunt of RAF Bomber Command's night offensive against Germany, from the middle of 1942 to the end of the war.

The origins of the Lancaster lay in the unsuccessful Avro Manchester. This latter had been designed, by a team led by Roy Chadwick, to a 1936 requirement for a twin-engined medium bomber powered by Rolls-Royce Vulture engines. The first prototype of the Manchester flew in July 1939, and performance soon proved to be good. The type was ordered into production and entered service in November 1940. But combat operations with the Manchester were unsuccessful: the engines had been rushed into service too quickly, and although powerful proved totally unreliable. Only 209 Manchesters were built, and the type was phased out of service in June 1942.

The problems with the Vulture engines led the Air Ministry in 1940 to consider a version with four lower-powered engines. These, coupled with the excellent Manchester airframe, promised to result in a good heavy bomber. The engine selected for the new model, which was to be known as the Manchester III, was the well-tried and reliable Rolls-Royce Merlin. The prototype of the new aircraft, fitted with a tall central fin and small fin and rudder units at the ends of the tailplane (inherited from the Manchester I), first flew in January 1941, and soon revealed an excellent performance. The original type of vertical tail surfaces was soon replaced by the larger endplate surfaces on a wider-span tailplane from the Manchester IA. The central fin was deleted. Exhaustive trials were conducted with the first two prototypes, and the type, now renamed Lancaster, was ordered into production.

The first production Lancaster I bombers, which differed from the prototypes in having dorsal and ventral machine-gun turrets and 1,280-hp Merlin XX engines in place of the earlier 1,145-hp Merlin X units, flew in October 1941, and squadrons began to receive their new aircraft early in 1942. The first combat operation was flown in March of that year, and from that time onwards the Lancaster quickly became the mainstay of RAF Bomber Command. A total of 3,425 Lancaster Is was built.

Early in the production life of the Lancaster there were fears that supplies of the Merlin would be insufficient to meet all the demands for the engine, hence the Lancaster B II. This differed from the initial version in being powered by four 1,650-hp Bristol Hercules VI radial engines. Performance with the Hercules engines differed little from that of the Merlin-engined B I, but as in the end there was no shortage of the latter engines, production of the B II amounted to only 301 machines.

From August 1943 there appeared the Lancaster B X. This was a version of the B I built by Victory Aircraft of Canada, and powered by Packard-built Merlin 28, 38 or 224 engines. A total of 430 of this mark was built. In Great Britain, meanwhile, production of the B I continued, later aircraft having 1,460-hp Merlin 20 and 22, or 1,640-hp Merlin 24 engines. The next British model of the Lancaster was the B III, which differed from the B I only in having Packard-built Merlin engines. Production of this model totalled 3,039 machines. To all intents and purposes the B III and B X were identical.

The B VI, which was built in very limited numbers in the summer of 1944 was the next model. This featured Merlin 87 engines with four-bladed propellers in place of the earlier marks' three-bladed units. The nose and dorsal turrents were also removed, the gaps thus left being faired over, and special equipment to jam German radar was installed. The last mark was the B VII with a new dorsal Martin turret fitted further forward up the fuselage than the earlier

Nash and Thompson turret; 180 were built. The last Lancaster was delivered to the RAF in February 1946, completing a grand total of 7,377 machines.

Two notable sub-marks of the B I were produced: the B I (Special) and the B I (FE). The first was designed to carry special loads such as the 'dam-buster' bomb, the 12,000-lb (5,443-kg) 'Tallboy' deep penetration bomb, and the 22,000-lb (9,979-kg) 'Grand Slam' earthquake bomb (the largest bomb used in the war); the second had the dorsal turret removed and a large saddle tank, extending from just behind the wing trailing edge to the cockpit, added to the top of the fuselage. This held 1,200 gallons (5,455 l) of fuel to allow the Lancaster to bomb Japan over long ranges; however, the B I (FE) was too late to see service in the war. (FE stood for Far East.) Final development of the Lancaster from the so-called B IV and B V led to the RAF's last piston-engined heavy bomber, the Avro Lincoln.

During the course of the war the Lancaster was fitted with a variety of radar aids to help bombing in cloud and fog conditions, and the record of the aircraft speaks for itself: more than 150,000 missions during which over 600,000 tons of bombs were dropped. Losses were also comparatively light: in 1943 one aircraft for each 132 tons of bombs dropped, compared with 56 tons for each Handley Page Halifax and 41 tons for each Short Stirling.

Growth potential had been built into the basic design; bombs of the 4,000-lb (1,814-kg) type were catered for in the first model but ever increased bomb-loads could be carried internally and only the 'Tallboy', 'Grand Slam' and 'dam-buster' bombs had to be carried externally. The aircraft itself was manoeuvrable for its size, and the one major fault which it shared with other British bombers was its lack of heavy-calibre defensive armament, especially after the ventral turret had been abandoned.

Below: Avro Lancaster heavy bombers at their dispersal points on a Bomber Command airfield

Avro Lancaster B I

The aircraft illustrated is machine G of No 15
Squadron (code-letters LS), serial number LM110,
which was flown by Flight-Lieutenant M Johnston,
Royal Australian Air Force. The aircraft was lost
on 13 September 1944 after it had flown 244 hours.
Camouflage is standard, with matt black under-
surfaces, extending three-quarters of the way up the
fuselage, and dark green and dark earth upper
surfaces.

Type seven-seat heavy bomber

Engines four Rolls-Royce Merlin 22 twelve-
cylinder liquid-cooled inlines, each rated at
1,460 hp at take-off

Armament defensive: two flexible 0.303-inch
(7.7-mm) Browning machine-guns in the nose
turret, two flexible 0.303-inch Browning machine-
guns in the dorsal turret, and four flexible
0.303-inch Browning machine-guns in the rear
turret (some aircraft also had one or two flexible
0.303-inch Browning machine-guns in a ventral
turret)

offensive: up to 18,000 lbs (8,165 kg) of bombs
(22,000 lbs (9,979 kg) on BI Specials)

Maximum speeds 275 mph at 15,000 feet (443 km/h
at 4,572 m) at maximum take-off weight; 245 mph
(394 km/h) at sea level at maximum take-off
weight; 287 mph (462 km/h) maximum

Cruising speed 200 mph at 15,000 feet (322 km/h
at 4,572 m)

Initial climb rate 250 fpm (76 m/minute)

Climb 41 minutes 36 seconds to 20,000 feet
(6,096 m)

Service ceiling 22,000 feet (6,706 m)

Range 2,530 miles (4,072 km) with 7,000-lb
(3,175 kg) bomb-load; 1,730 miles (2,784 km) with
12,000-lb (5,443 kg) bomb-load

Weights 36,900 lbs (16,738 kg) empty; 68,000 lbs
(30,845 kg) loaded; 72,000 lbs (32,659 kg) gross

Span 102 feet (31.09 m)

Length 69 feet 6 inches (21.18 m)

Height 20 feet 6 inches (6.25 m)

Wing area 1,297 square feet (120.45 m²)

Bristol Beaufighter

At a first glance the Bristol Beaufighter appears to be an ungainly and unattractive aircraft. Closer examination, however, reveals this great aircraft's better points: large wings for heavy load carrying, massive engines for high speed and performance, a sturdy fuselage to contain equipment and absorb battle damage, and a cockpit right at the front of the fuselage to afford the pilot an excellent field of vision forwards. In fact, despite its superficial ugliness, the Beaufighter looked right, and following the old airmen's adage that what looks right is right, it was a superlative aircraft.

The Beaufighter was designed in 1938 as a private-venture fighter aircraft, using as much of the unsuccessful Bristol Beaufort torpedo-bomber as possible including the wings, rear fuselage, empennage and many of the components. A new front fuselage and more powerful engines were fitted. Just before the first prototype flew in July 1939 the Air Ministry expressed an interest in the new type by ordering 300 'off the drawing board'. Initial flight trials were very successful, few modifications were found to be necessary and aircraft began to roll off the production lines in July 1940, reaching RAF squadrons in September.

These first aircraft were to the Mark IF standard, with four 20-mm cannon and six 0.303-inch (7.7-mm) machine-guns, which became the ordinary forward-firing armament for Beaufighter fighters. The new type's performance was good, with a top speed of 323 mph (520 km/h), and the new Air Interception Mark IV radar was fitted, the marriage of the two producing the world's first really effective night-fighter – the Blenheim had been an interim model without the performance to make it properly effective in this role. The AI Mark IV radar was distinguishable by its aerials: a double arrow-head on the nose and vertical aerials on the outer wing panels.

In the spring of 1941 the Beaufighter entered service with units in North Africa as a long-range day fighter. To provide the necessary range, extra fuel tanks were located in the fuselage; these were later moved to the outer wing bays, which necessitated the removal of the six Browning machine-guns previously located there. At about the same time, March 1941, a new model entered service with RAF Coastal Command as a long-range fighter. This was the Beaufighter IC, which featured extra radio and navigation equipment for long flights over water.

Fears that production of the Bristol Hercules radial engine would not be able to keep pace with Beaufighter deliveries led to the next model, the Beaufighter IIF. This had two 1,280-hp Rolls-Royce Merlin XX inlines in place of the Mark I's 1,425-hp Hercules III radials. The Merlin engines produced less drag, and performance was thereby improved slightly, but the loss of forward keel area made the Beaufighter's directional stability less than adequate. The answer, found after a series of exhaustive experiments, was to give the tailplane pronounced dihedral, and the modification was incorporated on this and subsequent models. Only 450 Beaufighter IIFs were built as production of the Hercules

radial engine proved sufficient to meet all aircraft production demands.

Among experiments carried out on the Beaufighter were the testing of a new centimetric radar with its aerial in a 'thimble' nose, an armament of two 40-mm cannon, and special air brakes. None of these reached production status early in the Beaufighter's development life and only the radar was widely used. In an effort to improve the type's firepower for night-fighting the Mark V was developed with a four-gun turret in a dorsal position over the wing. But the modification was not successful, and only two Beaufighter V aircraft were built. The next type to attain widespread service use was the Mark VI, built as the VIF and VIC for Fighter Command and Coastal Command respectively. Power for the Mark VI was provided by a pair of 1,650-hp Hercules VI or XVI radials. For the first time rearward defence was provided in the form of a single 0.303-inch (7.7-mm) Vickers K machine-gun in the observer's cockpit. The Mark VIC was also given vastly enhanced offensive power by the provision of gear enabling it to carry either rockets or a torpedo. The Mark VI entered service in summer 1942; in all 1,833 were built.

The Beaufighter III (to be powered by Hercules VI radials) and Beaufighter IV (to be powered by Rolls-Royce Griffon inlines) had not been built, and neither had the Beaufighter VII (to be powered by Hercules VIII radials) and Beaufighters VIII and IX (reserved for aircraft built in Australia). The Mark XIC, of which 163 were built, was an interim version of the VIC without torpedo-dropping gear.

The next major version was the Torpedo-Fighter X or TF X; 2,206 examples were built. The TF X appeared in 1943, and used two Hercules XVIII radials with cropped impeller blades for the low-altitude superchargers. The

TF X was the best anti-shipping strike fighter of the war, able to deliver a formidable quantity of rockets, bombs, torpedoes and cannon fire over very long ranges and at high speed. The chief external distinguishing marks of the TF X were the thimble nose, housing the centrimetric air-surface vessel search radar, and the dorsal fillet, extending the fin up the fuselage to improve directional stability. A total of 364 Beaufighters similar to the TF X was built in Australia as the Beaufighter 21. Production of the Beaufighter ceased in Great Britain in September 1945 after 5,562 machines had been built.

Although it had been the world's first truly effective night-fighter until supplanted by the de Havilland Mosquito, the Beaufighter found it real *métier* as a long-range strike fighter. In this role it was unsurpassed, and performed invaluable service in every theatre in which the RAF was involved.

Below: A Bristol Beaufighter TF X, aircraft T of 236 Squadron, RAF Coastal Command, in the air. Note the forward pair of shackles for the carriage of a torpedo under the pilot's cockpit, eight rockets carried on launchers under the outer wing panels (necessitating the deletion of the six 0.303-inch machine-guns normally carried in the wings), provision of defensive armament for the second crew member, and a pronounced dihedral angle on the tailplane. Later aircraft had a dorsal fillet extending the fin up the rear fuselage to increase directional stability. The excellent position of the pilot, right in the nose of the great fuselage where he enjoyed an unparalleled field of vision, is also apparent. Also noteworthy are the prominent 'invasion stripes' of all aircraft of the Allied Expeditionary Air Forces in the second half of 1944. The upper surface parts of these were often painted over

Bristol Beaufighter TF X

The aircraft illustrated is machine M of 404 Squadron (code-letters EE). Camouflage is a variation on the standard Temperate Sea Scheme, with Dark Slate Grey (appearing almost as green) and Medium Sea Grey (instead of the specified Extra Dark Sea Grey). The under surfaces are in Sky Grey. National markings are the usual ones. Note the black and white 'invasion' stripes, applied to all combat aircraft of the Allied Expeditionary Forces in June 1944

Type two-seat anti-shipping strike fighter

Engines two Bristol Hercules XVII fourteen-cylinder air-cooled radials, each rated at 1,770 hp at take-off

Armament four 20-mm Hispano cannon with 283 rounds per gun in the lower nose, plus one 1,650- or 2,127-lb (748- or 965-kg) torpedo, or eight 90-lb (41-kg) rockets and two 250-lb (113-kg) bombs

Maximum speed 303 mph at 1,300 feet (488 km/h at 396 m)

Cruising speed 249 mph at 5,000 feet (401 km/h at 1,524 m)

Climb 3 minutes 30 seconds to 5,000 feet (1,524 m)

Service ceiling 15,000 feet (4,572 m)

Range 1,470 miles at 205 mph at 5,000 feet (2,366 km at 330 km/h at 1,524 m)

Weights 15,600 lbs (7,076 kg) empty; unknown loaded; 25,200 lbs (11,431 kg) gross

Span 57 feet 10 inches (17.63 m)

Length 41 feet 8 inches (12.70 m)

Height 15 feet 10 inches (4.83 m)

Wing area 503 square feet (46.73 m²)

de Havilland Mosquito

Its versatility and basically wooden construction would be enough to ensure the immortality of the de Havilland Mosquito. And it deserves to be remembered, too, as an absolutely delightful aircraft – beautiful to look at and superb to fly. Although the Mosquito was originally designed as an unarmed high-speed bomber, relying on its pace to evade enemy fighters, the roles in which the aircraft eventually operated included those of bomber, fighter, fighter-bomber, night fighter, photographic-reconnaissance aircraft, minelayer, strike fighter, pathfinder, transport and trainer.

The de Havilland concern began design work on the aircraft that was to emerge as the Mosquito in October 1938 as a private venture high-speed bomber with two Rolls-Royce Merlin inline engines. Wooden construction was chosen as it was light and strong, because de Havilland had experience with it, and also because work of this type could be sub-contracted to other firms without disrupting an aircraft industry already fully extended. The Air Ministry began to display an interest in the de Havilland design in December 1939, and in the following March an order for 50 Mosquitoes was placed.

The exigencies of the Battle of Britain period of 1940 meant that Mosquito prototype construction enjoyed only a low priority; however, the first prototype flew in November 1940. It was a very clean, attractive aeroplane, and quickly showed itself to be possessed of exceptional performance and handling characteristics. Service trials were swiftly instituted, and so successful were these that the type was put into production – the order for 50 already mentioned being subdivided into 10 PR Mark 1, 10 B Mark IV and 30 NF Mark II aircraft. As the majority of Mosquitoes fall into one of these three categories (photographic-reconnaissance, bomber, and fighter), it is convenient to discuss the Mosquito according to type rather than in a strictly chronological order of marks.

The first Mosquitoes to enter service, in September 1941, were examples of the photographic-reconnaissance PR I mark. These aircraft were unarmed, but in deep-penetration missions over German-occupied Europe quickly showed themselves able to outpace even the latest German fighters. To improve the Mosquito's high-altitude performance the PR VIII was developed, powered by Merlin 61 engines with two-stage superchargers; but only five were built. In May 1943 the PR IX appeared, developed from the B IX high-altitude bomber mark and 90 examples were delivered. Late in 1943 the first pressurized version of the Mosquito for PR work appeared, the PR XVI; some 432 were produced making it the most numerous PR mark of the Mosquito. The last wartime version, the PR 34, was intended for very long-range missions with two drop-tanks under the wings and further fuel tanks in the bulged belly.

The second type of Mosquito to enter service was a bomber variant, the B IV, in November 1941. This carried 2,000 lbs (907 kg) of bombs, and was powered by a pair of 1,250-hp Merlin XXI engines. B IV aircraft were built in two series, the Series 2 differing from the Series 1 in having engine nacelles that extended aft of the trailing edge. Like the early PR aircraft, the unarmed B IV proved to be too fast for German fighters to catch, and its losses were therefore very light. Mosquitoes soon acquired an enviable reputation for their ability to deliver their bomb-loads with pinpoint accuracy over long ranges. In mid 1943 the B IX was introduced, with increased bomb capacity and an 'Oboe' radar aid for 'pathfinding'. The last major wartime variant, the B XVI, had a pressurized cockpit, enabling it to operate at altitudes of up to 40,000 feet (12,192 m) and a top speed of 415 mph (668 km/h), compared with the B IV's 380 mph (612 km/h). Some 1,200 of this mark were built, mostly for use in independent solo raids to disrupt German nights.

So spectacular was the performance of the Mosquito that very early in its career thought was given to producing a fighter version of the basic aircraft. The designers had catered for this, leaving the fuselage nose empty to enable cannon and machine-gun armament to be located there. The first fighter Mosquito, the NF II, entered service in January 1942. It had an armament of four 20-mm cannon and four 0.303-inch (7.7-mm) machine-guns in the nose, and was fitted with AI Mark IV (later Mark V) radar. The type proved an immediate success over northern Europe and in the Mediterranean theatre. The 97 NF XII fighters which followed were all conversions from NF II standard, with centimetric AI Mark VIII radar but no machine-gun armament – a feature of all night-fighter Mosquitoes with radar. The NF XII was succeeded by 270 NF XIIIs with underwing drop-tanks. The next model was the NF XVII – a redesignation of the 100 NF II aircraft re-equipped with the American AI Mark X radar. Similar radar was fitted to the NF XIII, but in this case 220 new aircraft were built as the NF XIX. The last wartime variant of the night-fighting Mosquito was the NF 30. This was essentially similar to the NF XIX except for the power units.

The success of the first armed Mosquito, the NF II, led to the development of a fighter-bomber variant, the FB VI, early in 1943. This entered service in May 1943, and became the most numerous of all Mosquito marks. Series 1 aircraft, of which 300 were built, were powered by 1,460-hp Merlin 21 or 23 engines, and carried a bomb-load of four 250-lb (113-kg) bombs in addition to a fixed armament of four 20-mm cannon and four 0.303-inch (7.7-mm) machine-guns. Series 2 aircraft, of which some 2,200 were built, had 1,635-hp Merlin 25 engines, and carried 500-lb (227-kg) bombs.

A total of 7,781 of this magnificent British aircraft was built before production ceased in November 1950.

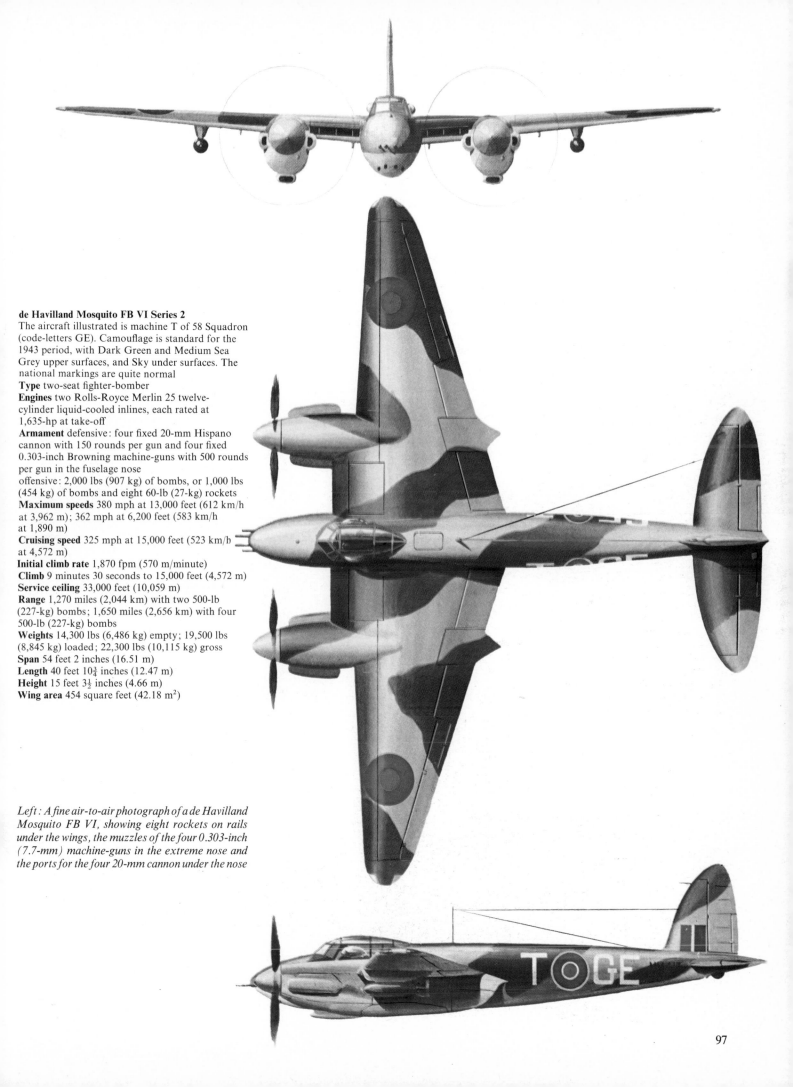

de Havilland Mosquito FB VI Series 2
The aircraft illustrated is machine T of 58 Squadron (code-letters GE). Camouflage is standard for the 1943 period, with Dark Green and Medium Sea Grey upper surfaces, and Sky under surfaces. The national markings are quite normal

Type two-seat fighter-bomber
Engines two Rolls-Royce Merlin 25 twelve-cylinder liquid-cooled inlines, each rated at 1,635-hp at take-off
Armament defensive: four fixed 20-mm Hispano cannon with 150 rounds per gun and four fixed 0.303-inch Browning machine-guns with 500 rounds per gun in the fuselage nose
offensive: 2,000 lbs (907 kg) of bombs, or 1,000 lbs (454 kg) of bombs and eight 60-lb (27-kg) rockets
Maximum speeds 380 mph at 13,000 feet (612 km/h at 3,962 m); 362 mph at 6,200 feet (583 km/h at 1,890 m)
Cruising speed 325 mph at 15,000 feet (523 km/h at 4,572 m)
Initial climb rate 1,870 fpm (570 m/minute)
Climb 9 minutes 30 seconds to 15,000 feet (4,572 m)
Service ceiling 33,000 feet (10,059 m)
Range 1,270 miles (2,044 km) with two 500-lb (227-kg) bombs; 1,650 miles (2,656 km) with four 500-lb (227-kg) bombs
Weights 14,300 lbs (6,486 kg) empty; 19,500 lbs (8,845 kg) loaded; 22,300 lbs (10,115 kg) gross
Span 54 feet 2 inches (16.51 m)
Length 40 feet $10\frac{3}{4}$ inches (12.47 m)
Height 15 feet $3\frac{1}{2}$ inches (4.66 m)
Wing area 454 square feet (42.18 m²)

Left: A fine air-to-air photograph of a de Havilland Mosquito FB VI, showing eight rockets on rails under the wings, the muzzles of the four 0.303-inch (7.7-mm) machine-guns in the extreme nose and the ports for the four 20-mm cannon under the nose

Fairey Swordfish

Although it was obsolescent by the beginning of World War II, the Fairey Swordfish remained in production until late in 1944; it performed both gallantly and usefully up to the end of hostilities in front-line service, and was in fact the last biplane combat aircraft to be used by the British armed forces. Nicknamed the 'Stringbag' by its crews, the Swordfish earned affection as an excellent torpedo-launching platform and as a remarkably sturdy and reliable aircraft which would get its crew home with damage that would have downed most other aircraft. The Swordfish was undeniably slow by World War II standards, but it was manoeuvrable for its size, very steady, and an ideal aircraft for operations from the small escort-carriers that came into service later in the war.

Derived from Fairey's Torpedo-Spotter-Reconnaissance I private-venture aircraft of 1933, the prototype Swordfish flew for the first time in April 1934. It was originally designated TSR II, and was developed to meet an Air Ministry request for a carrier-borne torpedo-bomber also capable of undertaking reconnaissance missions too. Trials with the new aircraft proved immediately successful with both wheel and float undercarriages, and it was ordered into production.

The Swordfish entered service with the Fleet Air Arm in July 1936, the main external difference between service and prototype aircraft being the three-bladed propeller of the former, in place of the two-bladed unit of the latter. By the beginning of World War II there were 13 squadrons equipped with the Swordfish, and during the war a further 13 were formed, the last in June 1943.

The Swordfish I, as the first production type was named, continued to be built up to 1943, when two improved marks appeared. The first of these, the Swordfish II, had metal skinning on the under surfaces of the lower wings, in place of the Mark I's cloth. This gave the lower wings enough strength to take eight 60-lb (27-kg) rockets, which proved very useful in anti-shipping strikes and attacks on U-boats. The 690-hp Pegasus IIIM 3 radial was retained on the first Mark IIs, but the improved 750-hp Pegasus 30 was installed on later aircraft of the Mark II series and all subsequent aircraft.

The second new mark to appear in 1943 was the Swordfish III. This featured the addition of Air-Surface Vessel Mark X radar, mounted in a large and clumsy radome under the fuselage between the undercarriage legs. This radar greatly improved the Swordfish's efficiency in the anti-shipping strike role. The last version of the Swordfish to appear was the Mark IV. This had an enclosed cockpit, and was intended for use in Canada. Total production of the Swordfish amounted to 2,392 aircraft, the last being delivered in August 1944.

In the war the Swordfish proved remarkably effective, its low speed and steadiness making it an excellent launching platform for torpedoes. Swordfish made the first torpedo strike of the war in April 1940, and continued to devastate German and Italian shipping with torpedoes and later rockets up to the end of hostilities.

Operating from escort-carriers in the mid-Atlantic, which land-based aircraft could not reach until the end of the war, the Swordfish proved an invaluable weapon in the final defeat of the U-boat menace in 1943. It was very effective against Axis surface vessels too: evidence for this need be sought no further than the crippling of the Italian battle fleet in Taranto in November 1940 and the damage inflicted on the German battleship *Bismarck* in May 1940, allowing elements of the British navy to close her and then sink her with gunfire and torpedoes. Perhaps the most courageous action fought by Swordfish aircraft was the vain attempt by six aircraft of 825 Squadron to disable the German battle-cruisers *Scharnhorst* and *Gneisenau*, and the heavy cruiser *Prinz Eugen* during their 'Channel dash' in February 1942. All six Swordfish torpedo-bombers were destroyed by AA gunfire and the massive German fighter screen. In conclusion, perhaps there can be no finer tribute to the qualities of the Swordfish than the fact that it outlived its supposed successor, the Fairey Albacore, as a front-line aircraft.

Above right: A Swordfish III, showing the large radome for the ASV X radar between the undercarriage legs
Below: This overhead photograph of a Swordfish reveals the type's angular flying surfaces, and the open nature of the triple cockpit. This last made long flights in poor weather very uncomfortable for the crew. The Swordfish IV, with an enclosed cockpit, was used in Canada

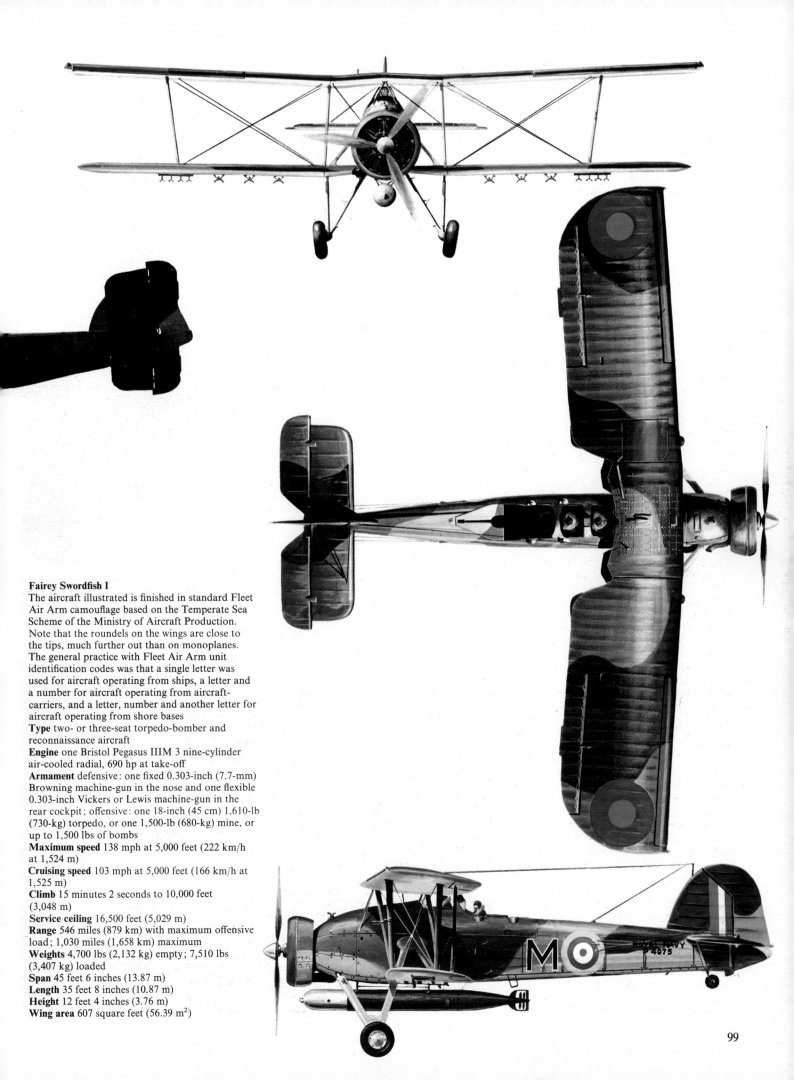

Fairey Swordfish I
The aircraft illustrated is finished in standard Fleet
Air Arm camouflage based on the Temperate Sea
Scheme of the Ministry of Aircraft Production.
Note that the roundels on the wings are close to
the tips, much further out than on monoplanes.
The general practice with Fleet Air Arm unit
identification codes was that a single letter was
used for aircraft operating from ships, a letter and
a number for aircraft operating from aircraft-
carriers, and a letter, number and another letter for
aircraft operating from shore bases
Type two- or three-seat torpedo-bomber and
reconnaissance aircraft
Engine one Bristol Pegasus IIIM 3 nine-cylinder
air-cooled radial, 690 hp at take-off
Armament defensive: one fixed 0.303-inch (7.7-mm)
Browning machine-gun in the nose and one flexible
0.303-inch Vickers or Lewis machine-gun in the
rear cockpit; offensive: one 18-inch (45 cm) 1,610-lb
(730-kg) torpedo, or one 1,500-lb (680-kg) mine, or
up to 1,500 lbs of bombs
Maximum speed 138 mph at 5,000 feet (222 km/h
at 1,524 m)
Cruising speed 103 mph at 5,000 feet (166 km/h at
1,525 m)
Climb 15 minutes 2 seconds to 10,000 feet
(3,048 m)
Service ceiling 16,500 feet (5,029 m)
Range 546 miles (879 km) with maximum offensive
load; 1,030 miles (1,658 km) maximum
Weights 4,700 lbs (2,132 kg) empty; 7,510 lbs
(3,407 kg) loaded
Span 45 feet 6 inches (13.87 m)
Length 35 feet 8 inches (10.87 m)
Height 12 feet 4 inches (3.76 m)
Wing area 607 square feet (56.39 m²)

Handley Page Halifax

Although it was not as successful a heavy bomber as the Avro Lancaster, the Handley Page Halifax nevertheless deserves more praise than it is usually given. The Halifax was the second of Great Britain's heavy bombers, becoming operational only a month after the unsuccessful Short Stirling, and was used for a variety of other tasks including transport, maritime reconnaissance and as a glider tug. It stayed in production after the end of the war.

The genesis of the Halifax was from the same 1936 requirement for a medium-heavy bomber powered by two Rolls-Royce Vulture engines that led to the ill-starred Avro Manchester. In 1937, however, the Air Ministry instructed Handley Page to redesign their contender to use four Rolls-Royce Merlins, as it was expected that Vulture production would not be able to match demand. Although Handley Page complied, the firm was unhappy about the decision. But the Air Ministry's directive was finally vindicated by the failure of the Vulture and the demise of the Manchester.

The prototype flew in October 1939, and the first production Halifax almost a year later. Service introduction followed in November, and the first operation mission was flown in March 1941. Naturally enough, these first production Halifaxes were built to Mark I standard, but in three groups, Series I, II and III. Top speed, with four 1,280-hp Merlin X engines, was 265 mph (426 km/h), and the three series differed from each other as follows: the Series I was stressed for take-off weights of 55,000 lbs (24,948 kg); the Series II for take-off weights of 60,000 lbs (27,216 kg); and the Series III had increased fuel tankage.

The lessons learned on operations were applied to the next Halifax model, the Mark II. This again was produced in three series. The Halifax II Series I (of which the prototype flew in July 1941 and the first production machine in September 1941) were powered by four 1,390-hp Merlin XX engines and had increased fuel tankage. A more radical departure from the Mark I standard, however, was the elimination of the two hand-held machine-guns in the waist position for beam defence, and their replacement by a Boulton Paul twin-gun turret in the dorsal position. Combat experience with this series led to the Series I (Special). The muffs which had previously been fitted to cut down exhaust flames were now removed as they reduced performance by an unacceptable margin; the little-used twin-gun nose turrent was removed, the gap thus left being faired over; and the dorsal turret was once again removed as its drag had affected performance adversely.

Further improvement was attained in the Halifax II Series IA. This series was powered by 1,460-hp Merlin 22 engines in improved cowlings; had a redesigned nose of perspex (mounting a single gun for forward defence), which lengthened the aircraft by 18 inches (45.7 cm) but produced far less drag than the old nose; and once again brought in a dorsal turret, this time a four-gun model which developed relatively little drag. These improvements raised the speed by 20 mph (32 km/h) compared with the

Mark I. Late production Series IA aircraft also introduced the rectangular vertical tail surfaces that became a hallmark of all later Halifaxes. The new surfaces eliminated the Halifax's tendency to yaw when the bomb-doors were open which reduced bombing accuracy. With these improvements the Halifax, now being built in large numbers, was one of the most useful types available to RAF Bomber Command. The efficiency of the Halifax was also improved by the introduction of the H2S radar blind-bombing and navigation device, which was pioneered in service by Halifax aircraft.

By the end of 1942 Halifax II Series IA aircraft were also serving with Coastal Command, under the designation Halifax GR II; all were armed with a 0.5-inch (12.7-mm) machine-gun in the nose, in place of Bomber Command aircraft's 0.303-inch (7.7-mm) weapons. The next Halifax model was the Mark V. This had a Dowty undercarriage in place of the earlier marks' Messier one – a change occasioned not by operational requirements but by a shortage of Messier units – but was otherwise identical with the Mark II. The Halifax V was built in two series, the Series I (Special) and Series IA, which corresponded to series of the same designation in the Mark II model. The type also served with Coastal Command as the Halifax GR V, with a 0.5-inch (12.7-mm) machine-gun in a ventral position when H2S was not carried.

The next model substituted a Bristol Hercules radial in place of the Rolls-Royce Merlin inline as the basic powerplant. The first example of the Mark III, which flew in July 1943, had four 1,615-hp Hercules XVI engines. The tailwheel was also made retractable for the first time, and

H2S or a ventral gun was made standard. On late production examples extended wingtips were introduced, raising the span to 104 feet 2 inches (31.76 m). This new wing was used on all subsequent Halifaxes. Despite all the early modifications and improvements the Halifax was now beginning to show its age as a combat aircraft, and it was increasingly relegated to attacks on less heavily defended targets from September 1943. The widespread introduction of the Halifax III, however, meant that the type was put back into full front-line service from February 1944. In October 1944 the Halifax VI appeared. This was intended for eventual operations against Japan, and was powered by 1,800-hp Hercules 100 engines. The last Halifax bomber model was the Mark VII, which was basically the same as the Mark VI except for its Hercules XVI engines.

It is worth noting that unlike the Lancaster the Halifax was also called upon to tow gliders (it was the only aircraft capable of towing the mighty General Aircraft Hamilcar glider), and to undertake the dropping of paratroopers and agents. Finally, amongst the other roles played by the Halifax, mention must be made of the vital job it did as a radio- and radar-countermeasures aircraft. In all, 6,176 Halifaxes were built.

Below: A Halifax II Series IA bomber with the rectangular vertical tail surfaces introduced in late production models
Bottom: A fine study of a Halifax II Series IA with the original vertical tail surfaces. Note the four-gun dorsal turret and the bulge for H2S radar under the fuselage

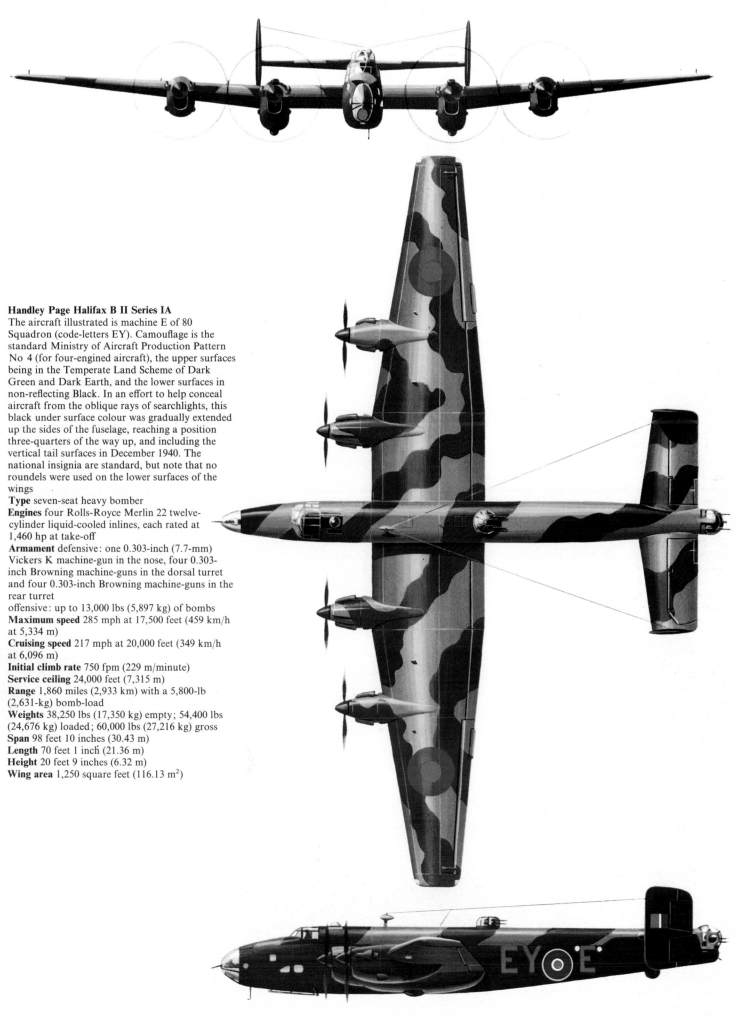

Handley Page Halifax B II Series IA
The aircraft illustrated is machine E of 80
Squadron (code-letters EY). Camouflage is the
standard Ministry of Aircraft Production Pattern
No 4 (for four-engined aircraft), the upper surfaces
being in the Temperate Land Scheme of Dark
Green and Dark Earth, and the lower surfaces in
non-reflecting Black. In an effort to help conceal
aircraft from the oblique rays of searchlights, this
black under surface colour was gradually extended
up the sides of the fuselage, reaching a position
three-quarters of the way up, and including the
vertical tail surfaces in December 1940. The
national insignia are standard, but note that no
roundels were used on the lower surfaces of the
wings
Type seven-seat heavy bomber
Engines four Rolls-Royce Merlin 22 twelve-
cylinder liquid-cooled inlines, each rated at
1,460 hp at take-off
Armament defensive: one 0.303-inch (7.7-mm)
Vickers K machine-gun in the nose, four 0.303-
inch Browning machine-guns in the dorsal turret
and four 0.303-inch Browning machine-guns in the
rear turret
offensive: up to 13,000 lbs (5,897 kg) of bombs
Maximum speed 285 mph at 17,500 feet (459 km/h
at 5,334 m)
Cruising speed 217 mph at 20,000 feet (349 km/h
at 6,096 m)
Initial climb rate 750 fpm (229 m/minute)
Service ceiling 24,000 feet (7,315 m)
Range 1,860 miles (2,933 km) with a 5,800-lb
(2,631-kg) bomb-load
Weights 38,250 lbs (17,350 kg) empty; 54,400 lbs
(24,676 kg) loaded; 60,000 lbs (27,216 kg) gross
Span 98 feet 10 inches (30.43 m)
Length 70 feet 1 inch (21.36 m)
Height 20 feet 9 inches (6.32 m)
Wing area 1,250 square feet (116.13 m²)

Hawker Hurricane

Although it is not as famous as the Supermarine Spitfire, the Hawker Hurricane should have as great, if not greater, claim to our remembrance: during the momentous days of the Battle of Britain, Hurricane fighters of RAF Fighter Command destroyed more enemy aircraft than all the other aircraft and ground defences involved. Apart from this, the Hurricane was the first eight-gun fighter to enter service with the RAF, and that force's first aircraft to be capable of a speed in excess of 300 mph (483 km/h) in level flight. The Hurricane was, moreover, an extremely sturdy machine, with viceless handling characteristics and excellent manoeuvrability at medium altitudes.

The origins of the Hurricane can be traced back to Sydney Camm's project for a 'Fury Monoplane', powered by a Rolls-Royce Goshawk engine, in October 1933. This project was shelved at the beginning of 1934 in favour of a revised version powered by a Rolls-Royce PV 12 (later the Merlin), renamed 'Interceptor Monoplane'. The Air Ministry soon became interested in the new type, and a prototype was ordered to two 1934 specifications early in 1935.

This flew for the first time in November 1935, and immediately displayed excellent performance and handling characteristics. An order for 600 of the new fighter was placed in June 1936 and raised to 1,000 in November 1938. The Hurricane was originally to be armed with four machine-guns, but this was altered to eight guns in July 1935. Experiments and assessments by the armaments branch of the Air Ministry had shown that the concentrated firepower of such an armament would be required to destroy the latest aircraft which, with their high speed, would only be in the fighter's gun-sights for a very short time.

Deliveries of production Hurricane I fighters started in October 1937, entering squadron service in December of the same year. These first machines had Merlin II engines, improved cockpit and exhausts, and modified undercarriage leg fairings. A small strake was subsequently fitted to the underneath of the rear fuselage to aid recovery from spins. As with the later Spitfire, the original fixed-pitch two-bladed wooden propeller was replaced first with a two-pitch three-bladed metal propeller and finally with a constant-speed three-bladed unit as they became available. The later propellers greatly aided the aircraft's rate of climb.

In comparison with other monoplane fighters of the World War II period, which were all-metal with a stressed-skin covering, the structure of the Hurricane was somewhat antiquated. A basic metal tube construction covered with fabric was used as the makers were very experienced in it, and thus the Hurricane could be brought into service more quickly and in greater numbers than would have otherwise been possible up to the early stages of the war. It is interesting to note that by the outbreak of war 497 Hurricanes had been delivered, compared with 310 Spitfires. By August 1940 deliveries were 2,309 and 1,400 respectively. The fabric-covered fuselage stayed with the Hurricane all its life, but later production examples had metal-skinned wings, which allowed a heavier armament to be carried, and higher diving speeds to be attained.

Much valuable combat experience was gained with the Hurricane during the 'Phoney War' period, and the type was the mainstay of the RAF fighter units in France after the invasion by Germany in May 1940, while the Spitfire was kept in Great Britain for metropolitan defence. During the Battle of Britain, the primary role of the Hurricane squadrons was the destruction of German bombers, while the Spitfires engaged the German fighters; the Hurricane was extremely successful, inflicting very heavy losses at a rate favourable to themselves.

Meanwhile the next model of the Hurricane, the Mark II, was under development. This had the 1,280-hp Merlin XX engine in place of the Mark I's 1,030-hp Merlin II or III, and also had a two-stage supercharger, giving a better performance at all altitudes. The armament, too, was revised. The first production Hurricane IIs, delivered in September 1940, retained the eight-gun armament of the Mark I, and were designated Hurricane IIA. But from April 1941 there appeared the Hurricane IIB, which had 12 0.303-inch (7.7-mm) machine-guns in the wings. In June 1941 there followed the Hurricane IIC, armed with four 20-mm cannon in place of the machine-guns. Other modifications of the period included provision of tropical equipment for use in the Middle Eastern and Mediterranean theatres, drop-tanks, and the ability to carry 250- or 500-lb (113- or 227-kg) bombs under the wings. Armed with bombs, the Hurricane became the 'Hurribomber', and as such soon proved itself an admirable fighter-bomber. It first went into service in Malta in September 1941, in Great Britain in October, and in North Africa in November. The Hurricane's armament was further improved in 1942, firstly by the addition of eight 60-lb (27-kg) rockets on underwing rails, and then by the fitting of 40-mm cannon. Rocket-armed Hurricanes entered service in the autumn of 1943, being preceded by the 'tank-busting' Hurricane IID. This mark was armed with a pair of 40-mm cannon, and entered service in North Africa during June 1942.

No Hurricane IIIs, intended to use Packard-built Merlins, were built, and thus the next model was the Mark IV. This had a Universal wing, which could carry 40-mm cannon, bombs, drop-tanks or rockets. It was at first designated Hurricane IIE. The final version of the Hurricane was the Mark V, of which only two were built. The Hurricane was also used at sea, the first being 'Hooked Hurricanes', converted from Mark II standard to carry an arrester hook. Full navalization led to the Sea Hurricane II, and later the Sea Hurricane XIIA, a carrier version of the Canadian Hurricane XIIA. Some 1,451 Hurricanes were built by the Canadian Car and Foundry Company, to a basic Mark II standard, as the Hurricanes X, XI, XII, and XIIA. British production of the Hurricane ended in September 1944, after a grand total of 14,223 had been built.

Below: An example of the Hurricane IV's predecessor, the Hurricane IIE (the designation was changed after 270 had been built). The IIE was the first model to have Universal wings, capable of taking 40-mm cannon, bombs, drop-tanks or rockets

Hawker Hurricane I
The aircraft illustrated is machine H of 32
Squadron (code-letters GZ), flown by Squadron-
Leader J Worrall, DFC, from Biggin Hill during
the opening stages of the Battle of Britain in July
1940. Standard upper surface camouflage of Dark
Green and Dark Earth (Temperate Land Scheme),
in Ministry of Aircraft Production Pattern No 1
for single-engined monoplanes, is carried. The
under surfaces are finished in a washed-out Sky
Blue. National insignia are the normal ones. Note
the red fabric patches doped over the gun ports
in the wing leading edge. These were applied
before take-off to reduce drag and thus improve
the climb to combat altitudes, and were shot
through on entering combat
Type single-seat fighter
Engine one Rolls-Royce Merlin III twelve-cylinder
liquid-cooled inline, 1,029 hp at 16,250 feet
(4,953 m)
Armament eight 0.303-inch (7.7-mm) Browning
machine-guns with 334 rounds per gun
Maximum speeds 328 mph at 20,000 feet (528 km/h
at 6,096 m); 280 mph (451 km/h) at sea level
Cruising speed unknown
Initial climb rate 2,300 fpm (701 m/minute)
Climb 8 minutes 30 seconds to 20,000 feet (6,096 m)
Service ceiling 34,200 feet (10,424 m)
Range 425 miles (684 km) on internal fuel; 900
miles (1,448 km) with drop-tanks
Weights 4,670 lbs (2,118 kg) empty; 6,600 lbs
(2,994 kg) loaded
Span 40 feet (12.19 m)
Length 31 feet 4 inches (9.55 m)
Height 13 feet 1½ inches (4.00 m)
Wing area 258 square feet (23.97 m²)

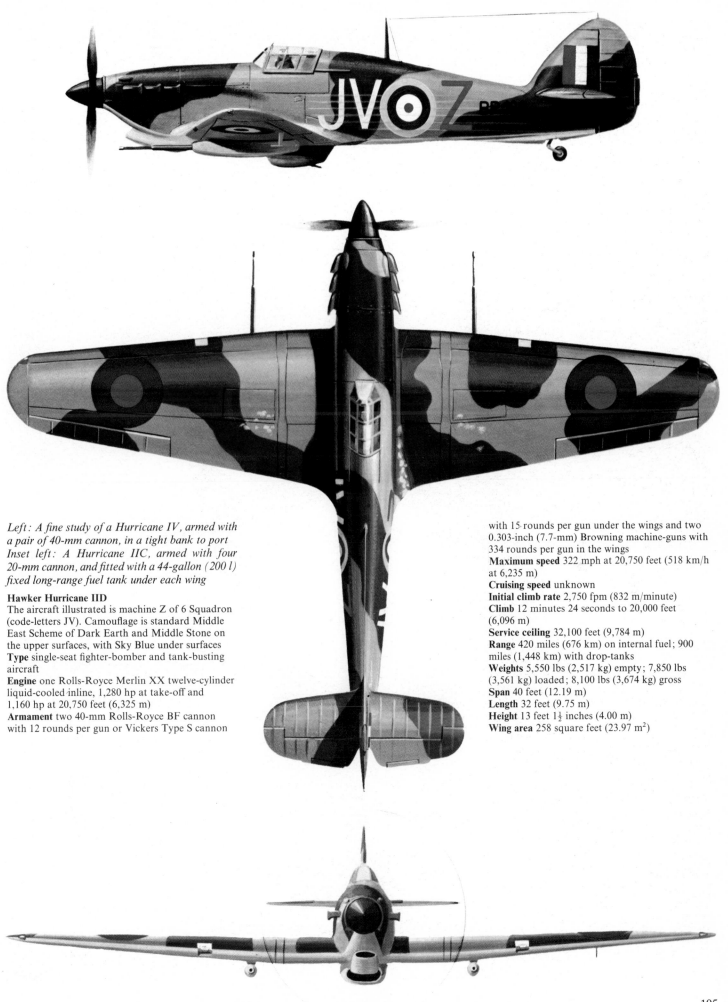

*Left: A fine study of a Hurricane IV, armed with
a pair of 40-mm cannon, in a tight bank to port
Inset left: A Hurricane IIC, armed with four
20-mm cannon, and fitted with a 44-gallon (200 l)
fixed long-range fuel tank under each wing*

Hawker Hurricane IID
The aircraft illustrated is machine Z of 6 Squadron
(code-letters JV). Camouflage is standard Middle
East Scheme of Dark Earth and Middle Stone on
the upper surfaces, with Sky Blue under surfaces
Type single-seat fighter-bomber and tank-busting
aircraft
Engine one Rolls-Royce Merlin XX twelve-cylinder
liquid-cooled inline, 1,280 hp at take-off and
1,160 hp at 20,750 feet (6,325 m)
Armament two 40-mm Rolls-Royce BF cannon
with 12 rounds per gun or Vickers Type S cannon
with 15 rounds per gun under the wings and two
0.303-inch (7.7-mm) Browning machine-guns with
334 rounds per gun in the wings
Maximum speed 322 mph at 20,750 feet (518 km/h
at 6,235 m)
Cruising speed unknown
Initial climb rate 2,750 fpm (832 m/minute)
Climb 12 minutes 24 seconds to 20,000 feet
(6,096 m)
Service ceiling 32,100 feet (9,784 m)
Range 420 miles (676 km) on internal fuel; 900
miles (1,448 km) with drop-tanks
Weights 5,550 lbs (2,517 kg) empty; 7,850 lbs
(3,561 kg) loaded; 8,100 lbs (3,674 kg) gross
Span 40 feet (12.19 m)
Length 32 feet (9.75 m)
Height 13 feet 1½ inches (4.00 m)
Wing area 258 square feet (23.97 m²)

Hawker Tempest

The Hawker Tempest was the result of an attempt to improve on the failings that manifested themselves early in the development career of the Typhoon. These failings in performance, especially at altitude, were largely attributable to the problems of compressibility, exaggerated by the thick, bluff wing-section of the aircraft. Hawker therefore proposed a Typhoon II, which would have an elliptical wing of laminar-flow section. This would delay the onset of compressibility problems and, coupled with the use of the latest Napier Sabre engine driving a four-bladed propeller, would guarantee a much higher performance at the altitudes at which interceptor fighters worked.

The idea was submitted to the Air Ministry in August 1941. It was approved and even expanded upon, but meanwhile the third Tornado, which had been modified to use a Bristol Centaurus radial engine, had been tested, with very encouraging results. With the cancellation of the Tornado programme, development of the Centaurus-powered derivative continued under the designation Typhoon II with a revised fuselage. The Air Ministry wished to explore the possibility of several powerplants for the elliptical wing Typhoon II, and to avoid confusion a new name was selected. This was Tempest, and the following prototypes were ordered: Tempest I with a Napier Sabre IV engine, Tempest II with a Bristol Centaurus engine, Tempest III and IV with Rolls-Royce Griffon engines, and Tempest V with a Napier Sabre II engine. Hawker elected to concentrate on the Tempest I, II and V, for which prototypes flew in February 1943, June 1943, and September

1942 respectively. The Tempest V preceded the others into the air as its engine was more readily available. The new thin-section laminar-flow wing of the Tempest could not accommodate the fuel tanks which had been placed there in the Typhoon, so extra fuel tankage had to be provided in a lengthened fuselage. A larger fin, provided by extending the Typhoon-type fin with a dorsal fillet, was required to compensate for the extra keel area.

The Tempest I, which had its radiators placed in the wings instead of the large chin radiator of the Typhoon and Tempest V, had an excellent performance and was ordered into large-scale production. Delays with the Sabre IV engines, however, led to the transference of Tempest I orders to the Tempest V. The first production Tempest V flew in June 1943, and the type entered squadron service in April 1944, proving to be an excellent low- and medium-altitude interceptor and fighter-bomber. As with the Typhoon, however, problems with the Sabre II had first to be eliminated.

Some 805 Tempest V fighters were built, the first 100 as Series 1 and the rest as Series 2 aircraft. Series 1 machines had a non-detachable rear fuselage and cannon that projected slightly in front of the wings, whereas Series 2 machines had a detachable rear fuselage, cannon that did not project ahead of the wing leading edge, smaller wheels, and spring tabs on the rudder and one aileron to increase manoeuvrability. Engine horsepower available eventually reached 2,260 with the Sabre IIC. Production ceased in August 1945. The Tempest VI was a development of the Mark V, with a 2,340-hp Sabre V engine and the

air intakes moved from the radiator to the wings. This was intended for tropical operations, and 142 were delivered between July 1945 and June 1947. None saw service during World War II.

The other major version of the Tempest to see service was the radial-engined Mark II. This was derived from the Bristol Centaurus-powered Tornado prototype, and eventually became the most powerful single piston-engined fighter to serve with the RAF. The engine used was the 2,520-hp Centaurus V or VI. A combination of vibration problems associated with the Centaurus installation and the production priority enjoyed by the Tempest V delayed production deliveries until October 1944. The Tempest II was intended primarily for operations in the Far East, but the first squadron to re-equip with the type did not do so until November 1945, after the end of the war; with a speed of 440 mph (708 km/h) and a range of 1,700 miles (2,736 km), it would have proved extremely useful had hostilities against Japan continued into 1946. The final expression of the Typhoon/Tempest design philosophy was reached in the postwar Hawker Fury and Sea Fury fighters, which were essentially lightened versions of the Tempest II aircraft.

Below: Three Hawker Tempest V Series 2 fighter-bombers. Series 2 aircraft were distinguishable by the fitting of Hispano Mark V short-barrelled 20-mm cannon, whose muzzles did not protrude in front of the wing leading-edge. Note the thin wings compared with the Typhoon's much thicker-section surfaces

Hawker Tempest V Series 1
The aircraft illustrated is machine N of 486
Squadron, Royal New Zealand Air Force. The
remarks on camouflage for the Hawker Typhoon
are also applicable here. Note that the AEAF
stripes have been replaced by camouflage on the
fuselage and the upper surfaces of the wings
Type single-seat fighter and fighter-bomber
Engine one Napier Sabre IIA, B or C twenty four-
cylinder liquid-cooled inline, 2,180 hp, 2,200 hp or
2,260 hp at take-off
Armament defensive: four 20-mm Hispano Mark II
cannon with 200 rounds per gun
offensive: up to 2,000 lbs (907 kg) of bombs,
two mines, napalm tanks or eight 60-lb (27-kg)
rockets
Maximum speeds 436 mph at 15,000 feet (702 km/h
at 4,572 m); 392 mph (631 km/h) at sea level
Cruising speed 391 mph at 18,800 feet (629 km/h
at 5,730 m)
Initial climb rate 4,700 fpm (1,433 m/minute)
Climb 5 minutes to 15,000 feet (4,572 m)
Service ceiling 36,500 feet (11,125 m)
Range 740 miles (1,191 km) on internal fuel;
1,530 miles (2,462 km) with drop-tanks
Weights 9,000 lbs (4,082 kg) empty; 11,500 lbs
(5,216 kg) loaded; 13,640 lbs (6,187 kg) gross
Span 41 feet (12.50 m)
Length 33 feet 8 inches (10.26 m)
Height 16 feet 1 inch (4.90 m)
Wing area 302 square feet (28.06 m²)

Hawker Typhoon

The Typhoon, like the Hurricane, was designed by Sydney Camm, Hawker's chief designer. Intended as an interceptor fighter to replace the Hurricane, the Hawker Typhoon was not successful in this role, and found its real *métier* as a ground-attack aircraft. In this latter role it was arguably the best ground-attack fighter of World War II.

Design work on the Typhoon began in 1937, the intention being to produce a stressed-skin all-metal fighter, powered by the new Napier Sabre engine of 2,000 hp. The Air Ministry was also looking into the possibility of a Hurricane replacement to be powered by either the Sabre or the Rolls-Royce Vulture, which was also intended to develop more than 2,000 hp. Thus when Hawker approached the Air Ministry with their project, the ministry instructed the firm to build four prototypes, two to be powered by each of the new engines. The Vulture-engined type, which appeared as the Tornado, was bedevilled by engine problems, and the type was abandoned after three examples had been built.

The Sabre-engined type, which became the Typhoon, first flew in February 1940. Although it had been hoped to have the new fighter in service by the middle of that year, production aircraft began to be delivered only in May 1941, entering service in September of the same year. These first aircraft were Typhoon IA fighters, armed with 12 0.303-inch (7.7-mm) Browning machine-guns in the wings.

But although the Typhoon was a welcome addition to Fighter Command's inventory, as the RAF's first fighter capable of a speed greater than 400 mph (644 km/h), its initial service career was far from smooth. This was to a great

extent the result of the type's too swift entry into service, before all the teething problems with the engine and the airframe had been eliminated. The two chief problems were the unreliability of the Sabre engine, which was especially dangerous at take-off, and a structural weakness in the rear fuselage, which resulted in a disastrous tendency for the empennage to shake itself off. The engine problems were finally solved after further testing and the structural ones by the addition of a band of strengthening fishplates right round the fuselage, but not before the withdrawal of the Typhoon had been seriously mooted. Fighter Command was disappointed with the Typhoon's low rate of climb and lack of performance at high altitude, and only the type's outstanding capabilities at low altitudes saved it. At this time, the end of 1941 and the beginning of 1942, the Focke-Wulf 190 had entered service with the *Luftwaffe*, and was engaged in making low-level hit-and-run raids on targets in the south of England. Only the Typhoon was able to catch the intruders, the latest mark of Spitfire, the Mark V, being too slow.

The Typhoon IA was soon replaced on production lines by the Mark IB, which had four 20-mm cannon instead of machine-guns as its chief armament. The new model went into action for the first time in August 1942. At the end of the same year models equipped to carry two 250-lb (113-kg) bombs under the wings also began to reach squadrons. During 1943 this bomb-load was increased from 500 to 2,000 lbs (227 to 907 kg), and rockets were added to the type's armament. With these weapons, the Typhoon quickly added to its laurels as a fast and very hard-hitting low-level attack aircraft, devastating

German transport all over northern Europe. With the Allied invasion of Europe in June 1944, the Typhoon really came into its own. Enough aircraft were now in service to allow 'cab-rank' patrols to be mounted. These could be called in by the ground forces at a moment's notice to blast any and every German tank, emplacement, gun position or other impediment to progress encountered.

The first production Typhoons had featured a framed cockpit canopy and a sideways-opening door for entry into the cockpit, but this cumbersome arrangement was replaced on later production aircraft by a sliding 'bubble' canopy, which greatly increased the pilot's all-round vision. Other modifications were the replacement of the earlier aerial mast behind the cockpit with a whip aerial and the provision of a four-bladed instead of a three-bladed propeller. Production of the Typhoon ceased in November 1945 with the delivery of the 3,330th and last machine. The importance of the Typhoon in the campaign in north-west Europe during 1944 and 1945 was very considerable. Its thick wings enabled it to carry a heavy offensive load in addition to its cannon armament, and its powerful engine bestowed an excellent low-altitude performance. The Typhoon was the scourge not only of German front-line units, but also of their corps and army headquarters, which it could attack with pinpoint accuracy.

Below: RAF groundcrew at work on a Hawker Typhoon IB. Note the barrels of the four cannon and the launching rails for eight 60-lb (27-kg) rockets. The drum-shaped object in the foreground is the radiator for the huge, but at times unreliable, Napier Sabre inline engine

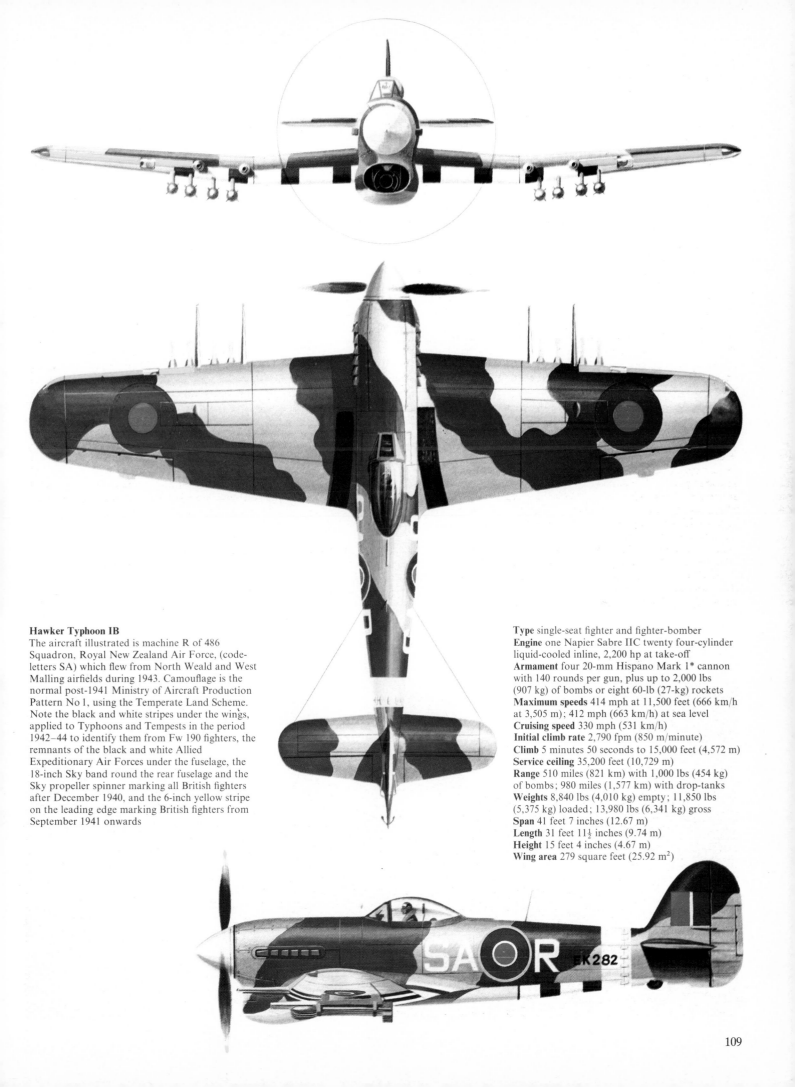

Hawker Typhoon IB

The aircraft illustrated is machine R of 486 Squadron, Royal New Zealand Air Force, (code-letters SA) which flew from North Weald and West Malling airfields during 1943. Camouflage is the normal post-1941 Ministry of Aircraft Production Pattern No 1, using the Temperate Land Scheme. Note the black and white stripes under the wings, applied to Typhoons and Tempests in the period 1942–44 to identify them from Fw 190 fighters, the remnants of the black and white Allied Expeditionary Air Forces under the fuselage, the 18-inch Sky band round the rear fuselage and the Sky propeller spinner marking all British fighters after December 1940, and the 6-inch yellow stripe on the leading edge marking British fighters from September 1941 onwards

Type single-seat fighter and fighter-bomber
Engine one Napier Sabre IIC twenty four-cylinder liquid-cooled inline, 2,200 hp at take-off
Armament four 20-mm Hispano Mark 1* cannon with 140 rounds per gun, plus up to 2,000 lbs (907 kg) of bombs or eight 60-lb (27-kg) rockets
Maximum speeds 414 mph at 11,500 feet (666 km/h at 3,505 m); 412 mph (663 km/h) at sea level
Cruising speed 330 mph (531 km/h)
Initial climb rate 2,790 fpm (850 m/minute)
Climb 5 minutes 50 seconds to 15,000 feet (4,572 m)
Service ceiling 35,200 feet (10,729 m)
Range 510 miles (821 km) with 1,000 lbs (454 kg) of bombs; 980 miles (1,577 km) with drop-tanks
Weights 8,840 lbs (4,010 kg) empty; 11,850 lbs (5,375 kg) loaded; 13,980 lbs (6,341 kg) gross
Span 41 feet 7 inches (12.67 m)
Length 31 feet 11½ inches (9.74 m)
Height 15 feet 4 inches (4.67 m)
Wing area 279 square feet (25.92 m²)

Short Sunderland

Although it was built in relatively limited numbers compared with other major RAF combat aircraft, the Short Sunderland holds an enviably high place in the annals of World War II air history. Its only contenders for the title of the best flying-boat of the war are the Japanese Kawanishi H8K 'Emily' and the American Consolidated PBY Catalina series. The Sunderland played a greater part than the Catalina in the defeat of Germany's U-boats in the Atlantic, and therefore played a more important role in the eventual Allied victory.

The Sunderland was a military derivation of the famous Short C class civilian flying-boats of the early 1930s, and was designed to a specification for a monoplane replacement for the Royal Air Force's elderly fleet of biplane maritime-reconnaissance flying-boats. The specification had been issued in 1933, and the first prototype flew in October 1937. Before this, however, the Air Ministry had placed orders for the new aircraft to a revised 1936 specification. The Sunderland entered service in the middle of 1938; by the outbreak of war three squadrons were flying the new machine and others followed as soon as production allowed.

The Sunderland I soon proved itself to be a useful anti-submarine aircraft and a formidable opponent in the air. With its two power-operated machine-gun turrets, the first to be fitted to a British flying-boat, a Sunderland often managed to shoot down or drive off several German fighters. The type's most vulnerable spot was the planing bottom of its hull, and to protect this the pilot normally flew as close to the water as possible when being attacked. Although its normal work was patrolling over the sealanes, the Sunderland was also called upon at times to serve as a rescue and transport aircraft. In the former capacity it picked up the crews of torpedoed ships, and in the latter capacity it

helped in the evacuation of Norway and Crete. It was even used to evacuate the wounded and sick from the second Chindit operation in Burma during 1944, flying off lakes far from the sea.

Production of the Sunderland I reached 90 before the next mark, the Sunderland II, began to appear in August 1941. The new model, which was powered by 1,065-hp Pegasus XVIII radials and had a power-operated twin-gun dorsal turret in place of the two hand-held beam guns, entered service at the end of 1941. After 43 examples had been built, the Mark II was replaced by the Mark III. The first production Sunderland III flew in December 1941. It differed from the Mark II in having a revised bottom to the hull, the forward step of the planing surface being reduced in depth. A total of 456 Sunderland III boats was built, making it the most numerous mark of the basic type.

The next version, the Sunderland IV, first flew in August 1944. This had 1,700-hp Bristol Hercules radial engines, and it was soon found that a larger fin and rudder and tailplane were needed. As it was realized that it would take some time to get this new model into full production, it was scheduled for use in the Pacific. Defensive armament was to include two 20-mm cannon and eight 0.5-inch (12.7-mm) machine-guns. Performance was disappointing, however, and only eight Seafords, as the Sunderland IV with all its modifications had been renamed, were built for military use.

The last Sunderland model was the Mark V. To obtain adequate performance with the Mark III it had been necessary to fly with the engines running flat out much of the time, and this wore out the Pegasus engines very quickly. Service pilots therefore suggested that 1,200-hp Pratt & Whitney Twin Wasp radials replace the Pegasus engines. The first of the new Mark V aircraft flew in March 1944, and the type entered squad-

ron service in February 1945. In all, 150 Sunderland V flying-boats were built before production ceased in June 1946, making a grand total of 739.

To improve the type as a reconnaissance aircraft, Sunderlands from the Mark II onwards had been fitted with air-surface vessel search radar. In the Mark II this had been ASV Mark II equipment, which was readily identifiable by its four masts rising vertically from the top of the hull, and the 16 transmitting loops in four rows of four, two on each side of the hull. On late production Mark III aircraft this radar was replaced by ASV Mark VIC, and this equipment was made standard on the Mark V. This later radar could be distinguished by the bulges underneath the wings outboard of the outer float bracing wires. Each of these two bulges housed a scanner. It is worth noting that the Sunderland's offensive armament was carried on racks in the hull. These had to be winched out under the wings before the bombs could be dropped.

The last Sunderlands were retired from RAF service in May 1959, after a career of 17 years. They had proved to be magnificent aircraft, acquiring for themselves a special niche in aviation history. Perhaps the Sunderland can best be described by the epithet bestowed upon it by German aircrew operating against it, *fliegende Stachelschwein* – Flying Porcupine – due to its formidable armament.

Below: A Short Sunderland Mark V long-range maritime-reconnaissance flying-boat in the air. This last production model of the Sunderland was distinguishable by the scanners for its air-to-surface vessel search radar, mounted in a small radome under each outer wing panel, and Pratt & Whitney Twin Wasp radials in place of earlier marks' Bristol Pegasus engines, with which the aircraft was slightly underpowered

Short Sunderland I

The aircraft illustrated is the 12th production
Sunderland, machine B of 204 Squadron, Coastal
Command (code-letters KG). Camouflage is
standard for the period 1941-mid 1942, with a
Temperate Sea Scheme of Dark Slate Grey and
Extra Dark Sea Grey on the upper surfaces, with
Sky Type 'S' on the under surfaces. National
insignia are the normal ones except for the fin
stripes, which at this time should have been three
equal stripes of red, white and blue in a block
24 inches wide and 27 inches high

Type ten-seat maritime patrol and reconnaissance
flying boat

Engines four Bristol Pegasus XXII nine-cylinder
air-cooled radials, each rated at 1,010 hp at take-off

Armament defensive: two flexible 0.303-inch
(7.7-mm) Browning machine-guns in the nose
turret, four flexible 0.303-inch Browning machine-
guns in the tail turret and two flexible 0.303-inch
Vickers K machine-guns, one in each of two beam
positions
offensive: up to 2,000 lbs (907 kg) of bombs

Maximum speed 210 mph at 6,500 feet (338 km/h
at 1,981 m)

Cruising speed 178 mph at 5,750 feet (286 km/h
at 1,753 m)

Initial climb rate 830 fpm (253 m/minute)

Service ceiling 17,000 feet (5,182 m)

Range 2,900 miles (4,667 km)

Weights 28,290 lbs (12,832 kg) empty; 44,600 lbs
(20,230 kg) loaded; 50,100 lbs (22,725 kg) gross

Span 112 feet 9 inches (34.37 m)

Length 85 feet 8 inches (26.11 m)

Height 32 feet 10½ inches (10.02 m)

Wing area 1,487 square feet (138.15 m²)

Supermarine Spitfire

The Supermarine Spitfire is certainly the most famous aircraft ever used by the Royal Air Force, and probably the most celebrated aircraft of World War II. It was a superlative fighter, a match for any of its opponents at the beginning of World War II, and still a match for any fighter powered by a piston engine at the end of that conflict. It had enormous development potential, and its successor, the Supermarine Spiteful, was the ultimate expression of the piston-engined fighter concept. Finally, the Spitfire's capabilities as a warplane were matched by its aesthetic qualities.

The designer of the Spitfire, R J Mitchell, who died just after it went into production, had been concerned with high-speed flight with monoplanes since the middle of the 1920s, when he had been responsible for the design of the Supermarine S 4 racing floatplane. Subsequently he had designed the S 5, S 6 and S 6B floatplanes which had won the Schneider Trophy for Great Britain. He had designed a single-seat monoplane fighter to a 1930 Air Ministry requirement, and was working on a more advanced design, to be powered by a Rolls-Royce Goshawk engine, with an enclosed cockpit and a retractable undercarriage, when two factors made him start afresh. These two factors were a 1934 Air Ministry requirement for a monoplane fighter armed with eight machine-guns, and the introduction of the 1,000-hp Rolls-Royce PV 12 engine, later the Merlin. Mitchell completely

redesigned his interim design to incorporate the new factors, and the result first flew in March 1936.

This was the prototype Spitfire, and its performance, combined with its handling characteristics, led to a first production order for 310 machines in June 1936. By October 1939 production orders totalled 4,000 machines. Production of the Spitfire I began in 1937, deliveries beginning in June 1938, the first squadron to re-equip with the new fighter doing so in July of the same year. These early Mark Is were fitted with a Merlin II engine with a fixed-pitch two-bladed wooden propeller, but improvements in these latter matched those already described for the Hurricane. The first few aircraft, designated Spitfire I, had only four machine-guns and an unbulged cockpit like the prototype's. Later machines had a domed cockpit canopy, and the Spitfire IA introduced an eight-gun armament. The Spitfire IB, of which 30 were delivered in August 1940, had two 20-mm cannon and four machine-guns. Spitfire I production totalled 1,583 aircraft before production was changed to the next model.

This was the Spitfire II, which was powered by a Merlin XII of 1,175-hp. It entered service in August 1940, and two major versions were built: 750 Mark IIAs with eight machine-guns, and 170 Mark IIBs with two 20-mm cannon and four 0.303-inch (7.7-mm) Browning machine-guns. The designation Spitfire IIC was used for

the Mark II variant in service with air/sea rescue squadrons. Apart from being used as a fighter, the Spitfire was also employed as a photographic-reconnaissance aircraft under the designations A, B, C, D, E, F, and G. The first definitive PR Spitfire was the PR IV, with a 1,100-hp Merlin 46; 229 were built.

The Spitfire III proved a useful development aircraft, but did not enter production. It was strengthened to take a 1,480-hp Merlin XX, and had clipped wings of 30 feet 6 inches (9.3 m) span. The Spitfire IV tested a Rolls-Royce Griffon IIB installation. With the introduction of the PR IV, the Griffon-engined Mark IV became the Mark XX. The Mark IV/XX prototype also had the mock-up of a six-cannon wing armament.

The Spitfire V, the next major production model, entered service in February 1941. This was powered by a 1,440-hp Merlin 45 series engine, and was the first model to be fitted with tropical equipment for service in the Mediterranean and Middle Eastern theatres, and the first to be used as a fighter-bomber, with one 500- or two 250-lb (227- or 113-kg) bombs. Production of the Spitfire V totalled 6,479 aircraft, in three major versions: the VA with eight machine-guns, the VB with two cannon and four machine-guns, and the VC with the Universal wing, capable of accepting either A or B armament, or four cannon. With the decline of Axis air strength, the Spitfire V was used increasingly for

Left: RAF groundcrew at work on three Spitfire VC fighter-bombers of 253 Squadron in the Middle East theatre. Note the details of the engine installation, made visible by the removal of the Merlin, and the belt of 20-mm cannon shells ready for loading into the ammunition tank in the starboard wing. Visible under the nose of the middle aircraft is the Vokes air-filter so essential for operations in dusty climates to prevent the engines from wearing out too soon

Supermarine Spitfire IA
The aircraft illustrated is machine D of 603 'City of Edinburgh' Squadron, Royal Auxiliary Air Force. The squadron was based at Dyce, Hornchurch and Montrose during the Battle of Britain. Camouflage is the standard Ministry of Aircraft Production Pattern No 1, in the Temperate Land Scheme of 1940, with Dark Green and Dark Earth upper surfaces and an unusual under surface finish of white. National insignia are normal

Type single-seat fighter
Engine one Rolls-Royce Merlin III twelve-cylinder liquid-cooled inline, 1,030 hp at take-off
Armament eight 0.303-inch (7.7-mm) Browning machine-guns with 300 rounds per gun
Maximum speed 362 mph at 19,000 feet (583 km/h at 5,791 m)
Cruising speed 315 mph at 20,000 feet (507 km/h at 6,096 m)
Initial climb rate 2,530 fpm (771 m/minute)
Climb 9 minutes 24 seconds to 20,000 feet (6,096 m)
Service ceiling 31,900 feet (9,723 m)
Range 395 miles (636 km) normal; 575 miles at 210 mph (925 km at 338 km/h)
Weights 4,810 lbs (2,182 kg) empty; 5,784 lbs (2,624 kg) loaded
Span 36 feet 10 inches (11.23 m)
Length 29 feet 11 inches (9.12 m)
Height 8 feet 10 inches (2.69 m)
Wing area 242 square feet (22.48 m²)

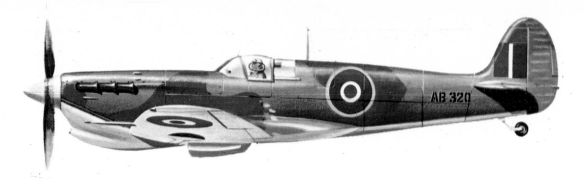

low-level attacks. In this capacity it was fitted with Merlin 45M, 50M, or 55M engines and clipped wings of 32 feet 2 inches (9.80 m). Other Spitfire variants of this time were the production versions of the F and G PR models as the PR VI and PR VII. An increasingly difficult problem for the RAF from 1941 onwards was that of intercepting high-altitude German raiders and reconnaissance aircraft. To meet this threat the Spitfire VI was developed with a Merlin 47 engine of 1,415 hp at 14,000 feet (4,267 m) and a pressurized cockpit. Production of the Spitfire VI, which could reach 40,000 feet (12,192 m), totalled 100 aircraft. The wingtips were extended, to give a span of 40 feet 2 inches (12.24 m).

The Spitfire VI was essentially an interim model, the Spitfire VII being intended as the definitive high-altitude interceptor. The first of the 140 built flew in April 1942. The Mark VII used the 1,700-hp Merlin 60 series of engines, with a two-stage supercharger. The new engine needed a revised cooling system and the two underwing radiators were made symmetrical. The area of the fin and rudder also had to be increased to compensate for the increased area forward of the centre of gravity, resulting in a wider and slightly more pointed fin and rudder. The FR VII fighter-reconnaissance model was derived from the PR IV and was powered by a Merlin 45 or 46, with an armament of eight machine-guns. Some 16 of these FR VII aircraft were later converted to low-level PR XIIIs, with 1,645-hp Merlin 32 engines.

The modifications incorporated in the Mark VII, with the exception of the pressurized cockpit, were also incorporated in the Spitfire VIII. This was basically similar to the Mark VII in function, but intended for operations at lower altitudes. The type was introduced into service in August 1943, and 1,658 were built in three major versions: the F VIII with standard wings and a Merlin 61 or 63 engine, the HF VIII with extended wings and a Merlin 70 engine, and the LF VIII with clipped wings and a Merlin 66.

With the introduction of the Focke-Wulf in 1941 the Spitfire V was definitely outclassed, and Supermarine gave thought to a radically improved version of the Spitfire. Pending deliveries of the Mark VII and VIII, an interim model based on the Spitfire VC, using the Merlin 60 series of engines, was developed. This became the Mark IX, and despite the fact that it was intended only as a stopgap, 5,665 were built, making it the most numerous Spitfire mark. It was built in F, LF, and HF versions, with only the engines distinguishing the three sub-marks. The Mark IX was an improvement on the Mark V, but was still not quite a match for the Fw 190. Later in the Mark IX's production, the C wing was replaced by the E wing, with the cannon

moved outboard and the four 0.303-inch (7.7-mm) machine-guns replaced by a pair of 0.5-inch (12.7-mm) guns. The PR X and PR XI – the former with, and the latter without, a pressurized cockpit – were developed from the Mark IX.

The final version of the Spitfire to be powered by a Merlin engine was the LF XVI. This had a Packard-built Merlin 266, enlarged vertical tail surfaces, and a bubble canopy for the cockpit, together with a cut-down rear fuselage. This last greatly improved the pilot's field of vision. A total of 1,054 Mark XVIs was built with C or E wings.

It had been intended to number Griffon-engined Spitfires from XX onwards, but in the event the first Griffon version was the Spitfire XII. This was based on the Mark V, and 100 were built. The type was powered by a Griffon III or IV engine rated for low-altitude work, and was intended as a counter to Fw 190 sneak-raiders over southern England. The Spitfire XII was put into service from the spring of 1943. Tests with a Griffon-engined Mark VIII had proved so encouraging that another interim model, the Spitfire XIV powered by a Griffon 65, was produced, entering service in January 1944. This had the vertical tail surfaces widened still further, and had either a C or an E wing. Mark XIV production totalled 957. A further development of the Mark XIV idea led to the Mark XVIII, with fuselage and undercarriage strengthened to allow more fuel to be carried. By the end of the war 100 F XVIII and 200 FR XVIII models had been built. The Griffon-engined PR XIX was based on the Spitfire XIV with a Mark VC type of wing.

With the Mark 21 the Spitfire underwent a radical change, losing its elliptical wing planform for an aerodynamically superior wing allowing higher diving speeds. The Mark 22 was basically similar, but had a cut-down rear fuselage and a bubble canopy. The Mark 21 appeared in February 1944 and entered service just before the end of hostilities. The Mark 22 appeared in March 1945, and 278 were built. The last version, the Mark 24, appeared after the war, 54 being built. Total Spitfire production reached 20,334 before it ceased in October 1947.

Naval versions of the Spitfire were also built, but the outward retracting undercarriage, with its inherently narrow track, always proved a weakness. The Seafire IB was derived from the Spitfire VB, the Seafire IIC from the Spitfire VC, the Seafire III was the first model with folding wings, the Seafire XV had a Griffon engine but was otherwise similar to the Seafire III, and the final wartime Seafire was the Mark XVII, basically a Seafire XV with a cut-down rear fuselage and bubble canopy.

Supermarine LF VB
The aircraft illustrated is finished in standard Ministry of Aircraft Production Pattern No 1 in the Middle East Scheme of Dark Earth and Middle Stone upper surfaces and Sky Blue under surfaces. The 18-inch Sky Type 'S' fighter band round the rear fuselage was not used in the Middle East. National insignia are standard
Type single-seat fighter and fighter-bomber
Engine one Rolls-Royce Merlin 50M twelve-cylinder liquid-cooled inline, 1,585 hp at 2,750 feet (838 m)
Armament defensive: two 20-mm Hispano cannon with 60 or 120 rounds per gun and four 0.303-inch Browning machine-guns with 350 rounds per gun offensive: up to 500 lbs (227 kg) of bombs
Maximum speeds 357 mph at 6,000 feet (575 km/h at 1,829 m); 332 mph (534 km/h) at sea level
Cruising speed 272 mph at 5,000 feet (438 km/h at 1,524 m)
Initial climb rate 4,750 fpm (1,448 m/minute)
Climb 7 minutes to 20,000 feet (6,096 m)
Service ceiling 35,500 feet (10,821 m)
Range 470 miles (756 km) on internal fuel; 1,135 miles (1,827 km) with drop-tank
Weights 5,050 lbs (2,291 kg) empty; 6,650 lbs (3,016 kg) loaded; 6,710 lbs (3,044 kg) gross
Span 32 feet 2 inches (9.80 m)
Length 29 feet 11 inches (9.12 m)
Height 9 feet 11 inches (3.02 m)
Wing area 231 square feet (21.46 m²)

Supermarine Seafire III
The aircraft illustrated is finished in the Temperate Sea Scheme of Dark Slate Grey and Extra Dark Sea Grey upper surfaces with white under surfaces. The national insignia are those used by the British Pacific Fleet, with the markings placed as on American aircraft. Note that the roundels contain no red, to avoid confusion with the Japanese *hinomaru* marking
Type single-seat naval fighter and fighter-bomber
Engine one Rolls-Royce Merlin 55 twelve-cylinder liquid-cooled inline, 1,470 hp at take-off
Armament defensive: two 20-mm Hispano cannon with 120 rounds per gun in the wings and four 0.303-inch (7.7-mm) Browning machine-guns with 350 rounds per gun in the wings offensive: up to 500 lbs (227 kg) of bombs
Maximum speed 352 mph at 12,250 feet (567 km/h at 3,734 m)
Cruising speed 218 mph at 20,000 feet (351 km/h at 6,096 m)

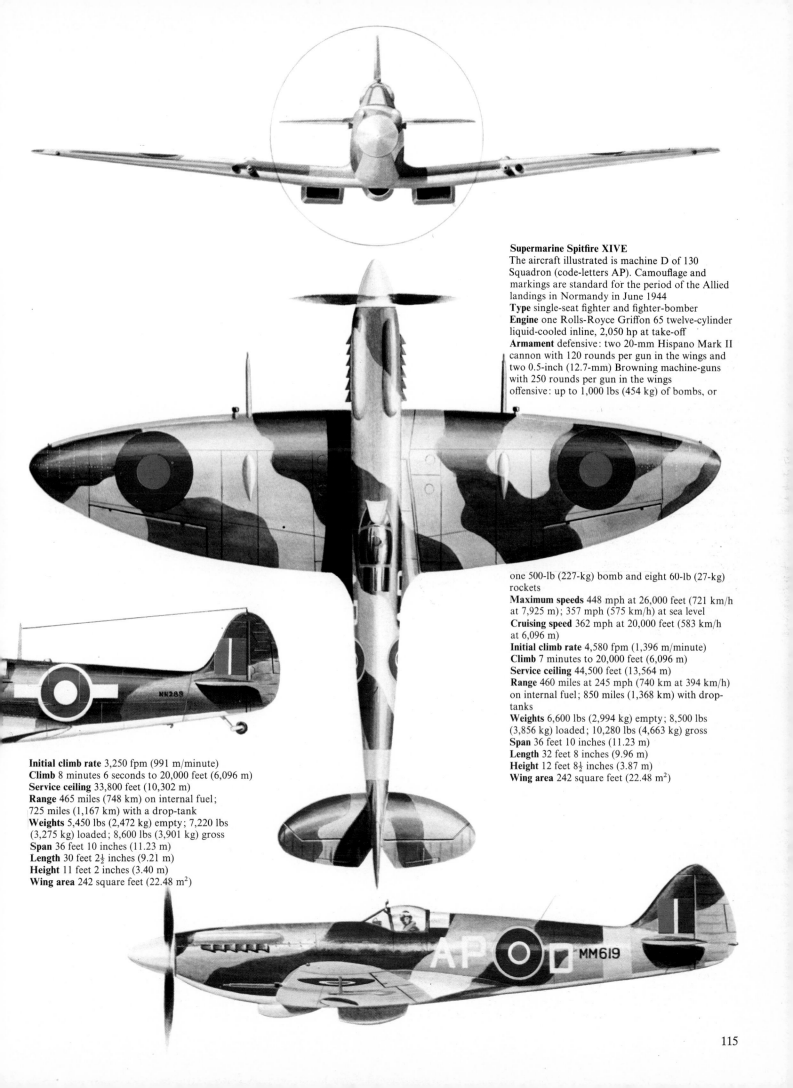

Supermarine Spitfire XIVE
The aircraft illustrated is machine D of 130
Squadron (code-letters AP). Camouflage and
markings are standard for the period of the Allied
landings in Normandy in June 1944
Type single-seat fighter and fighter-bomber
Engine one Rolls-Royce Griffon 65 twelve-cylinder
liquid-cooled inline, 2,050 hp at take-off
Armament defensive: two 20-mm Hispano Mark II
cannon with 120 rounds per gun in the wings and
two 0.5-inch (12.7-mm) Browning machine-guns
with 250 rounds per gun in the wings
offensive: up to 1,000 lbs (454 kg) of bombs, or
one 500-lb (227-kg) bomb and eight 60-lb (27-kg)
rockets
Maximum speeds 448 mph at 26,000 feet (721 km/h
at 7,925 m); 357 mph (575 km/h) at sea level
Cruising speed 362 mph at 20,000 feet (583 km/h
at 6,096 m)
Initial climb rate 4,580 fpm (1,396 m/minute)
Climb 7 minutes to 20,000 feet (6,096 m)
Service ceiling 44,500 feet (13,564 m)
Range 460 miles at 245 mph (740 km at 394 km/h)
on internal fuel; 850 miles (1,368 km) with drop-
tanks
Weights 6,600 lbs (2,994 kg) empty; 8,500 lbs
(3,856 kg) loaded; 10,280 lbs (4,663 kg) gross
Span 36 feet 10 inches (11.23 m)
Length 32 feet 8 inches (9.96 m)
Height 12 feet 8½ inches (3.87 m)
Wing area 242 square feet (22.48 m²)

Initial climb rate 3,250 fpm (991 m/minute)
Climb 8 minutes 6 seconds to 20,000 feet (6,096 m)
Service ceiling 33,800 feet (10,302 m)
Range 465 miles (748 km) on internal fuel;
725 miles (1,167 km) with a drop-tank
Weights 5,450 lbs (2,472 kg) empty; 7,220 lbs
(3,275 kg) loaded; 8,600 lbs (3,901 kg) gross
Span 36 feet 10 inches (11.23 m)
Length 30 feet 2½ inches (9.21 m)
Height 11 feet 2 inches (3.40 m)
Wing area 242 square feet (22.48 m²)

Ilyushin Il-2 Shturmovik

The Ilyshin Il-2 *Shturmovik* was the most celebrated, and perhaps the best, aircraft used by the Red Air Force during World War II. So successful was the type that the designation *Shturmovik*, meaning ground-attack aircraft, was applied only to the Il-2, in much the same way as the epithet *Stuka*, meaning dive-bomber, was applied only to the Junkers 87.

Design work on ground-attack aircraft began in Russia during 1930, but so stringent were the provisions of the requirement that no suitable aircraft was forthcoming. The main reason for this was that while the demands for protection and firepower could be met, those for high speed and manoeuvrability could not with the fairly low-powered engines then available. The first aircraft to approach the performance required was Sergei V Ilyushin's *TsKB*-55 of 1938 (*TsKB* stands for *Tsentralnoye Konstruktorskoye Byuro* or Central Design Bureau.) From this the design team evolved the *TsKB*-57 late in 1939. This can be considered the true progenitor of the Il-2. Initial flight trials, however, proved disappointing as the 1,370-hp Mikulin AM 35 was too low-powered for so massive an aircraft. A far more satisfactory performance was achieved with the 1,680-hp AM 38 engine in October 1940.

The most interesting feature of the *TsKB*-57 was its excellent armour protection. This in fact formed the basis of the structure of the forward fuselage, and consisted of an armour-plate 'bath', between 5 and 12 mm thick, forming the bottom and sides of the fuselage between the rear of the cockpit and the front of the engine. Armament consisted of two 20-mm cannon, two 7.62-mm machine-guns, eight 82-mm rockets, and up to 882 lbs (400 kg) of bombs. The *TsKB*-57 was ordered into production as the Il-2 in March 1941. Only 249 had been delivered by the time of the German invasion in June 1941, but these proved very useful in hampering the progress of the German armoured columns. But it proved

impossible to halt the German advance before the winter of 1941–1942, and in the evacuation of Russian industry from western Russia to the Ural mountains area, production of the Il-2 ceased for two months.

By the early summer of 1942 certain complaints were being voiced about the Il-2. The two most important of these were the lack of rear defence at a time of almost total German air superiority, and the increasing inadequacy of the 20-mm cannon against the latest German armoured vehicles. The first complaint was dealt with by the addition of a second crew member, a rear gunner, armed with a single 12.7-mm BS or UBT machine-gun. The gunner was located behind the pilot, and to protect him the armoured bath was extended to the rear. The second complaint was remedied by the replacement (already tested on the Il-2 Modified) of the 20-mm cannon with 23-mm VJa cannon, which had a considerably higher muzzle velocity, and therefore penetrative power. As the weight of the aircraft was increased, the power of the engine was boosted to 1,750 hp by increasing the compression ratio.

With these modifications the new type entered service in August 1942 as the definitive Il-2m3. (The 'm3' stood for model 3.) As the addition of the gunner's cockpit improved the aerodynamic lines of the fuselage, top speed rose to 252 mph (405 km/h) despite the increase in loaded weight. In parallel with the Il-2m3 was produced the Il-2U trainer, with duplicated controls in the rear cockpit.

The main armament needed revision again in 1943 to deal with improved German armour. The VJa cannon were therefore replaced by a pair of 37-mm N-37 or P-37 cannon with good armour-piercing capabilities; a container for 200 small 5½-lb (2.5-kg) hollow-charge anti-tank bombs was installed, as was a grenade-launcher which fired grenades on small parachutes in

front of pursuing aircraft. These modifications were incorporated in the Il-2m3 (Modified), which entered service just in time to wreak terrible devastation on the latest German *PzKpfw* V and VI tanks in the Battle of Kursk in July 1943.

At the same time structural modifications were effected to the basic airframe. The original type, which had featured a wooden rear fuselage, was now designated the Basic type. A new structure of metal, introduced in the spring of 1944, was used on the Il-2m3 (Modified). This also had a rear bulkhead for the armoured bath in place of the gunner's previous front and back plates. During 1944 provision was also made for the carriage of 132-mm instead of 82-mm rockets for use against strongpoints, and an increased bomb-load of 1,323 lbs (600 kg) in the wing bays. The Il-2 was also used by the Red Naval Air Force as the Il-2T. This carried a 21.7-inch (55-cm) torpedo beneath the fuselage. The final development of the Il-2 occurred after the end of the war.

In combat the Il-2 *Shturmovik* proved a devastating weapon. It usually operated at extremely low altitudes, so that its hail of cannon shells and rockets hit the target horizontally, taking the Axis forces completely by surprise. The most favoured tactic for Il-2 units was the 'circle of death'. In this the unit would cross the lines and attack the target from the rear, flying past it towards the lines and then circling back to attack it again until it was destroyed or all the ammunition expended. In this tactic the target could be kept under continued fire for up to 30 minutes. To the Russians the Il-2 was the *Ilyusha*, the Flying Tank, the Flying Infantryman, or the Hunchback. To the Germans the Il-2 was, with very great justification, the *schwarz Tod* or Black Death.

Below : Line-up of the Red Air Force's superlative Il-2m3 on a Russian airfield

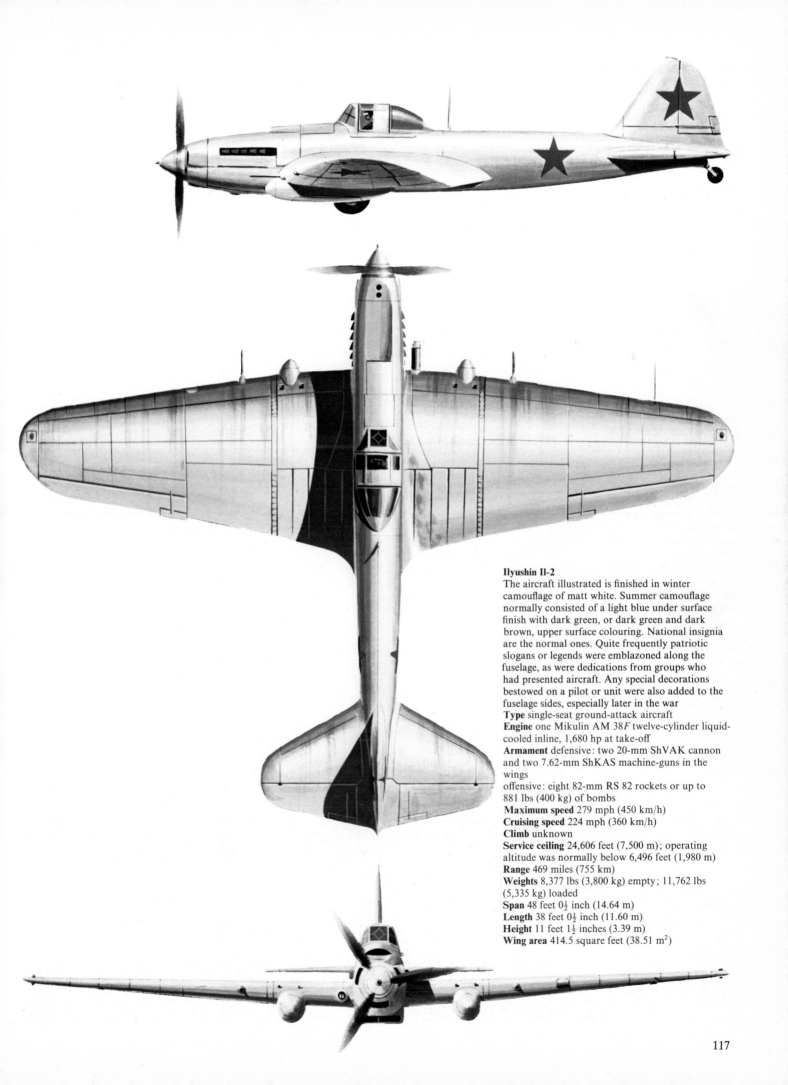

Ilyushin Il-2
The aircraft illustrated is finished in winter
camouflage of matt white. Summer camouflage
normally consisted of a light blue under surface
finish with dark green, or dark green and dark
brown, upper surface colouring. National insignia
are the normal ones. Quite frequently patriotic
slogans or legends were emblazoned along the
fuselage, as were dedications from groups who
had presented aircraft. Any special decorations
bestowed on a pilot or unit were also added to the
fuselage sides, especially later in the war
Type single-seat ground-attack aircraft
Engine one Mikulin AM 38*F* twelve-cylinder liquid-
cooled inline, 1,680 hp at take-off
Armament defensive: two 20-mm ShVAK cannon
and two 7.62-mm ShKAS machine-guns in the
wings
offensive: eight 82-mm RS 82 rockets or up to
881 lbs (400 kg) of bombs
Maximum speed 279 mph (450 km/h)
Cruising speed 224 mph (360 km/h)
Climb unknown
Service ceiling 24,606 feet (7,500 m); operating
altitude was normally below 6,496 feet (1,980 m)
Range 469 miles (755 km)
Weights 8,377 lbs (3,800 kg) empty; 11,762 lbs
(5,335 kg) loaded
Span 48 feet 0½ inch (14.64 m)
Length 38 feet 0½ inch (11.60 m)
Height 11 feet 1½ inches (3.39 m)
Wing area 414.5 square feet (38.51 m²)

117

Petlyakov Pe-2

Vladimir Petlyakov's Pe-2 was without doubt the best light bomber of World War II. Moreover, so sound was the basic structure and so good the performance that the Pe-2 also bid fair to equal Germany's Junkers Ju 88 and Great Britain's de Havilland Mosquito in the multitude of roles it fulfilled: light bomber, dive-bomber, day fighter, night fighter, reconnaissance aircraft, and advanced trainer. That the type did not undertake further roles was the result of the simplicity of Red Air Force operations rather than any limitations on the part of the aircraft.

The origins of the Pe-2 lay in a Red Air Force requirement of the late 1930s for a high-altitude bomber interceptor. To meet this Petlyakov produced his *VI*-100. (*VI* stands for *Vysotnyi Istrebitel* or High-Altitude Fighter.) The prototype *VI*-100 was ready in the spring of 1939, but was never flown, the Red Air Force cancelling its requirement for such an aircraft, issuing in its place a requirement for a high-altitude bomber. Petlyakov decided to respond to this with a design based on the *VI*-100, using the same turbo-supercharged engines, the same type of pressurized cockpit, and a modified airframe to allow the carriage of bombs in an internal bomb-bay, and remote-control dorsal and ventral defensive machine-guns.

Before a prototype could be built, however, the Red Air Force once again altered its requirement, the accuracy of high-altitude bombing being in doubt. Thus Petlyakov was now instructed to modify his high-altitude bomber into a dive-bomber, the efficiency of which had been proved in the Spanish Civil War. The change in altitude performance required meant that the turbo-supercharged engines could be abandoned, and with them the cabin pressurization equipment. This allowed more room in the aircraft, and meant that the defensive armament could be operated directly by the crew. The new aircraft emerged in December 1939 as the *PB*-100. (*PB* stands for *Pikiruyushchii Bombardirovshchik* or Dive-Bomber.) After service trials, during which the area of the vertical tail surfaces was increased by one-third, the *PB*-100 was pronounced an excellent aircraft, with good diving characteristics when the slatted dive-brakes were extended and a fair turn of speed with them retracted.

The Pe-2, as the *PB*-100 was now designated, was put into large-scale production early in 1940, the tempo of deliveries gaining pace rapidly in 1941. Although only two machines were delivered during 1940, the grand total built finally reached 11,426. The original machine-gun armament consisted of four 7.62-mm weapons, but this was later standardized as three 12.7-mm and two 7.62-mm weapons. The bomb-load was also increased from 1,323 lbs to 2,205 lbs (600 kg to 1,000 kg). The Pe-2's performance was also improved during 1943, when aircraft powered by Klimov VK-105*RF* engines supplanted Klimov M-105*R*-powered machines on the production lines in February. At the same time the airframe was considerably 'cleaned up' aerodynamically by giving the undercarriage doors a better fit, improving the lines of the engine nacelles, and reducing the gap between fixed and movable surfaces. These modifications raised the maximum speed by 25 mph (40 km/h).

As noted above, the Pe-2 was an extremely versatile aircraft, and was modified to perform several roles other than bombing. The first of these, which appeared in the first half of 1941, was the Pe-3. This was structurally akin to the *VI*-100, and was intended as a multi-role fighter. Only limited production of this variant was undertaken as a result of the high priority given to the basic Pe-2. The Pe-3 was powered by the M-105*R* inlines of the early production Pe-2, but was armed with two fixed 20-mm ShVAK cannon and two fixed 12.7-mm UBK machine-guns, and two flexible 12.7-mm machine-guns.

The next Pe-2 variant was the Pe-2*R*. (*R* stands for *Razvedchik* or Reconnaissance.) This reconnaissance aircraft had three cameras in the bomb-bay and a directional autopilot to hold the machine steady during the photography run. Fuel tankage was increased to give a range of 1,056 miles (1,700 km), and the Pe-2*R* was intended for employment by day or night. The Pe-2*UT* was an advanced trainer variant. (*UT* stands for *Uchebno Trenirovochnyi* or Advanced Trainer.) This was intended for operational conversion flying, and had a second cockpit for the instructor, complete with full controls, behind the original cockpit.

For its size the Pe-2 was quite agile, and proved a devastating weapon as a dive-bomber or level bomber. The type's three vices, if they may be called that, were a high landing speed, a tendency to spin after stalling, and extreme sensitivity during landing. In the last, a heavy landing was likely to cause the Pe-2 to bounce high in the air, with disastrous consequences for all but very experienced pilots.

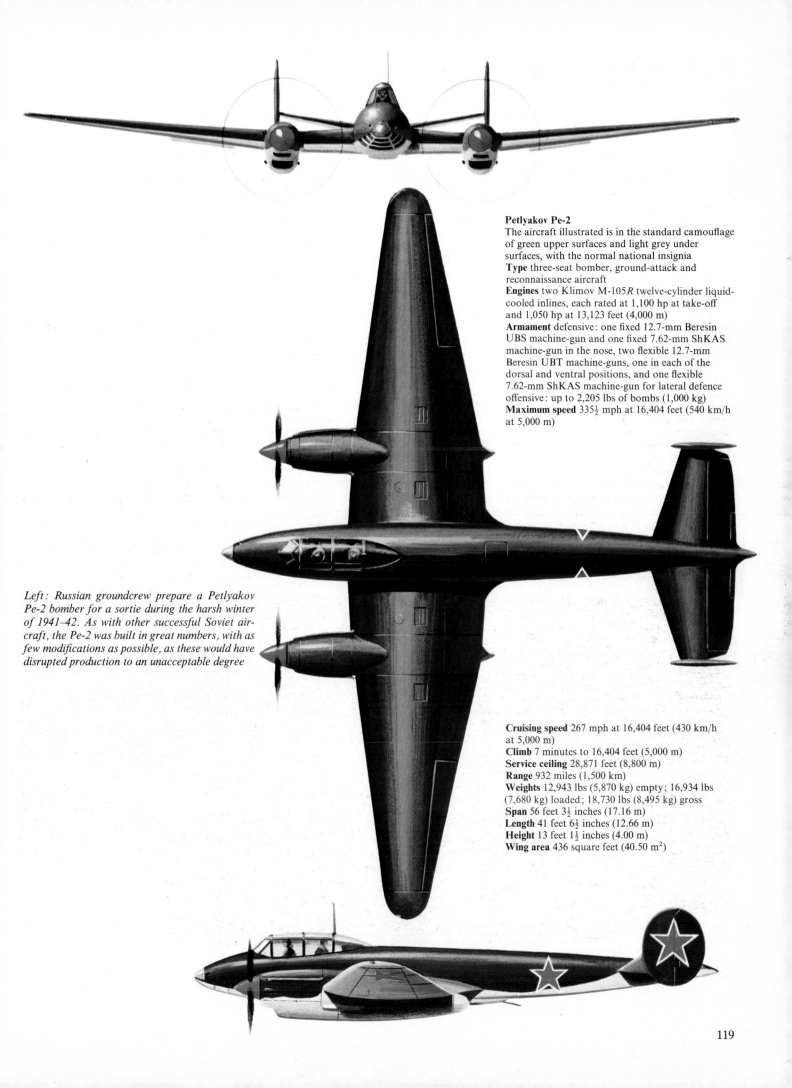

Petlyakov Pe-2
The aircraft illustrated is in the standard camouflage of green upper surfaces and light grey under surfaces, with the normal national insignia
Type three-seat bomber, ground-attack and reconnaissance aircraft
Engines two Klimov M-105*R* twelve-cylinder liquid-cooled inlines, each rated at 1,100 hp at take-off and 1,050 hp at 13,123 feet (4,000 m)
Armament defensive: one fixed 12.7-mm Beresin UBS machine-gun and one fixed 7.62-mm ShKAS machine-gun in the nose, two flexible 12.7-mm Beresin UBT machine-guns, one in each of the dorsal and ventral positions, and one flexible 7.62-mm ShKAS machine-gun for lateral defence offensive: up to 2,205 lbs of bombs (1,000 kg)
Maximum speed 335½ mph at 16,404 feet (540 km/h at 5,000 m)

Left: Russian groundcrew prepare a Petlyakov Pe-2 bomber for a sortie during the harsh winter of 1941–42. As with other successful Soviet air-craft, the Pe-2 was built in great numbers, with as few modifications as possible, as these would have disrupted production to an unacceptable degree

Cruising speed 267 mph at 16,404 feet (430 km/h at 5,000 m)
Climb 7 minutes to 16,404 feet (5,000 m)
Service ceiling 28,871 feet (8,800 m)
Range 932 miles (1,500 km)
Weights 12,943 lbs (5,870 kg) empty; 16,934 lbs (7,680 kg) loaded; 18,730 lbs (8,495 kg) gross
Span 56 feet 3½ inches (17.16 m)
Length 41 feet 6½ inches (12.66 m)
Height 13 feet 1½ inches (4.00 m)
Wing area 436 square feet (40.50 m²)

119

Yakovlev Fighters

The Yakovlev series of aircraft was the most widely used of Russian fighters in World War II, and continued in service with the Red Air Force and the services of the Russian satellites long after the end of hostilities. Although its performance seems low, and its structure crude, compared with Western types, the Yak-9 series reigned supreme in the role for which it was designed: low- and medium-altitude tactical fighter. Below 16,404 feet (5,000 m) the Yak-9 had a combination of performance and manoeuvrability that could not be matched by any German fighter.

Design work on the basic aircraft that was developed through the Yakovlev series of fighters began in 1938, in response to a Red Air Force requirement for a replacement for the Polikarpov I-16. Three design teams produced prototypes to meet this need, and all three entered production, the I-26 as the Yak-1, the I-22 as the LaGG-3, and the I-200 or I-61 as the MiG-1. The Yak-1 first flew in March 1939, and quickly attracted the interest of the Russian authorities, including Stalin himself. The type was ordered into production as quickly as possible, and the first unit to re-equip with the new fighter took part in the May Day parade of 1940.

Production Yak-1 fighters were also known as Yak-1IPs. (IP stands for *Istrebitel Pushka* or Cannon Fighter.) Once its initial teething problems had been corrected in the summer and autumn of 1941, the Yak-1 proved to be one of the few Soviet types able to take on Germany's Messerschmitt Bf 109F and Focke-Wulf Fw 190A on anything approaching equal terms, and quickly became one of the most valued fighters in the Red Air Force's inventory. Meanwhile, the need for an operational trainer for the new generation of fighters had led to the introduction of the Yak-7V, later redesignated Yak-7U. This trainer variant was also known as the UTI-26, and was powered by the Klimov M-105PF of 1,260 hp, the powerplant that was adopted in

late series Yak-1s. With the M-105PF engine, the Yak-1 became the Yak-1M. (M stands for *Modificatsion* or Modification.) The Yak-1M could be distinguished from its predecessor by its cut down rear fuselage, new all-round vision cockpit canopy and lack of an engine-mounted cannon; production ceased in 1942. The type was later developed into the Yak-3, a parallel version of the Yak-9.

In the autumn of 1941 the Red Air Force formulated a requirement for a single-seat night fighter. Alexander Yakovlev responded to the requirement by producing his Yak-7A, basically a Yak-7U with the second cockpit removed and the armament improved. With the standardization of the M-105PF engine and the cut-down rear fuselage, production examples of the Yak-1M were from this time onwards redesignated Yak-7B. Two variants of the Yak-7 were the experimental Yak-7VRD, with a Merkulov ramjet under each wing, and the Yak-7DI. (DI stands for *Distantsyonnyi Istrebitel* or Long-Range Fighter.) Only a few examples of the Yak-7DI were built before the type was replaced by a newer variant.

This was designated Yak-9, and was based on the Yak-7DI. Production aircraft started to come off the production lines in December 1942. The powerplant was the standard M-105PF, and the armament one 20-mm cannon and one 12.7-mm machine-gun. In May 1943 the basic Yak-9 was joined by the Yak-9M, which had a second 12.7-mm machine-gun in the nose. At the same time another variant, the Yak-9B, was introduced. (B stands for *Bombovoy* or Bomber.) This bomber model had the same gun armament as the basic Yak-9, but featured an internal bomb-bay for a load of up to 992 lbs (450 kg) of bombs. Both the Yak-9M and Yak-9B were built in very substantial numbers. By the middle of 1943, Yakovlev fighters in service exceeded both Lavochkin and Mikoyan-Gurevich types by a very handsome margin.

The majority of Russian fighters had been designed to operate over short ranges but as the Red Army began to push forward in 1943, the need for models with increased ranges was strongly felt. Light alloys were now available in fair quantities, and Yakolev again redesigned the wing of his fighter to produce the Yak-9D, which had bigger fuel tanks in the wings, and a range increased by 317 miles (510 km) over that of the basic Yak-9. (D stands for *Distantsyonnyi* or Long-Range.) Armament was similar to that of the Yak-9, but the ShVAK cannon was replaced by a MPSh cannon of the same calibre. The Yak-9D was further modified with additional internal fuel tankage and provision for a drop-tank under the fuselage, raising the range of the Yak-9DD, as the new type was designated, to 1,367 miles (2,200 km). (DD stands for *Dalnodistantsyonnyi* or Very Long-Range.)

Late in 1943 the Red Air Force called for a fighter able to deal with the latest generation of German tanks. Yakovlev responded with the Yak-9T. (T stands for *Tankovoy* or Tank.) The Yak-9T was a derivative of the Yak-9M with a 37-mm NS-37 cannon mounted in place of the 20-mm ShVAK cannon. The final Yakovlev fighter variant to use the well-tried M-105 engine was the Yak-9L, which had the supercharged M-105PD of 1,050 hp at 20,997 feet (6,400 m). (L stands for *Lyogkii* or Light.)

The next model, the Yak-9U, was powered by the 1,600-hp Klimov VK-107A engine. (U stands for *Ulutshennyi* or Improved.) The Yak-9U was basically the same aircraft as its predecessors, but was a stronger machine, being of all-metal stressed-skin construction; it began to enter service in the autumn of 1944, and was the last major variant of the Yakovlev piston-engined fighter line. The last Yak-9 variant was the Yak-9P. (P stands for *Perekhvatchik* or Interceptor.) This differed from the Yak-9U only in having a transparent cover for the direction-finding loop behind the cockpit.

Yakovlev Yak-1

The aircraft illustrated right is finished in the alternative summer camouflage of dark green and dark brown upper surfaces, with light grey under surfaces. National insignia are the usual ones

Type single-seat fighter and fighter-bomber

Engine one Klimov VK-105*PA* twelve-cylinder liquid-cooled inline, 1,100 hp at take-off

Armament one 20-mm ShVAK cannon with 120 rounds firing through the propeller shaft and two 7.62-mm ShKAS machine-guns with 375 rounds per gun in the nose, plus six 82-mm RS 82 rockets

Maximum speeds 364 mph at 16,404 feet (586 km/h at 5,000 m); 310 mph (500 km/h) at sea level

Cruising speed 149 mph at 9,842 feet (240 km/h at 3,000 m)

Initial climb rate unknown

Climb 4 minutes 30 seconds to 16,404 feet (5,000 m)

Service ceiling 32,808 feet (10,000 m)

Range 435 miles at 323 mph (700 km at 520 km/h)

Weights 5,137 lbs (2,330 kg) empty; 6,217 lbs (2,820 kg) loaded

Span 32 feet 9¾ inches (10.00 m)

Length 27 feet 9¾ inches (8.48 m)

Height 8 feet 8 inches (2.64 m)

Wing area 184.5 square feet (17.14 m²)

Left: Yakolev Yak-9DD long-range fighters on an airfield in Yugoslavia. Early in the war, emphasis on high performance at short ranges was all important for the Russians, but as the war turned against Germany and the Red Army advanced rapidly, the Red Air Force found itself increasingly in need of longer-ranged tactical aircraft

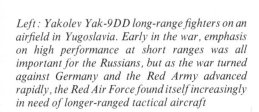

Yakovlev Yak-9D

The aircraft illustrated has standard markings. For details see the Yak-1

Type single-seat escort fighter

Engine one Klimov VK-105*PF* twelve-cylinder liquid-cooled inline, 1,210 hp at take-off and 1,180 hp at 8,858 feet (2,700 m)

Armament one 20-mm MPSh cannon with 120 rounds firing through the propeller shaft and one 12.7-mm Beresin UBS machine-gun with 120 rounds in the nose

Maximum speeds 373 mph at 11,483 feet (600 km/h at 3,500 m); 336 mph (540 km/h) at sea level

Cruising speed 292 mph (470 km/h)

Initial climb rate unknown

Climb 4 minutes 54 seconds to 16,404 feet (5,000 m)

Service ceiling 32,808 feet (10,000 m)

Range 808 miles (1,300 km)

Weights 6,052 lbs (2,745 kg) empty; 6,867 lbs (3,115 kg) loaded

Span 32 feet 9¾ inches (10.00 m)

Length 27 feet 11½ inches (8.52 m)

Height 9 feet 10 inches (3.00 m)

Wing area 186.75 square feet (17.35 m²)

Boeing B-17 Flying Fortress

The Boeing B-17 Flying Fortress, which served with the US air forces throughout the World War II period, is perhaps the most celebrated aircraft operated by the United States during the war. Its development during the early 1930s marked the American enthusiasm for pinpoint heavy bombing at a time when most European bomber designs were in the medium bomber category.

The B-17 was designed in 1934 in response to a requirement issued in May by the US Army Air Corps for a multi-engined bomber capable of delivering at least 2,000 lbs (907 kg) of bombs over a minimum range of 1,020 miles at a speed of 200 mph (1,642 km at 322 km/h) or above. As the company was also working on another, larger bomber, the Model 294 or XB-15, the decision to compete for the new aircraft was a risky one. Design and construction work proceeded rapidly, and the prototype Model 299, as the new aircraft was designated by Boeing, first flew in July 1935. This prototype is sometimes erroneously referred to as the XB-17. Power was provided by four 750-hp Pratt & Whitney R-1690 Hornet radials, the defensive armament consisted of five single 0.30-inch (7.7-mm) machine-guns, and a bomb-load of 4,800 lbs (2,177 kg) could be carried. Although the prototype was destroyed in an accident, its performance had been so encouraging that the USAAC ordered a pre-production batch of 14 YB-17s, later redesignated Y1B-17s. The first of these was delivered in December 1936, with 930-hp Wright GR-1820 radials. The first 13 Y1B-17s were finished to this standard, whilst the 14th was completed as the sole Y1B-17A, with turbo-superchargers for its engines. These boosted maximum speed to 311 mph (501 km/h) and service ceiling to over 30,000 feet (9,144 m), and were incorporated on all subsequent B-17 models.

At the end of their trials the Y1B-17s were redesignated B-17s and the Y1B-17A the B-17A. As the US Navy objected to an aircraft that would pre-empt its right to defend America's shores, plans for large-scale procurement of the B-17 by the USAAC had to be cut back. In 1938 the first true production model, the B-17B with a larger rudder, larger flaps and a modified nose, was ordered. Some 39 B-17Bs were built. Production of the B-17C, 38 of which were ordered, began in 1939. This model had a greater take-off weight, improved engines and better armament. The B-17C was followed by 42 B-17Ds in 1941. The B-17D differed only slightly from its predecessor and was the first Flying Fortress variant to enter combat with the USAAF, suffering heavy losses on the ground in the Japanese strikes on Hawaii and the Philippine islands in December 1941.

The next model to enter service was the B-17E, a much modified type incorporating lessons learned in combat by Royal Air Force crews. In 1941 the RAF had received ten B-17Cs, which it renamed Fortress I, and combat experience had shown that the defensive armament of one 0.30-inch (7.7-mm) and six 0.50-inch (12.7-mm) machine-guns was totally inadequate. The first of the 512 B-17Es built was delivered to the USAAF in October 1941, and featured a completely revised defensive armament and a new set of vertical tail surfaces, with much greater area to help control at high altitudes. The armament of this new model now included twin 0.50-inch (12.7-mm) turrets in the tail, dorsal and ventral positions, together with two 0.50-inch waist guns and two 0.30-inch (7.7-mm) nose guns. The bomb-load, which had been 10,496 lbs (4,761 kg) in the B-17C, was increased to 17,600 lbs (7,983 kg) for short ranges. Surprisingly, although the loaded weight had risen 6,350 lbs to 53,000 lbs (2,880 kg to 24,041 kg) and the powerplants were still the 1,200-hp Wright R-1820-65 radials of the B-17C, the B-17E attained a maximum speed of 317 mph at 25,000 feet (510 km/h at 7,620 m), compared with the earlier model's 291 mph (468 km/h) at the same altitude. The B-17E became operational in the Pacific theatre in December 1941, and in the European theatre in July 1941. It was used in the US Eighth Air Force's first raid in Europe on 17 August 1942.

In May 1942, meanwhile, there had appeared the B-17F, based on the combat lessons of the B-17Ds operating in the Pacific in the months immediately after Japan's strike on Pearl Harbor. A new one-piece perspex nose was introduced, and improved R-1820-97 engines, together with a strengthened undercarriage, allowed take-off weight to increase from 54,000 lbs to 65,000 lbs (24,494 kg to 29,484 kg) and finally to 72,000 lbs (32,659 kg). Further additions were made later during production and by front-line units, usually to the amount of armour carried, the defensive armament, and to the fuel tankage in the wings. Finally, the reintroduction of underwing racks allowed a maximum of 20,800 lbs (9,435 kg) of bombs to be carried over very short ranges. Production of the B-17F totalled 3,405 aircraft. Despite these modifications, however, the B-17F still suffered very heavy losses in combat over Europe, especially to German fighters which had discovered that the Flying Fortress's weak spot was the nose.

In an effort to produce a counter to the German head-on attacks prompted by the B-17's poor nose armament, Boeing developed the B-17G, which first flew in July 1943. This model featured a twin 0.50-inch (12.7-mm) machine-gun chin turret, also used on the last B-17Fs, and later production models had improved turbosuperchargers which raised the service ceiling 5,000 feet to 35,000 feet (1,524 m to 10,668 m). Many other modifications were also carried out by front-line units. Production of the B-17G, the last variant of the basic B-17, totalled 8,680 aircraft.

Total production of the B-17 reached 12,731 aircraft, and the Flying Fortress served with distinction as the USAAF's standard daylight heavy bomber over Europe and in South-East Asia and the South-West Pacific. By 1946, however, only a few hundred were left in service. The main failing of the B-17 was that it was designed as a medium bomber, and although later in the war it could carry very heavy bombloads, it was only at the expense of range. Another fault was that the type tended to ignite all too easily when hit by enemy gunfire.

Below: B-17G bombers of the 533rd Bombardment Squadron, 381st Bombardment Group, 1st Combat Wing, 1st Air Division, US 8th Army Air Force, set off on a mission over occupied Europe from their base in Great Britain

Boeing B-17G Flying Fortress

The aircraft illustrated is machine D of the 401st
Bombardment Squadron (code-letters LL), of the
91st Bombardment Group (marking a black A in a
white triangle on the fin), of the 1st Combat Wing
of the 8th Air Force's 1st Air Division. The spacing
of the individual letter and the squadron letters
on each side of the fuselage national insignia show
that the period should be before late July 1943, and
the group marking that it is after June 1943. This
particular aircraft was built by Douglas at Long
Beach in California, and was written off after a
crash landing at Cambridge on 21 December 1943.
Camouflage is the standard olive drab upper
surfaces and light grey under surfaces. National
insignia, on top of the port wing, under the
starboard wing, and on each side of the fuselage,
are normal for the period after 17 September 1943,
when the blue outline, in place of the earlier red
one, was adopted for the white bar

Type ten-seat heavy bomber

Engines four Wright R-1820-97 Cyclone 9 nine-
cylinder air-cooled radials, each rated at 1,200 hp
at take-off and 1,000 hp at 25,000 feet (7,620 m)

Armament defensive: two flexible 0.50-inch
(12.7-mm) Browning M2 machine-guns in the chin
turret, two flexible 0.50-inch Browning M2
machine-guns in the ventral turret, two flexible
0.50-inch Browning M2 machine-guns in the dorsal
turret, two flexible 0.50-inch Browning M2
machine-guns in the tail turret, and four 0.50-inch
Browning M2 machine-guns, one in each of the
two nose cheek positions and two waist positions
offensive: up to 17,600 lbs of bombs (7,983 kg)

Maximum speed 287 mph (462 km/h) at 25,000 feet
(7,620 m) with normal bomb-load

Cruising speed 160 mph (258 km/h) at 25,000 feet
(7,620 m) with 4,000-lb (1,814-kg) bomb load

Climb 37 minutes to 20,000 feet (6.096 m)

Service ceiling 35,600 feet (10,851 m)

Range 1,800 miles (2,897 km) at 160 mph (258 km/h)
with 4,000-lb (1,814-kg) bomb-load; 3,400 miles
(5,472 km) without war load

Weights 36,135 lbs (16,391 kg) empty; 55,000 lbs
(24,948 kg) loaded; 65,500 lbs (28,421 kg) gross

Span 103 feet 9½ inches (31.64 m)

Length 74 feet 9 inches (22.78 m)

Height 19 feet 1 inch (5.82 m)

Wing area 1,420 square feet (131.92 m²)

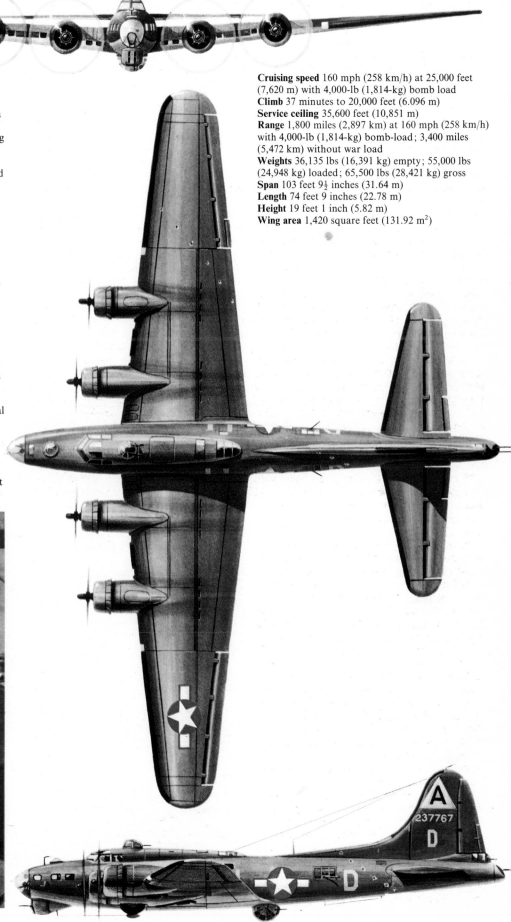

Boeing B-29 Superfortress

If for no other reason, the Boeing B-29 Superfortress will always be remembered as the only aircraft to have used atomic weapons in combat, when Hiroshima and Nagasaki were bombed in August 1945 in the final stages of the war with Japan. The B-29 was also an excellent aircraft, with many advanced features, including remote-control gun turrets and large-scale pressurization of the crew compartments.

US interest in a bomber able to carry a worthwhile load over considerable ranges at high speeds reached back to such designs as the Boeing XB-15 of 1933. Although official interest in such a weapon flagged during the second half of the decade, Boeing continued basic design work on a number of similar projects, culminating in the Model 341, which was estimated to be able to deliver 2,240 lbs (1,016 kg) of bombs over a range of 7,000 miles (11,266 km) at a speed in excess of 400 mph (644 km/h). With the outbreak of World War II in Europe, however, and the possibility of US involvement, the US Army Air Corps once again developed an interest in any weapon that could enable the United States to bomb its enemies over very long ranges. Thus in February 1940 a requirement for a 'Hemisphere Defense Weapon' was issued. This called for a bomber able to deliver 2,000 lbs (907 kg) of bombs over 5,333 miles (8,583 km) at a speed of 400 mph (644 km/h). The bomber also had to have self-sealing fuel tanks, considerable armour protection, a heavy defensive armament, and the ability to carry 16,000 lbs (7,257 kg) of bombs.

Boeing developed its Model 341 design into the Model 345, which met all the requirements but that for speed. Two prototypes, to be called XB-29, were ordered in August 1940. The mock-up was approved in April 1941, and prototype construction began. With the constant deterioration of the world situation in late 1941 and early 1942, the B-29 programme was given top priority in the spring of 1942.

The first XB-29 made its maiden flight in September 1942, preceded by orders for a batch of 14 pre-production YB-29s and more than 1,500 production aircraft. The design was extremely clean, with no steps in the nose outline, and the engine nacelles received special attention. Each of the Wright R-3350 radials used had two turbo-superchargers. The first prototype had no defensive armament, but the second XB-29 was fitted with the system that was intended for production models. This consisted of remote-control Sperry turrets sighted with periscopes. The turrets on production models were also intended to be retractable. The third XB-29 prototype had a system of General Electric turrets controlled from small astrodome bubbles near each turret. This latter system was adopted for production aircraft.

Delivery of the 14 pre-production YB-29s began in June 1943, and units began to work up with the new bomber. Production deliveries began in the autumn of 1943. At the end of the year it was decided not to use B-29s against targets in Europe, but concentrate instead on Japanese targets, in the bombing of which the B-29's great range would be most useful. Pre-production YB-29 aircraft had R-3350-21 radials, but production B-29s had R-3350-23, 23A, or 41 radials, and were allowed to operate at a gross weight of 138,000 lbs (62,595 kg), compared with the 120,000 lbs (54,432 kg) of the XB-29. Production of the B-29 reached 2,527 before the next model, the B-29A, was introduced. This had a wing of 12 inches (30.5 cm) greater span, R-3350-57 or 59 radials, reduced fuel tankage, and a four-gun, instead of a two-gun, front dorsal turret. This turret had also been introduced on the last B-29s, which had dispensed with the 20-mm cannon in the tail turret. In all, 1,119 B-29A bombers were built before production ceased in May 1946.

The first B-29 operation took place in June 1944, and thereafter the tempo of B-29 operations increased rapidly from bases in India and China, and then from the Marianas after their capture. After a relative lack of success with high-explosive bombs, operations with incendiary bombs proved far more successful, devastating vast areas of Japanese cities. With the decline in Japanese airpower, it proved possible to strip all defensive armament and its ancillary equipment, except the tail turret, from the B-29s. This enabled a greater offensive load to be carried. So successful did this field modification prove that a production equivalent, the B-29B, was developed; 311 such aircraft were built.

The last wartime variant of the B-29 was the F-13A, a photographic-reconnaissance aircraft needed to assess the results of B-29 raids on Japan. Additional fuel was carried in the bombbay. Variants that achieved only prototype form or project status were the XB-39, with four Allison V-3420 inline engines; the XB-44, with four Pratt & Whitney R-4360 radials, which became the prototype of the B-50 series; and the B-29C, which was to have had improved engines. Development also continued after the war, with cargo, inflight refuelling, air-sea rescue, drone, and reconnaissance variants. By the end of hostilities some 2,000 B-29 models had been delivered to the USAAF. A further 5,000 were cancelled, but production reached a total of 3,960 before ceasing in May 1946.

The B-29 was one of the outstanding aircraft of the war, and played an all-important part in hastening the defeat of Japan. It was an extremely sound, clean design, with good performance and load-carrying capabilities, and excellent defensive armament so long as it was needed.

Below: B-29 Superfortress heavy bombers unload their bombs over a Japanese target. The Superfortress bore the brunt of the long-range US air offensive against Japan, and proved most devastating when using incendiary bombs dropped in clusters at low altitude. Japanese cities, built largely of wood, had little or no defence against such attacks

Boeing B-29 Superfortress

The aircraft illustrated is a machine of the 499th Bombardment Group of the US 20th Air Force. The group markings were a black V above an outlined black square, later changed to a black V alone. The finish of the aircraft is natural metal, camouflage being deemed unnecessary after the virtual elimination of the main strength of the Japanese fighter arm. The natural metal finish also improved the maximum speed. National insignia are the normal ones

Type ten-seat heavy bomber
Engines four Wright R-3350-57 Cyclone eighteen-cylinder air-cooled radials, each rated at 2,200 hp at take-off
Armament defensive: four 0.50-inch (12.7-mm) Browning machine-guns in the front upper turret, two 0.50-inch Browning machine-guns in the rear upper turret, two 0.50-inch Browning machine-guns in the front lower turret, two 0.50-inch Browning machine-guns in the rear lower turret, and two 0.50-inch Browning machine-guns and a 20-mm M2 Type B cannon in the tail turret
offensive: up to 20,000 lbs (9,072 kg) of bombs
Maximum speed 358 mph at 25,000 feet (576 km/h at 7,620 m)
Cruising speed 230 mph (370 km/h)
Climb 38 minutes to 20,000 feet (6,096 m)
Service ceiling 31,850 feet (9,708 m)
Range 3,250 miles (5,231 km)
Weights 70,140 lbs (31,815 kg) empty; 133,500 lbs (60,555 kg) loaded; 138,000 lbs (62,596 kg) gross
Span 142 feet 3 inches (43.36 m)
Length 99 feet (30.18 m)
Height 29 feet 7 inches (9.02 m)
Wing area 1,736 square feet (161.28 m²)

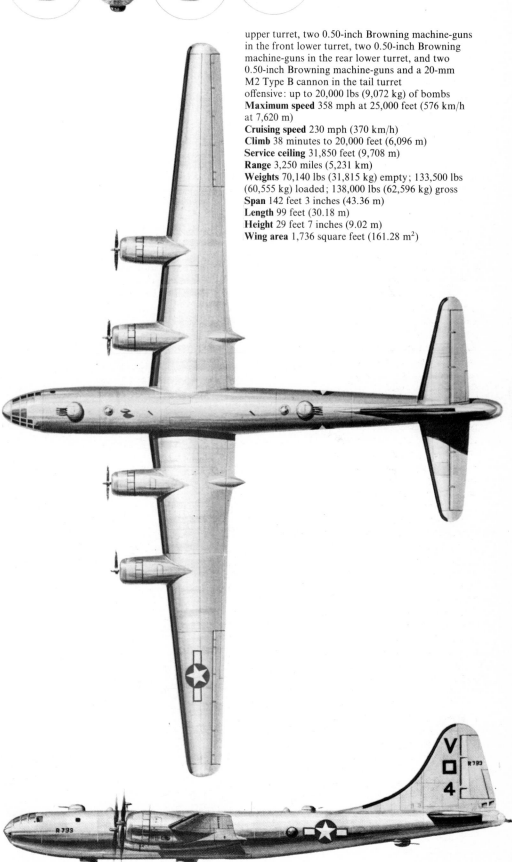

Consolidated B-24 Liberator

Although not as famous as its companion heavy bomber, the Boeing B-17 Flying Fortress, the Consolidated B-24 Liberator was in many respects a superior aircraft. It could not carry the bomb-load of the Flying Fortress, but it did have distinct aerodynamic advantages: a tricycle undercarriage and wings of very high aspect ratio. The first made take-off and landings considerably easier, and the second produced high lift for the minimum drag, resulting in good overall performance. The Liberator also possessed an auto-pilot, and although this proved temperamental at times, it allowed the Liberator to be used to the full advantage of its long range as a maritime-reconnaissance bomber.

The flying surfaces that were the basis of the Liberator's design had first appeared on the Consolidated P4Y flying-boat, and with the US Army Air Corps' interest in long-range heavy bombers with excellent performance at altitude, Consolidated engineers were able to produce a mock-up and plans for a high-performance bomber by combining the wings and tail surfaces of the P4Y with a new fuselage by January 1939. The USAAC insisted on several alterations during February, but in March the first prototype of what was to become the B-24 was ordered.

Prototype construction advanced quickly and smoothly, and the XB-24 first flew in December 1939. This could carry up to 8,000 lbs (3,629 kg) bombs in its capacious fuselage, and had an armament of six hand-held 0.30-inch (7.7-mm) Browning machine-guns. As prototype construction was getting under way, the USAAC had ordered seven YB-24 pre-production aircraft for service evaluation, and these aircraft were delivered during 1941. The only major differences between the two models was the higher take-off weight and the provision of de-icing equipment on the wings and tail for the YB-24s.

During 1940 the USAAC also ordered its first production Liberators under the designation B-24A. Only nine of this model were delivered, as an improved model was being developed. This featured heavier armament and superior engines. The latter had been tested on the XB-24, which had been redisgnated XB-24B when the original Pratt & Whitney R-1830-33 Twin Wasps, with mechanically-driven super-

chargers, had been replaced by R-1830-41 units, with exhaust-driven turbo-superchargers. At the same time the engine oil-coolers had been relocated on each side of the engine from positions under each power unit, giving the Liberators' engine nacelles their distinctive elliptical shape when viewed from the front. With these modifications a total of nine production aircraft appeared in 1941 as B-24C Liberators.

Next into service was the first large-scale production version, the B-24D. This had take-off weight increased to 56,000 lbs (25,401 kg), and was powered by R-1830-43 engines, giving the model a top speed of 303 mph at 25,000 feet (487 km/h at 7,620 m) compared with the B-24A's 292 mph at 15,000 feet (469 km/h at 4,572 m). Armament was by now 10 0.50-inch (12.7-mm) machine-guns, and the bomb-load 8,800 lbs (3,991 kg) compared with the B-24A's 4,000 lbs (1,814 kg). Range was also increased by 650 miles (1,046 km) to 2,850 miles (4,586 km). Production of the B-25D began late in 1940, and eventually 2,738 were produced.

The Liberator was about to be declared operational when Japan attacked Pearl Harbor in December 1941. The United States immediately held back delivery of some Liberators ordered by Great Britain, and the type was pressed into service as quickly as possible. The first operational sortie by a B-24 was flown in January 1942 from Java – British Liberators, however, had already flown operationally during 1941. By the middle of 1942 the B-24 was in operation with USAAF units in the Pacific, Alaska, India and the Middle East. During this year the decision was made to concentrate Liberator activities on the Pacific, where their long range, autopilot capability and reliability was to prove invaluable. The type did continue in service elsewhere, however, notably in Europe.

The B-24E was basically the same as the B-24D, but had improved propellers. It was built by Consolidated, Douglas and Ford. The next model, the B-24G, was at first built by North American. The initial 25 were to all intents and purposes identical with the B-24D, but subsequent examples of the 430 built had a nose turret with two 0.50-inch (12.7-mm) machine-guns in a redesigned fuselage. This modification had

been proved essential by combat over Europe, where German fighters had found that the most vulnerable point on both the Liberator and the Flying Fortress was the nose, attacked head-on.

The B-24H was similar to the B-24G, but was built by Douglas, Ford and Consolidated; deliveries totalled 3,100 aircraft. The B-24J was again almost identical with the B-24G and B-24H, and was the most numerous B-24 type – production reached 6,678 aircraft. In place of the Consolidated or Emerson nose-turret used on the two earlier marks, the B-24J introduced a Motor Products turret, and an improved auto-pilot and bombsight were fitted. In fact many B-24G and B-24H aircraft retrofitted with these items were redesignated B-24J. The B-24L featured a Consolidated tail position with two manually-operated 0.50-inch (12.7-mm) machine-guns, and the B-24M had a Motor Products tail turret with two 0.50-inch (12.7-mm) guns. Production of these two models totalled 1,667 and 2,593 respectively. These were the last production Liberator bomber variants, although several other experimental models had been produced.

The Liberator was also used by the US Navy in two patrol-bomber models and three transport models. The bomber variants were the PB4Y-1, basically similar to the B-24D, with an armament of eight 0.50-inch machine guns and a bomb-load of 8,000 lbs (3,628 kg); and the PB4Y-2 Privateer, with a single tail fin and rudder assembly, and an increased armament.

Thus although the Liberator's offensive load was inferior to Allied heavy bombers, this medium bomber served the US Army Air Forces and the US Navy well in a variety of guises, its principal advantages being its excellent range, high speed, and admirable performance at altitude. Production of the Liberator, which also served extensively with the Royal Air Force, exceeded 18,000 making it the most numerous US aircraft of World War II.

Below: A Consolidated B-24J Liberator of the 565th Bombardment Squadron, 389th Bombardment Group, 2nd Combat Wing, 2nd Air Division, US 8th Army Air Force. The high-set wings and elliptical nacelles are shown to advantage

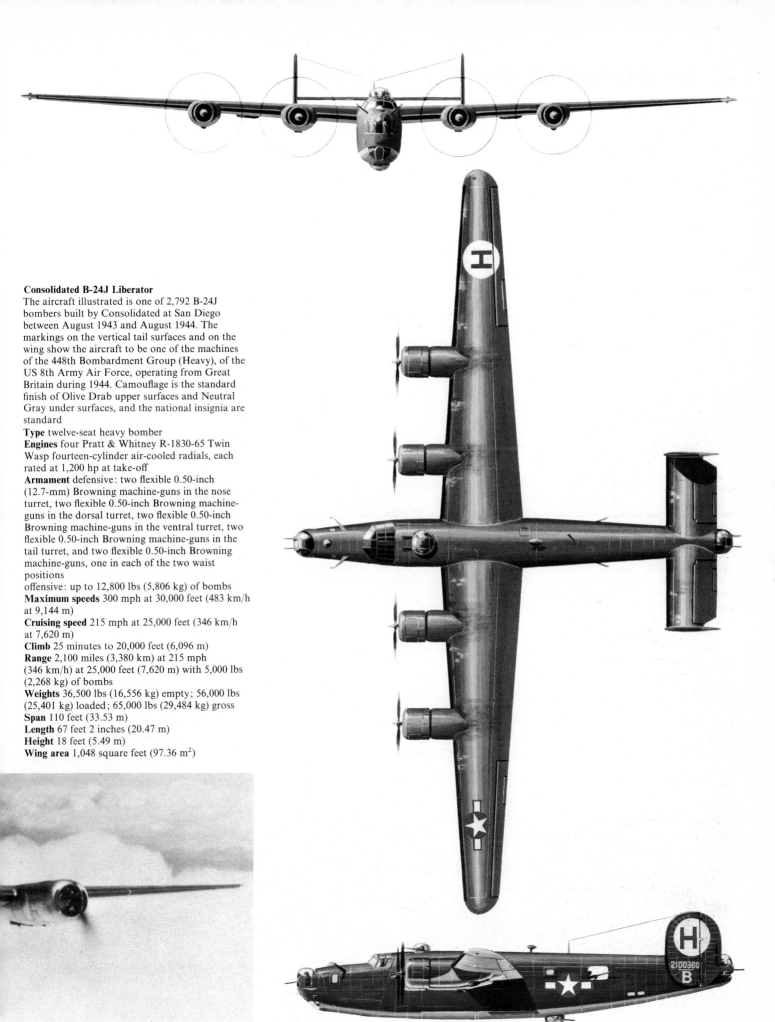

Consolidated B-24J Liberator
The aircraft illustrated is one of 2,792 B-24J bombers built by Consolidated at San Diego between August 1943 and August 1944. The markings on the vertical tail surfaces and on the wing show the aircraft to be one of the machines of the 448th Bombardment Group (Heavy), of the US 8th Army Air Force, operating from Great Britain during 1944. Camouflage is the standard finish of Olive Drab upper surfaces and Neutral Gray under surfaces, and the national insignia are standard

Type twelve-seat heavy bomber
Engines four Pratt & Whitney R-1830-65 Twin Wasp fourteen-cylinder air-cooled radials, each rated at 1,200 hp at take-off
Armament defensive: two flexible 0.50-inch (12.7-mm) Browning machine-guns in the nose turret, two flexible 0.50-inch Browning machine-guns in the dorsal turret, two flexible 0.50-inch Browning machine-guns in the ventral turret, two flexible 0.50-inch Browning machine-guns in the tail turret, and two flexible 0.50-inch Browning machine-guns, one in each of the two waist positions
offensive: up to 12,800 lbs (5,806 kg) of bombs
Maximum speeds 300 mph at 30,000 feet (483 km/h at 9,144 m)
Cruising speed 215 mph at 25,000 feet (346 km/h at 7,620 m)
Climb 25 minutes to 20,000 feet (6,096 m)
Range 2,100 miles (3,380 km) at 215 mph (346 km/h) at 25,000 feet (7,620 m) with 5,000 lbs (2,268 kg) of bombs
Weights 36,500 lbs (16,556 kg) empty; 56,000 lbs (25,401 kg) loaded; 65,000 lbs (29,484 kg) gross
Span 110 feet (33.53 m)
Length 67 feet 2 inches (20.47 m)
Height 18 feet (5.49 m)
Wing area 1,048 square feet (97.36 m²)

Consolidated PBY Catalina

The Consolidated PBY flying-boat, named Catalina by the Royal Air Force, was one of the best aircraft of its type during World War II together with the British Short Sunderland and the Japanese Kawanishi H8K 'Emily'. But being smaller and therefore lighter than the other two types, the PBY was also capable of adaptation into an amphibian, and as such is still in service today with several operators, and is bidding fair to rival the ubiquitous Douglas DC-3 Dakota for longevity.

The origins of the Catalina lay in a requirement issued by the US Navy during 1933 for a replacement for its first generation of monoplane and sesquiplane flying-boats. The new boats were to make the fullest use of the latest technological advances, and to be possessed of a high performance. Both Consolidated and Douglas built prototypes, but only the Consolidated type entered widespread service.

Originally designated XP3Y-1, and designed by Isaac M Laddon (later the chief designer of the B-24 Liberator bomber), the new flying boat was ordered in October 1933 and first flew in March 1935. It was a handsome aircraft, with a parasol wing mounted on a pylon above the fuselage, braced by four struts, and the unusual feature of retractable floats at the wingtips. This saved a considerable amount of drag, with benefits to the overall performance. Power was provided by a pair of Pratt & Whitney R-1830-58 Twin Wasp radials of 825 hp each, and armament consisted of four flexible 0.30-inch (7.7-mm) Browning machine-guns and up to 2,000 lbs (907 kg) of bombs.

Prototype flight trials were so encouraging that the type was ordered into production in June 1935 as the PBY-1. As the new production line was being readied, the XP3Y-1 was modified to an improved standard as the XPBY-1, with

a less angular fin and rudder and the more powerful R-1830-64 engines of 900 hp each. The revised prototype flew in May 1936, and was handed over to the navy in October, at about the same time as production PBY-1s began to enter service. PBY-1 production totalled 60 aircraft; it was replaced by the PBY-2 (50 built), PBY-3 (66 built), and PBY-4 (33 built) which were constructed during 1937 and 1938. The later models were similar to the PBY-1 in all respects except the powerplant – 1,000-hp R-1830-66 radials in the PBY-3 and 1,050-hp R-1830-72 radials in the PBY-4.

The PBY-5 was powered by a pair of 1,200-hp R-1830-92 radials and had a revised shape to the vertical tail surfaces. More immediately apparent, however, was the replacement of the sliding hatches for the waist guns by prominent blisters on each side of the hull midway between the wings and the tailplane. These blisters had been pioneered on the PBY-4, all but one of which had had the new positions. Deliveries of the PBY-5 began in September 1940.

Before production of the PBY-5 was complete, Consolidated had unveiled their latest version of the series, which was an amphibious model with a retractable tricycle undercarriage, the main members pulling up to positions on the sides of the hull, and the nose-wheel up into a compartment in the under surface of the bows. The whole arrangement was very neat, and although it reduced performance slightly, this was more than counterbalanced by the versatility it bestowed on the type. The US Navy immediately converted the last of its orders for the PBY-5 to the PBY-5A, as the new type was designated, and placed orders for another 134 PBY-5A boats in November 1940, only three days after the first flight of the prototype.

Further orders for the type, now named

Catalina in agreement with the British, were placed in 1941 and 1942: 586 PBY-5s, 627 PBY-5As, and 225 PBY-5Bs, the last for transference to Great Britain under Lend-Lease. By this time the offensive armament of the type had been increased from the 2,000-lb (907-kg) bombload of the PBY-1 to 4,000 lb (1,814 kg) of bombs, depth-charges or torpedoes on the PBY-5A, with increases in the defensive armament to two 0.50- (12.7-mm) and three 0.30-inch (7.7-mm) machine-guns.

Production was also undertaken in Canada by Vickers and Boeing. The former built 230 Catalinas as OA-10A amphibians for the USAAF, and 149 as Cansos for the Royal Canadian Air Force. Boeing built 362 as Catalinas and Cansos, the latter being the RCAF designation for the aircraft. In the United States, meanwhile, the Naval Aircraft Factory had undertaken an improvement programme for the type, and this in 1941 led to the introduction of the PBN-1 Nomad. This had an improved hull and float design, and a taller fin and rudder assembly. A 0.50-inch (12.7-mm) machine-gun replaced the 0.30-inch (7.7-mm) weapon in the bows, and deliveries, including 138 for Russia, began in February 1943. This model was also built by Consolidated as the PBY-6A with two 0.50-inch (12.7-mm) guns in the bows and search radar mounted in a radome over the cockpit.

Contracts for Catalina production were cancelled at the end of the war in Europe, after 3,290 examples had been built in Canada and the United States. This production alone made the Catalina the most numerous flying-boat type of all time, and many more were built under licence in Russia. The Catalina proved an admirable type, with excellent range characteristics, good cruise, and a powerful offensive armament.

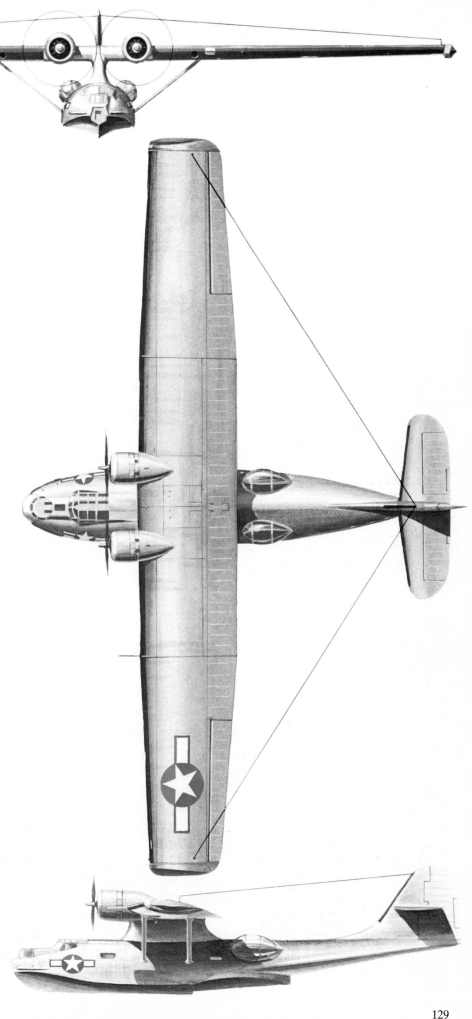

Consolidated PBY-5 Catalina
The aircraft illustrated is finished in an overall
light grey colour scheme. Note the positioning of
the national insignia on the bows rather than
behind the wings – a feature common to all US
Navy patrol flying-boats
Type seven- to nine-seat patrol-bomber flying boat
Engines two Pratt & Whitney R-1830-92 Twin
Wasp fourteen-cylinder air-cooled radials, 1,200 hp
each at take-off
Armament defensive: two flexible 0.50-inch
(12.7-mm) Browning machine-guns, one in each
of the two waist positions, one flexible 0.30-inch
(7.7-mm) Browning machine-gun in the bow turret,
and one flexible 0.30-inch Browning machine-gun
in the ventral tunnel
offensive: up to 4,000 lbs (1,814 kg) of bombs, two
torpedoes or four 325-lb (147-kg) depth charges
Maximum speed 189 mph at 7,000 feet (304 km/h
at 2,134 m)
Cruising speed 115 mph (185 km/h)
Initial climb rate 690 fpm (210 m/minute)
Climb unknown
Service ceiling 18,100 feet (5,517 m)
Range 2,990 miles (4,812 km)
Weights 17,526 lbs (7,950 kg) empty; 26,200 lbs
(11,884 kg) loaded; 34,000 lbs (15,422 kg) gross
Span 104 feet (31.70 m)
Length 63 feet 10 inches (19.46 m)
Height 20 feet 2 inches (6.15 m)

*Below: A Naval Air Factory PBN-1 Nomad
patrol flying-boat. This revised version of the
Catalina featured improved armament and height-
ened vertical tail surfaces. An equivalent version,
designated PBY-6A, was built by Consolidated.
This was an amphibious model, and also had sea
search radar mounted in a small radome above the
cockpit*

Grumman TBF Avenger

Introduced into combat during the Battle of Midway in June 1942, just as the United States' tide of defeat was beginning to turn, the Grumman TBF Avenger had a disastrous initial career. But once its crews had learned the best way in which to use their aircraft, the Avenger was destined to become, with the Curtiss SB2C Helldiver, one of the major scourges of Japanese ships, both naval and mercantile. The Avenger was also used with great success by several of the United States' allies, and served with the US Navy itself in a variety of roles up to 1954.

The Avenger was designed early in 1941 in answer to a navy requirement for a replacement for its Douglas TBD Devastator torpedo-bomber. Although the company had never built such a type before, the designers set to work with a will, basing their work on the F4F Wildcat fighter: a tubby fuselage, mid-mounted wings and angular flying surfaces. Two prototype XTBF-1s were ordered in April 1940, and construction soon began. The offensive load of one torpedo or 2,000 lbs (907 kg) of bombs could be carried in the capacious internal bomb-bay, and a defensive armament of one fixed forward-firing 0.50-inch (12.7-mm) machine-gun on the engine cowling, one flexible 0.50-inch gun in a powered dorsal turret, and one flexible 0.30-inch (7.7-mm) gun in a ventral position was incorporated.

The navy had already placed orders for 286 production aircraft some eight months before the first prototype flew in August 1941, and the TBF was accepted for service in December 1941. The first production aircraft reached the navy in January of the following year, and units began to work up on the new torpedo-bomber as quickly as possible. Despite the disaster of its first air combat, in which five of the six TBF-1s despatched were shot down, orders for the type grew, with Grumman unable to match production with demand. The Eastern Aircraft Division of the General Motors Corporation was therefore asked to undertake production of the Avenger, as well as continuing production of the other Grumman type it was building, the Wildcat fighter. Eastern began to deliver Avengers, with the designation TBM-1, in November 1942, eight months after orders had been placed. Grumman also continued production until early in 1944, in that time building 1,525 TBF-1s and 764 TBF-1Cs, the latter having two fixed 0.50-inch guns in the wings in place of the initial single gun in the engine cowling. Eastern built 550 TBM-1s and 2,332 TBM-1Cs to a similar specification. Other versions of the basic TBF-1 mark were the TBF-1D with radar, the TBF-1CP with special cameras as a reconnaissance aircraft, the TBF-1E with radar, and the TBF-1L with a small searchlight in the bomb-bay; Eastern built similar models. The Royal Navy accepted 395 Avengers of the TBF-1B type under the designations first of Tarpon and then of Avenger I, and then 334 TBM-1Cs as Avenger IIs.

The last Avenger models built by Grumman were three prototypes: one XTBF-2, with a Wright XR-2600-10 radial, and two XTBF-3s, with Wright R-2600-20 engines. The former was not persevered with, but the latter went into production in Eastern factories as the TBM-3. Eastern itself built another four prototypes as TBM-3s. Apart from their more powerful engines, delivering an additional 200 hp, the aircraft of the TBM-3 family were similar to the TBM-1 aircraft, and were built in the same sub-series, with D, P, E and L suffixes to their designations. The TBM-3H incorporated a special search radar set. The final wartime version of the Avenger was to have been the TBM-4, but only three XTBM-4 prototypes were built to test the strengthened airframe.

Total Avenger production reached 9,839, with Grumman contributing 2,293 and Eastern the other 7,546. British orders for the type amounted to 1,058 aircraft, but only 921 were delivered to the Royal Navy, a further 63 going to the Royal New Zealand Air Force. In British service the TBM-3 was designated Avenger III, the TBM-3E Avenger AS Mark 4, and the cancelled TBM-4 Avenger IV.

After the war the type gained great popularity as an anti-submarine aircraft, fitted with radar in a radome under the fuselage and with the dorsal turret deleted. As such it was supplied to several US allies. A transport version, the TBM-3R, with a capacity of seven passengers, was also produced for ferrying out personnel to aircraft-carriers at sea.

Below: An Eastern-built TBM-3, in service with the Fleet Air Arm as an Avenger III. The 0.30-inch (7.7-mm) machine-gun in the ventral 'step' came as a severe shock to many Axis fighter pilots, who took the type for an F4F or F6F

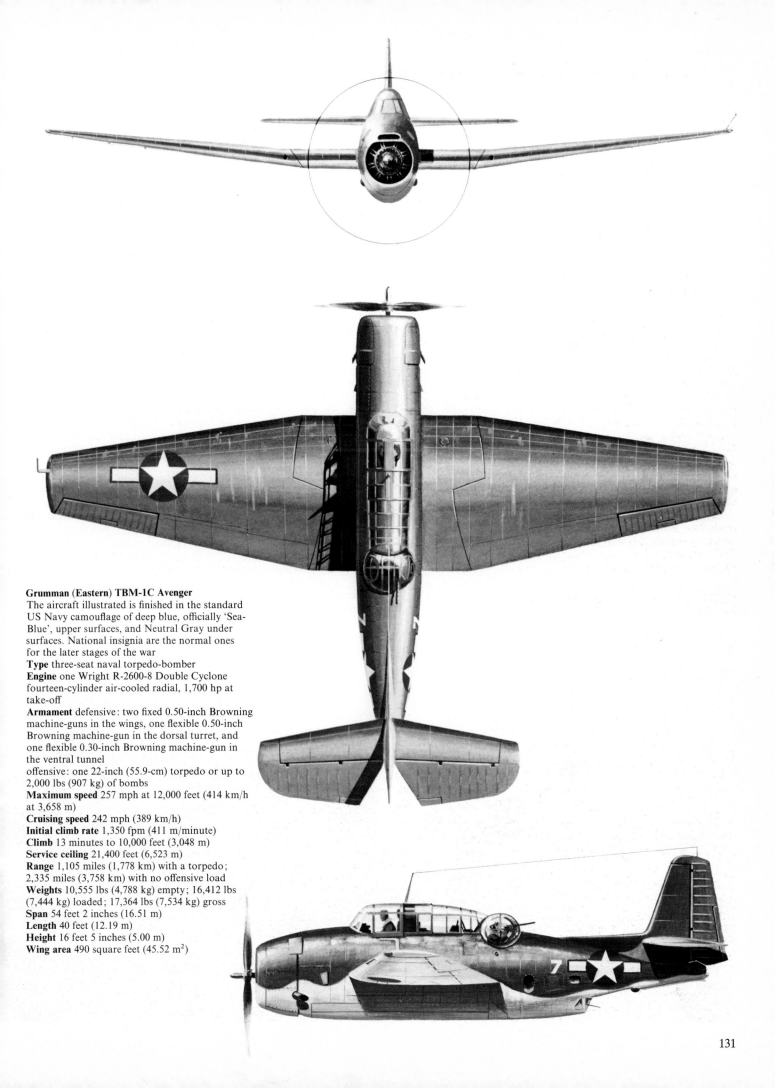

Grumman (Eastern) TBM-1C Avenger
The aircraft illustrated is finished in the standard
US Navy camouflage of deep blue, officially 'Sea-
Blue', upper surfaces, and Neutral Gray under
surfaces. National insignia are the normal ones
for the later stages of the war
Type three-seat naval torpedo-bomber
Engine one Wright R-2600-8 Double Cyclone
fourteen-cylinder air-cooled radial, 1,700 hp at
take-off
Armament defensive: two fixed 0.50-inch Browning
machine-guns in the wings, one flexible 0.50-inch
Browning machine-gun in the dorsal turret, and
one flexible 0.30-inch Browning machine-gun in
the ventral tunnel
offensive: one 22-inch (55.9-cm) torpedo or up to
2,000 lbs (907 kg) of bombs
Maximum speed 257 mph at 12,000 feet (414 km/h
at 3,658 m)
Cruising speed 242 mph (389 km/h)
Initial climb rate 1,350 fpm (411 m/minute)
Climb 13 minutes to 10,000 feet (3,048 m)
Service ceiling 21,400 feet (6,523 m)
Range 1,105 miles (1,778 km) with a torpedo;
2,335 miles (3,758 km) with no offensive load
Weights 10,555 lbs (4,788 kg) empty; 16,412 lbs
(7,444 kg) loaded; 17,364 lbs (7,534 kg) gross
Span 54 feet 2 inches (16.51 m)
Length 40 feet (12.19 m)
Height 16 feet 5 inches (5.00 m)
Wing area 490 square feet (45.52 m²)

Lockheed P-38 Lightning

The Lockheed P-38 fighter was one of the most controversial aircraft of World War II, being for the most part either greatly liked or intensely disliked by its pilots. It was built in lesser numbers than either the Republic P-47 Thunderbolt or the North American P-51 Mustang, yet served in more theatres and proved a more versatile aircraft. It was not as manoeuvrable as other single-seat fighters, nor as fast, yet earned a healthy respect from German pilots, who nicknamed the Lightning the *gabelschwanz Teufel* or 'forked-tail Devil'.

The P-38 was designed in 1937 by a team under H L Hibbard to a USAAC requirement for a high-altitude interceptor. As no single engine with the requisite power was available, the Lockheed team opted for the twin-engined format that was currently in vogue for single-seaters with European designers. (This trend produced several interesting designs, including the British Westland Whirlwind and the German Focke-Wulf 187.) The question of basic layout was neatly solved by twin booms which contained the engines, turbo-superchargers and radiators, and the main members of the tricycle undercarriage, as well as supporting the tail surfaces. An armament of one 23-mm cannon and four 0.50-inch (12.7-mm) machine-guns grouped in the nose of the central nacelle, which also housed the pilot, was intended. This was very heavy for US aircraft of the time, yet despite this, the unorthodox layout and the very high loaded weight, the USAAC ordered a prototype XP-38 in June 1937.

Construction of the XP-38 began a month later, and it first flew in January 1939. The performance of the XP-38, which was powered by a pair of 960-hp Allison V-1710-11/15 inlines, was good and 13 pre-production YP-38s were ordered, despite the total destruction of the XP-38 during flight trials and trouble with tailplane buffeting. The YP-38s were powered by Allison V-1710-27/29 engines of 1,150-hp each, and had a revised armament of one 37-mm Oldsmobile cannon, two 0.50-inch Browning and two 0.30-inch (7.7-mm) Colt machine-guns. Production contracts had been awarded in September 1939, and the first P-38, with armament restored to that of the XP-38, flew in June 1941. Only 30 P-38s were built, the rest of the first batch of 66 being finished as P-38Ds, the initial combat model. The incidence of the tailplane was altered on the latter, it having been discovered that this was principally to blame for the buffeting encountered by earlier aircraft. Production of the P-38E, with a 20-mm Hispano cannon and revised nose, totalled 210; the first was delivered in March 1942, but 99 of these became F-4 models for photographic-reconnaissance, with cameras replacing the armament in the nose. The Lightning, as all models after the D were named, was ordered by Great Britain; the order was cancelled, however, after two examples had been tested as performance without the turbo-superchargers, which were not released for export, was too low for British requirements.

Airframes built to the British order were bought by the USAAF after the cancellation of the British requirement and finished as P-38Fs, with 1,325-hp V-1710-49/53 engines. The P-38F for the USAAF had also replaced the P-38E in production early in 1942, and featured racks under the centre section for two 1,000-lb (454-kg) bombs, two 22-inch (55.9-cm) torpedoes or drop-tanks. A combat setting for the flaps was also introduced on the P-38F to give the type enhanced manoeuvrability, especially in turns. Of the 527 P-38Fs built, 20 were converted to F-4A photographic-reconnaissance aircraft by replacing the armament with cameras. The P-38F was the first model to enter combat, in August 1942, but the type was not used in substantial numbers until the Allied landings in French North Africa during November 1942.

The P-38G, which differed from the P-38F in having V-1710-51/55 engines and some equipment changes, replaced the P-38F in production during June 1942; 1,082 examples were built before production ceased in March 1943. It was G-model Lightnings that were involved in the type's most celebrated single action of the war: in April 1943 fighters of this type, operating from Henderson Field on Guadalcanal, intercepted and shot down a transport carrying the Imperial Japanese Navy's commander-in-chief, Admiral Yamamoto, over 500 miles (805 km) from their base. As with other Lightnings, photographic-reconnaissance models of the P-38G were produced.

In May 1943 the first of 601 P-38Hs entered service. This model was powered by a pair of 1,425-hp V-1710-89/91 engines, and could carry a maximum of 1,600 lbs (726 kg) on each of the two underwing pylons. When very long-range fuel tanks were carried on these pylons, the already excellent operating radius of the Lightning was extended yet further from 850 miles (1,368 km) of the P-38G. The F-5C, of which 128 were built, was the photographic-reconnaissance

model of the P-38H. In August 1943 the P-38J appeared, and in this model the external appearance of the Lightning was substantially altered for the first time. Powered by a pair of the same powerplants as its predecessor, the P-38J introduced 'chin' radiators under each engine. The improved cooling allowed the engines to develop their full power, boosting the P-38J's speed to 420 mph (676 km/h). Of the 2,970 P-38Js built, several hundred were converted to the F-5E and F-5F photographic-reconnaissance model before the P-38L appeared in June 1944. This was the most numerous P-38 model, 3,923 being built. It was powered by a pair of 1,600-hp V-1710-111/113 engines, and was the first Lightning model to carry rocket projectiles, five 5-inch (12.7-cm) weapons on 'Christmas tree' installations under each wing. Again, several hundred were converted to F-5E, F-5F and F-5G photographic-reconnaissance standard. The last P-38 model to see service, in the closing stages of the war against Japan, was the P-38M. This was a conversion of the P-38L to make a two-seat night-fighter.

Captain Richard Bong, the leading US ace with 40 kills, flew only the Lightning, so the type was clearly an excellent machine in the right hands. Yet the strength of feeling both for and against the type raged during the war, and has abated little since amongst ex-pilots and air historians. It would seem fair to assess the type as being less forgiving than most other types to inexperienced pilots, but in the right hands an excellent aircraft for the high-altitude interception role for which it was designed.

Below: A beautiful study of a Lockheed P-38H Lightning. Note the turbo-superchargers on top of each boom and the radiators on each side of the booms. Armament is one 20-mm cannon and four 0.50-inch (12.7-mm) machine-guns

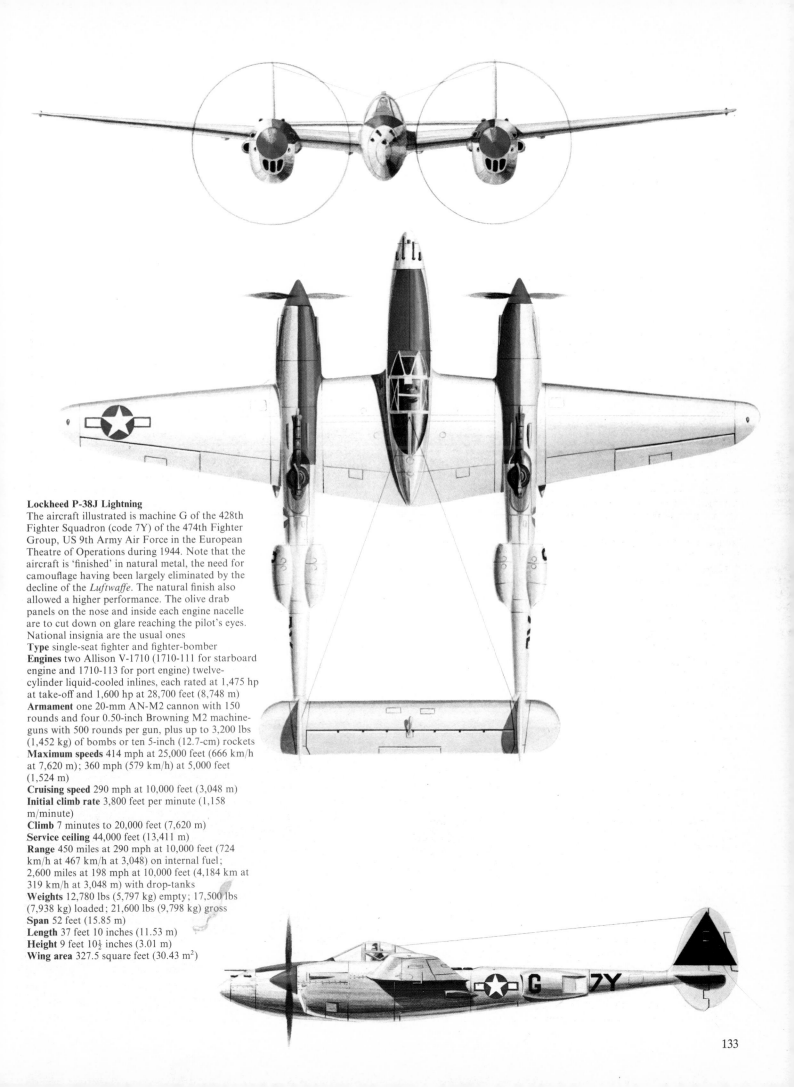

Lockheed P-38J Lightning
The aircraft illustrated is machine G of the 428th Fighter Squadron (code 7Y) of the 474th Fighter Group, US 9th Army Air Force in the European Theatre of Operations during 1944. Note that the aircraft is 'finished' in natural metal, the need for camouflage having been largely eliminated by the decline of the *Luftwaffe*. The natural finish also allowed a higher performance. The olive drab panels on the nose and inside each engine nacelle are to cut down on glare reaching the pilot's eyes. National insignia are the usual ones
Type single-seat fighter and fighter-bomber
Engines two Allison V-1710 (1710-111 for starboard engine and 1710-113 for port engine) twelve-cylinder liquid-cooled inlines, each rated at 1,475 hp at take-off and 1,600 hp at 28,700 feet (8,748 m)
Armament one 20-mm AN-M2 cannon with 150 rounds and four 0.50-inch Browning M2 machine-guns with 500 rounds per gun, plus up to 3,200 lbs (1,452 kg) of bombs or ten 5-inch (12.7-cm) rockets
Maximum speeds 414 mph at 25,000 feet (666 km/h at 7,620 m); 360 mph (579 km/h) at 5,000 feet (1,524 m)
Cruising speed 290 mph at 10,000 feet (3,048 m)
Initial climb rate 3,800 feet per minute (1,158 m/minute)
Climb 7 minutes to 20,000 feet (7,620 m)
Service ceiling 44,000 feet (13,411 m)
Range 450 miles at 290 mph at 10,000 feet (724 km/h at 467 km/h at 3,048) on internal fuel; 2,600 miles at 198 mph at 10,000 feet (4,184 km at 319 km/h at 3,048) with drop-tanks
Weights 12,780 lbs (5,797 kg) empty; 17,500 lbs (7,938 kg) loaded; 21,600 lbs (9,798 kg) gross
Span 52 feet (15.85 m)
Length 37 feet 10 inches (11.53 m)
Height 9 feet 10½ inches (3.01 m)
Wing area 327.5 square feet (30.43 m²)

North American B-25 Mitchell

The North American B-25 Mitchell formed, with the Douglas A-20 Havoc and the Martin B-26 Marauder, the mainstay of the tactical support units of the USAAF during World War II. The Mitchell, in particular, turned out to be a versatile and popular aircraft. Although its bomb-load was not very high, it was capable of carrying a heavy gun armament for both offensive and defensive purposes, and was much feared by German, Italian and Japanese pilots. It was a Mitchell unit, also, that made the daring raid on Tokyo from the carrier USS *Hornet* in April 1942 – despite the fact that the Mitchell had never been intended for carrier operations, being a large, land-based medium bomber.

The genesis of the B-25 series lay in a 1938 USAAC requirement for a medium bomber, to which North American designed their private-venture NA-40. This was a neat three-seat aircraft, with a shoulder-mounted wing, twin vertical tail surfaces, a heavy defensive armament and two 1,100-hp Pratt & Whitney R-1830-56C3-G radial engines. The NA-40 flew for the first time in January 1939, and after its engines had been replaced by 1,350-hp Wright GR-2600-A71 units in February, the type was handed over to the USAAC for official testing in March. The NA-40 was lost in an accident soon after the trials began, but so impressive had been its performance that the USAAC instructed North American to proceed with a larger version. This emerged as the NA-62, with a wider fuselage, double the bomb-load, the wings dropped slightly, and the crew increased to five.

North American completed the redesign by September 1939, and the USAAC immediately ordered 184 production machines, designated B-25, without the normal lengthy programme of prototypes and pre-production machines. Work began as quickly as possible, and the first B-25 was ready for flight in August 1940. It was powered by two 1,700-hp Wright R-2600-9 radials and a weight of 27,310 lbs (12,388 kg) half as much again as that of the NA-40. Early flight trials were successful apart from a lack of

directional stability, which was cured by reducing the dihedral on the outer wing panels. As there were no prototypes as such, the first production B-25s were retained for testing, the initial nine having full dihedral, and the subsequent 15 having the reduced dihedral outer panels. These 24 aircraft should be considered as prototype, testing and evaluation models, the first combat type being the B-25A, of which 40 were built.

The B-25A was basically similar to the later B-25s, but had armour protection for the flight crew and self-sealing fuel tanks; combat experience in Europe, passed on to the Americans by the British, had shown that these were absolutely essential for fighting aircraft. Deliveries to the USAAF began in 1941, and at the end of the year several units were operational with the Mitchell. The B-25B was also produced in 1941, 120 being built in all. Again this was similar to its predecessor, but had certain armament differences: Bendix turrets with two 0.50-inch (12.7-mm) machine-guns in each for the dorsal and ventral positions, and the deletion of the single hand-held 0.50-inch gun in the tail position. Gross weight had also risen to 28,460 lbs (12,909 kg). It was Mitchells of this model that took part in the Doolittle raid on Tokyo already mentioned. In 1941 production of the next model, the B-25C, began in California while at the same time an almost identical model, the B-25D, was built in Texas.

Three experimental models followed, all based on the B-25C. The XB-25E tested a thermal de-icing device, whilst the XB-25F tested an electrical de-icing device. And the XB-25G had a trial installation of one of the heaviest guns to be used by any aircraft in World War II – an M4 75-mm field gun obtained from the army. The tests with this gun proved so successful that the B-25G, armed with a 75-mm gun, was put into production. Each of the 21 shells carried weighed 15 lbs (6.8 kg), and had to be loaded individually by the navigator. With this gun, which was aimed with the aid of a pair of 0.50-inch (12.7-mm) machine-guns in the nose, the 405 B-25Gs

became devastating anti-shipping weapons, when the target could be hit.

The B-25G was followed into production by the B-25H, which was fitted with the lighter T13E1 75-mm gun and a multitude of other guns to make it the most heavily armed B-25 model of all. Although 1,000 B-25Hs were built, the 75-mm gun did not prove very successful in the Pacific and Far East, where most B-25Hs were deployed.

The model that followed, the B-25J, was the most numerous Mitchell derivative, some 4,318 being built. This had the older type of forward fuselage, with a considerable amount of glazing, and an armament of one flexible and two fixed 0.50-inch machine-guns. The rest of the aircraft was the same as the B-25H. The powerplants which had been R-2600-13 or -29 radials in the B-25H, were replaced by R-2600-92 engines in the B-25J. With the decline in Japanese air power in 1944, B-25s could operate at very low level, where the bombardier or bomb-aimer was not needed, and a new nose with eight 0.50-inch guns was designed. At the same time the Mitchell was given the capability of carrying eight 5-inch (12.7-cm) rocket projectiles under the wings.

The Mitchell was built in considerable numbers, the USAAF receiving 9,816 and others of the Allies some 2,500 more. For its size the Mitchell was relatively agile, and this proved a great asset in the roles in which it excelled: low-level bombing and 'on the deck' attack on strongpoints and shipping. All in all the Mitchell played a part that would be difficult to over-estimate. Moreover, unlike many other medium bombers and attack aircraft, the Mitchell was able to rely on its own defences to protect itself against enemy fighters, and could therefore dispense with fighter escort to a great extent.

Below: A North American B-25J Mitchell in service with the Royal Air Force as a Mitchell III. Note the restoration of the 'bombardier' nose in place of the 75-mm gun of the B-25H which had not proved very successful

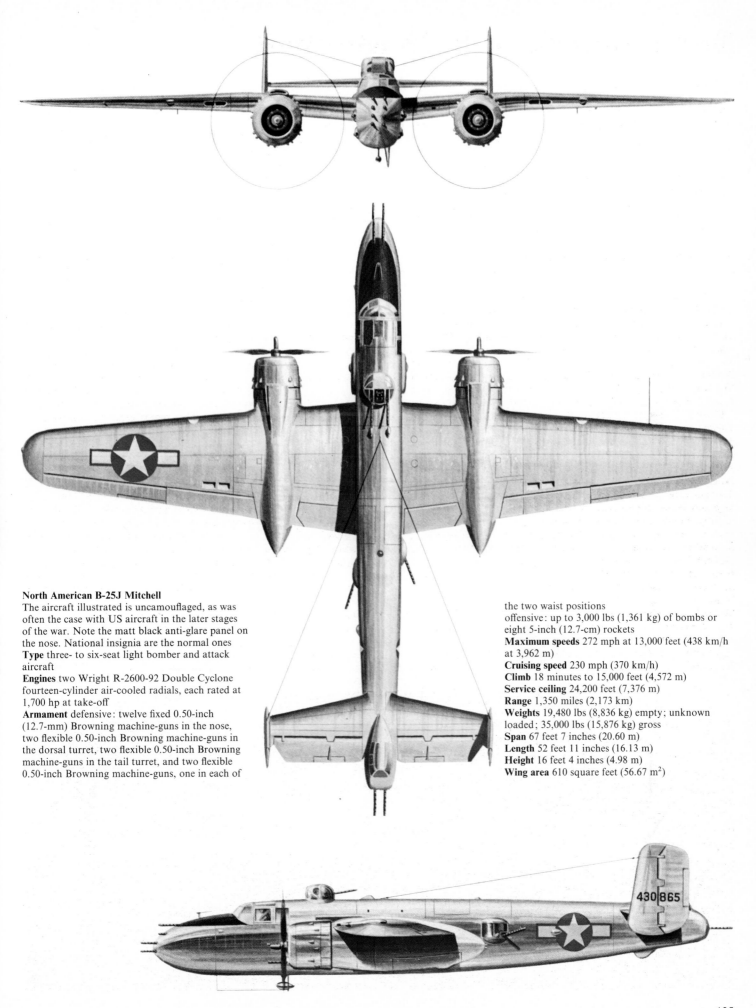

North American B-25J Mitchell
The aircraft illustrated is uncamouflaged, as was
often the case with US aircraft in the later stages
of the war. Note the matt black anti-glare panel on
the nose. National insignia are the normal ones
Type three- to six-seat light bomber and attack
aircraft
Engines two Wright R-2600-92 Double Cyclone
fourteen-cylinder air-cooled radials, each rated at
1,700 hp at take-off
Armament defensive: twelve fixed 0.50-inch
(12.7-mm) Browning machine-guns in the nose,
two flexible 0.50-inch Browning machine-guns in
the dorsal turret, two flexible 0.50-inch Browning
machine-guns in the tail turret, and two flexible
0.50-inch Browning machine-guns, one in each of

the two waist positions
offensive: up to 3,000 lbs (1,361 kg) of bombs or
eight 5-inch (12.7-cm) rockets
Maximum speeds 272 mph at 13,000 feet (438 km/h
at 3,962 m)
Cruising speed 230 mph (370 km/h)
Climb 18 minutes to 15,000 feet (4,572 m)
Service ceiling 24,200 feet (7,376 m)
Range 1,350 miles (2,173 km)
Weights 19,480 lbs (8,836 kg) empty; unknown
loaded; 35,000 lbs (15,876 kg) gross
Span 67 feet 7 inches (20.60 m)
Length 52 feet 11 inches (16.13 m)
Height 16 feet 4 inches (4.98 m)
Wing area 610 square feet (56.67 m²)

North American P-51 Mustang

The North American P-51 Mustang is one of the truly great aircraft of all time. Although the early Mustang models, powered by an Allison inline engine, were good low-level aircraft, it was not until the introduction of the Rolls-Royce Merlin engine in later models that the Mustang came into its own. The basic simplicity of the design, coupled with its beautiful lines, had great potential for development, and the Mustang was to excel in two fields: as a hard-hitting low-level fighter-bomber, and a long-range high-altitude escort fighter. In the former capacity the Mustang could deliver a formidable volume of gunfire, rockets and bombs, and in the latter, with the aid of drop-tanks, became the first Allied fighter to penetrate as far as Berlin or Tokyo. The Mustang was a great fighter; what makes this all the more remarkable is the fact that it was designed to a British specification, and that it was one of few aircraft to be designed during the war to enter very widespread service.

At the beginning of 1940 the British were shopping for combat aircraft in the United States. Failing to find a fighter that could meet the requirements that combat had shown to be essential, the British asked North American, who had little experience in the field, if it could produce a fighter to British specifications within the remarkably short time of 120 days. The aircraft had to have good performance, an armament of eight machine-guns, armour protection for the pilot, self-sealing fuel tanks, and an inline engine, the last in keeping with all British single-engined fighters of the period.

The prototype NA-73, as the design was called, was ready three days before the British deadline and could immediately be seen to possess exceptional lines, with laminar-flow wings, low-drag fuselage features, and an overall cleanliness of airframe. After the 1,100-hp Allison V-1710-P3R inline had been fitted, the prototype made its maiden flight in October 1940 and entered immediate production, the first deliveries beginning in December. These Mustang I aircraft had an armament of four 0.30-inch (7.7-mm) and two 0.50-inch (12.7-mm) machine-guns in the wings, and two 0.50-inch guns in the fuselage.

As part of the original export permission, it had been specified that two NA-73s should be supplied to the US army for evaluation and the fourth and tenth aircraft were handed over and tested as XP-51s. The USAAF ordered 150 of this model, armed with four 20-mm cannon, as P-51s so that they could be supplied to Great Britain as Mustang IAs under Lend-Lease. After the Japanese attack on Pearl Harbor, however, the USAAF kept some examples.

The first Mustang model ordered for the USAAF themselves was the A-36A, a ground-attack version which had first flown in September 1942. Armament consisted of six 0.50-inch guns in the wings and two 500-lb (227-kg) bombs under the wings; deliveries of the 500 ordered were completed by March 1943. Because of the type of Allison engine fitted to these early models, the first Mustangs were used by the USAAF and RAF as low-level ground-attack and army co-operation aircraft respectively, but some urgency was now attached to giving the Mustang an engine that would deliver its best power at a higher altitude. A partial solution was found in the Allison V-1710-81 of 1,200 hp, which was used in the P-51A; a total of 310 of this type was ordered in 1942. The uprated Allison engine had only partially solved the problem of the Mustang's lack of adequate performance above medium altitude and a new solution had to be found. The answer in fact lay in a British proposal to abandon the Allison engine in favour of the Rolls-Royce Merlin. Experimental installations were carried out in the United States and Great Britain with engines built in each country; the American version was selected for major production. Conclusive trials, which had shown that the Merlin boosted the Mustang's top speed by some 50 mph (80 km/h) to 441 mph (710 km/h) and generally altered the type's high-altitude performance out of all recognition, were concluded in September 1942, and the type was ordered into large-scale production. Two identical models, the P-51B and the P-51C, were built in California and Texas. At first deliveries were made of aircraft with 1,300-hp V-1650-3 engines, but later the V-1650-7 of 1,695 hp was

fitted. Armament of both the P-51C and D started as four 20-mm cannon, but was later altered to six 0.50-inch (12.7-mm) guns. Drop-tanks could be carried, increasing the maximum range to 2,080 miles (3,348 km). Production of the P-51B reached 1,988, and of the P-51C 1,750.

The next model, the P-51D, was built in greater numbers than all other Mustangs put together. The main distinguishing feature of this model was a complete revision of the cockpit lines to improve the pilot's field of vision. The rear fuselage was cut down, and a smoothly lined one-piece perspex canopy was fitted in place of the earlier framed hood. The six-gun armament was standardized, as was the V-1650-7 engine, and after a few aircraft had been delivered, a dorsal fillet was added to the fin to aid directional stability. This fillet was also added retrospectively to many P-51B and C aircraft. Production of the P-51D amounted to 7,956 aircraft, of which 280 were supplied to the RAF as Mustang IVs.

The final production model was the P-51H with power provided by a 2,218-hp V-1650-9 engine, the cockpit shortened, extra fuel tankage provided, and a taller fin and rudder assembly fitted. The P-51H was 1,100 lbs (499 kg) lighter than the P-51D and was the fastest of all Mustang variants at 487 mph (784 km/h). Only 555 had been built before further orders were cancelled after the surrender of Japan.

The Mustang was in every respect a great aircraft, well loved by its pilots and the crews of bombers it escorted, and greatly feared by German and Japanese pilots. With the Merlin engine the Mustang possessed great speed, rate of climb and acceleration. Combined with a high level of manoeuvrability, this made the type a fighter to be respected – and its lines made it a type to be remembered.

Below: Four US 8th Air Force North American P-51 Mustang fighters. Three distinct types are visible: leading is a D without a dorsal fillet; nearest is a D with such a fillet; and furthest away is a B with the original type of framed cockpit canopy

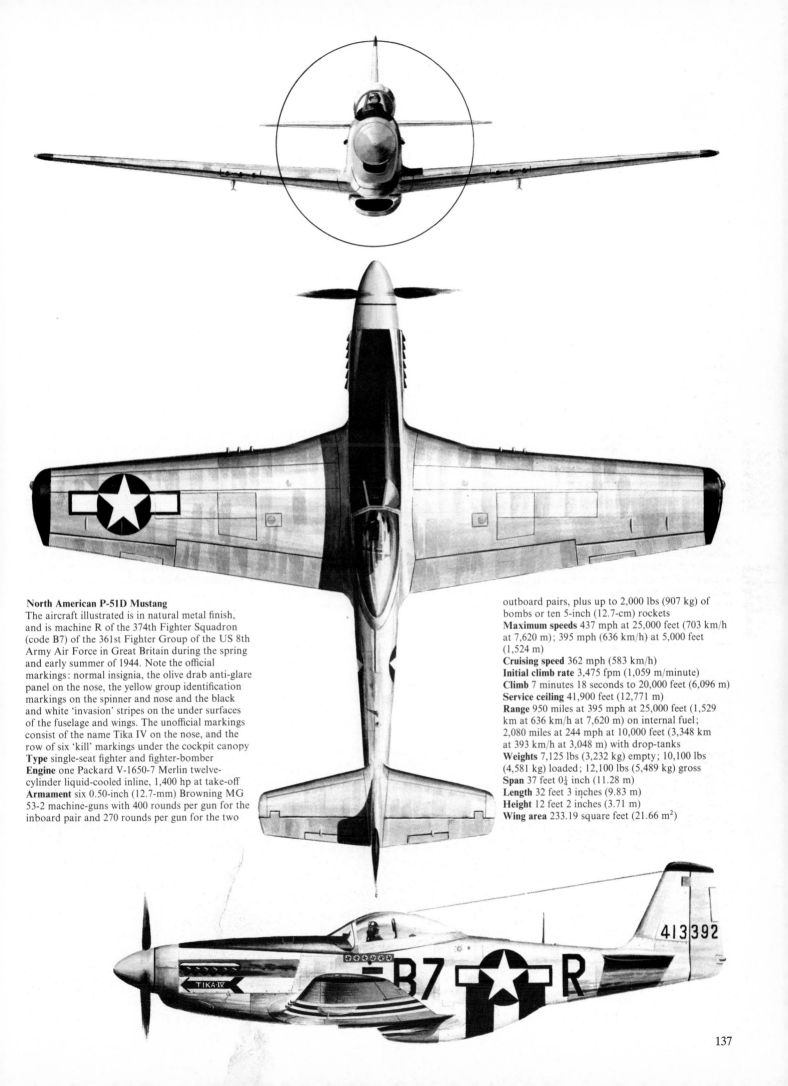

North American P-51D Mustang
The aircraft illustrated is in natural metal finish, and is machine R of the 374th Fighter Squadron (code B7) of the 361st Fighter Group of the US 8th Army Air Force in Great Britain during the spring and early summer of 1944. Note the official markings: normal insignia, the olive drab anti-glare panel on the nose, the yellow group identification markings on the spinner and nose and the black and white 'invasion' stripes on the under surfaces of the fuselage and wings. The unofficial markings consist of the name Tika IV on the nose, and the row of six 'kill' markings under the cockpit canopy
Type single-seat fighter and fighter-bomber
Engine one Packard V-1650-7 Merlin twelve-cylinder liquid-cooled inline, 1,400 hp at take-off
Armament six 0.50-inch (12.7-mm) Browning MG 53-2 machine-guns with 400 rounds per gun for the inboard pair and 270 rounds per gun for the two outboard pairs, plus up to 2,000 lbs (907 kg) of bombs or ten 5-inch (12.7-cm) rockets
Maximum speeds 437 mph at 25,000 feet (703 km/h at 7,620 m); 395 mph (636 km/h) at 5,000 feet (1,524 m)
Cruising speed 362 mph (583 km/h)
Initial climb rate 3,475 fpm (1,059 m/minute)
Climb 7 minutes 18 seconds to 20,000 feet (6,096 m)
Service ceiling 41,900 feet (12,771 m)
Range 950 miles at 395 mph at 25,000 feet (1,529 km at 636 km/h at 7,620 m) on internal fuel; 2,080 miles at 244 mph at 10,000 feet (3,348 km at 393 km/h at 3,048 m) with drop-tanks
Weights 7,125 lbs (3,232 kg) empty; 10,100 lbs (4,581 kg) loaded; 12,100 lbs (5,489 kg) gross
Span 37 feet 0¼ inch (11.28 m)
Length 32 feet 3 inches (9.83 m)
Height 12 feet 2 inches (3.71 m)
Wing area 233.19 square feet (21.66 m²)

Republic P-47 Thunderbolt

The Republic P-47 Thunderbolt was the largest and heaviest single-seat, single-piston engined fighter ever to enter service, and was excelled in size and weight only by the experimental Boeing XF8B-1 shipboard fighter of 1943. Like North American's P-51 Mustang, the Thunderbolt was conceived and built wholly during the war years, but was also the logical conclusion of the series of barrel-shaped Republic fighters that had started in the 1930s with the P-35 and progressed to the P-43 Lancer of 1940. The P-47 was also the last radial-engined fighter to serve in quantity with the USAAF.

The first two designs to bear the designation P-47, the XP-47 and XP-47A, in fact bore little resemblance to the eventual Thunderbolt, being designed in 1940 to meet USAAC requirements for a light fighter. Although the USAAC evinced interest in both types, reports of air combat over Europe convinced the authorities that they would have to re-equip American fighter units with a machine that would excel the 400-mph (644 km/h) performance of the XP-47 and XP-47B, as well as possess a far heavier armament and be fitted with armour protection and self-sealing fuel tanks.

In view of the new requirements, the Republic team under Alexander Kartveli undertook a complete reworking of the initial designs to produce the XP-47B. This was powered by a 2,000-hp Pratt & Whitney R-2800 Double Wasp radial, and no effort was made to pare down weight at the expense of performance or combat capacity. In fact the armament proposed – eight 0.50-inch machine-guns in the wings – was extremely heavy by the standards of the time. Although the projected gross weight of 12,000 lbs (5,443 kg) would make the type the heaviest fighter to date ordered, the USAAF gave Republic the order to go ahead with a prototype in September 1940.

The mechanical centre of the new fighter was its large radial engine and its associated turbo-supercharger; Kartveli started with the problem of where to place the latter, and then built up the fuselage around the two major components. To help balance the aircraft the supercharger was placed in the rear fuselage. This in turn meant that the air for the supercharger to compress had to be drawn in through the nose, ducted back to the supercharger and then led forward again to the engine; the engine exhaust gases to drive the supercharger were led back from the engine, and after use exhausted under the rear fuselage. To utilize the engine's output efficiently a four-bladed propeller of large dimensions was needed and this entailed provision of a long undercarriage to enable the propeller to clear the ground. A large amount of fuel had to be carried, and the structure necessary to deal with the recoil forces of the eight machine-guns needed to be sturdy, and so the XP-47B, which flew for the first time in May 1941, was of necessity a very bulky, heavy aircraft. Top speed was 412 mph (663 km/h), fully justifying the order for 773 production models placed by the USAAF during the previous September.

Deliveries of the P-47B, which differed from the prototype in having a sliding instead of a hinged cockpit canopy and an R-2800-2 engine, began in 1942, and eventually 171 were built. The P-47B was used in combat for the first time over Europe, and experience against German fighters in April and May 1943 showed that although the new fighter lacked adequate manoeuvrability and rate of climb, its weight bestowed a phenomenal dive, and its structure the ability to absorb battle damage that would destroy any other fighter.

Production of the 602 P-47Cs began in the last quarter of 1942. This model had provision for a drop-tank under the fuselage, and the fuselage itself was lengthened by some 13 inches (33 cm) to increase manoeuvrability. The drop-tank increased range from 550 to 1,250 miles (885 to 2,012 km), and the installation of the R-2800-59 engine of 2,300 hp added to the P-47C's rate of climb considerably, as well as improving other performance figures. This engine, with water injection to boost power to 2,535 hp for emergency combat use, was standardized on later production examples of the next model, the P-47D. This was built in larger numbers (12,608) than any other model, and also had a pylon under each wing for additional drop-tanks. These gave the P-47D a range of 1,800 miles (2,897 km), enabling Thunderbolts to play a useful part in long-range escort duties. Later in the P-47D's career, the drop-tank pylons were converted to enable the type to carry bombs up to a total weight of 2,500 lbs (1,134 kg); with these the P-47 became an effective fighter-bomber from the end of 1943. To improve vision a bubble canopy was introduced on late P-47Ds.

The introduction of the latest German aircraft and the V-1 flying bomb led to the development of the P-47M late in 1944. This model was intended only as a fighter, and all fighter-bomber equipment was removed from the 130 models built. The last Thunderbolt production model – the P-47N – was intended for use in the Pacific theatre, in which very long range was essential. This was similar to the P-47M, but had wings increased in span by 22 inches (55.9 cm) to 42 feet 7 inches (12.98 m). The engine was the 2,800-hp R-2800-77, and increased fuel capacity made the P-47N the longest-ranged Thunderbolt of all at 2,350 miles (3,782 km). Fighter-bomber equipment was restored, and the dorsal fillet was larger than that pioneered on the P-47D. Production of the P-47N amounted to 1,816 before the end of the war against Japan brought cancellation of the remaining 5,934 Thunderbolts on order. In all, production of the Thunderbolt had amounted to 15,683 aircraft.

The type was also used by the Free French, Russian and British air forces. The British designated the 340 early P-47Ds delivered Thunderbolt I, and the 590 late P-47Ds and subsequent models Thunderbolt II.

Below: The largest piston-engined single-seat fighter to serve in World War II: the Republic P-47 Thunderbolt. Shown here is a D model, the first to have a bubble canopy

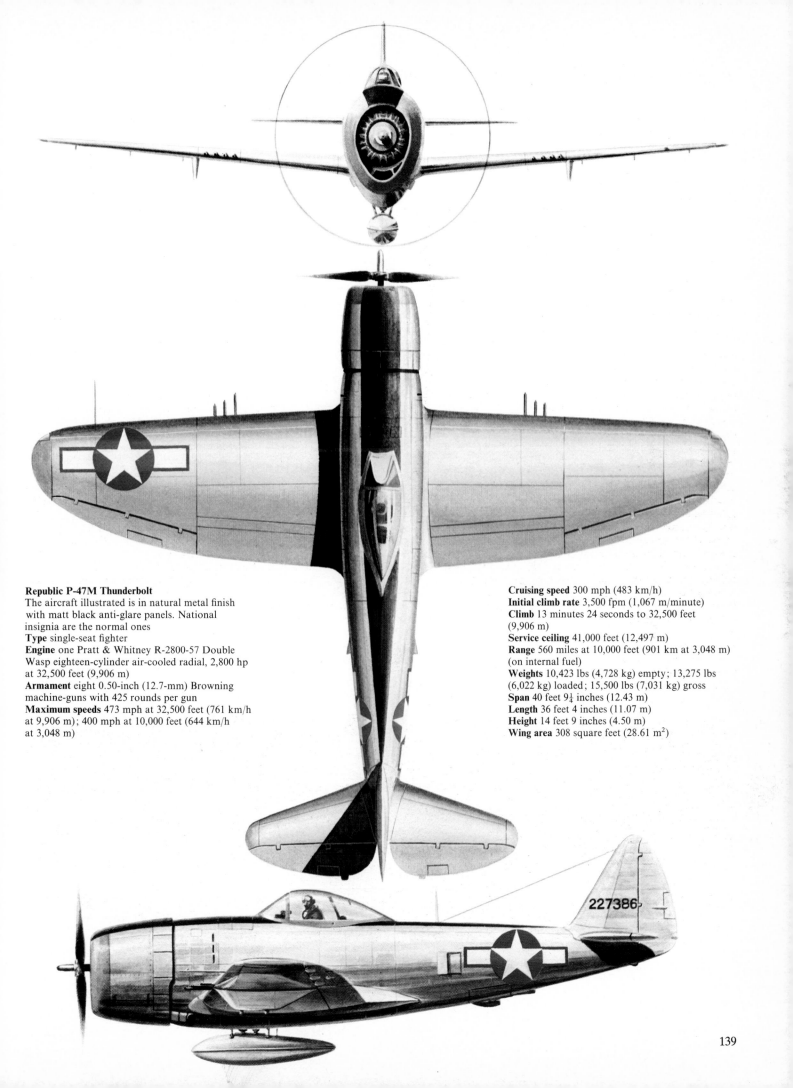

Republic P-47M Thunderbolt
The aircraft illustrated is in natural metal finish
with matt black anti-glare panels. National
insignia are the normal ones
Type single-seat fighter
Engine one Pratt & Whitney R-2800-57 Double
Wasp eighteen-cylinder air-cooled radial, 2,800 hp
at 32,500 feet (9,906 m)
Armament eight 0.50-inch (12.7-mm) Browning
machine-guns with 425 rounds per gun
Maximum speeds 473 mph at 32,500 feet (761 km/h
at 9,906 m); 400 mph at 10,000 feet (644 km/h
at 3,048 m)

Cruising speed 300 mph (483 km/h)
Initial climb rate 3,500 fpm (1,067 m/minute)
Climb 13 minutes 24 seconds to 32,500 feet
(9,906 m)
Service ceiling 41,000 feet (12,497 m)
Range 560 miles at 10,000 feet (901 km at 3,048 m)
(on internal fuel)
Weights 10,423 lbs (4,728 kg) empty; 13,275 lbs
(6,022 kg) loaded; 15,500 lbs (7,031 kg) gross
Span 40 feet 9¼ inches (12.43 m)
Length 36 feet 4 inches (11.07 m)
Height 14 feet 9 inches (4.50 m)
Wing area 308 square feet (28.61 m²)

Vought F4U Corsair

The Vought F4U was undoubtedly the best carrier-borne fighter of World War II, and could with some justification make a bid for the title of best fighter of the war. It was an extremely potent fighter, and as a fighter-bomber proved so efficient against the Japanese that they nicknamed it the 'Whistling Death'.

The origins of the Corsair lay in a 1938 US Navy requirement for a fighter that could match the performance of any landplane. Vought produced the V-166B design to meet this requirement, and in June 1938 the company received a contract to build one prototype. The design had been produced by a team under Tex B Beisel, and was very striking in appearance. To obtain the necessary high performance the new fighter was designed around the Pratt & Whitney XR-2800 Double Wasp radial, with the fuselage being kept to the minimum dictated by the engine. The wing arrangement was very ingenious, the inverted gull planform providing the necessary area in a reduced overall span. As the wing also folded at its angle, this helped keep the folded height of the aircraft down. The backward-retracting undercarriage was also located at the angle of the wing, which enabled the length of the legs to be kept short, with resultant saving in weight.

The first Corsair, the XF4U-1 prototype, made its maiden flight in May 1940, and quickly showed its paces, being capable of more than 400 mph (644 km/h). At the time it was the only US fighter that could fly at this speed. Armament consisted of one 0.30- (7.7-mm) and one 0.50-inch (12.7-mm) gun in the fuselage, and one 0.50-inch gun in each wing, as well as 10 small bombs to be dropped on enemy bomber formations. At the end of June 1941 the navy placed orders for 584 production F4U-1 models.

The first of these flew in June 1942, and deliveries began in October. These aircraft were powered by the R-2800-8 engine in place of the

prototype's R-2800-4, and had two more guns in the wings. The most noticeable difference was the relocation of the cockpit three feet (91 cm) further back, to allow extra fuel to be carried in the fuselage. This unfortunately reduced the forward view of the pilot when the aircraft was on the ground, and the navy decided that the Corsair could not be operated from aircraft-carriers. The first F4U-1s therefore went to units of the US Marine Corps operating from land bases and entered combat with the marines for the first time in February 1943.

The Vought production facilities could not match demand, and the Corsair was accordingly manufactured by Brewster as the F3A-1 and by Goodyear as the FG-1. Later models built by all three companies had the raised cockpit canopy introduced on Vought's 689th Corsair. Other early models were: the FG-1A with fixed wings; the F4U-1C with four 20-mm cannon in place of earlier production models' six wing-mounted 0.50-inch machine-guns; and the F4U-1D/FG-1D/F3A-1D with water-injected R-2800-8W engines, provision for a drop-tank under the fuselage, and shackles for one 1,000-lb (454-kg) bomb or four 5-inch (12.7-cm) rockets under each wing to turn the Corsair into a fighter-bomber. Production of these first models by the three companies involved totalled 8,663, and of these 370 were delivered to the Royal New Zealand Air Force and 2,012 to the Royal Navy's Fleet Air Arm. The first Corsair operations from carrier decks were by the Fleet Air Arm in April 1944, although successful trials had been carried out some nine months before. It was at this time that the US Navy finally cleared the Corsair for carrier operations.

As the Corsair was beginning to make its mark on operations in the Pacific, work on a night-fighter version, the XF4U-2, was making progress. This prototype was not in fact completed; and although work on three XF4U-3s, using the

turbo-supercharged R-2800-16 engine, started in March 1942, the first aircraft did not fly until 1946. Only 13 of the 27 similar Goodyear FG-3s were completed. The next production model was therefore the F4U-4, the first of which flew in April 1944. Power was provided by the 2,100-hp R-2800-18W engine with water injection. The extra 350 hp of this engine, when water injection was used, raised top speed of the Corsair by 21 mph (34 km/h) to 446 mph (718 km/h). Other versions of the F4U-4 were the F4U-4C armed with four 20-mm cannon; the F4U-4N night fighter with four cannon and APS-5 radar in a wing-mounted pod; the F4U-4E with four cannon and APS-4 radar; the Goodyear FG-4 equivalent of the F4U-4; and the F4U-4P photographic-reconnaissance model with cameras. Total production of the F4U-4 series reached 2,556 aircraft including the 200 FG-4s.

These were the last wartime variants of the Corsair, and although many aircraft contracts were cancelled in September 1945, the excellent Vought fighter was kept in production, with development plans slightly curtailed. The last Corsair was delivered in December 1952, after the type had been in production for more than 10 years. In combat the Corsair had served principally with the US Navy and Marine Corps in the Pacific theatre, some 64,051 missions being flown in all. Corsairs achieved the remarkable ratio of 11 kills to one loss in action against Japanese fighters, destroying 2,140 aircraft for the loss of only 189 of their own number. And in the fighter-bomber role the Corsair also achieved remarkable results, being able to deliver its large offensive load with considerable speed and great accuracy.

Below: Vought F4U-4 fighter-bombers, perhaps the US Navy's most versatile aircraft of World War II, and certainly the most successful naval fighter of that war

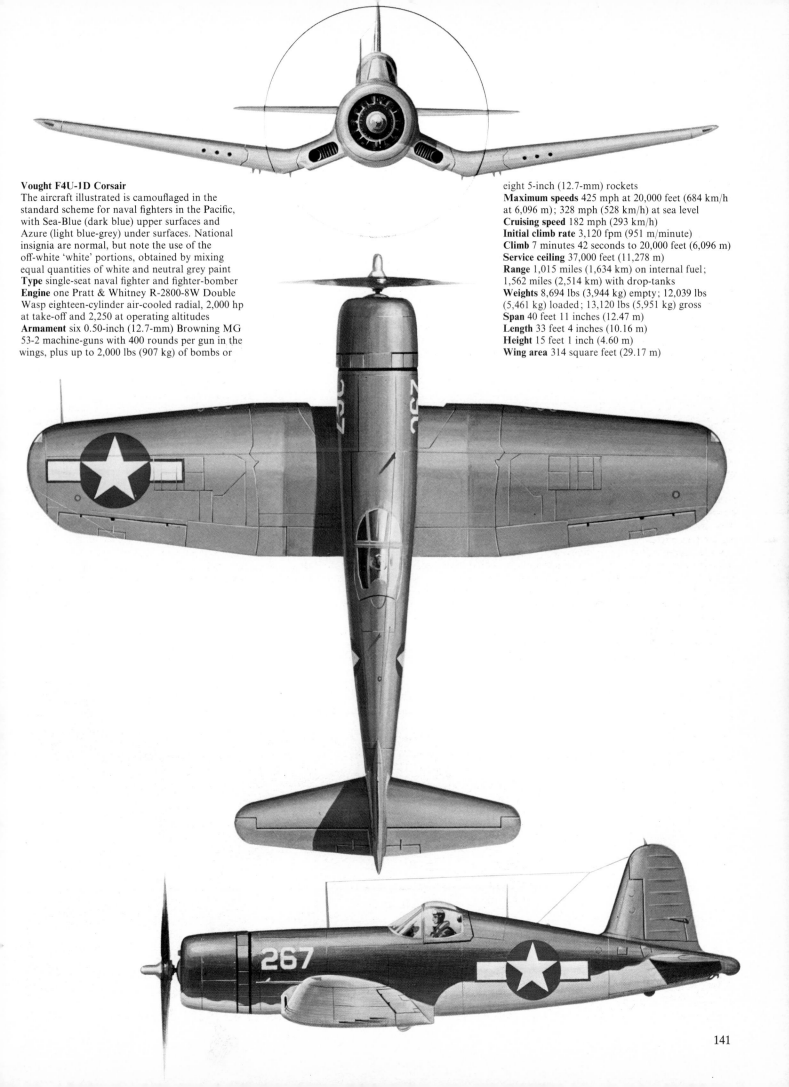

Vought F4U-1D Corsair
The aircraft illustrated is camouflaged in the standard scheme for naval fighters in the Pacific, with Sea-Blue (dark blue) upper surfaces and Azure (light blue-grey) under surfaces. National insignia are normal, but note the use of the off-white 'white' portions, obtained by mixing equal quantities of white and neutral grey paint
Type single-seat naval fighter and fighter-bomber
Engine one Pratt & Whitney R-2800-8W Double Wasp eighteen-cylinder air-cooled radial, 2,000 hp at take-off and 2,250 at operating altitudes
Armament six 0.50-inch (12.7-mm) Browning MG 53-2 machine-guns with 400 rounds per gun in the wings, plus up to 2,000 lbs (907 kg) of bombs or eight 5-inch (12.7-mm) rockets

Maximum speeds 425 mph at 20,000 feet (684 km/h at 6,096 m); 328 mph (528 km/h) at sea level
Cruising speed 182 mph (293 km/h)
Initial climb rate 3,120 fpm (951 m/minute)
Climb 7 minutes 42 seconds to 20,000 feet (6,096 m)
Service ceiling 37,000 feet (11,278 m)
Range 1,015 miles (1,634 km) on internal fuel; 1,562 miles (2,514 km) with drop-tanks
Weights 8,694 lbs (3,944 kg) empty; 12,039 lbs (5,461 kg) loaded; 13,120 lbs (5,951 kg) gross
Span 40 feet 11 inches (12.47 m)
Length 33 feet 4 inches (10.16 m)
Height 15 feet 1 inch (4.60 m)
Wing area 314 square feet (29.17 m)

NAVAL VESSELS

Germany Italy Japan Great Britain USA

Germany: Capital Ships

After the end of the First World War, Germany was left with none of the excellent dreadnoughts of the High Seas Fleet – only a handful of old pre-dreadnoughts, useful for training but little else. She was not allowed to build any warship larger than 10,000 tons (10,160 tonnes), carrying more than 11-inch (280-mm) guns. The intention

was to keep the German Navy at the level of the Scandinavian navies, whose largest ships were small armoured vessels with a few heavy guns for coastal defence, known only by courtesy as battleships.

Germany's answer to these restrictions was to produce a new type of warship, called an

armoured ship but generally known as a pocket battleship. This type combined the armament of a coastal defence battleship, two triple 280-mm turrets, torpedo tubes and a secondary armament of 150-mm guns, with the hull and protection of

Graf Spee

The 'pocket battleship' Admiral Graf Spee seen just before the war. The 'Seetakt' gunnery radar aerial is visible on the front face of the fire control on the control tower; the use of this radar in the Battle of the River Plate marked the first use of radar in surface action. She was sunk too early to be given the raked bow and funnel cap added to her two sisters. The Heinkel biplane shown on the photograph was replaced at the outbreak of war by an Arado monoplane, as depicted in the illustration below

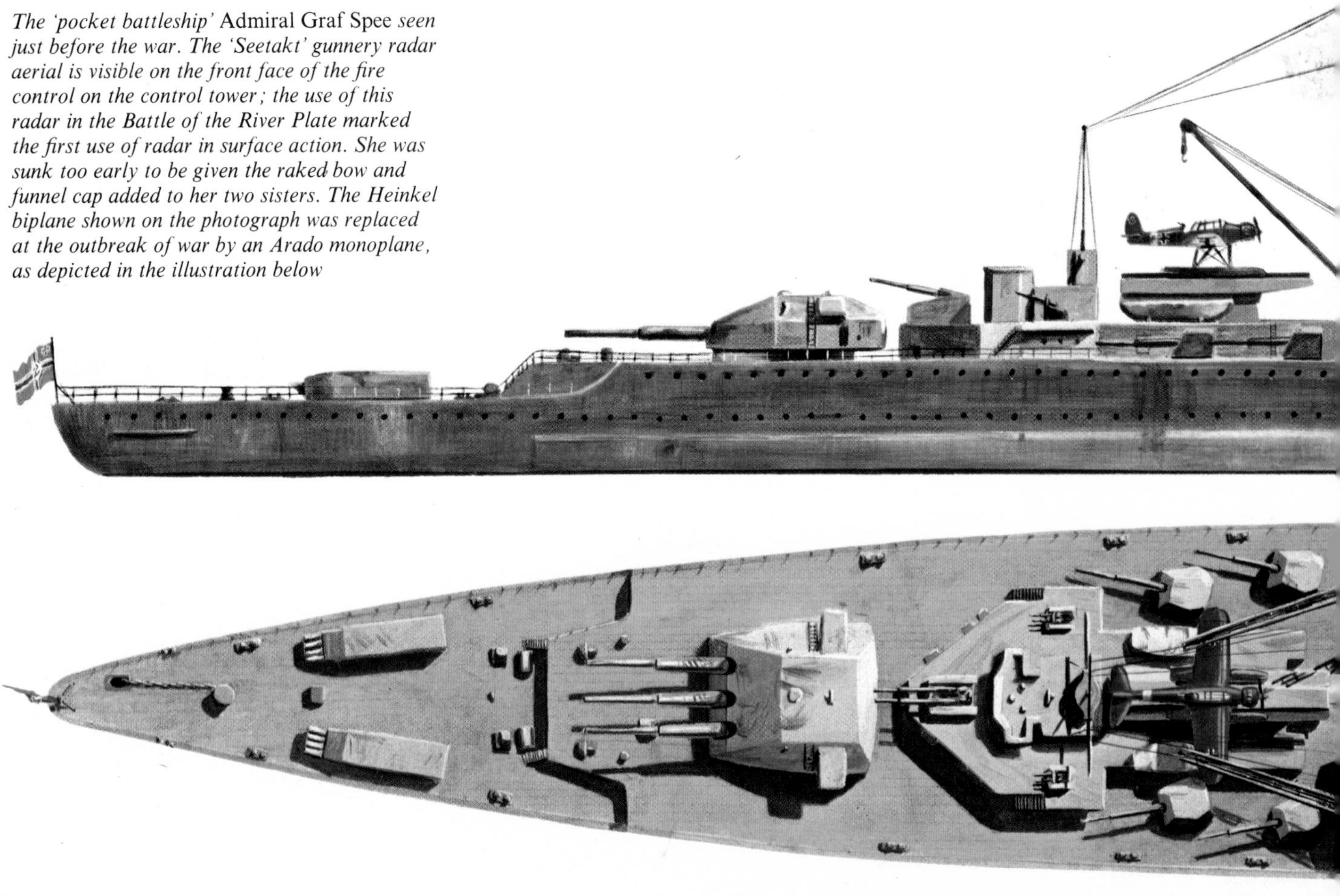

an armoured cruiser. A startling innovation was made in the engine room, for diesel engines were used for propulsion; these gave the pocket battleships a greater speed than the battleships of the day (though less than battle-cruisers and cruisers) and a very respectable range (though less than was claimed at the time). Other technical innovations, such as the widespread conviction to the stated weight of 10,160 tonnes, though in fact the laden tonnage was well over half that again.

The three pocket battleships, the *Deutschland*

(later renamed *Lutzow*), *Graf Spee* and *Scheer*, caused a furore in naval circles when they first appeared. They seemed to be the perfect type of long-range commerce raider, faster than nearly every ship powerful enough to sink them but strong enough to defeat nearly every warship fast enough to catch them. In fact they were not as formidable as they looked. With only two main turrets it was difficult to split their fire between more than one adversary, which was the *Graf Spee*'s downfall at the River Plate. In addition they were little larger, and not much

better protected, than contemporary 8-inch (203-mm) cruisers, but they had the prestige of battleships. Vessels fitted with more 203-mm guns, and with better speed and perhaps better protection, might have proved better investments for Germany. Still, the pocket battleships did worry other navies at the time, and although no other navy copied the ships, much effort was put into devising anti-raider tactics. The Germans considered building improved versions later, but other factors intervened and the designs were never taken very far.

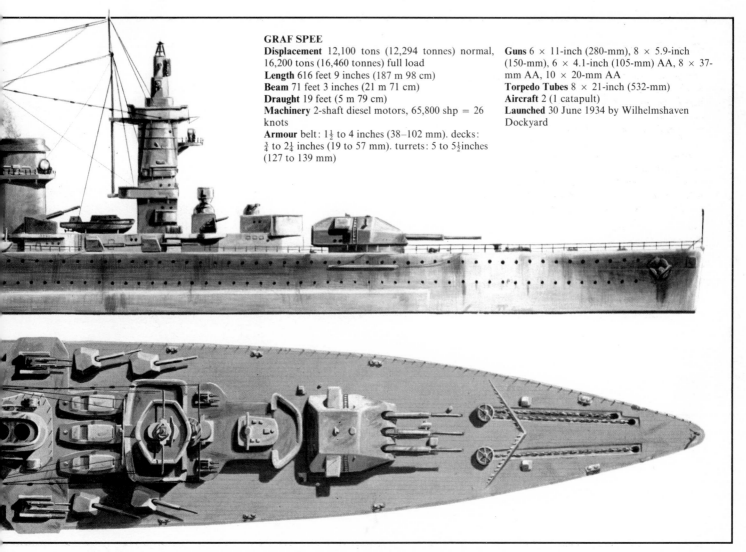

GRAF SPEE
Displacement 12,100 tons (12,294 tonnes) normal, 16,200 tons (16,460 tonnes) full load
Length 616 feet 9 inches (187 m 98 cm)
Beam 71 feet 3 inches (21 m 71 cm)
Draught 19 feet (5 m 79 cm)
Machinery 2-shaft diesel motors, 65,800 shp = 26 knots
Armour belt: $1\frac{1}{2}$ to 4 inches (38–102 mm). decks: $\frac{3}{4}$ to $2\frac{1}{4}$ inches (19 to 57 mm). turrets: 5 to $5\frac{1}{2}$ inches (127 to 139 mm)

Guns 6 × 11-inch (280-mm), 8 × 5.9-inch (150-mm), 6 × 4.1-inch (105-mm) AA, 8 × 37-mm AA, 10 × 20-mm AA
Torpedo Tubes 8 × 21-inch (532-mm)
Aircraft 2 (1 catapult)
Launched 30 June 1934 by Wilhelmshaven Dockyard

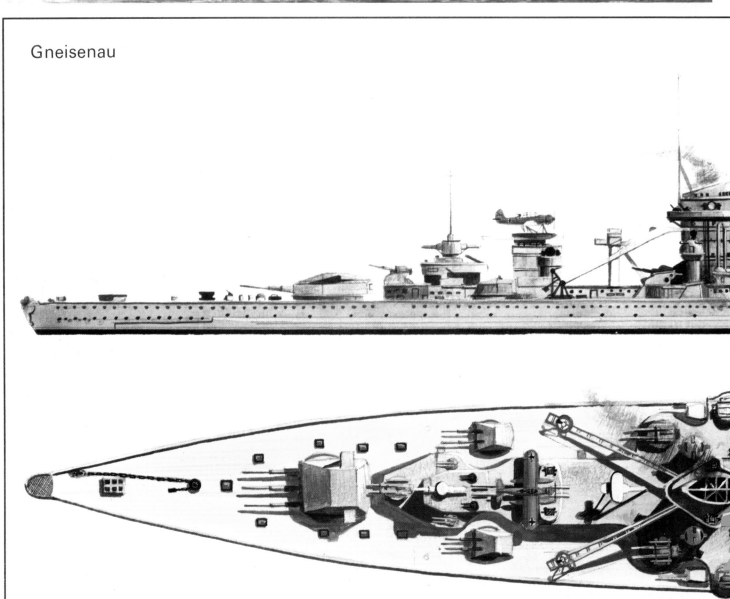

Gneisenau

The next German heavy ship design was a much more effective concept. The two armoured ships *Gneisenau* and *Scharnhorst*, like the pocket battleships, caused some problems in classification, some authorities rating them as battle-cruisers, others battleships. Their armour was of battleship standard, but their high speed of 32 knots fitted the battle-cruiser definition better, and their main armament, nine of the same 280-mm guns as the *Graf Spee* and her sisters, was lighter than contemporary battleships. Twin 380-mm guns had been proposed as an alternative to the triple 280-mm, but these turrets were not available when the ships were built. The secondary armament consisted of the same 150-mm guns as in the pocket battleships,

The crew of the Scharnhorst *man the side to cheer the* U-47, *a Type VIIB U-boat. (Under the command of Gunther Prien, U-47 penetrated the defences of Scapa Flow in October 1939 and torpedoed the British battleship* Royal Oak.) *At this stage both battleships still had a catapult on the after turret. The drawing below shows* Gneisenau *without the second catapult after wartime modifications*

but the anti-aircraft armament of fourteen 105-mm guns was much heavier. For light anti-aircraft weapons the Germans had the sense to adopt the Bofors design from the start (but using 37-mm ammunition instead of 40-mm) and also the 20-mm heavy machine-gun, well before the Allies did so.

To obtain their high speed these ships adopted steam turbines rather than their predecessors' diesels. Their lack of range was their worst feature, although they made useful sorties against the Allied convoy routes; inadequate bunkers were always a worry, as was also the unreliability of their high-pressure steam installation. Nonetheless, their high speed made them a particular threat to the Allied navies. Even though their armament was inadequate for taking on a battleship, they were still formidable opponents. In the Battle of North Cape on 26 December 1943, in which *Scharnhorst* was finally sunk, it was fortunate for the British that it proved possible to slow her down so the *Duke of York* could engage her, for once this happened she was doomed.

Scharnhorst resembled the pocket battleships, with a straight stem and a flat-topped funnel,

a rather sinister and ugly silhouette. She (and the surviving pocket battleships) were soon, however, altered to look like the *Gneisenau*, which was built with the clipper bow and funnel cap which became the trade mark of the Second World War German heavy ship. This change made them both more handsome in appearance and very difficult to tell apart, a fact which confused the British on several occasions.

GNEISENAU

Displacement 31,800 tons (32,310 tonnes) normal, 38,900 tons (39,524 tonnes) full load
Length 771 feet (235 m)
Beam 100 feet (30 m 47 cm)
Draught 27 feet (8 m 22 cm)
Machinery 3-shaft geared steam turbines, 160,000 shp = 32 knots
Armour belt: 5 to 13 inches (127 to 330 mm). decks: 2 to 4¼ inches (51 to 108 mm). turrets: 9¾ to 14¼ inches (246 to 362 mm)
Guns 9 × 11-inch (280-mm), 12 × 5.9-inch (150-mm), 14 × 4.1-inch (105-mm) AA, 16 × 37-mm AA
Torpedo Tubes 6 × 21-inch (532-mm)
Aircraft 4 (2 catapults)
Launched 8 December 1936 by Deutsche Werke, Kiel

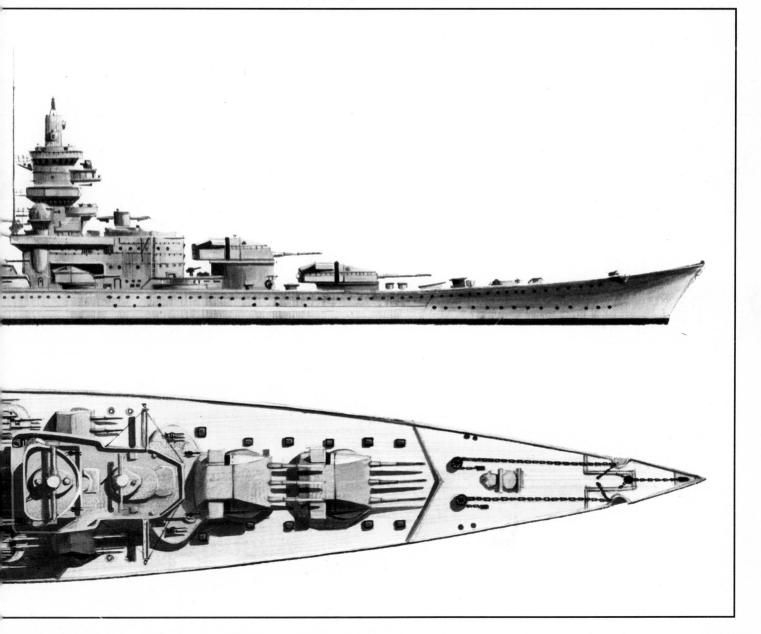

While neither the pocket battleships nor even the *Scharnhorst* and *Gneisenau* were fully equal to foreign battleships, the Germans made a determined effort with the *Bismarck* and her near-sister the *Tirpitz* to produce warships second to none. To a certain extent they succeeded, for these two were certainly impressive in appearance, and had a greater tonnage than any Allied battleships until the American *Iowa* class appeared. Their armour was thick, and they were certainly difficult to sink. However – and this is much more important in a battleship – they were not as difficult to knock out of action as they should have been. As we have already seen, the hull and protection design was basically no more than an enlargement of the quarter-century-old *Baden*, and this gave far too little protection to vital internal communications, particularly as the protective deck was too low.

Though the *Bismarck*'s gunnery against the *Hood* was superb and reaped its reward in the latter's sinking, the *Bismarck* achieved no success at all against *Rodney* and *King George V* on 27 May 1941. After half an hour's pounding, she had not only failed to damage her adversaries, but was a battered wreck incapable of retaliation. After this her sinking was inevitable, and the argument as to whether it was British torpedoes or a German scuttling party which finally caused her to founder is of very little significance.

For all her size the *Bismarck* was a poor sea boat, and her main armament was no better than older and smaller foreign battleships. A lot of the extra displacement was taken up by having, unlike British and American contemporaries, both a secondary armament of 150-mm guns and a tertiary battery of 105-mm high-angle weapons, instead of a dual-purpose secondary armament. However, the tertiary armament did have the exceptionally good complement of six separate directors (the more directors, the more targets can be engaged at one time, good fire control being more important than number of guns). The light anti-aircraft armament was also excellent for its day.

Tirpitz was basically similar to *Bismarck* except in having greater range and in carrying torpedo tubes. One weakness of the German heavy ships not immediately evident was that their shells had a distressingly high proportion of failures; most of those that hit the *Prince of Wales* in her action against the *Bismarck* and *Prinz Eugen* failed to explode. In the First World War it was the British who were handicapped by poor-quality projectiles, whereas in the second conflict it was the Germans who had this trouble.

In short *Bismarck*, though by no means a failure as a fighting ship, was far from being the paragon of excellence she is often claimed to be. If her gunnery had not been so good in the opening minutes of her engagement with the *Hood* it is quite possible that her career might have been even shorter than it was, as the British ship's armour should have proved quite adequate to withstand shelling by the Germans at closer ranges.

Two large battleships to be armed with 406-mm guns were laid down early in the war, but abandoned by the end of 1940. Later battleship and battle-cruiser designs did not develop beyond the project stage, for by that time Germany was sensibly concentrating on U-boat development.

Germany actually launched an aircraft carrier, the *Graf Zeppelin*, and began building another, but the problems of designing this type of ship with no practical experience proved more than the Germans had bargained for. This, combined with the *Luftwaffe*'s hostility to a separate naval air arm, ensured that neither ship was completed.

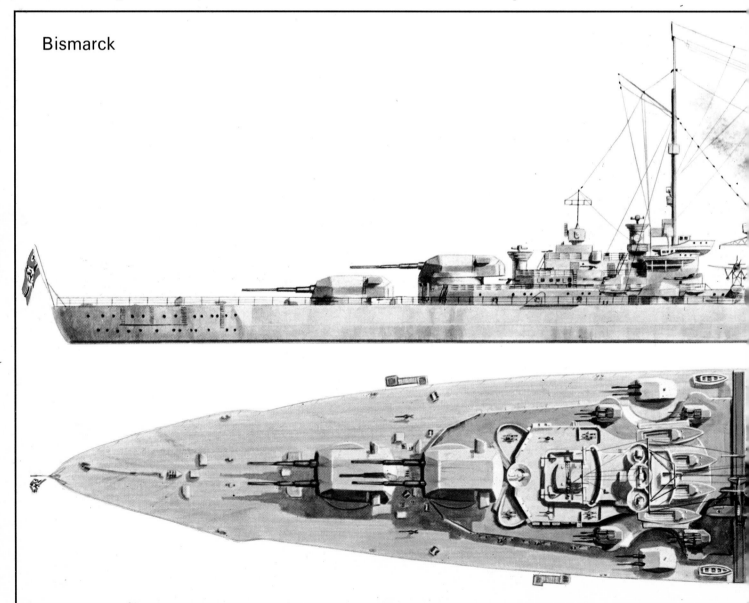

Bismarck

BISMARCK

Displacement 41,700 tons (42,369 tonnes) normal, 50,900 tons (51,717 tonnes) full load
Length 822 feet 9 inches (250 m 77 cm)
Beam 118 feet 3 inches (36 m)
Draught 29 feet 6 inches (9 m)
Machinery 3-shaft geared steam turbines, 138,000 shp = 29 knots
Armour belt: 12¾ inches (323 mm). decks: 2 to 4½ inches (51 to 114 mm). turrets: 12½ to 14 inches (319 to 356 mm)
Guns 8 × 15-inch (380-mm), 12 × 5.9-inch (150-mm), 16 × 4.1-inch (105-mm) AA, 16 × 37-mm AA, 36 × 20-mm AA
Torpedo Tubes none
Aircraft 3 (1 catapult)
Launched 14 February 1939 by Blohm & Voss, Hamburg

The Fuhrer inspects the new battleship Bismarck *in 1941. The radar mattress on the after fire control is clearly visible at top left and the aircraft crane can be seen on the right. The drawing shows how the fixed cross-deck catapult divided the forward and after superstructure. The* Tirpitz *was similar in appearance, apart from having a higher catapult, quadruple torpedo tubes abaft the catapult, and extra anti-aircraft guns*

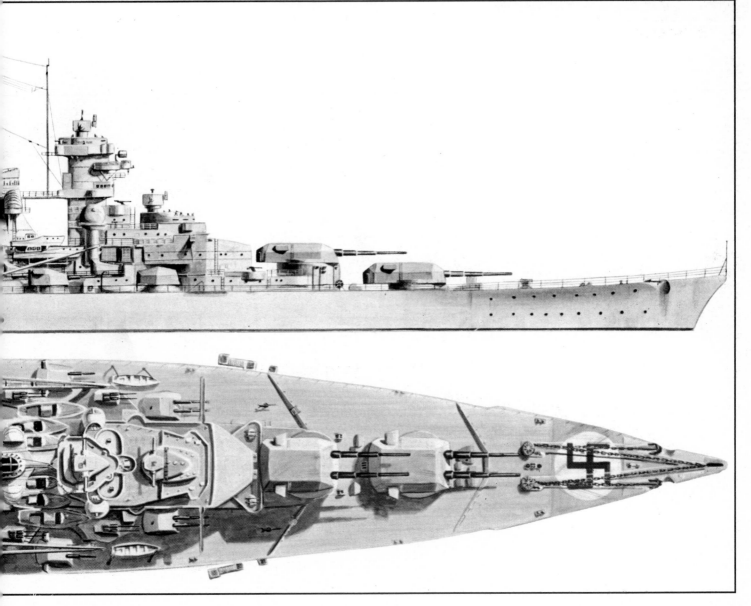

Germany: Submarines

The Germans were more successful in keeping a certain continuity in the design of submarines after the end of the First World War than they were with any other type of vessel. This is one of the reasons why the U-boats were the most satisfactory of all German warship types. The other eminently successful and well-designed German warship type, the *S-Boat* or MTB ('E-Boat') should not be ignored, even though space does not permit any description of them.

Submarines were the only type of ship in which the German Navy of the First World War had outnumbered the Royal Navy. There was variety, too, in the German submarine fleet; besides the medium-sized vessels which she had continued to develop throughout the war, Germany had the large 'U-cruisers' armed with 150-mm guns and capable of crossing the Atlantic, the small minelayers of the 'UC' classes, and the coastal boats of the 'UB' group, which started small, but evolved into a design which was to be the basis of the standard Second World War U-boat. With the end of the First World War, Germany lost all these submarines, but the teams which designed them were kept at work in exile in other countries – Finland, Spain, Holland and Sweden. Germany was not allowed to have any submarines until 1934, but her designers were ready with improved versions of vessels built abroad for foreign navies, which themselves were in a direct line of descent from the best First World War designs. Fortunately for Britain, full advantage was not taken of the opportunity to build these boats before the war. German admirals were dreaming grandiose dreams of super-battleships and gave little thought to the building or use of the one type of vessel that could win the war for them, if used in sufficient numbers and with adequate skill. The U-boats did remarkably well in the early part of the war, though handicapped by the failure of their over-complicated and insufficiently developed torpedoes. During the period from 1941 to 1943, when the deficiencies in both torpedoes and submarine numbers had been overcome, the U-boats came close to winning. However, as time went on the sheer quantity of Allied shipbuilding production began to tell, and, more important, the Allies began to win the scientific battle. New types of radar were developed, ahead-throwing weapons like 'Hedgehog' and 'Squid' made surface escorts more deadly, and rockets and acoustic homing torpedoes did the same for aircraft. One of the most effective weapons against U-boats was their own radio chatter with their bases, used by Allied ships to track them down.

It was not that the U-boats did not have new weapons of their own, such as homing and pattern-running torpedoes, decoys like the *'pillenwerfer'* to give false echoes on Asdic, radar detectors, and extra 20-mm guns to turn the boats into flak traps for Allied aircraft. Despite all these, the U-boats were overwhelmed and by

Right: Incomplete Type XXI hulls at Bremen and a scuttled VIIC and XXI in dry dock; the Type XXI was an advanced design, in effect a true submarine

the end of 1943 decisively defeated in the chief battleground, the North Atlantic. The number of skilled commanders and crews on the German side dropped, whereas the Allies' experience and skill grew. Right at the end of the war the Germans were ready to attempt a comeback with radically new designs of submarine, but they were far too late. The Schnorkel had been brought into use rather earlier and gave the U-boats a greatly extended range underwater, but it was essentially a defensive innovation, whose use helped to prevent U-boats being sunk but was of little good in assisting them to sink enemy ships.

The first submarines built for the Kriegsmarine were the Type I, ocean-going boats based on a design built in Spain for Turkey, of which only two were built, and the Type II, small coastal boats of more use for training than anything else.

The mainstay of German submarine building throughout the war was the next design to appear, the Type VII. These were developed, via a Finnish boat, from the later First World War 'UB' boats. The Type VIIs were the smallest possible design for ocean going, well armed and with a good diving performance. The Type VIIB version (of which the U-47 which sank the Royal Oak was one) was a slightly improved version of the original Type VIIA. They were slightly bigger and more seaworthy, and had more powerful diesels. The VIIC which followed was improved by the addition of extra torpedo reloads and a better light anti-aircraft

armament, but was otherwise unchanged. This design became the standard production version, and was built in greater numbers than any other submarine type. The concomitant of this was that, by the end of the war, more vessels of this type had been lost in action than of any other warship class at any time or anywhere. They had, however, also achieved a similarly record number of merchant ships (and a fair number of warships) sunk.

As the war went on, design alterations were made on the stocks and during refits. More 20-mm and 37-mm guns were added, usually with the removal of the 88-mm deck gun. Some 'Flak-Trap' U-boats carried an impressive total of these automatic cannon in an attempt to discourage the increasingly deadly long-range anti-submarine aircraft the Allies were using. This was, in the event, a mistaken move; U-boats which stayed on the surface to fight it out were liable to be kept there till the aircraft that found them had summoned other aircraft, or even warships, to make a concerted attack. After numbers of U-boats had been lost in this way the experiment was abandoned.

The Schnorkel was more successful, but only appeared towards the end of the war, when it gave some respite to the battered survivors of the defeat in the battle of the convoys. Later models of the Type VII were given stronger hulls to increase the already impressive maximum diving depth. This was greater for German boats than for other nations' submarines. The Type VIID minelaying version had an extra section

fitted with vertical mine tubes abaft the conning tower. The Germans and French preferred these vertical tubes for minelaying, but the British and Americans preferred rails laid on top of the pressure hull and covered by a casing, laying the mines through ports in the stern. The VIIF design also had an extra section added amidships, but this time to carry extra torpedoes.

The variants of the Type VII had been extremely successful designs in their day, but by the end of the war they had become obsolete and were easy meat for their opponents. They were also small for oceanic warfare, and, though this gave them excellent underwater manoeuvrability, important in the evasion of depth charge attacks, it also meant that the crews lived in badly cramped conditions.

U-47
Displacement 753 tons (765 tonnes) surfaced, 857 tons (870 tonnes) submerged
Length 218 feet 3 inches (66 m 52 cm) waterline
Beam 20 feet 3 inches (6 m 17 cm)
Draught 5 feet 6 inches (1 m 67 cm)
Machinery surfaced: 2-shaft diesel-electric, 2,800 bhp = $17\frac{1}{4}$ knots. submerged: 2-shaft electric, 750 shp = 8 knots
Guns 1 × 3.5-inch (88-mm), 1 × 20-mm AA
Torpedo Tubes 5 × 21-inch (532-mm)
Launched 29 October 1938 by Germania Yard, Kiel

Two main types of U-boats fought the Battle of the Atlantic. U-47 (below) a Type VIIB, was developed into the standard workhorse Type VIIC while the larger, long-range Type IXB (right) patrolled more distant waters

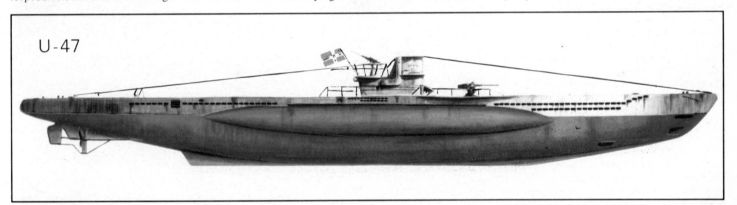

U-47

The Type VIIs also had insufficient endurance for the longer patrols which were necessary in a world war. The larger and longer-range German standard production type developed to fill this gap was the Type IX. This traced its ancestry through the Type I (of which it was an enlargement), via the Spanish-built Turkish *Gür* to the *U-81* class of the First World War.

The initial group, the Type IXA, carried an impressive number of reloads for their six tubes, 22 torpedoes in all, or could carry mines instead. The Type IXB was merely a similar design with improved bunkerage and therefore increased radius, while the next development, the IXC, was further improved in this respect. These larger and clumsier boats were, in general, not as popular with their crews as the Type VIIs, but were in fact the most successful of all U-boats in the total of merchant ship tonnage sunk per submarine.

The first two of the IXD type were special cargo submarines, designed for communicating with Japan and capable of carrying small quantities of certain vital commodities. Their engine installation was designed for a high surface speed, but proved unsatisfactory and had to be replaced. The second type of IXD was also designed for operation in distant seas, but was armed with torpedoes (with an alternative mine armament if required).

The Type XBs (Type XA was a design that was never built) were large minelayers, fitted with only a couple of stern tubes and a defensive gun armament in addition to their 66 mines, in external and internal vertical tubes. They were more often used as supply boats to extend the endurance of other boats than for minelaying.

The role of 'Milch Cow' submarine tankers and supply boats gained greater importance as Allied successes in the North Atlantic drove the U-boats further afield in search of easier pickings, a search which proved delusive. A special type of submarine tanker, the Type XIV, was therefore developed. These ships had shorter and fatter hulls, though much the same tonnage as the IXDs. They were comparatively easy targets, and thanks to good intelligence many of them were caught and sunk, particularly by US escort carriers operating in the South Atlantic.

Towards the end of the war, Germany made giant strides in submarine design and produced boats which were true submarines designed to operate almost entirely below the surface, instead of being submersibles intended chiefly for surface operations and brief dives. This was done by streamlining the hull for underwater speed, providing greatly increased battery power for high and sustained underwater speed, and *Schnorkels* for recharging the batteries. The larger versions of this new concept were known as the Type XXI, and a smaller coastal version was the Type XXIII. Both types made extensive use of prefabrication, and some that were completed were useless because of this.

The Germans also made many experiments with the closed-circuit Walther hydrogen peroxide turbine system, theoretically ideal for submarines, but the building of a series of type XVIIA and B boats powered entirely by these turbines, and others with combined diesel and hydrogen peroxide propulsion, was premature. Even after the war, when the British built a couple of submarines on this system and made many experiments, the turbines never worked completely satisfactorily. The Germans put much energy into a whole series of other diverse projects, such as closed-circuit diesel submarines and many other fascinating designs, but one cannot help feeling that this was a mistaken diversion of resources.

U-64
Displacement 1,051 tons (1,068 tonnes) surfaced, 1,178 tons (1,197 tonnes) submerged
Length 251 feet (76 m 50 cm)
Beam 22 feet 2 inches (6 m 76 cm)
Draught 15 feet 4 inches (4 m 70 cm)
Machinery surfaced: 2-shaft diesel, 4,400 bhp = $18\frac{1}{4}$ knots. submerged: electric motors, 1,000 shp = $7\frac{1}{4}$ knots
Guns 1 × 4.1-inch (105-mm), 1 × 37-mm AA, 1 × 20-mm AA (a second 20-mm gun was later added, and in some cases one quadruple and two twin 20-mm mounts or one 37-mm AA and two 20-mm AA mounts)
Torpedo Tubes 6 × 21-inch (532-mm), four bow, two stern
Launched 20 September 1939 by AG Weser, Bremen

Below left: The Type II was the most numerous U-boat type at the beginning of the war.
Below: U-883, a Type IXD2, lies alongside three Type VIIC boats after the surrender at Wilhelmshaven

U-64

Italy: Capital Ships

In the early 1930s, the only battleships that the Italians possessed were four old, slow, lightly armed and lightly armoured vessels which, though possibly a match for their French equivalents, were certainly no use against the new *Dunkerque* class. They were therefore reconstructed, emerging as completely different vessels. In order to raise the speed by seven knots the hull was lengthened by more than 9 metres by fitting a new bow section. The centre turret was removed to make room for entirely new machinery and boilers of three times the power, driving two instead of four screws. A new superstructure was fitted and the armament was remodelled. The heavy guns were bored out from 305 mm to 320 mm and a new secondary antiaircraft battery was fitted. The new Pugliese system of underwater protection was introduced and the horizontal armour was strengthened, but it was still inadequate, and nothing could be done about the thin side armour.

The first pair, the *Conte Di Cavour* and *Giulio Cesare*, were converted between 1933 and 1937. The second pair, *Andrea Doria* and *Caio Duilio*, converted between 1937 and 1940, were fitted with a modified secondary armament and a much improved anti-aircraft battery. Their appearance had changed dramatically, for when completed in the First World War they had widely spaced tall funnels and very tall tripod masts like contemporary British dreadnoughts. The midships triple 305-mm gun turret had divided the superstructure into two separate sections, in the same manner as the first Italian dreadnought *Dante Alighieri*. Now all four ships had a forecastle deck which extended for two-thirds of the length, and in place of the midships turret were two smaller funnels with clinker-screens. The tripod masts and small bridge gave way to a prominent bridge with a control tower above it. The anti-aircraft guns were sited on the forecastle deck and the old broadside battery was completely suppressed. The first pair of vessels could be easily distinguished from the second because the later ships had their anti-aircraft guns in single turrets, closely arranged.

Wartime alterations were mostly minor, for the Italian Navy did not have sufficient battle experience to know how many changes were needed. Radar aerials were fitted late in the war and the three survivors were painted in a series of camouflage schemes. Numerous light anti-aircraft guns were added on 'B' turret, the quarter-deck and the superstructure to cope with increased air attacks. The *Conte Di Cavour* never completed her rebuilding and repairs after Taranto, so in December 1941 she went to sea with a new camouflage scheme and extra anti-aircraft guns, but no big guns in her turrets as she was merely in transit from Taranto to Trieste where she would be out of reach of British bombers. The two *Caio Duilio* ships, being completed later, had a more elaborate control tower and more light anti-aircraft guns.

As in the Royal Navy, the Italians drew on the expertise of marine artists in designing camouflage schemes. In the autumn of 1941 the *Andrea Doria* was painted in a four-colour scheme devised by an artist named Claudius; it was a disruptive pattern of saw-toothed black areas over the central part of the superstructure and hull, with panels of dark and light grey and light blue. But the most spectacular design of all was the 'dorsal fin' camouflage scheme worn by the *Duilio* in 1941, with enormous light green arrowheads pointing inwards from both ends of the ship against a dark grey background. The *Giulio Cesare* and *Cavour* both used schemes designed by Claudius in 1941 and 1942, but in 1942–43 the *Cesare*, *Duilio* and *Doria* changed to lighter-coloured patterns. In the post-war Italian Navy the *Duilio* and *Doria* adopted a scheme resembling the Royal Navy's post-war colours, a dark grey hull and light grey upperworks.

Although the conversions were a very successful technical achievement it is doubtful whether the results justified the time and money involved. It is true that Italy needed numbers as well as quality to counteract the five old French battleships, and Washington Naval Treaty tonnage restrictions would have caused problems if new battleships had been laid down without scrapping the old. However, the *Cavour* and the *Duilio* vessels, as reconstructed, were far too weakly protected to stand up even to the old British 15-inch (380-mm) battleships. Also, the underwater protection was inadequate, as was shown at Taranto, when *Cavour* sank and

Duilio was badly damaged.

Giulio Cesare, *Caio Duilio*, and *Doria* survived the war, and were among the last battleships in service, *Cesare* in the Soviet and *Duilio* and *Doria* in the Italian Navy. The latter two were not finally taken out of service till 1956, about the time that the ex-*Guilio Cesare* was mined and sunk by the Soviet Navy. Though *Cavour* was raised, she was never returned to service and was eventually sunk by an American air raid in 1945.

The problem with battleships was that they represented too big an investment in capital to be discarded. The Italian conversions were not as extreme as the Japanese but they still demonstrate the folly of putting new wine into old bottles. But it must be remembered that the political climate of the 1920s and 1930s, both inside and outside Italy, favoured disarmament. It was therefore inconceivable that the major powers would have agreed to any relaxation of the treaties to allow navies to start building battleships. The whole series of reconstructions in the 1930s must be looked on as attempts to modernize fleets in spite of a hostile climate, and in that light they were justifiable. But in the case of the *Conte di Cavour* and her sisters the original design was poor, and so any amount of reconstruction was unlikely to produce a front-rank battleship capable of facing foreign ships. The obsession with speed did nothing to help the designers. There is no doubt that a more modest speed would have allowed for at least some extra deck armour.

CONTE DI CAVOUR
Displacement 26,140 tons (26,559 tonnes) normal, 29,032 tons (29,498 tonnes) full load
Length 611 feet 6 inches (186 m 38 cm)
Beam 54 feet 4 inches (16 m 55 cm)
Draught 30 feet (9 m 14 cm)
Machinery 2-shaft geared steam turbines, 75,000 shp = 26 knots
Armour belt: 9¾ inches (245 mm). decks: 3⅖ inches (87 mm). turrets: 11 inch (280 mm)
Guns 10 × 12.6-inch (320-mm), 12 × 4.7-inch (120-mm), 8 × 3.9-inch (100-mm) AA, 8 × 37-mm AA, 12 × 20-mm AA
Aircraft none
Launched 10 August 1911 by La Spezia Dockyard

Conte di Cavour

The *Littorio* class were much more impressive ships. The first two, *Littorio* (renamed *Italia* in 1943) and *Vittorio Veneto*, were laid down in 1934 and the second group, *Impero* and *Roma*, in 1938. Because their designers ignored the 35,500-tonne treaty limitation it is not surprising that these were powerful ships, although the extra 2,000 or more tonnes did not give them as much advantage over their British and American contemporaries as might have been expected. The second group differed from the first mainly by having a different bow to improve the seaworthiness.

These ships were well armed and armoured, with an unusually high command for the after 380-mm turret. Their weakest point, apart from the short range usual in Mediterranean vessels, was their underwater protection. As in the *Cavour* and *Duilio* classes, the Pugliese system was employed, which utilized an empty cylinder to absorb the shock of a torpedo's explosion. This did not work as well in practice as the various systems used by other countries, since the compartmentation was not fully watertight. The first pair of ships were completed just before Italy entered the war, and these fast modern vessels might have had a considerable effect on the war in the Mediterranean if they had been used more adventurously. *Impero* was never completed, and *Roma*, finished near the end of 1943, saw no active service apart from gaining the unfortunate distinction of being the only battleship to be sunk by a guided missile. She

was sunk by a German 1400 X glider bomb on her way to surrender at Malta in September 1943, and *Italia* (ex-*Littorio*) was damaged by a hit and a near miss on the same occasion. It is interesting to note that there were proposals to use *Vittorio Veneto* and *Italia* to reinforce the British Far Eastern Fleet near the end of the war, but their short range and anticipated problems with equipment and spares prevented this.

In appearance the *Littorio* vessels differed widely from the older ships, although the compact control tower and small capped funnels stamped them as coming out of the same stable. The most obvious recognition point was the after 380-mm triple gun turret, which was on the same level as 'B' turret, and the aircraft catapult on the quarterdeck. Apart from the addition of 20-mm anti-aircraft guns on the superstructure and on the 152-mm gun turrets, and radar aerials on the control tower, little was done to alter the *Littorio* vessels between 1940 and 1943.

In the spring of 1941 the *Littorio* was painted in a 'fish-tail' camouflage scheme, but using a very dark grey background. Her sister *Vittorio Veneto* adopted the same scheme but used the lighter grey that was tried in the *Duilio*. In 1943 there was more variation, with the *Littorio* (now renamed *Italia* in an effort to purge memories of Fascism) painted in two tones of grey, with dark irregular patterns, whereas the *Vittorio Veneto* had a series of dark triangular patterns. On her last voyage the luckless *Roma*

was painted with rhomboidal patches all over her hull and superstructure.

The *Littorio* class were unusual in carrying not only floatplanes for reconnaissance but a fighter to shoot down enemy reconnaissance planes. The floatplane was the 311 km/h IMAM Ro 43 biplane, and the fighter was the 531 km/h Reggiane 2000 Falco Serie II monoplane. The idea was sound, and resembled the policy of the Japanese, who developed a floatplane fighter for similar purposes, but in the Mediterranean the Italian shipboard aircraft were far more likely to run into carrier-based fighters than the lumbering Walruses and Seafoxes that the Falco fighter was supposed to defeat. No protection was given to the aircraft on the catapult, either from the sea or from the blast of the 380-mm turret, and there are many photographs to show how badly the aircraft suffered.

The two survivors, the *Italia* and *Vittorio Veneto*, sailed for Malta after the surrender and were laid up in the Bitter Lakes on the Suez Canal. Their disposal was complicated by the fact that Italy was now a gallant Ally. After the abortive discussions about 'tropicalizing' them to act as fast carrier escorts in the Far East, it was reluctantly agreed among the Allies that it would be better to scrap them. This was almost certainly dictated by a desire to prevent one of them from falling into Soviet hands, as the Soviets staked their claim to a fair share of Italian tonnage by way of reparations. Instead, the Soviets were given the *Giulio Cesare*, while

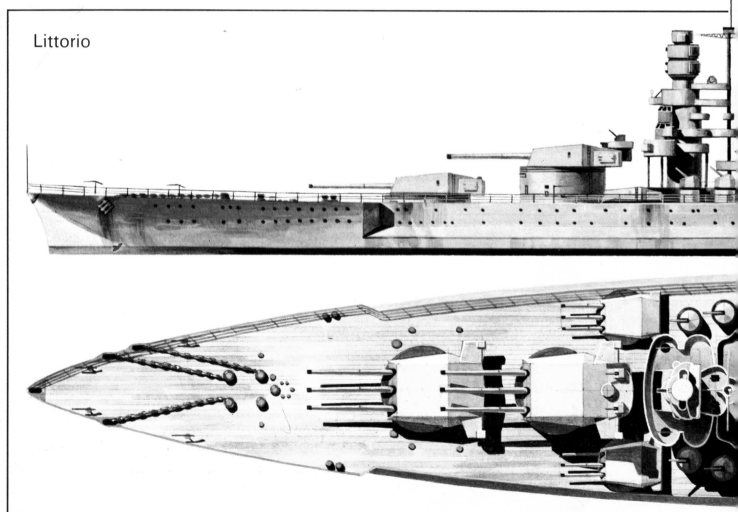

Littorio

the elegant but ineffective *Littorio* vessels went to the breakers' yards. By 1951 the demolition work was completed at La Spezia.

The *Littorio* class were among the best-looking warships of the Second World War, and although by no means the best battleships of their day they could well have given a good account in action. Their secondary armament was too crowded for efficiency, with the triple 152-mm turrets crowding the anti-aircraft turrets into a serried rank on the broadside where they had restricted arcs of fire. Looking back, they had restricted arcs of fire.

LITTORIO

Displacement 41,377 tons (42,041 tonnes) normal, 45,963 tons (46,700 tonnes) full load
Length 780 feet 8 inches (237 m 94 cm)
Beam 108 feet (32 m 91 cm)
Draught 31 feet 5 inches (9 m 56.5 cm)
Machinery 4-shaft geared steam turbines, 130,000 shp = 28 knots
Armour belt: 13¾ inches (348 mm). deck: 3.9 to 8.1 inches (100 to 204 mm). turrets: 13¾ inches (348 mm)
Guns 9 × 15-inch (380-mm), 12 × 6-inch (152-mm), 12 × 3.5-inch (88 mm) AA, 4 × 4.7-inch (120-mm) (for starshell), 20 × 37-mm AA, 28 × 20-mm AA
Aircraft 3 (1 catapult)
Launched 22 August 1937 by Ansaldo, Genoa

The Littorio *in her 1943 camouflage scheme with two RO43 biplane reconnaisance aircraft. The illustration shows a Reggiane 2000 monoplane fighter on the catapult*

Japan: Aircraft Carriers

Under the provision of the Washington Treaty it had been intended that the incomplete battlecruisers *Amagi* and *Akagi* should not be scrapped as originally proposed, but completed as carriers to match the American *Lexington* and *Saratoga*. Unfortunately the hull of *Amagi* was so badly damaged by an earthquake in 1923 that it had to be scrapped, and the hull of the incomplete *Kaga*, one of the companion class of battleships also due to be scrapped under the Washington Treaty, was used instead. As finally converted, *Kaga* was 12 m 17 cm shorter, 2,000 tonnes heavier and 3 knots slower than *Akagi*, but they carried virtually the same number of aircraft, and usually operated together. Indeed, after her 1936–38 refit, *Akagi* was fitted with her bridge on the port side instead of the normal starboard side (as it was on *Kaga*), so that when

they operated together the landing circuits of their aircraft would be in opposite directions. It was hoped that this would avoid accidents and speed the rate of recovery of the aircraft. *Soryu* had her bridge to starboard and her half-sister *Hiryu* had hers to port for the same reason. When these four ships operated together at the Battle of Midway, their formation was arranged to take advantage of this.

However, having the bridge on the port side was not a success. Air turbulence caused problems and increased the rate of landing accidents, so no other carrier had the bridge to port. Both *Kaga* and *Akagi* retained a thick waterline belt, and each was armed initially with ten 203-mm guns and had three flight decks forward.

Originally *Kaga* had two long funnels, one on either side of main flight deck, exhausting astern.

During a major refit from 1934–36 this was replaced with a single funnel angled slightly downwards exhausting amidships. In contrast to the original arrangement this gave little trouble. Bulges were fitted, and the ship was lengthened 8.5 m at the stern. New machinery was fitted, raising the speed slightly. At the same time the 203-mm guns were removed and the main flight deck extended from bow to stern, the subsidiary flight decks being removed. This enabled the hangars to be enlarged, and the number of aircraft carried was increased from 60 to 90. A navigating bridge was erected on the previously flush flight deck. The two existing lifts were enlarged and a third added forward.

Akagi's refit was slightly less extensive. As time and money were at a premium, bulges were fitted but only four 203-mm were landed. Even

Kaga

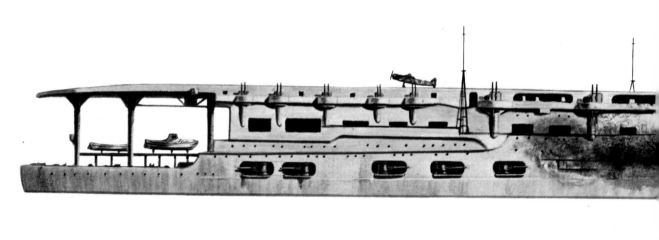

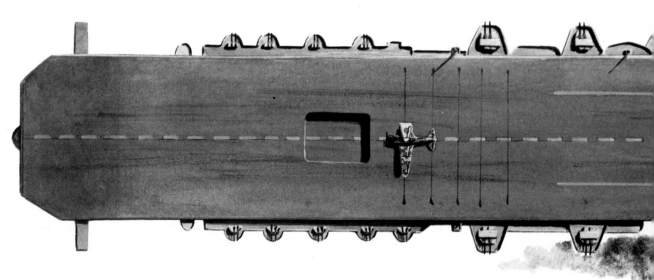

so the main flight deck was extended from bow to stern, and additional hangar space raised the aircraft complement from 60 to 91. The two original lifts were enlarged and a third was added forward, and a navigating bridge erected. All the boilers were converted to oil firing which raised the power slightly. A little smaller and somewhat slower than *Lexington* and *Saratoga*, after their 1930s facelift *Kaga* and *Akagi* compared favourably with them.

Laid down in 1929, the next carrier, *Ryujo*, was completed in 1933. Originally designed to displace about 7,620 tonnes to take advantage of the fact that the Washington Treaty did not limit the number of carriers of less than 10,160 tonnes that each country could build, she was altered while being built to include two hangar decks instead of one. Too much was attempted on too small a displacement, and she was top-heavy, a fault that many Japanese interwar designs suffered from. The dangers of this were highlighted in March 1934, when the torpedo boat *Tomozuru* capsized in a storm from this cause. Immediately afterwards four of the 127-mm anti-aircraft guns on the *Ryujo* were removed and a ballast keel fitted. Then in September 1935 the Japanese Combined Fleet encountered a storm in the Pacific; almost all the ships were damaged, and two destroyers were lost. After this, the hulls of most Japanese warships were strengthened and topweight was removed. *Ryujo* herself had her forecastle raised by one deck to improve her seaworthiness. All these modifications raised her displacement to 10,776 tonnes, but she would have been a more successful design if that had been her designed tonnage.

KAGA
Displacement 38,200 tons (38,813 tonnes) normal, 43,000 tons (43,690 tonnes) full load
Length 812 feet 4 inches (247 m 59 cm)
Beam 100 feet (30 m 47 cm) over flight deck
Draught 31 feet (9 m 44 cm)
Machinery 4-shaft geared steam turbines, 127,400 shp = 28 knots
Armour belt: 11 inch (280 mm) probably retained. deck: 4 to 6 inches (105 to 152 mm)
Guns 10 × 8-inch (203-mm), 16 × 5-inch (127-mm) DP, 22 × 25-mm AA
Aircraft 72 (2 catapults)
Launched 17 November 1921 by Kawasaki Co., Kobe

The aircraft carrier **Kaga** *shows traces of her battleship origin. Note the 203-mm guns in casemates, the small island superstructure and the downward-curved funnel*

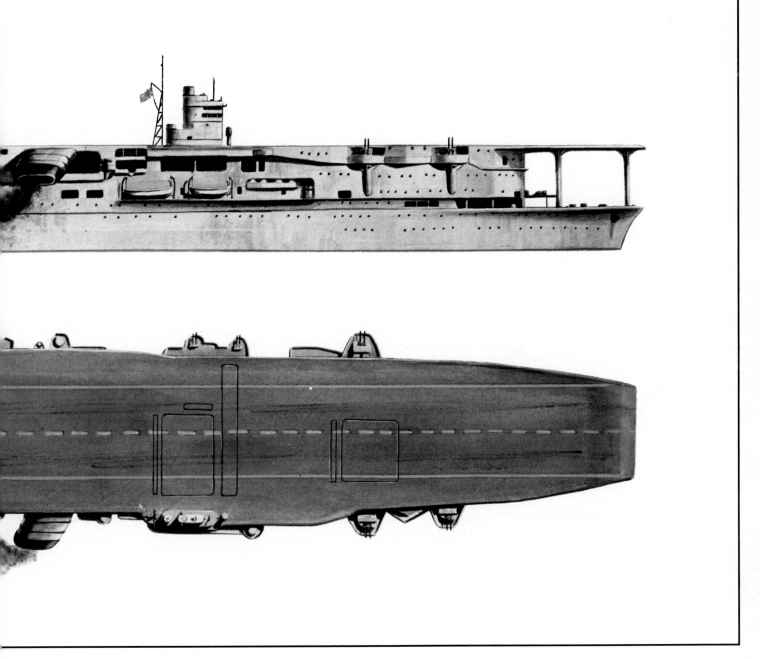

In any case, *Ryujo* was far too small for a fleet carrier. Much more successful was the 16,150-tonne *Soryu*, laid down in 1934; she was only able to be built because Japan had so continuously understated her carrier tonnage that there appeared to be enough left under the terms of the Washington Treaty to build another one which was not in fact the case. Nevertheless, *Soryu* was built, and she formed the basis of the design of most subsequent Japanese Navy carriers. With a speed of more than 34 knots and able to carry over 50 aircraft, she was a formidable vessel.

Her half-sister *Hiryu* was very similar but was built after the expiry of the terms of the Washington Treaty, so the tonnage limitations no longer applied. Thus she was able to take advantage of the lessons of the great storm in 1935, and was modified to improve her seaworthiness. She had 900 mm more beam, her forecastle was one deck higher, her hull was stronger and her displacement was nearly 1,525 tonnes greater. Even so she was smaller and could carry fewer aircraft than her American contemporaries of the *Yorktown* class. As previously noted, *Hiryu* shared with *Akagi* the dubious distinction of being the only carriers with a bridge to port of the flight deck.

Although *Hiryu* was built after the end of the treaty restrictions her size had been governed by that of *Soryu*. The next pair of fleet carriers, *Shokaku* and *Zuikaku*, were the first Japanese carriers since *Hosho* whose design was governed solely by operational requirements.

Basically enlarged and improved versions of the *Hiryu*, they each displaced over 25,400 tonnes and could operate over 80 planes. Utilizing the same sort of bulbous bow as the contemporary *Yamato*, they had a maximum speed of more than 34 knots and an extended range. The 160,000 shaft horsepower developed by their engines was the largest of any Japanese warship. In addition, they possessed the heavy (for 1941) anti-aircraft armament of sixteen 127-mm and thirty-six 25-mm anti-aircraft guns. Each had three lifts (*Soryu* had only two), and after the unhappy experiences with *Akagi* and *Hiryu*, both had their bridges on the starboard side of the flight deck. When they were completed a few months before Pearl Harbor they were the most powerful carriers in the Pacific. Well-balanced designs, they were the most successful of all the Japanese carriers, and their enforced absence from the Midway operation due to battle damage and lack of trained pilots was a misfortune for the Japanese.

However, in one respect neither they nor any other Japanese or American carriers of the late 1930s measured up to their British contemporaries. The first shortfall was the lack of an armoured flight deck, which was by deliberate choice. Royal Navy carriers would be forced to operate for much of the time within range of shore-based aircraft which would be available in numbers sufficient to swamp any fighter defence the carriers could put up. Therefore the defence of the British carrier rested ultimately on its own anti-aircraft armament and as much horizontal armour as possible. Because armoured flight decks put a lot of weight high up in a ship, the hangars had to be small to avoid top-heaviness. Therefore the number of planes carried was small. In the Pacific the problems were different. Distances were too great for land-based aircraft to be considered the prime threat. The greatest need was for a large aircraft-carrying capacity to provide overwhelming strike force as well as sufficient fighters for escort and carrier defence. Therefore armoured flight decks were not fitted.

Wartime experience showed that this was the wrong decision. Whereas British carriers with armoured flight decks survived to be repaired, and frequently were able to continue operating

Hiryu

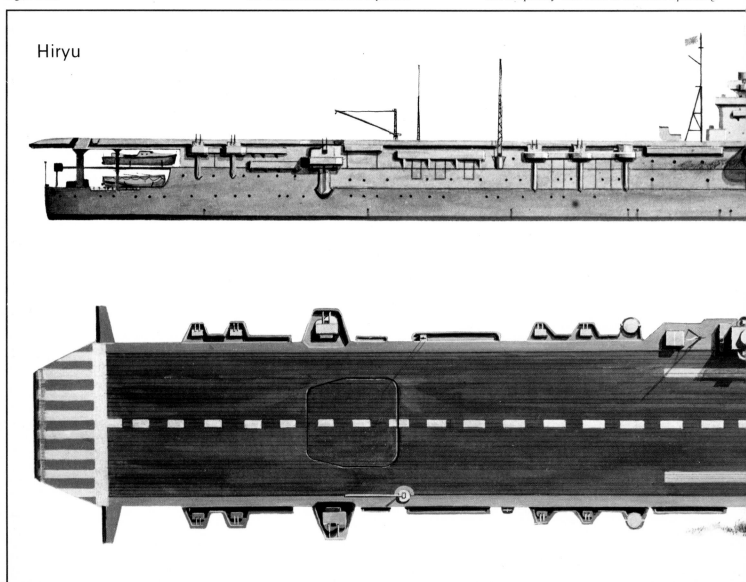

aircraft even after quite large bomb hits, the
unarmoured flight decks of their Japanese and
American contemporaries were easily put out of
action by even minor damage, and the carriers
themselves were much more easily sunk by air
attack. Although *Shokaku* survived two battles
(Coral Sea and Santa Cruz) at which her flight
deck was so badly damaged as to render her
incapable of operating aircraft, such resistance
to battle damage was rare among Japanese
carriers.

HIRYU

Displacement 17,300 tons (17,577 tonnes) normal,
21,000 tons (21,337 tonnes) full load
Length 746 feet (227 m 38 cm)
Beam 88 feet 6 inches (26 m 97 cm) over flight deck
Draught 25 feet 4 inches (7 m 72 cm)
Machinery 4-shaft geared steam turbines,
152,000 shp = 34½ knots
Armour unknown, but probably a waterline belt
and deck protection
Guns 12 × 5-inch (127-mm) DP, 31 × 25-mm AA
Aircraft 73 (2 catapults)
Launched 16 November 1937 by Yokosuka
Dockyard

*Hiryu on trials in April 1939; note the distinctive
port-side island*

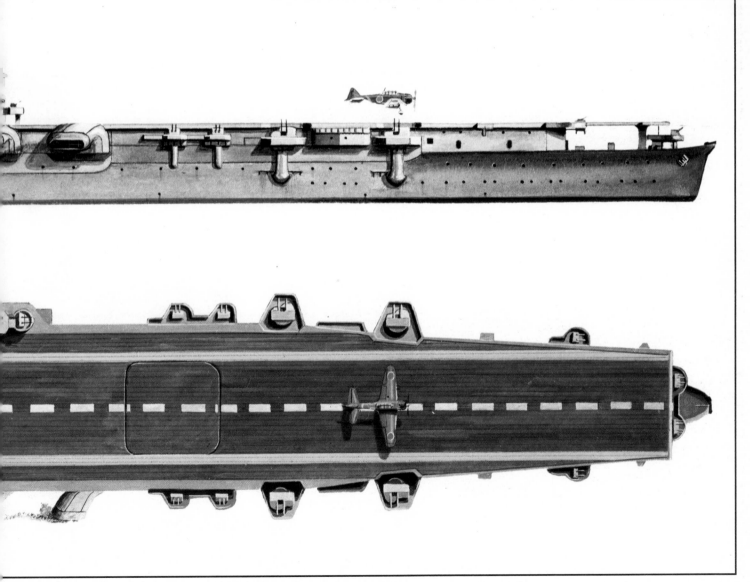

Shoho

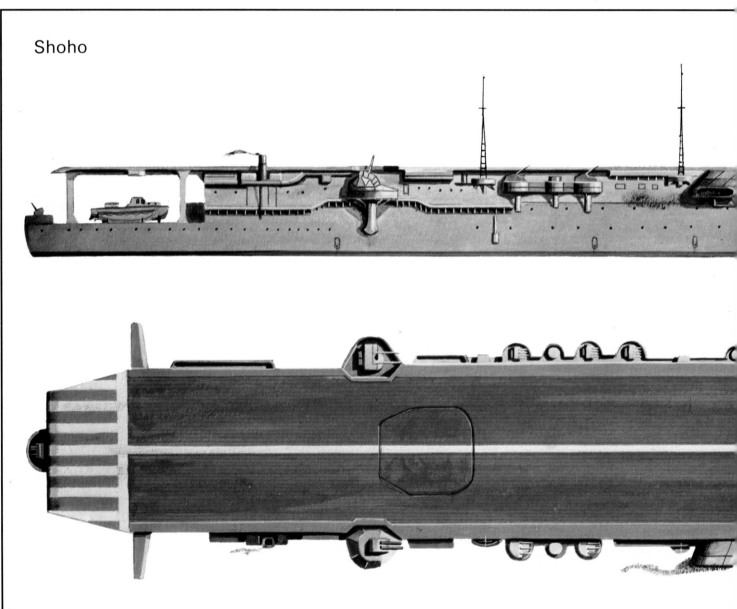

Realizing that there would be neither time nor shipbuilding capacity available if Japan became involved in a major war, the naval high command had arranged that a number of fleet auxiliaries and large liners should be designed in such a way that they could swiftly and easily be converted into light carriers if the need arose, and in 1940 the first steps were taken to convert them. The *Shoho* and *Zuiho* (ex-*Tsurugizaki* and *Takasaki* respectively) had been laid down in 1934 as high-speed oilers, but it was later decided that they should be completed as submarine tenders. *Tsurugizaki* was actually completed in this form in 1938 and her conversion into a carrier did not start till early 1941. *Takasaki* was still under construction when in January 1940 it was decided to complete her as a carrier. These ships were originally fitted with

Shoho *was built as the submarine depot ship* Tsurugizaki. *She was not renamed until December 1941, two days after this photograph was taken. Note the raised barrier on the flight deck and the hinged radio masts which would be lowered during flying operations*

diesels because the potential advantages of this type of engine – lower fuel consumption and less weight – were what were needed to provide the ships with greater range while at the same time releasing a greater proportion of the displacement for armament and protection. Like the Germans, the Japanese made extensive experiments with diesels in the interwar period, but the Japanese never managed to get their diesels to perform with sufficient reliability for active service. For this reason *Shoho* and *Zuiho* were fitted with turbines when they were converted into carriers. No armour was fitted because this would have reduced the ships' performance, which was already very low for vessels intended to act with the fleet. The slightly larger *Ryuho* (ex-*Taigei*), laid down in 1931 as a submarine tender, was converted in the same way as *Shoho* and *Zuiho*. Designed and built in a hurry, the extensive electrical welding used to speed her construction gave trouble, as did her extremely unreliable diesels which were replaced with turbines during reconstruction. Partly because of this the conversion, planned to take three months, in fact took 12. Completed in late 1942,

she was never used operationally and was one of the four Japanese carriers that survived the war.

Designed to be convertible into high-speed oilers, submarine tenders, seaplane carriers or aircraft carriers, *Chiyoda* and *Chitose* were completed in 1938 as high-speed seaplane tenders, with four catapults apiece and a mix of diesel and steam turbine engines that they retained for the rest of their career. With the loss of four large carriers at Midway, Japan's need for carriers became pressing, and conversion of both *Chitose* and *Chiyoda* was begun in late 1942 and early

SHOHO
Displacement 11,262 tons (11,442 tonnes) normal, 15,000 tons (15,240 tonnes) full load
Length 712 feet (217 m)
Beam 75 feet 6 inches (23 m) over flight deck
Draught 21 feet 9 inches (6 m 62 cm)
Machinery 2-shaft geared steam turbines, 52,000 shp = 28 knots
Armour none
Guns 8 × 5-inch (127-mm) DP, 8 × 25-mm AA
Aircraft 30 (2 catapults)
Launched 1 June 1935 (as *Tsurugizaki*) by Yokosuka Dockyard

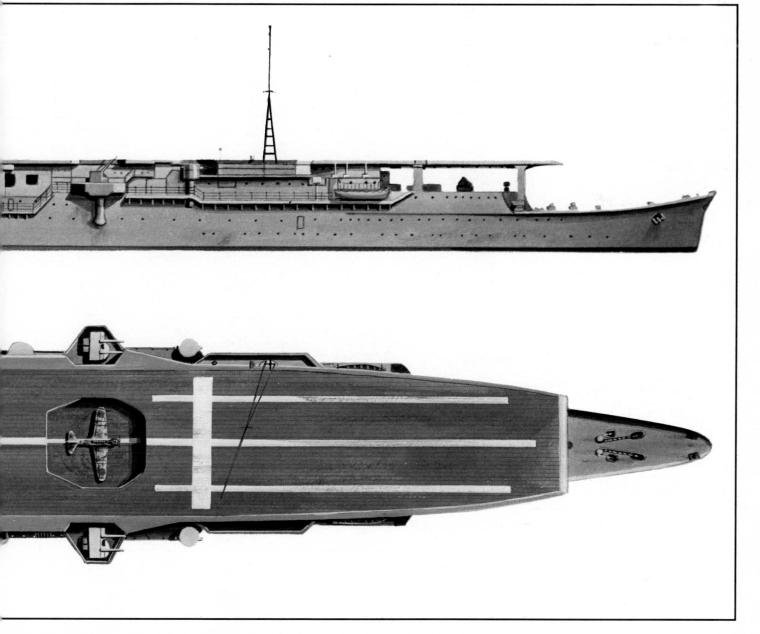

1943. As converted they resembled the *Shoho* class closely, except for their mixed propulsion.

Taiyo, Chuyo and *Unyo* (ex-*Kasuga Maru, Nitta Maru* and *Yawata Maru* respectively) were converted into carriers. *Taiyo* was converted in 1941 and *Unyo* from January to May 1942, but the conversion of *Chuyu* was delayed because she was intended to carry a Japanese delegation to a proposed conference with President Roosevelt in late 1941. In the event, her conversion was not completed until November 1942. Because they lacked catapults and arrestor gear, these ships were not suitable for service with the fleet, while for escort and training duties they were unnecessarily large and fast. They were mostly used as aircraft ferries and training carriers, and their large size merely served to provide a large target for the submarines that eventually sunk all three. Considerably better fitted for fleet work were the *Hiyo* and *Junyo*. Converted in an early stage of construction, these ships (originally intended as the luxury liners *Izumo Maru* and *Kashiwara Maru* respectively) were over 6,000 tonnes larger and nearly five knots faster than the *Taiyo* class. Most nearly comparable with the British light fleet carriers, these were the first carriers in the Japanese Navy to have both the bridge and funnel mounted above the flight deck, and were valuable additions to the fleet.

Also converted from liners were *Kaiyo* and *Shinyo*. *Kaiyo* (ex-*Argentina Maru*) was completed as a liner in 1939 and her conversion was finished in late 1943. She was the smallest liner the Japanese converted, and in an effort to increase her speed they replaced her existing engines with a set of destroyer turbines, but even so she could only make 23 knots. This would have been more than adequate for escort work, but the Japanese mistakenly intended to use all these conversions for fleet work, for which purpose she, like the *Taiyo*, was too slow. Like them, she was used for training and as an aircraft ferry. Her sister *Brazil Maru* was sunk as a transport before she could be converted.

Shinyo was a conversion of the German liner *Scharnhorst*, caught in Far Eastern waters by the outbreak of war. She had been the test ship for the new German high-pressure boilers, which proved as unreliable in her as in all the German ships they were used in; they were replaced shortly after conversion. As completed she was similar to the ships of the *Taiyo* class, except that she was fitted with bulges and a radar aerial. Steel for her conversion was taken from the incomplete hull of the forth *Yamato*-class battleship.

ZUIHO
Displacement 11,262 tons (11,442 tonnes) normal, 15,000 tons (15,240 tonnes) full load
Length 712 feet (217 m)
Beam 75 feet 6 inches (23 m) over flight deck
Draught 21 feet 9 inches (6 m 62 cm)
Machinery 2-shaft geared steam turbines, 52,000 shp = 28 knots
Armour none
Guns 8 × 5-inch (127-mm) DP, 8 × 25-mm AA
Aircraft 30 (2 catapults)
Launched 19 June 1936 (as *Takasaki*) by Yokosuka Dockyard

The carrier Zuiho, *a sister of the* Shoho, *seen shortly before she sank during the Battle of Leyte Gulf. The camouflage scheme tried to give the impression of a battleship*

Zuiho

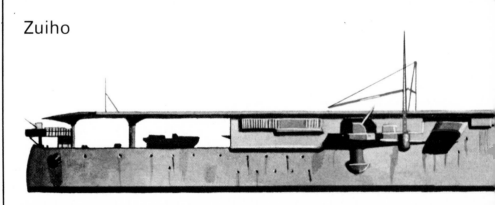

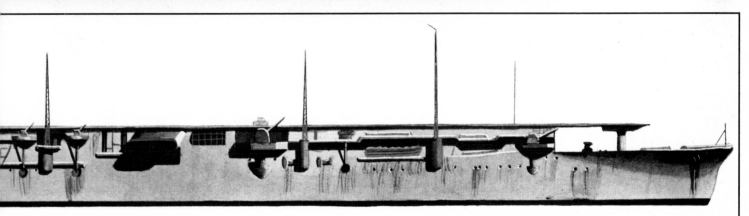

Taiho, laid down in 1941 but not completed until 1944, was the first Japanese fleet carrier to be completed that incorporated the results of combat experience from the war in the Atlantic and in the Mediterranean and from Japan's own experience in the Pacific. Much the same size as *Shokaku*, she had one deck less owing to having an armoured deck (though this was only a deck, and not a box as in British carriers) and therefore carried only two-thirds the number of aircraft. She also carried a large anti-aircraft armament and was the first Japanese fleet carrier to have her bridge and funnel above the flight deck. The bow was also plated up to this level, giving superior seaworthiness in heavy seas. While *Taiho* was a competent design, she was not perhaps quite as good as one might expect of a carrier completed so late in the war. Four slightly larger variants were ordered in the two emergency programmes following Midway, and a further three were proposed, but they were all cancelled. *Taiho* was eventually lost after being torpedoed because of poor damage control, to which the badly thought-out fuel storage and distribution arrangements contributed.

Laid down in 1942, *Unryu* was a very slightly altered *Hiryu* with the bridge moved to the starboard side of the flight deck and an augmented anti-aircraft armament. Five more were laid down after Midway, of which only *Amagi* and *Katsuragi* were completed. *Kasagi* was almost finished when work stopped in April 1945, but *Aso* and *Ikoma* had not even been fitted with hangars by the end of the war. Only two lifts were fitted in these ships to simplify construction, and because there were no suitable large engines, *Aso* and *Katsuragi* were fitted with destroyer turbines which reduced the power by thirty per cent and lowered the speed by two knots. Eleven more were ordered, but they were all cancelled before being laid down. Although the *Hiryu* was a reasonable design for the mid-1930s, by 1944 it had become somewhat dated, and the *Unryu* class were too small and too badly protected for their designed function as Pacific fleet carriers in the later part of the war.

Following these vessels came two warship conversions. The first, *Shinano*, was laid down in May 1940 as the third *Yamato*-class battleship. After Midway the design was altered and the virtually complete hull was fitted with an armoured flight deck. As first recast, her design did not envisage her operating any aircraft of her own. Instead she was intended to act as a base for the planes from other carriers, refuelling, repairing and maintaining them at sea. Because of this she was to be fitted with only a small amount of hangar space, but would have large stocks of fuel, bombs, torpedoes and spare parts stored in the spaces where her turrets were to have been. In time it was recognized that she would need some planes of her own for self-protection, and so provision was made for her to operate some, but she never had the chance to use them in action for she was torpedoed and sunk on her maiden voyage. Hit by four torpedoes aft, from the American submarine *Archerfish*, she proceeded at 16 knots for her destination; *Shinano* still had her battleship protection, and it was thought that she would be able to survive. However, her crew were untrained, and production standards as well as the quality of materials had deteriorated during the war. As a result, many compartments that ought to have been watertight were not, and some watertight doors were missing. At 16 knots water poured into the hull, and she sank after a few hours.

The other warship conversion, *Ibuki*, had been laid down in 1942 as a heavy cruiser. Owing to the pressing shortage of tankers, it was at first decided to complete her as a high-speed oiler, but this was never put into effect. In late 1943 it was decided to convert her into a carrier, but work proceeded very slowly and she was only eighty per cent complete when Japan surrendered. If she had been finished she would have been similar to the American *Saipan* carriers.

The last Japanese wartime carrier conversions to be projected were the oil tankers *Otakisan Maru*, *Shimane Maru*, *Chisusa Maru* and *Yamishio Maru* which were built in 1944, the latter two for the army. It was intended to fit them with flight decks to act as escort carriers, but early in 1945 it was decided to complete them as coal-burning cargo ships, since Japan no longer had any oil supplies; all were sunk before they could be completed.

Japan was the first country in the world to fit sonar to its carriers. Starting with *Shokaku*, all Japanese carriers completed after 1940 had passive sonar, which enabled them to detect nearby submarines and helped evasion of torpedoes. However, until the middle of the war, no Japanese carrier had radar, and in this respect the Americans, whose carriers had it from the start, had an enormous advantage. If Japanese carriers had been fitted with radar at Midway the four fleet carriers *Kaga*, *Akagi*, *Soryu* and *Hiryu* might not all have been lost, despite incompetent leadership and lack of armoured decks.

TAIHO

Displacement 29,300 tons (29,770 tonnes) normal, 33,000 tons (33,529 tonnes) full load
Length 855 feet (260 m 60 cm)
Beam 98 feet 6 inches (30 m) over flight deck
Draught 31 feet 6 inches (9 m 60 cm)
Machinery 4-shaft geared steam turbines, 160,000 shp = 33 knots
Armour belt: $2\frac{1}{4}$ to 6 inches (56 to 152 mm). deck: $3\frac{3}{4}$ inches (94 mm)
Guns 12 × 3.9-inch (100-mm) DP, 51 × 25-mm AA
Aircraft 74
Launched 7 April 1943 by Kawasaki Co., Kobe

SHINANO

Displacement 62,000 tons (62,995 tonnes) normal, 70,755 tons (71,890 tonnes) full load
Length 872 feet 9 inches (266 m)
Beam 131 feet 3 inches (40 m) over flight deck
Draught 33 feet 9 inches (10 m 28 cm)
Machinery 4-shaft geared steam turbines, 150,000 shp = 27 knots
Armour belt: $6\frac{1}{4}$ to $15\frac{3}{4}$ inches (158 to 398 mm). deck: 3 to 9 inches (76 to 227 mm)
Guns 16 × 5-inch (127-mm) DP, 145 × 25-mm AA, 12 × 28-barrelled rocket-projectors
Aircraft 47
Launched 8 October 1944 by Yokosuka Dockyard

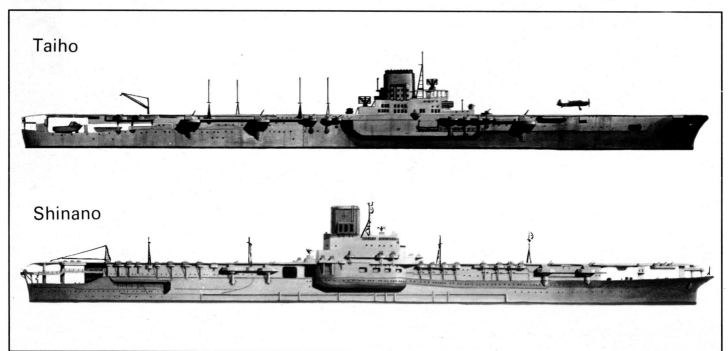

Taiho

Shinano

Japan: Capital Ships

The oldest effective Japanese battleships in World War II were the four *Kongo*-class fast battleships. *Kongo* herself had been built in Britain between 1910 and 1913 to a design that owed much to the Royal Navy, but which had been modified to suit Japanese conditions and combat experience in consultation with the major British private shipbuilders. *Haruna*, *Hiei* and *Kirishima* were built to the same design in Japan. As first completed they were lightly armoured battle-cruisers. In 1917, Britain wished to use them in the European theatre of operations, but the Japanese refused.

By the standards of the mid-1920s, the *Kongo*-class vessels were far too lightly armoured, and because Japan was unable to build any new ships under the terms of the Washington Treaty, they (except *Hiei*, which was disarmed as a training ship) were extensively rebuilt between 1927 and 1932. Torpedo bulges were fitted, one funnel was removed and the old boilers were replaced by a smaller number of new ones (though they were still coal-fired). The horizontal armour was also thickened, and the range of the 356-mm guns was extended by increasing the elevation. However the power was not increased so the speed fell by two knots to nearly 26 knots. The complicated and distinctive 'pagoda' masts fitted to these and the other Japanese battleships in the 1930s were simply the rather less tidy Japanese equivalent of the large bridges that the British and Americans fitted onto their rebuilt vessels; they had the unfortunate effect of increasing topweight very high up in the ship. Their sole advantage was the high command they gave to the forward fire control, enabling them to see the enemy at a greater range than before, but of course these massive structures could also be seen at long range by an enemy.

It was soon realized that it would be an advantage if these vessels could act as a unit with the fast fleet carriers. As originally converted they were too slow, so between 1935 and 1940 they were taken in hand again and lengthened by 7.6 m. At the same time a smaller number of oil-fired boilers replaced the first conversion's coal-fired ones; as a result the speed was raised to about 30 knots, and they were redesignated fast battleships. At the same time, 'pagoda' masts were fitted. *Hiei* was included in this rebuilding, and was brought up to the same standard as the other three. Even after the second rebuilding they were no match for a modern battleship, mainly because their armour was very weak. Japan had fully intended replacing them after the First World War with modern ships, but had been foiled by the Washington Treaty. They were, however, among the best interwar conversions, providing Japan with a much-needed and otherwise unattainable protection for the fast carriers. The weakness of their protection is demonstrated by the loss of *Hiei*, crippled in a scrappy night action off Guadalcanal by the gunfire of two cruisers and finished off by destroyers with torpedoes, and the fate of *Kongo*, sunk by a single torpedo from a submarine. Their effectiveness is shown by the speed with which *Kirishima* crippled the modern *South Dakota*, before she herself was destroyed by the radar-equipped *Washington*.

The Yamato *being fitted out in 1941. This huge vessel was the result of many years' planning; she and her sister* Musashi *were the largest World War II battleships*

The next class, *Fuso*, were Japan's first super-dreadnoughts. *Fuso* and *Yamashiro*, laid down in 1912 and 1913 respectively, were contemporaries of the American *Pennsylvania* ships, but whereas the American ships mounted their twelve 14-inch (356-mm) guns in four triple turrets, the Japanese were in six twin turrets. Theoretically this gave a higher rate of fire, but it also meant a longer ship with thinner armour to stretch over the greater number of magazines. In the 1930s both ships were extensively rebuilt, but without the same measure of success as the *Kongo* ships. Their horizontal armour was increased, torpedo bulges were added, the stern was lengthened by 7.6 m, and one funnel and the old boilers and turbines were removed and replaced by modern oil-burning machinery, which increased the range by one-third. However, virtually doubling the power only raised the speed by 1.7 knots. The guns' elevation was increased and a 'pagoda' mast fitted. They were too slow to be of much use in the war, and were eventually blasted to pieces by their American contemporaries in the Battle of the Surigao Straits in 1944.

Ise and *Hyuga*, laid down in 1914, were in essence improved versions of the *Fuso*-class ships, the major difference being that the two centre turrets were superimposed aft of the second funnel, instead of fore and aft of it. Their conversion between 1934 and 1937 was also virtually identical to that of the *Fuso* ships, but they were still too slow to be of any use in the carrier actions at the start of the Pacific war. Then from late 1942 to late 1943 they were both converted into carrier-battleships. Obsessed after Midway with the need to have as many aircraft carriers as possible, the Japanese wasted a valuable amount of their extremely limited shipbuilding capability on producing two hybrids whose only value was to act as bait for the American carrier planes, a role they were quite capable of performing in their original guise.

Instead of removing all the heavy armament and attempting to provide a complete flight deck, even of the crudest kind, the two aft turrets were removed and a short deck with catapults for operating floatplanes was erected in their stead, combined with an elaborate hangar and lift. The floatplanes could not land on the deck; they had to land on the water and were hoisted inboard on cranes. As it turned out, it did not matter that these two hybrids had been converted so badly, for, by the time they were ready, Japan no longer had any trained pilots to operate from them. After conversion their best feature was their heavy anti-aircraft armament.

ISE
Displacement 34,700 tons (35,257 tonnes) normal. 39,000 tons (39,626 tonnes) full load
Length 698 feet (212 m 73 cm)
Beam 108 feet 6 inches (33 m)
Draught 31 feet 9 inches (9 m 67 cm)
Machinery 4-shaft geared steam turbines, 75,000 shp = 24 knots
Armour belt: 4 to 12 inches (101 to 305 mm). deck: 7 inches (176 mm). turrets: 8 to 12 inches (203 to 305 mm)
Guns 12 × 12-inch (305-mm), 14 × 6-inch (155-mm), 8 × 5-inch (127-mm) DP, 16 × 25-mm AA
Aircraft 3 (1 catapult)
Launched 28 March 1914 by Kure Dockyard

Right: The battleship Fuso *on trials in the Bungo Straits in 1933 after her reconstruction. The 'pagoda' mast was a series of platforms built around the original tripod mast. There is a catapult on 'C' turret between the bridge and funnel. Below: The* Ise *and her sister* Hyuga *were reconstructed during 1943 with a flight deck in place of the two after 356-mm gun turrets. The drawing depicts them in 1944, by which time the floatplane had been replaced by light anti-aircraft guns, although the catapults were retained until October 1944. In 1943 the 'mattress' radar aerial was added to the control tower*

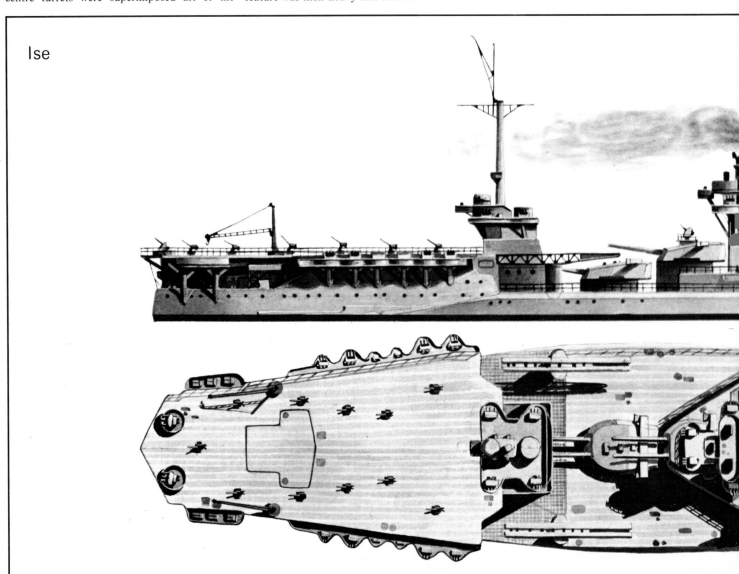

Ise

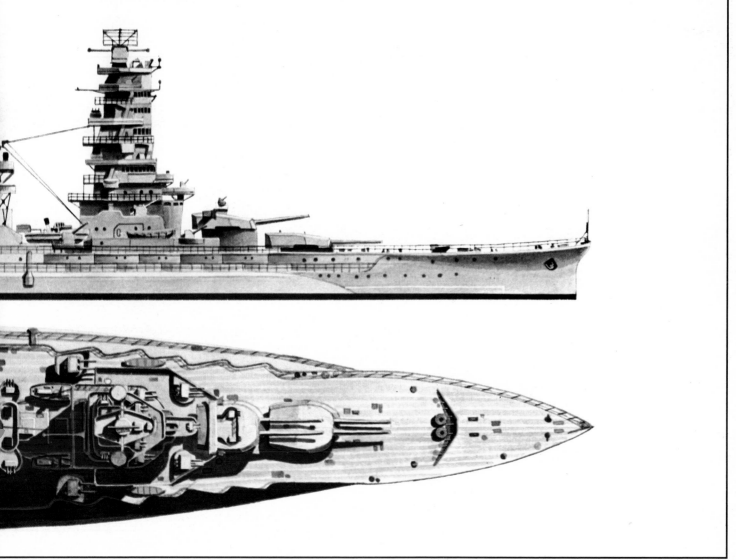

Laid down in 1916, *Nagato* and *Mutsu* were the first dreadnoughts to carry 406-mm guns. Fast, with a sensibly arranged main armament and with (for that time) moderately good armour protection, there is no doubt that they were by far the best Japanese battleship design. They were well-balanced ships, capable of taking on any foreign contemporary. Altered in the mid-1920s, they were throughly rebuilt in the mid-1930s. Horizontal armour was thickened where necessary, torpedo bulges were fitted, a funnel was removed and new engines and boilers were fitted. In addition, the hull was lengthened by 8.6 m, enabling speed to be maintained at 25 knots. The elevation of the guns was increased at the same time. Although slow by modern standards, these ships were still reasonably effective fighting units. *Mutsu* blew up in 1943 from unknown causes, the only Second World War battleship to do so, though several battleships had blown up in harbour in the First World War. Where cause could be established for these,

spontaneous ignition (usually owing to deterioration) of the ammunition was found to be the cause. *Nagato* only once took part in a surface action, at Leyte Gulf. After the war she was sunk during the second American atom bomb test at Bikini Atoll.

NAGATO
Displacement 39,130 tons (39,758 tonnes) normal, 44,000 tons (44,706 tonnes) full load
Length 738 feet (224 m 94 cm)
Beam 113 feet 6 inches (34 m 70 cm)
Draught 31 feet (9 m 44 cm)
Machinery 4-shaft geared steam turbines, 82,000 shp = 25 knots
Armour belt: 4 to 12 inches (101 to 305 mm). deck: $3\frac{1}{2}$ to 7 inches (88 to 176 mm). turrets: 14 inches (356 mm)
Guns 8 × 16-inch (406-mm), 18 × 5.5-inch (140-mm), 8 × 5-inch (127-mm) DP, 20 × 25-mm AA
Aircraft 3 (1 catapult)
Launched 9 November 1919 by Kure Dockyard

Above: The battleship Nagato *after modernization in 1936, with a 'Pagoda' mast and a single funnel. Right: The drawing depicts the* Nagato *as she was at the end of the war. Her light anti-aircraft armament had been increased from 25 to 98 25-mm guns, and air-warning and surface-gunnery radar had been added. Her sister ship* Mutsu *was lost in June 1943, after an accidental explosion in her magazines*

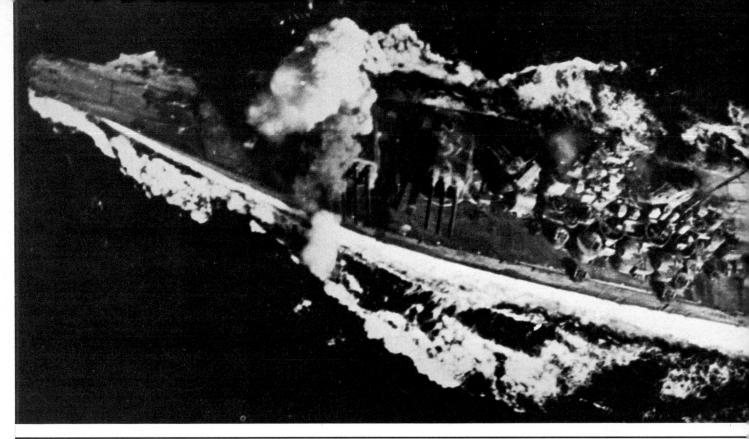

Yamato

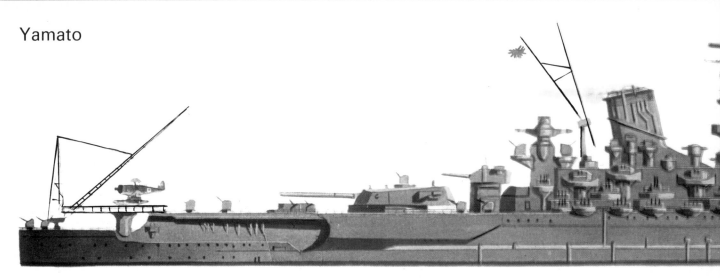

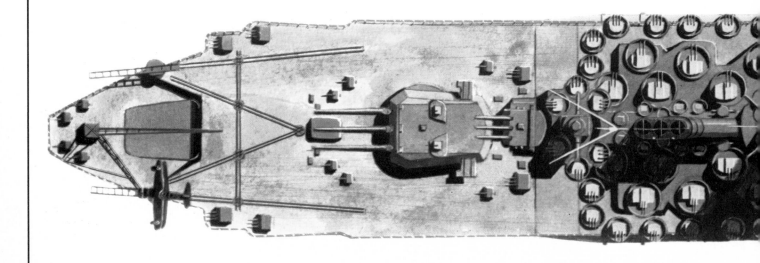

During the later 1920s and early 1930s, Japanese naval designers refined their ideas of a battleship capable of defeating the Americans by individual superiority after producing a number of more or less credible designs. Plans for a battleship with 460-mm guns and a speed of 30 knots were called for in late 1934, on the grounds that the Americans would not build a battleship too large to go through the Panama Canal, and that any new American battleship would have a speed of 25 knots. The Japanese had calculated that the maximum size of battleship that could go through the Panama Canal would be a 64,000-tonne ship with ten 406-mm guns and a speed of about 23 knots. (It is interesting to note that both these predictions were wrong. The *Washington* class had a speed of 28 knots, and the *Montana*, though it was not built, would have been too large for the canal, as the large American carriers are today.)

The initial design to meet the Japanese naval staff's requirements would have displaced over 70,000 tonnes and was considered to be too big. Some requirement would have to be dropped, and eventually it was decided that speed could be reduced to 27 knots. By July 1936 a suitable design had been worked out. However, this was intended to be diesel powered to give a good range, and because the diesels on other Japanese warships were proving highly unsatisfactory, the design had to be reworked for steam turbines. It was just as well that this was done, because it had been intended to cover the diesels with nearly 203 mm of armour, making their extraction in case of breakdown virtually impossible.

In March 1937 the final design was prepared.

YAMATO
Displacement 64,000 tons (65,027 tonnes) normal, 69,988 tons (71,111 tonnes) full load
Length 863 feet (263 m)
Beam 127 feet 9 inches (38 m 92 cm)
Draught 34 feet 3 inches (10 m 44 cm)
Machinery 4-shaft geared steam turbines, 150,000 shp = 27 knots
Armour belt: 7.9 to 16.1 inches (200 to 405 mm). deck: 7.9 to 9 inches (200 to 228 mm). turrets: 9.8 to 25.6 inch (247 to 650 mm)
Guns 9 × 18-inch (460-mm), 12 × 6-inch (155-mm) (6 removed 1943), 12 × 5-inch (127-mm) DP, 24 × 25-mm AA
Aircraft 6 (2 catapults)
Launched 8 August 1940 by Kure Dockyard

Yamato *seen under air attack during the Battle of Leyte Gulf. The armament had been altered, with the triple 155-mm gun turrets removed and twin dual-purpose guns added*

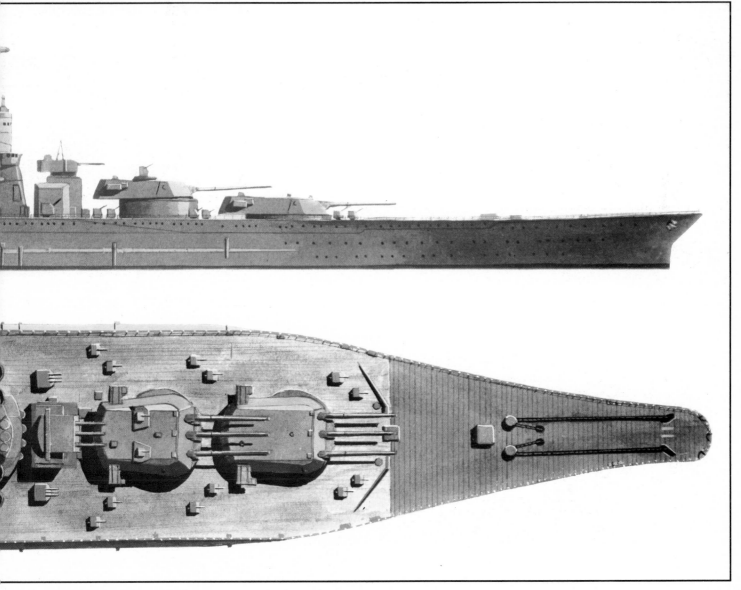

By completely ignoring the Washington and London treaties, a battleship of nearly double the treaty size was planned. But her size was to cause many problems to the designers and constructors. She had to be big; each triple 460-mm turret alone weighed about 3,050 tonnes and armour to resist 460-mm gunfire has to be very thick. However, Japanese home waters are very shallow, so the ship's depth could not exceed 8.2 m. Therefore she would have to have a large beam, which needed more power to maintain the intended speed, which itself meant more weight. Although the Japanese weight-saving methods were not as good as those used in Britain and the United States, some ingenious methods were employed.

Unfortunately for the Japanese, the damage caused by the storm during maneouvres in 1935 had shown that with the techniques they were then employing they could not trust to electrical welding for important structural members, so that method of saving weight was partially barred. However, it was possible to utilize the armour itself as a structural member, and this was done.

Another method of saving weight much favoured by the Japanese was to make the weather deck (the deck on which the superstructure is mounted) continuous, instead of breaking it in a step where a change of level was needed. This resulted in the wavy profile of most large Japanese interwar warships. This was claimed to save weight because a continuous deck is stronger than the same thickness of deck with a break in it. This is true, but when a continuous deck changes level, so much additional material is needed that frequently a broken

deck line would weigh less.

As much time and trouble was taken in building the ships as in working out their design. Only one Japanese yard, Mitsubishi's Nagasaki shipyard, was large enough to build one of these ships, and even there the slipway had to be heavily reinforced to take the weight. Yet facilities were needed to build four vessels. Three yards had therefore to be built. Buildings had to be enlarged, old cranes strengthened and new ones built. A special ship was even built to transport the guns and their turrets.

In the event, only two of these battleships, *Yamato* and *Musashi*, were completed as battleships. *Shinano*, as has already been described, was converted into an aircraft carrier, and steel from the incomplete hull of the fourth vessel was used to complete other more urgently needed vessels. Yet after all this expenditure of time, money and intellect, the end results were not particularly impressive as fighting vessels. The hull form was excellently thought out – for example, the use of a very large bulbous bow helped the *Yamato* class to attain their designed speed – but the same was not true of some of the other details. Although the armour was intended to withstand 460-mm gunfire, for example, it was not realized until too late that the 155-mm gun, taken from the *Mogami* class cruisers when they were rearmed with 203-mm guns and re-used on the *Yamato* vessels, only had light armour protection. Again, the underwater protection, the effectiveness of which on any ship depends on its width, ought to have been superb, for the *Yamato* class had a greater beam than any other battleship. Yet it was not as good as it should have been. Both *Yamato* and *Musashi* took a

The battle-cruiser Hiei *is shown demilitarised to comply with the London Naval Treaty of 1932, with only three main turrets. She was brought up to standard in 1936–40*

great deal of punishment, but they were very big ships. In the end, they were both overwhelmed by a succession of small blows. This undermines the basic concept behind these ships, for in order to beat the superior numbers of American battleships, it was essential that not only should the Japanese ships have had a better armament than their opponents but that they should also have been able to withstand the greater number of hits that the superior numbers of enemy ships ought to be able to achieve. It is doubtful that the *Yamato* ships could have withstood these without impairing their own fighting capabilities, and because there were bound to be fewer of them than of their American opponents, any losses the Japanese sustained would make the situation of the remaining ships that much worse. No other country seriously considered building such ships; Germany produced mere pipedreams, and even the American *Montana* class, much better balanced ships, would have been 5,000 tonnes smaller. Even without hindsight about the deadliness of carrier-borne aircraft, ships of this size were too vulnerable to a greater number of smaller ones to warrant gambling such a large proportion of a country's design effort and, even more important, shipbuilding capacity, on them.

Two battle-cruisers of 33,000 tonnes with nine 311-mm guns and a speed of 33 knots were ordered, but because of the overriding need for carriers, they were cancelled in 1942.

Japan: Submarines

Japan had a sizable submarine force at the beginning of the war. Well handled, it ought to have achieved considerable results. Although some successes were achieved early in the war, particularly against the American carriers, the end results were disappointing. Poor doctrine, with an overemphasis on attacking warships, resulted in an almost total failure to disrupt any of the US invasion fleets that were gradually mopping up Japanese conquests in the Pacific. Then the Japanese submarines were frittered away in a vain attempt to provide sufficient men and materials to keep the Japanese garrisons in being. Used as transports, they lost their chance to permanently discourage the American advance. Although the Japanese submarines were by no means the best in the world, they were quite good enough to have given Japan a chance to achieve stalemate, if they had only been properly employed.

Almost all the Japanese interwar submarines were of two main types. First there were the *Kaidai*-type submarines, mostly of about 1,620 tonnes surface displacement, with a radius of action of over 16,000 km and a surface speed of over 20 knots. These were intended to take part in fleet actions, hence the high surface speed. The other type were intended to act as long-range scouting submarines, and had an even greater radius of action and a surface displacement of over 2,030 tonnes. The later versions also carried aircraft. The first type was developed from British, German and French designs, while the latter was very directly developed from the large German First World War cruiser submarines. The first one to be fitted with an aircraft (not, initially, very successfully) was *I 5*, launched in 1931.

Odd men out were the *I 121* class. Practically identical to the German First World War *U 125*, they were smaller and slower than most of the other Japanese submarines completed in the late 1920s. In 1940 these four submarines were fitted with external petrol tanks to refuel the main fleet's floatplane reconnaissance aircraft.

Another odd class were the two 710-tonne surface displacement submarines of the *RO 33* class, launched in 1934 and 1935. In the late 1930s, Japan developed a successful midget submarine, and several of the large scout submarines were adapted to carry them. Their only success in the war was the torpedoing of HMS *Ramillies* in Diego Saurez harbour.

When war became imminent a new type of coastal submarine, the *RO 100* class of 533 tonnes surface displacement, were hastily developed. They were intended for close defence of Japanese outposts and home waters, and they had a very restricted radius of action of 5,800 km while surfaced. Only one more medium-sized attack submarine class was built by the Japanese Navy. These were the *RO 35s*. Eighteen were built between 1941 and 1944 and a further 28 were cancelled in 1943. These submarines were of 975 tonnes surface displacement and had a radius of action of 8,050 km. American success in destroying Japanese submarines forced the Japanese to abandon active submarine warfare. The only submarines built after this were for

coastal transport and large cruiser submarines, both of which were intended for highly specialized roles.

The *I 361* class of supply submarines were intended for running supplies to invested island garrisons, for which purpose they could carry 82 tonnes of cargo and two landing craft on the coaming aft of the conning tower. Towards the end of the war, they were modified (as were many

Three Japanese submarines lie moored alongside the American submarine tender Proteus *after the surrender in September 1945. On the left are the sister vessels* I 400 *and* I 401, *the largest submarines in the world at that time. On the right is the* I 14, *also large even though it was only two-thirds the size of the* I 400s. *Note the aircraft catapult and hanger which can be seen on each of the boats*

171

surviving Japanese submarines) to carry *Kaiten* human torpedoes.

These boats were succeeded by the slightly modified *I 373*s, which could carry up to 260 tonnes of cargo. Both the *I 361*s and the *I 373*s were armed but the last type of transport submarine, the *Ha 101* class, were intended purely to carry cargo, and on a surface displacement of 375 tonnes they could carry 60 tonnes of cargo for 4,800 km. They were intended for ease of production and some of them were completed in five months. The building of all remaining types of submarine other than these and suicide craft was discontinued in March 1945 so as to expedite their construction.

Despite the urgent need for large numbers of submarines during the war, the Japanese persisted in building specialized craft. The most famous of these were the very large submarines of the *I 13* and *I 400* classes. The *I 13*s were the largest submarines that the Japanese had built up to that time. On a surface displacement of 2,635 tonnes they carried an armament of one 140-mm and seven 25-mm guns, six 530-mm torpedo tubes and two aircraft. The surface speed was 16 knots and they had the immense radius of action of 21,000 miles (39,000 km). Ordered in 1942, it had been intended that these should be cancelled because of American successes against the large Japanese submarines. However, Admiral Yamamoto issued a direct order that they should be continued, and two were completed in 1945.

The *I 400* class were also only built because of a direct order from Admiral Yamamoto. Over half as big again as the *I 13*s, these were the world's largest submarines at the time when they were built. They were intended to fulfil all the Japanese submarine's designed roles except that of transport. Their aircraft were intended to be used to attack the Panama Canal. The most peculiar feature of their design was the shape of their hull. In order to keep the draught as shallow as possible the hull was constructed as two side-by-side cylinders. They were fitted with a *schnorkel*, and were sometimes fitted with a dummy funnel as a disguise when sailing on the surface in home waters.

Quite apart from the vulnerability of these large submarines, there was no excuse for wasting a large amount of shipbuilding capacity on their construction, for this capacity was needed for vessels much more important to Japan's survival. There was some excuse for wasting time and effort on the *Yamato* class, for no one knew how soon war would be declared, or even if there would be a war at all. The building of the *I 13*s and the *I 400*s did not even have this justification.

In 1937 a small highly streamlined experimental submarine, *No 71*, was laid down in Japan and on test she achieved the underwater speed of 21.25 knots. After the tests were completed she was scrapped in 1940. This marked a breakthrough in submarine design. Although her underwater endurance was limited, she came close to being a true submersible. In 1943 the first of the *I 201* class, which were based on the results of *No 71*, were laid down. These antedated the German Type XXI submarines and had an underwater speed of 19 knots, which they could maintain for 55 minutes.

In 1943 and 1944 the Japanese Army also built a number of transport submarines, the *Yu 1* class and the slightly larger *Yu 1001*s, which were built so that the army could supply its own garrisons without needing to call upon the navy for assistance.

The last underwater craft built in Japan in the closing stages of the war were an immense number of small suicide craft, intended to slow down, if not to turn back, the anticipated American invasion. Very few of these were ever used in action.

I 400
Displacement 5,223 tons (5,306 tonnes) surfaced, 6,560 tons (6,665 tonnes) submerged
Length 400 feet 3 inches (121 m 99 cm)
Beam 39 feet 4 inches (11 m 98 cm)
Draught 23 feet (7 m)
Machinery surfaced: 2-shaft diesel-electric, 7,700 bhp = $18\frac{3}{4}$ knots; submerged: 2-shaft electric, 2,400 shp = $6\frac{1}{2}$ knots
Guns 1 × 5.5-inch (140-mm), 10 × 25-mm AA
Torpedo Tubes 8 × 21-inch (532-mm) (20 torpedoes carried)
Aircraft 3 (1 catapult)
Launched 1944 at Kure Dockyard

Top right: The submarine I 53, *a vessel of the KD3A class, renumbered* I 153 *in 1942. She was built in 1925–27. Right:* Kairyu *suicide craft after the surrender*

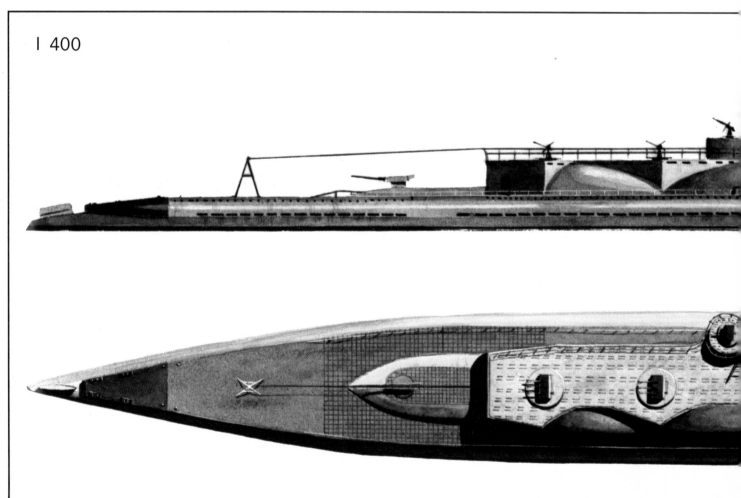

I 400

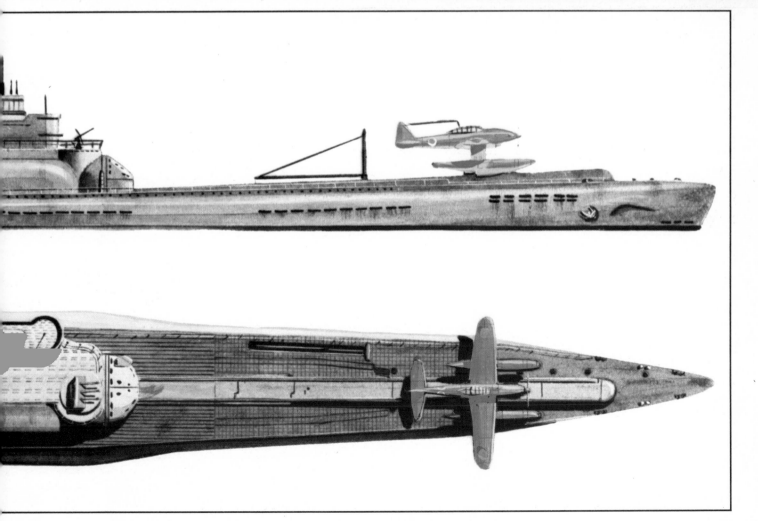

Great Britain: Aircraft Carriers

The aircraft carrier was developed in Britain, as were the earliest techniques of deck landing. Yet in 1939 Britain had the least effective naval air arm of the three major powers which possessed this vital addition to naval strength. This had nothing to do with the quality of British aircraft carriers, arguably the best and certainly the most thoroughly designed in the world. Certainly it also had nothing to do with the quality of the aircrew. The Fleet Air Arm was superbly trained, and indeed had to be: 'They say in the Air Force a landing's okay/if the pilot he gets up and walks right away/but in the Fleet Air Arm the prospects are dim/if the landing is poor and the pilot can't swim,' as one song put it. It was in the quality and quantity of the aircraft available that the Royal Navy fell behind the Americans and Japanese.

The basic reason for this was the decision on April Fool's Day 1918 to found a separate air force. At one blow not only was the navy deprived of its air arm – which was not returned to naval control until 1937, far too late to rectify the years of neglect – but also of most of its air-minded officers. The RAF, intent on preserving its independence, paid little attention to developing its seaborne forces, while the Navy tended to concentrate on developing spotting aircraft which might be able to manage a torpedo attack as a sideline. The worst deficiency of all was the failure to produce a carrier-borne single-seat fighter capable of matching its land-based contemporaries. When war came the Royal Navy's carriers had to rely on obsolete aircraft such as the Swordfish, converted landplanes like the Seafire, American imports like the Wildcat, Hellcat and Avenger, or home-produced oddities like the Barracuda. It was not until after the end of the war that the first really adequate British carrier fighter, the Sea Fury, entered service.

Despite these handicaps, British carriers and their aircraft more than justified themselves. Fleet Air Arm Skuas, operating from an airfield, bombed the German cruiser *Königsberg*, the first major warship sunk by air attack. A tiny force of obsolete Swordfish achieved the most economical victory of the war, crippling the Italian fleet in its base at Taranto, while fighters helped to preserve convoys and defend landings in the Mediterranean.

At the outbreak of the war nearly all British carriers were built on hulls which had not only been constructed during the previous conflict, but also were not originally designed for operating aircraft. Three had been conceived as light battle-cruisers, designed for use in a far-fetched scheme to land troops in the Baltic. Two of these, *Courageous* and *Glorious*, originally had two twin 15-inch (380-mm) turrets each, and were converted to aircraft carriers in the 1920s. Both were sunk early in the war, and had little chance to prove themselves. The third ship, *Furious*, was intended to carry two 18-inch (457-mm) guns. In the event only one was fitted, and a flying-off deck fitted forward. This was used for the first-ever carrier landings, but was obviously inadequate. Soon a landing-on deck was built aft, in place of the 18-inch (457-mm) gun. However, the funnel and bridge structure

were obviously unnecessary excrescences in the middle of the ship, and so *Furious* was completely rebuilt with a completely flush flight deck. There was a small retractable navigating bridge but nothing else stood out above the flight deck, the smoke being ejected through vents below deck level aft. This was not the last alteration to this much-changed ship, as she was rebuilt and modernized just before the Second World War.

Two smaller carriers came into service just after the end of the First World War. One, *Argus*, had been built as a passenger liner, and was given, like the *Furious*, a flight deck with nothing sticking out above it. However, she did not have the bigger ship's speed, and was mainly used for training and ferrying tasks during the later conflict. The second ship, *Hermes*, was much more interesting, being the first carrier designed and built as such. Unlike *Furious* and *Argus* she had an 'island', incorporating the bridge and funnel, offset to one side of the ship; this was a more sensible solution to the problems of accommodating the command facilities of the ship and getting rid of the boiler gasses. Unfortunately *Hermes* was a small and relatively slow ship, and could only carry a few aircraft. The last of the older generation of aircraft carriers was the *Eagle*, built on a hull which was to have been a Chilean battleship. She, too, had an island, but was unusual for a carrier in having two funnels. Like the *Hermes* she was rather slow for a carrier, but sturdy.

The first of the new carriers built during the years of rearmament in the 1930s was the *Ark Royal*. A great deal of thought and research went into her design, and that of her successors. The British were most thorough, and took great care over the aerodynamic design of the island and flight deck to avoid eddies in the air-flow which might endanger aircraft landing and taking off. British carriers also had much better precautions against fire and protection of aviation fuel supply lines than their American and Japanese equivalents. All this went into the *Ark Royal* as well as a powerful anti-aircraft armament of 4.5-inch (114-mm) guns. Purely as a carrier of aircraft she was the best equipped of all the wartime British carriers, thanks to her two-level hangar, which gave her a capacity equivalent to the big American carriers. If she had not been lost comparatively early in the war, due to poor damage control, she could have taken advantage of wartime developments in aircraft stowage to carry even more.

The later British fleet carriers had a much smaller aircraft complement because of their exceptionally good protection. It has often been said that the best feature of the *Illustrious* class was their armoured flight decks. This is not the whole truth, as some of all nation's major carriers had flight deck armour, although the British ships had the thickest. What distinguished the *Illustrious* and her sisters was that the whole hangar, the most vulnerable area of the ship above the waterline, was enclosed in an armoured box. In the context of the time when these ships were designed this was a wise decision. These carriers were going to operate in the Mediter-

ranean and North Sea with fighters of inferior performance against superior enemy air forces. With the early warning facilities given by radar, and the better carrier fighters that came later, the balance between greater weight of armour and more aircraft (the *Illustrious* class only had a single hangar deck against the *Ark Royal's* two) might have been different. As it was, the *Illustrious's* survival against massed *Stuka* attacks and heavy bomb damage in the Mediterranean in 1941 proved the decision a sensible one. Later, radar and a good combat air patrol of fighters gave equally good protection against conventional air attack, as the Americans proved in the Pacific. However, towards the end, the British armoured carriers came into their own again when they continued operating against a scale of *kamikaze* attacks which disabled several American carriers for a long time.

It is interesting that even before this experience the Americans were impressed enough by

ILLUSTRIOUS

Displacement 23,207 tons (23,579 tonnes) standard, 28,619 tons (29,078 tonnes) full load
Length 743 feet 9 inches (226 m 69 cm)
Beam 95 feet 9 inches (29 m 18 cm)
Draught 24 feet (7 m 31 cm)
Machinery 3-shaft geared turbines, 111,000 shp = 30½ knots
Armour belt: 4½ inches (114 mm). deck: 4½ inches (114 mm) hangar side, 1½ to 3 inches (38 to 76 mm) flight deck
Aircraft 36
Guns 16 × 4.5-inch (114-mm) DP, 6 × 8-barrelled 40-mm pom-poms
Launched 5 April 1939 by Vickers-Armstrong, Barrow

Eagle, Formidable *and* Indomitable *escort the allied* Pedestal *convoy in August 1942*

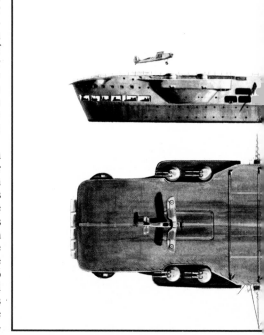

Illustrious

the British design to offer to exchange some of their *Essex*-class carriers for an equal number of British fleet carriers. The British, for their part, equally impressed by the American ships' aircraft capacity, were prepared to take part in the exchange. However, for a variety of reasons, this exchange, which had been seriously discussed in 1943, never came off.

Illustrious had two sisters, *Victorious* and *Formidable*. The fourth ship of the class was the *Indomitable*, but her design was modified so that she became in effect the prototype of two more ships, *Implacable* and *Indefatigable*. In order to take account of the criticisms of the small number of aircraft carried by her predecessors, *Indomitable* was given an extra half hangar deck aft, below the main hangar. To compensate for this extra weight the armour on the hangar sides was made thinner. Originally the two final ships were to have had a full-length lower hangar deck, but as the capacity for aircraft stores and armament would have been inadequate for so many planes, they were only given a half hangar, like *Indomitable*.

Because of stability problems all three of these later ships had less height in their hangars, which meant that there were types of aircraft that could not be operated by them. Also, after the war, as aircraft size continued to grow, it was the earlier ships that were kept in service. The first four ships had a triple shaft installation, new to British major warships, and one that gave

considerable trouble, whereas *Implacable* and *Indefatigable* had four shafts.

Considered purely as ships rather than as platforms for operating aircraft these British fleet carriers were the best of their type built, and it is significant that many of their best features, the built-up bow and armoured hangars especially, were adopted by the Americans in their later construction. However, the transatlantic flow of information was not all one-way, and the British adopted the superior American flight-deck operation techniques, as well as American aircraft. They were also considering putting deck-edge lifts, an American concept, into their biggest carriers, the *Malta* class, which were never built, though two other large carriers, *Ark Royal* and *Eagle*, were completed after the end of the war.

Although the six ships of the *Illustrious* group were the only British major fleet carriers completed during the war, other, smaller carriers were built. Besides the escort carriers which we will consider later, there were the light fleet carriers. These had mercantile hulls with a view to converting them to merchant ships after the war was over (none were, in the event); they carried only close-range anti-aircraft guns and no armour, but were otherwise small versions of the fleet carriers. Unfortunately, they were completed too late to play a part in the war, but subsequently proved a very effective concept. They have been sold or given to a wide variety

of navies, and several are still in service.

One very useful smaller ship was being built before the war began, though not completed until 1943. This was the *Unicorn*, designed as an aircraft maintenance ship, but capable of acting as an ordinary carrier at a pinch, which she did, with some success, in the Mediterranean in 1943. Later she proved so useful in her designed role with the British Pacific Fleet that two of the light fleet carriers then being built were converted for the same purpose.

INDOMITABLE

Displacement 24,680 tons (25,076 tonnes) standard, 29,730 tons (30,207 tonnes) full load
Length 754 feet (229 m 81 cm)
Beam 95 feet 9 inches (29 m 18 cm)
Draught 25 feet (7 m 61 cm)
Machinery 3-shaft geared turbines, 111,000 shp = 30½ knots
Armour belt: 4½ inches (114 mm). deck: 1½ inches (38 mm) hangar side, 1½ to 3 inches (38 to 76 mm) flight deck
Aircraft 48
Guns 16 × 4.5-inch (114-mm) DP, 6 × 8-barrelled 40-mm pom-poms, 8 × 20-mm AA

The aircraft carrier Indomitable *in the Indian Ocean in 1942. British fleet carriers differed from the* Essex *class of the US Navy in having an enclosed 'hurricane' bow and the 4.5-inch (114-mm) guns at the four corners of the flight deck*

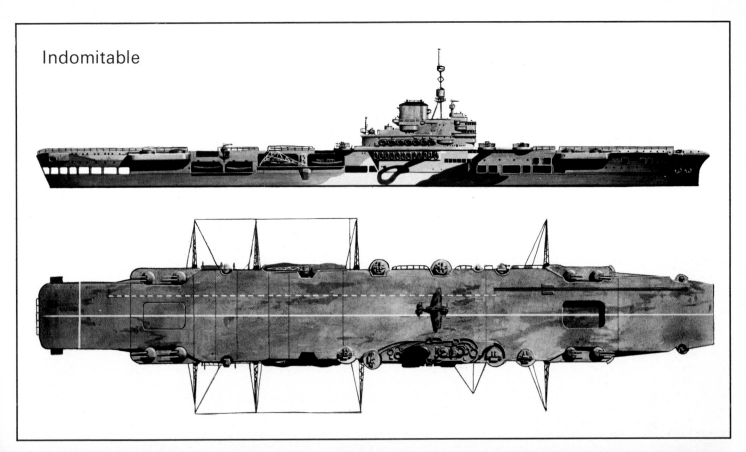

Indomitable

The German's most dangerous attack on Britain was the attack on her maritime communications. The possibility of defeat in the Battle of the Atlantic was the one which scared Churchill the most. The chief enemy was the U-boat, but the depredations of long-range bombers, the Focke-Wulf Condors, were also a serious threat. Air cover was needed, especially as aircraft proved to be getting the highest score of submarines sunk. Long-range patrol aircraft were in very short supply early in the war because of the demands of the strategic bomber offensive against Germany. It was not until 1943 that aircraft were provided which could cover the entire North Atlantic convoy route from shore bases.

Meanwhile another answer to the problem of air cover for the convoys had been tried successfully. This was to provide aircraft carriers for the purpose. Fleet carriers were too few, too vitally needed elsewhere, and too precious to use in this role. Therefore the possibility of building smaller aircraft carriers for escort purposes was examined. The possibility of mercantile conversions had been discussed before the war, but mainly in terms of the largest liners (especially the *Queen Mary* and the *Queen Elizabeth*). These proved to be too valuable in their role as troop transports and so smaller and slower ships were chosen.

The trial conversion was, ironically, a captured German ship. The *Hannover* was a brand-new diesel ship captured at the beginning of the war, and at first named *Empire Audacity*. Her superstructure was cut down and a simple wooden flight deck fitted; this was a fairly rudimentary conversion, with no lift or hangar, so that aircraft had to be stowed and serviced on deck. As she was primarily intended to provide cover against aerial shadowers and

EMPIRE FAITH
Displacement 7,061 tons (7,174 tonnes) full load
Length 431 feet (131 m 36 cm)
Beam 57 feet 5 inches (17 m 49.5 cm)
Machinery 1-shaft diesel, 688 shp = 11 knots
Guns light AA only
Launched 4 March 1941 by Barclay Curle, Glasgow

Empire Faith

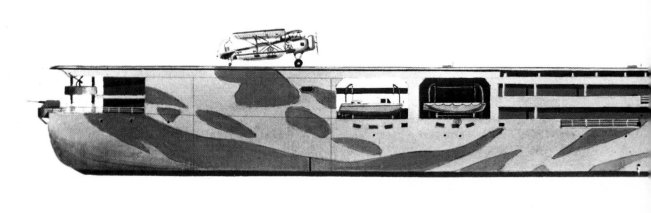

Audacity

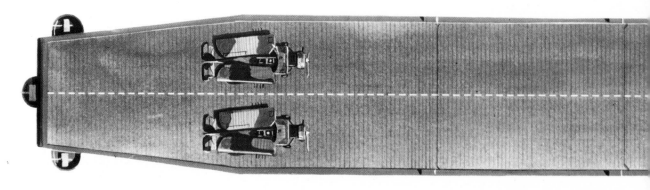

bombers the six aircraft she carried were all Grumman Martlet fighters (the English name for the Wildcat). Completed in mid-1941, she was immediately put on the Gibraltar convoy run.

Audacity was torpedoed and sunk before the year was out, but not before she had proved how invaluable even the smallest carrier could be. Condors had been shot down and U-boats harried by her aircraft. British yards were too occupied to do more than a few escort carrier conversions, and these were generally rather too elaborate, but the basic ideas were passed over to the United States, which soon started to produce escort carriers for itself and the British in large numbers. These designs will be discussed in greater detail in the American section, but it may be worth noting that a considerable amount of inter-Allied friction was caused by British delays in putting their American-built escort carriers into service because of their insistence on more stringent safety precautions.

The British eventually received some 39 escort carriers from the Americans, but many of these were diverted to other purposes, especially the support of amphibious landings. The need for integral air support for convoys remained, however, and the 'MAC' ships were evolved to meet this need. These were reasonably fast merchant ships, either grain ships or oil tankers, which did not need large hatches to load their cargoes, and could therefore have a flight deck added without impairing their ability to carry a cargo. They were manned by the Merchant Navy, not the Royal Navy, except for the aircraft contingent. The oil tankers had six obsolescent Swordfish, the grain-ships only four (the Swordfish was one of the few aircraft which could take off from their very short flight decks) but the grain-ships had the advantage of a lift and a small hangar. These ships were more like the *Audacity* than the later elaborate escort carriers, but arrived a little late to play a vital part in the Battle of the Atlantic, which had to a great extent been won before they arrived.

In the desperate days of 1941 any expedient which provided some degree of air cover to convoys was better than none, particularly one which provided some protection against other aircraft. This desperate need produced the 'CAM' ships, of which *Empire Faith* was one. These were the Catapult Aircraft Merchantmen, which carried a single Hurricane fighter on a catapult forward. This was a one-shot weapon. Once catapulted the pilot could only 'ditch' in the sea, or bale out when his petrol ran out, hoping to be picked up by the convoy escorts. If he was lucky enough to be near to land he might be able to fly to a land base, but in any event the aircraft was no longer any use to the convoy. Obviously the moment to catapult the fighter had to be chosen with great care if it was to achieve worthwhile results. The method was expensive in scarce fighters and in even scarcer pilots, and also expensive in the ships themselves. Over one-third were lost, so it is not surprising that the 'CAM'-ship concept was dropped as soon as numbers of escort carriers became available.

However, they did have a certain value: some German aircraft were shot down, and their presence exercised a beneficial effect on the morale of the convoys and dissuaded German aircrews from attacking. The 'CAM'-ships, and also the Fighter Catapult Ships, which were naval auxiliaries fitted with catapults and naval fighters, were only stopgaps, but they fulfilled this function properly. When looking at the illustration of the *Empire Faith* it should be remembered that the artist has shown her rather high out of the water; in normal service, even unladen, her decks would be far nearer the waterline.

AUDACITY
Displacement 10,200 tons (10,363 tonnes) full load
Length 467 feet (142 m 34 cm)
Beam 56 feet (17 m)
Draught 18 feet (5 m 48 cm) mean
Machinery 2-shaft diesels, 4,750 bhp = 16 knots
Armour none
Aircraft 6
Guns 1 × 4-inch (102-mm) AA, 6 × 20-mm AA

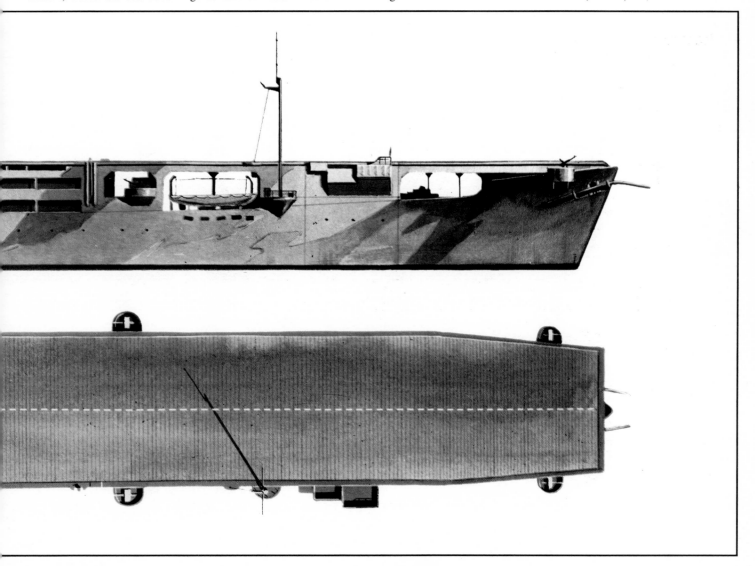

Great Britain: Capital Ships

Hood *seen after her last refit with new twin 4-inch (102-mm) A/A mountings*

At the beginning of the war the Royal Navy had a numerically powerful force of battleships. They were, however, all quite old. The majority had served in the First World War and some remained virtually unaltered since those days. Others had been heavily altered. The *Nelson* and *Rodney* were the only battleships in the world incorporating the full lessons of the First World War, but they were no longer in the first flush of their youth, and rather slow by current standards. The first of Britain's new class of battleships, the *King George V*, was still fitting out.

Three of Britain's capital ships were, strictly speaking, not battleships at all, but battle-cruisers. This was a type developed by the Royal Navy before the First World War in an attempt to extend the capabilities of the largest cruisers, the armoured cruisers, by giving them a battleship's gunpower, while retaining cruiser speeds and standards of protection. This was an unfortunate move, as it proved, because it meant that the ships would be treated as fast battleships when they were not capable of standing up to a proper battleship's fire, and their speed would not always be sufficient protection. The fact that the three British battle-cruisers lost at the Battle of Jutland blew up due to inferior cordite and poor magazine-stowage arrangements, rather than thinner armour, does not really affect this argument. Jutland initiated a reaction against the battle-cruiser, though two 15-inch (380-mm) ships – the *Repulse* and *Renown* – were at a too advanced stage to cancel. Both were altered between the wars and given more protection; the *Renown*, indeed, was almost completely rebuilt just before war broke out and she had a very distinguished career in the war. Neither, however, were really considered to be a match for a battleship, especially as they only had six 15-inch (380-mm) guns apiece.

This view, however, was modified for their immediate successor, the *Hood* – for a long time the largest warship in the world, and the most handsome capital ship ever built. There were originally to have been four ships of her class,

Hood

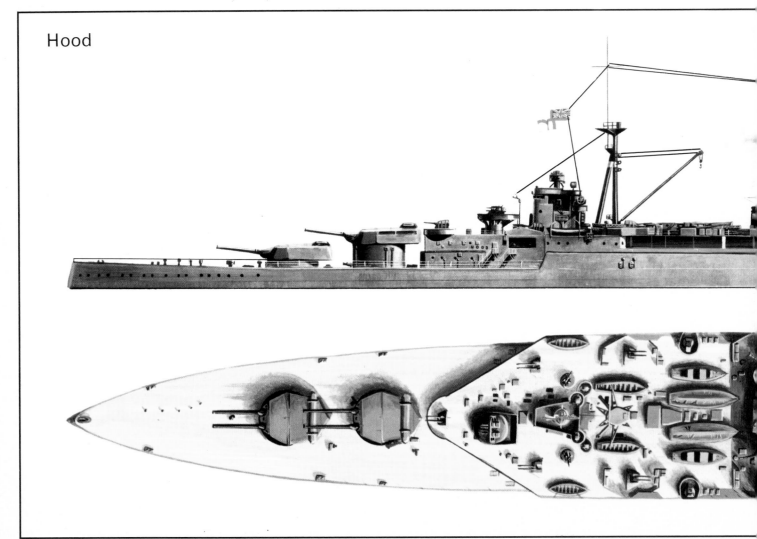

designed before Jutland was fought but modified after that battle to incorporate considerably more protection, and thereby losing some freeboard – becoming lower in the water – and two knots in speed from the original target of 33 knots.

The other three ships were cancelled before the end of the First World War but *Hood* was completed despite the misgivings of the new chief designer – the Director of Naval Construction, Sir Eustace Tennyson D'Eyncourt – because it was felt that she would have some experimental value. But it should not be thought that the *Hood* was badly protected. The alterations to her had produced what was in effect a fast battleship rather than a battle-cruiser. She was at least as well armoured against bombs and shells plunging down on her – an increasing danger thanks to the great range at which actions were fought – as contemporary battleships such as those of the *Queen Elizabeth* class. Her armour was, however, spread over a wide area of her hull, and therefore comparatively thin, whereas by 1918 it was becoming increasingly obvious that armour should be concentrated to protect the really vital points – a system already adopted by the Americans and called 'all or nothing'. The *Hood* also had the disadvantage of her enormous length, necessary for her original great designed speed and the powerful engines and boilers which that speed required.

By 1939 *Hood* was overdue for a complete rebuild, but this was prevented by the outbreak of war. By the time of her loss in 1941 she had been changed from her original appearance. Her unusual original secondary armament of single 5.5-inch (140-mm) guns had been removed, and instead five of the ubiquitous twin 4-inch (102-mm) anti-aircraft gun mountings were substituted. The main armament, eight 15-inch (380-mm) guns in mountings slightly different to those in the other British ships of the same generation, was retained. On top of B turret (immediately in front of the bridge) and also between the 4-inch (102-mm) mounts were the oddly-shaped tubes of a rather useless anti-aircraft weapon. This was a rocket projector which was a stop-gap until enough light anti-aircraft guns could be produced. Thanks to the increase in weight of the ship she lay noticeably deeper in the water, so that in any sort of a sea, or at speed, the low-lying quarterdeck was usually awash. Her top speed was less than 30 knots by then, but she was still a useful unit.

It was her bad luck that the superb gunnery of the *Bismarck* found one of her weaknesses so early in the Denmark Strait action. Unfortunately her torpedo tubes, which were situated above water, had been left undisturbed by refits. It can never be known for sure just why she exploded and sank, but the *Bismarck*'s hit was amidships, and the fire which started there possibly set off the torpedoes. This seems more likely to have caused the catastrophe than the rocket or 4-inch (102-mm) ready-use ammunition – or a penetration of the magazines which should not have been pierced or set off with such ease.

HOOD
Displacement 42,100 tons (42,775 tonnes) standard, 46,200 tons (46,941 tonnes) full load
Length 860 feet 6 inches (262 m 28 cm)
Beam 105 feet 3 inches (32 m)
Draught 28 feet 6 inches (8 m 68 cm)
Machinery 4-shaft geared steam turbines, 144,000 shp = 31 knots
Armour belt: 5 to 12 inches (127 to 305 mm). deck: 1½ to 2 inches (38 to 51 mm). turrets: 11 to 15 inches (280 to 380 mm)
Guns 8 × 15-inch (380-mm), 10 × 4-inch (102-mm) AA, 3 × 8-barrelled (40-mm) pom-pom AA, 4 × 4-barrelled MGs
Torpedo Tubes 4 × 21-inch (530-mm) above water
Launched 22 August 1918 by John Brown, Clydebank

The oldest operational battleships in the Royal Navy were the famous *Queen Elizabeth* class. The ships of this class were the finest battleships of the First World War, several knots faster than any of their predecessors, and the first ships designed to take the superlative twin 15-inch (380-mm) mounting. This gun deserves a special mention on its own account. After World War II the US Navy conducted a thorough comparison of all heavy gun mountings; the conclusion was that despite the fact that it was old, that it did not have the range or the weight of shell of 16-inch (404-mm) or 18-inch (457-mm) mountings, its accuracy, rate of fire and the simplicity and reliability of its mounting more than made up for this.

Because of their speed and power the class were used as a special fast squadron of their own, co-operating with the battle-cruisers. For a while at Jutland they virtually took on the German High Seas Fleet singlehanded, and gave out and received a considerable amount of punishment. During the 1920s the handsome silhouette of the class was altered for the worse by trunking back the foremost of the two funnels into the after one; more significantly, external bulges were added against torpedo attack. Two of the

class, *Barham* and *Malaya*, were left basically in this state when war broke out, though with the addition of extra anti-aircraft guns and a seaplane catapult. Like the 'R' class battleships (see next section) these two were not altered much during the war, and *Barham* was finally lost to a submarine's torpedo.

The *Warspite* was refitted at Portsmouth between 1934 and 1937, and what emerged from this process was virtually a new ship. The turrets were retained, but with 10° more elevation which gave them greater range. The armour was also kept, though there was a considerable amount of extra horizontal protection added on the decks. A block-like tower bridge replaced the old armoured conning tower and multiple-layer bridge. The whole interior of the ship was gutted and new boilers and engines put in. These gave more power for less weight, and the boiler uptakes could be led to a single funnel. The 6-inch (152-mm) secondary armament in its old-fashioned casemates in the hull was still retained, but was supplemented by 4-inch (102-mm) anti-aircraft guns in twin mounts, and by the formidable but short-ranged eight-barrelled pom-poms.

Armour plate and guns and gun mountings

were the most difficult parts of a new battleship to produce, and took the longest time. Because the immediate need for ships fit to meet modern conditions was so pressing in the late 1930s, the conversion of the *Warspite* was probably justified, despite the time and money required. These were not far off the requirements for a new ship, which would, in the long run, have been a better investment. In the circumstances, though, and in view of the *Warspite*'s magnificent war record, one can hardly complain. Sent in to Narvik Fjord in a calculated risk, her heavy salvoes smashed the German destroyers trapped there. Later she fought the Italians as Admiral A B Cunningham's flagship, most notably at the Battle of Matapan. Hit by a glider bomb off Italy, she was patched up to serve at the bombardments of D-Day and Walcheren.

Her two other sisters, *Queen Elizabeth* and *Valiant*, had even more elaborate refits. They had their 6-inch (152-mm) batteries removed and were fitted instead with countersunk 4.5-inch (114-mm) twin high-angle mountings similar to those fitted in *Renown* and the *Illustrious* class of carriers. Like *Warspite* these two battleships had distinguished war records, and were continually altered to take new anti-aircraft guns

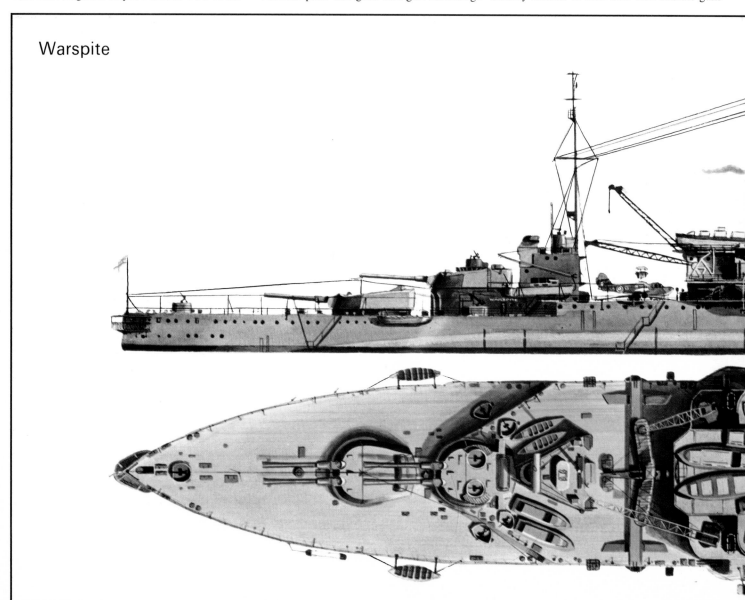

Warspite

and radar; unlike her, both suffered from the attentions of Italian human torpedoes in Alexandria Harbour and had to be refitted in the USA.

The *Queen Elizabeth* class will continue to exert a fascination on everyone who loves large warships. No other twentieth-century battleship combined such drastic alterations with distinguished service in both world wars.

WARSPITE

Displacement 30,600 tons (31,091 tonnes) standard, 34,500 tons (35,053 tonnes) full load
Length 643 feet 9 inches (196 m 21 cm)
Beam 104 feet (31 m 69 cm)
Draught 30 feet 9 inches (9 m 37 cm)
Machinery 4-shaft geared turbines, 80,000 shp = 24½ knots
Armour belt: 8 to 13 inches (203 to 330 mm). deck: 1¼ to 3 inches (31 to 76 mm). turrets: 5 to 13 inches (127 to 330 mm)
Guns 8 × 15-inch (380-mm), 8 × 6-inch (152-mm), 8 × 4-inch (102-mm) AA, 4 × 8-barrelled 40-mm pom-poms
Torpedo Tubes removed
Launched 26 November 1913 at Devonport Dockyard

Quadruple 2-pounder pom-pom guns of the type fitted in British warships

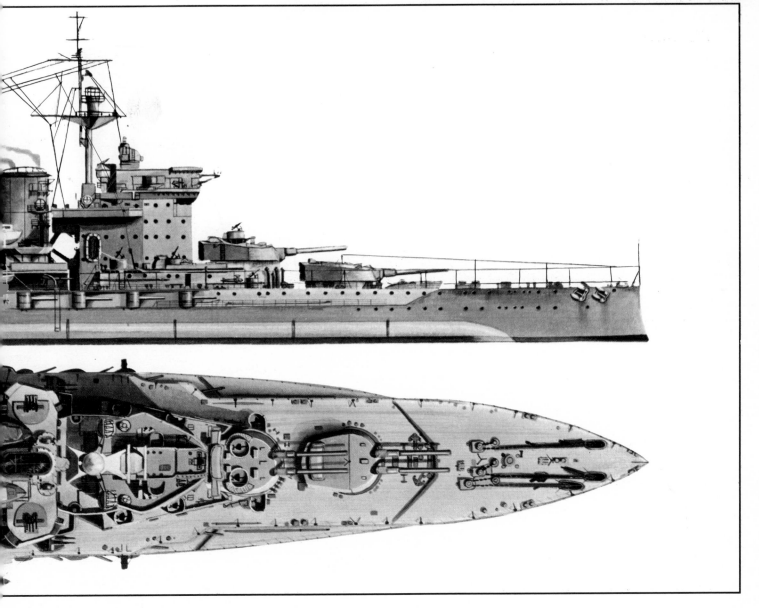

Although slightly later than the *Queen Elizabeth* class, the five ships of the *Royal Sovereign* class did not receive the complete rebuilds of the three ships previously referred to. This was mainly because the 'Rs', *Revenge, Resolution, Royal Oak, Ramillies* and *Royal Sovereign*, were shorter and slower. They were an excellent design when they were conceived at the outbreak of the First World War. They carried the same armament as the *Queen Elizabeth* class, but were originally intended for coal fuel (this was changed to oil while they were being built) and were given less stability, which meant that they were steadier gun platforms. Because of this reduced stability the armour protection was raised higher in these ships; this meant that it would be less likely for a shell hit to start flooding.

All in all, the 'Rs' were an excellent design for their day, sturdy, powerfully armed, with a handsome pyramidal appearance and single

Royal Oak *at the outbreak of war, with an added aircraft catapult and modern A/A guns*

Royal Oak

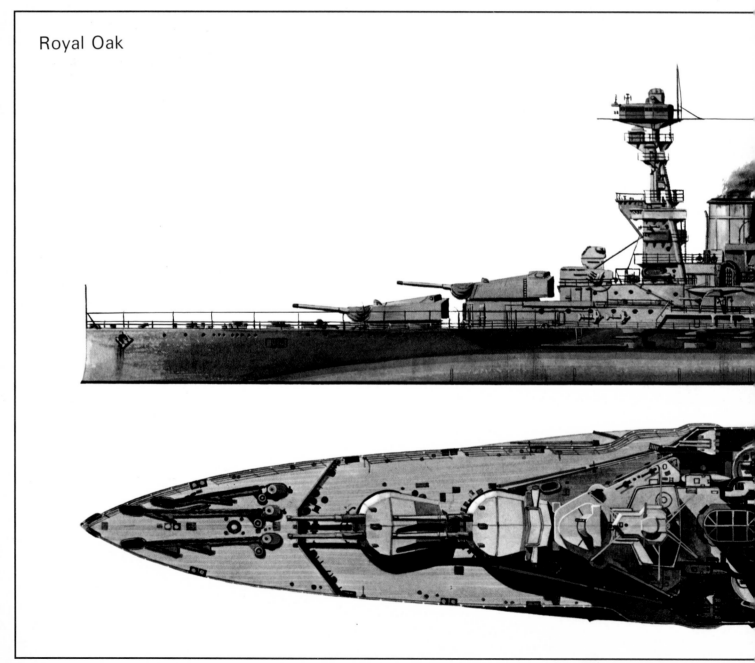

capped funnel. By 1939 they were all obsolescent and due for retirement. Refits during the inter-war period had added bulges against submarine attack, installed seaplane catapults and augmented the anti-aircraft armament, but basically they were not altered much. Almost certainly the decision not to rebuild them was wise, as the resources which this would have taken were better employed in building new ships. This is not to say that the 'Rs' were useless; far from it, though they could only be considered as second-line battleships. They were vulnerable to air attack because of their lack of horizontal protection, even after the usual wartime light anti-aircraft guns had been added, so they had to be kept away from enemy bases. They were not really a match for a modern enemy battle-ship, but could be usefully employed in guarding convoys, where an enemy raider might well shy away from another capital ship, however old and weak. This was in fact what happened several times during the war when German heavy ships avoided action with British convoys because of

the presence of an old battleship. At a pinch the old 'R' ships could be added to a fleet, as happened in the desperate days of 1941–42. In this employment, however, their age told against them; they were plagued with minor breakdowns and could not make their nominal full-load speed of 21 knots. A more sensible employment was shore bombardment, which is how most of the class ended their active careers. One, *Royal Sovereign*, was transferred on loan to the Russians in 1944 as the *Archangelsk*. She was returned after the war in a dreadful state, covered in rust, all her guns loaded with live ammunition and much of it rusted in place.

The ship illustrated, however, did not survive long enough to build any sort of fighting record during the Second World War. On 14 November 1939 the German submarine *U-47* managed to penetrate the unfinished defences of Scapa Flow and her second salvo of torpedoes sank the *Royal Oak*. A minor mystery is why no one apart from the anxious submariners heard the bang of one of the dud torpedoes exploding but the result is

not in doubt; allegations of sabotage seem improbable when it is known that *U-47* was inside Scapa Flow, and did fire two salvoes of torpedoes. The *Royal Oak* herself still rests on the bottom of the Flow, undisturbed because she is officially held to be a war grave for the large number of her crew who went down with her.

ROYAL OAK
Displacement 29,150 tons (29,617 tonnes) standard, 33,500 tons (34,037 tonnes) full load
Length 624 feet 3 inches (190 m 27 cm)
Beam 102 feet 6 inches (31 m 24 cm)
Draught 28 feet 6 inches (8 m 68 cm)
Machinery 4-shaft steam turbines, 40,000 shp = 22 knots
Armour belt: 6 to 13 inches (152 to 330 mm). deck: 1¾ to 2 inches (45 to 51 mm). turrets: 4¼ to 13 inches (108 to 330 mm)
Guns 8 × 15-inch (380-mm), 12 × 6-inch (152-mm), 8 × 4-inch (102-mm) AA, 2 × 8-barrelled 40-mm pom-poms
Torpedo Tubes 4 × 18-inch (456-mm) above water
Launched 17 November 1914 at Devonport Dockyard

After the end of the First World War all the lessons of that war were taken into account, as well as the findings from experiments with captured German ships. The result was a series of original designs culminating in the 'G3' design which was ordered, but then cancelled as a result of the Washington Naval Treaty. This class would have had high speed and strong protection, both in armour (which would have been on the 'all or nothing' principle) and in a system of internal bulges against torpedo attack. These magnificent ships would have looked very odd, with all the gun armament forward, but with the first two triple 16-inch (406-mm) turrets separated from the third by the bridge. They would, however, have been more than a match for any of the Japanese or American ships being built at the time, and would have been at least equal in fighting power to the much later *Bismarck*.

The design appeared in a modified and reduced form in the *Nelson* and *Rodney*, smaller and much slower ships, but still with excellent protection, which included special arrangements against underwater damage which worked excellently when tested by action damage in the Second World War. These two ships had all three main turrets in front of the bridge, making them look rather like immense angry oil tankers. They also had their secondary armament 6-inch (152-mm) guns in twin turrets on the upper deck; this proved to be a successful innovation.

The Admiralty deliberately played down the less visible aspects of this original and successful design, and the ships have never been given enough credit. In all respects except speed (they could only do 23 knots) they were the equals of much later foreign designs. It must, however, be admitted that the 16-inch (406-mm) was not as successful a gun or mounting as the earlier 15-inch (380-mm); the guns wore out much faster, and had more than their fair share of teething troubles.

British battleship design did not stop short with *Nelson* and *Rodney*. A whole series of studies were made in the years between the wars, but financial stringency and the provisions of treaties prevented anything coming of them till the mid-1930s when the threats of Japan, Italy, and rearming Germany were becoming too obvious to be ignored. The result was the building of the *King George V* class, of which *Howe* was a later example. Like *Nelson* and *Rodney*, this class, the only recently designed British battleships to serve in the Second World War, have perhaps been given less than their due as designs. They did not appear to be very spectacular ships, and this aesthetic impression was reinforced by the fact that they carried a smaller calibre of gun than any foreign equivalent. This was because their design was prepared at a time when the naval treaties still held sway, and the Admiralty suspected that new ships might be restricted to 14-inch (356-mm) guns. An adequate design of gun from the First World War period was adapted, and the Admiralty decided to compensate for the slight loss in range and hitting power by carrying more guns. (Stories that the 14-inch (356-mm) was a brand-new design which mysteriously possessed superior qualities to other navies' 15-inch (380-mm) or 16-inch (406-mm) guns were just a propaganda 'blind'.) Originally the new class was to have

carried 12 guns in three quadruple turrets, but the increasing need for heavier protection on the decks against long-range shelling and bombs led to one quadruple turret being dropped in favour of a twin to save weight.

The quadruple turret had been first adopted by the French, and another innovation in the new British class had also appeared first in the *Dunkerque* class. This was the merging of the secondary anti-destroyer armament with the tertiary anti-aircraft armament in one high-angle/low-angle gun. The *King George V* class had a twin 5.25-inch (133-mm) gun, a rather complicated mounting and rather too heavy for effective anti-aircraft fire. However, the idea was a good one, and later became standard.

Where the *King George V* class shone in comparison with their foreign contemporaries was in their heavy, simple and effective armour protection. This, particularly the horizontal armour, was heavier than in any foreign equivalent. The US Navy, which had invented the 'all or nothing' system, did not armour its later ships particularly heavily (most published figures on this are wrong). The British disposition of protection was far more sensible than that of the *Bismarck*; despite legends to the contrary, British armour was at this time equal in quality to German (as was proved in comparative trials after the war) and thicker.

The *King George V* class turned out to be an effective design when they were tested in action. There was a lot of teething trouble with the quadruple 14-inch (356-mm) mountings, particularly noticeable in the *Prince of Wales* when she met the *Bismarck* before she was fully worked up. But what is often ignored by commentators on this action is that the German battleship and *Prinz Eugen* would have had a great problem in trying to 'finish off' the British ship as so many have suggested they should. Because of faults in the mountings the *Prince of Wales* would not have been able to make much of a reply to the German fire, but her powerful protection was intact, her machinery functioning, and her only serious hit was by a German shell on the bridge – a shell which, incidentally, did not explode. She would have been very difficult to sink, and reinforcements were on their way.

The sinking of the *Prince of Wales* by Japanese air attack was due, more than any other technical factor, to the lack of consideration given before the war to the problem of shock from near-

misses exploding underwater. It was this shock which knocked out most of the *Prince of Wales'* auxiliary power and thereby deprived her of her hitherto effective anti-aircraft barrage (the 5.25-inch (133-mm) guns were in powered mountings), and, later, of vitally needed pumps. The later ships of the class, *Anson* and *Howe*, were still being built at the time of the *Prince of Wales'* loss, and as a result were fitted with improved damage control arrangements, including auxiliary machinery mounted flexibly to reduce shock damage.

The fact that they were only armed with the 14-inch (356-mm) gun seemed to make little practical difference to the effectiveness of *King George V*'s shooting against *Bismarck*, or *Duke of York*'s against *Scharnhorst*. Because of the piecemeal nature of wartime additions to anti-aircraft armament and radar, not one of the five ships was exactly the same as another, and all changed their appearance slightly during the course of their war service.

The increasing importance of carriers and then aircraft, which by the end of the war had reduced the remaining ships in the *King George V* class to the status of large anti-aircraft escorts and fast bombardment ships for the British Pacific Fleet, also meant that the next class of British battleships were never completed. These were to have been known as the *Lion* class, larger and improved versions of the *King George V* with triple 16-inch (406-mm) turrets.

However, one other battleship was built, specifically designed as a fast battleship with the Pacific in mind, the *Vanguard*. To speed up delivery she used spare 15-inch (380-mm) gun mountings built during the First World War (the story that she was built to take advantage of the availability of these turrets is, however, false). Though these were old guns, they were, as we have seen, excellent, and in every other way the *Vanguard* was a very up-to-date ship. Her raised bow gave her an advantage in seaworthiness over her predecessors; she was also a better sea-boat than the larger American *Missouri* class, which made the American ships' advantage in speed a marginal one. *Vanguard* had probably the best system of battleship protection ever devised. She, rather than *Bismarck*, the clumsy *Yamato*, or the *Iowa*, was probably the best all-round battleship design produced by the war. Alas, she had only one disadvantage: she was completed too late to serve in it.

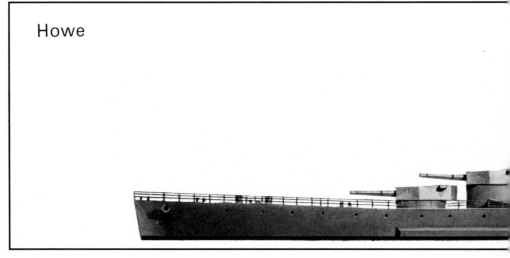

Howe

HOWE
Displacement 36,830 tons (37,421 tonnes) standard,
40,990 tons (41,648 tonnes) full load
Length 745 feet (227 m)
Beam 103 feet (31 m 39 cm)
Draught 28 feet (8 m 53 cm)
Machinery 4-shaft geared steam turbines,
110,000 shp = 29¼ knots
Armour belt: 14 to 15 inches (356 to 380 mm).
deck: 2½ to 6 inches (64 to 152 mm). turrets: 9 to 16
inches (227 to 405 mm)
Guns 10 × 14-inch (356-mm), 16 × 5.25-inch
(133-mm) DP, 6 × 8-barrelled 40-mm pom-poms
Torpedo Tubes none
Launched 9 April 1940 by Fairfield, Govan

Above: Howe *passing through the Suez Canal
in 1944.* Right: Duke of York *steams at speed
with the Home Fleet in 1943*

Great Britain: Cruisers

It has always been difficult to find an adequate short definition for the cruiser as a type. Historically the word has covered virtually everything between the huge and powerful armoured cruisers of 1900, as big as battleships, down to small vessels difficult to distinguish from sloops or gunboats. Also there is no clear line of development such as there is in the evolution of the battleship or the destroyer. However, by the end of the First World War there was some degree of order in the types of cruiser in the Royal Navy. The old kind of armoured cruiser was vanishing, though most cruisers had some form of protective plating, usually deck and side armour. There were a number of small fast cruisers designed primarily for the North Sea. By 1939 the earlier surviving examples of these (the 'C' class) had all been converted, or were undergoing conversion, to anti-aircraft ships. Armed with high-angle 4-inch (102-mm) guns they proved very effective in this role. The later class, the 'D' ships, were not heavily rebuilt, but in general used for second-line duties. The exception to the rebuilding rule was the *Delhi*, which was converted in the USA to a main armament of five of the excellent American 5-inch (127-mm) destroyer guns in place of her original 6-inch (152-mm) mounts. This was a trial installation, as the Admiralty was seriously considering the possibility of using this weapon in British destroyers.

The older type of trade-route cruiser was the original 'Town' type, of which only one, the Australian *Adelaide*, survived to serve in the Second War. These were armed with 6-inch (152-mm) guns, as were two fast cruisers still being built at the end of the war, the *Emerald* and *Enterprise*. However, the most influential vessels being built then were a class of larger cruisers armed with 7.5-inch (190-mm) guns, the *Cavendish* class. It was these ships which were responsible for the adoption of 8-inch (203-mm) guns as the maximum calibre for cruisers in the interwar naval treaties, and also the 10,000-ton limitation on tonnage. Other than this, their importance was not great, as they were merely enlarged versions of the smaller cruisers, retaining single gun mounts.

The first post-war ships were very different. These were the 'Counties', the original 'treaty cruisers'. Because of their high freeboard and their archaic-looking triple funnels, and also because of the fact that the British did not cheat on displacement as blatantly as most other naval powers, this large group of ships came to be looked upon as inferior to their foreign contemporaries. However the 'Counties' were to prove excellent fighting ships; their twin 8-inch (203-mm) mounting was a very powerful and effective weapon indeed, their speed and endurance were both adequate to meet most demands, and despite a propensity to roll a lot, they were

good sea-boats. Their protection was also reasonable, the magazines were armoured, and so was half of the machinery space. The last two of the 'Counties' were to have been built with a two-knot drop in speed, traded for an increase in armour thickness and extent. Unfortunately these two interesting ships, the *Northumberland* and *Surrey*, were cancelled.

The 'Counties' were all described as 'A'-class cruisers under the treaty definitions but there was also provision for 8-inch (203-mm) cruisers of the 'B' type, a kind of cheap version. The length and breadth of the 'County' design were reduced, and three as against four 8-inch (203-mm) turrets were fitted. Freeboard was generally reduced, and the flush deck of the 'Counties' was abandoned for a cut-down after deck. Three funnels were replaced by two, though the power of the machinery was not changed.

Only two ships of this kind were built, the *York* and the *Exeter*. The *Exeter* differed from her slightly earlier sister by having a lower bridge and unraked funnels, and she also had two fixed catapults angled outwards abaft the funnels. In all cruisers of this time great importance was given to the aircraft arrangements, which were indeed to prove useful early in the war for isolated cruisers on patrol in the oceans. Later the increasing availability of carrier aircraft lessened the need for the amphibians catapulted

Exeter

from battleships and cruisers.

HMS *Exeter*, like all the 'Counties' and most other British cruisers, had a secondary anti-aircraft armament of high-angle 4-inch (102-mm) guns, and also carried 21-inch (530-mm) torpedo tubes. It was, however, her excellent protection which was probably her greatest asset in her most famous action, against the *Graf Spee*. This enabled her to continue to divert the pocket battleship's fire from *Ajax* and *Achilles* even after virtually all her armament was out of action and she had suffered other heavy damage. She thus played her part to the limit in the carefully planned anti-raider tactics which had been developed by the Admiralty to deal with the pocket battleships before the war. It was definitely not a brilliant improvisation

by the local commander which had the three British cruisers dividing into two forces, for this was a manoeuvre practiced on several occasions before the war by all British cruiser squadrons.

After *Exeter*, Britain built no more cruisers armed with 8-inch (203-mm) guns mainly because it was considered that the rate of fire and ease of handling of 6-inch (152-mm) guns more than compensated for that weapon's lesser range, particularly if the cruiser carrying such guns was armoured to resist 8-inch (203-mm) gunfire. Nevertheless, 8-inch (203-mm) shells fired from 'County'-class cruisers inflicted vital damage on two German capital ships. In the case of the *Bismarck* it was her fire control which was knocked out, while the *Scharnhorst*'s radar was irreparably damaged.

Exeter *firing at aircraft, showing her added tripod masts and heavy a/a armament*

EXETER

Displacement 8,390 tons (8,524 tonnes) standard, 10,500 tons (10,668 tonnes) full load
Length 575 feet (175 m 25 cm)
Beam 58 feet (17 m 67 cm)
Draught 17 feet (5 m 18 cm)
Machinery 4-shaft geared steam turbines, 80,000 shp = $32\frac{1}{4}$ knots
Armour belt: 2 to 3 inches (51 to 76 mm). deck: 2 inches (51 mm). turrets: $1\frac{1}{2}$ to 2 inches (38 to 51 mm)
Guns 6 × 8-inch (203-mm), 4 × 4-inch (102-mm) AA, 2 × 2-barrelled 40-mm pom-poms
Torpedo Tubes 6 × 21-inch (530-mm)
Launched 18 July 1929 at Devonport Dockyard

Ajax

By 1930 the majority of British 6-inch (152-mm)-gun light cruisers were becoming obsolete, and various other navies were producing modern cruiser designs, such as the German *Königsberg* class, with enclosed gun-houses and other modern refinements. This was the background against which the *Leander* class were designed. There were five, named *Achilles*, *Ajax*, *Leander*, *Neptune* and *Orion*, handsome symmetrical ships with a single trunked funnel. The most important design considerations were an armament of eight 6-inch (152-mm) guns and a speed of 32 knots. The twin mounting with its enclosed gun-house was developed from that fitted in the cruiser *Enterprise* and then the battleships *Nelson* and *Rodney*.

Unlike some of their contemporaries, particularly the Italian 152-mm cruisers, the *Leanders* had a reasonable amount of armour protection, which paid off when *Ajax* and *Achilles* had to take on *Graf Spee*. *Neptune* demonstrated the efficiency of her underwater protection by setting off four mines before sinking in a Mediterranean minefield.

One disadvantage of the *Leander* class, otherwise excellent and well-balanced fighting ships, was that their machinery was not on the unit system; in other words, boiler rooms adjoined one another and could all be knocked out by a single hit. This was rectified in the next design, the 'Modified *Leander*' class with machinery spaces in the sequence of boiler room – engine room – boiler room – engine room. This necessitated a return to two funnels, giving the new class a less massive but perhaps more elegant appearance. All three were transferred to the Royal Australian Navy as the *Hobart*, *Perth* and *Sydney*.

The next class of ships to appear were reduced versions of the previous one. The *Arethusa* class were intended first and foremost for trade protection, and were of the minimum size compatible with seaworthiness. They had an armament of six 6-inch (152-mm) guns, adequate against an armed merchant raider, and a speed of about 32 knots, which was necessary as they

AJAX
Displacement 6,985 tons (7,097 tonnes) standard, 8,950 tons (9,073 tonnes) full load
Length 554 feet 3 inches (168 m 93 cm)
Beam 55 feet 9 inches (16 m 99 cm)
Draught 16 feet (4 m 87 cm)
Machinery 4-shaft geared turbines, 72,000 shp = $32\frac{1}{2}$ knots
Armour belt: 2 to 4 inches (51 to 102 mm). deck: 2 inches (51 mm). turrets: 1 inch (25 mm)
Guns 8 × 6-inch (152-mm), 8 × 4-inch (102-mm) AA, 4 quadruple MGs
Torpedo Tubes 8 × 21-inch (530-mm)
Launched 1 March 1934 by Vickers-Armstrong, Barrow

Ajax after her 1940 refit with tripod masts fitted. The catapult and aircraft have been removed. The prominent knuckle forward was a feature of most British cruisers, but the unusual single trunked funnel led the Graf Spee to confuse her and her sister Achilles with destroyers early in the River Plate action. The fire control carries gunnery radar and the small tower abaft it supports a surface radar search. In common with her surviving sisters she had an X turret replaced by light A/A guns in 1944

Penelope

were also intended to act as fleet cruisers if required.

They were 50 feet (15.2 m) shorter than the preceeding class, and had only one twin turret aft, but otherwise were very similar, except for their 'chopped off' look aft. They were attractive little ships and an excellent design. They could do anything bigger cruisers could do, but were cheaper and required a smaller crew. It is a pity that Britain did not build more of these instead of the later 'Town' class, impressive ships though the latter undoubtedly were. The *Arethusa* ships' anti-aircraft armament was much the same as their bigger sisters', and the armour protection was only slightly less. One interesting feature was that, for the first time in British ships of this type, welding played an important part in construction in order to save weight.

Ironically this class were mainly employed in fleet work in the confined waters of the Mediterranean, and saw little of the trade routes for which they were designed. *Penelope*, in particular, operating from Malta, had an impressive record and it is she who is immortalized in C S Forester's famous novel *The Ship* as HMS *Artemis*.

Later, when the Admiralty required a small cruiser design primarily intended for anti-aircraft work, the *Arethusa* design was modified

Penelope entering Grand Harbour, Malta probably in 1942 after bomb damage had been repaired at Gibraltar. The artwork depicts this ship before the outbreak of war, except for the tripods. These ships were too small to carry the catapult and aircraft normally considered necessary for cruisers of the Second World War period

to fit. Instead of a main armament of 6-inch (152-mm) guns and a secondary high-angle outfit of 4-inch (102-mm) guns, the new class was given ten dual-purpose 5.25-inch (133-mm) guns in twin mounts. These weapons were perhaps a little heavy for anti-aircraft work, though perfectly adequate if a little complicated as low-angle weapons. The new ship class, the *Dido* vessels, were handicapped by a shortage of mountings and two, the *Scylla* and *Charybdis*, had eight 4.5-inch (114-mm) guns each instead of 5.25-inch (133-mm) weapons. Although they were known as the 'toothless terrors', they were more useful than their sisters for anti-aircraft duties. As ten guns were found to fire off the ammunition rather faster than was prudent a second improved group were given eight guns instead, as well as upright instead of raked funnels. All gave good service in the war, especially in the Mediterranean, and proved the basic soundness of the design and concept of this particular type of light cruiser.

PENELOPE
Displacement 5,270 tons (5,342 tonnes) standard, 6,715 tons (6,819 tonnes) full load
Length 506 feet (154 m 22 cm)
Beam 51 feet (15 m 54 cm)
Draught 14 feet (4 m 26 cm)
Machinery 4-shaft geared turbines, 64,000 shp = 32¼ knots
Armour belt: 2 to 2¾ inches (51 to 70 mm). deck: 2 inches (51 mm). turrets: 1 inch (25 mm)
Guns 6 × 6-inch (152-mm), 8 × 4-inch (102-mm) AA, 2 quadruple MGs
Torpedo Tubes 6 × 21-inch (530-mm)
Launched 15 October 1935 by Harland & Wolff, Belfast

From the lighter 6-inch (152-mm) cruisers we now shift to the heavier ones. Japan, with the *Mogami* class, and the United States with the *Brooklyn* class, had both produced very large 6-inch (152-mm) cruisers, fully the equal of the older 8-inch (203-mm) treaty cruisers. Britain followed suit, though in slightly more conservative fashion, as her heavy 6-inch (152-mm) cruisers only had 12 as opposed to 15 guns. Ironically these ships, because of their guns, continued to be known as 'light' cruisers despite their large size.

The British, like their rivals, adopted triple turrets, though with the special feature of having the central gun further back than the two outer weapons, to avoid blast interference problems. The first group of ships built for the Royal Navy with this turret were known by the old 'Town' names, and were called the *Southampton* class. In many ways they were enlarged versions of the *Amphion* or Australian 'Improved *Leander*' class. Armour protection was improved and thickened, and a hangar built on either side of the forefunnel. These were heavy and powerful ships, but towards the end of the war the addition of topweight in the form of radar and extra light guns caused the superimposed turret aft to be removed to preserve the ships' stability. This modification was also applied to the later 'Colony' class, but not to the survivor (*Belfast*) of the two improved 'Towns' which were the largest British cruisers of the war.

These two ships looked quite different from the other 'Towns', as the machinery was moved further aft, the after turrets were mounted higher, and two extra twin 4-inch (102-mm) high-angle mountings added. There was a somewhat unsightly gap between bridge and forefunnel, but these were very powerful ships indeed, having been lengthened and given extra armour protection. Because she broke her back when mined early in the war, *Belfast* was rebuilt with external bulges, which did not add to the beauty of her appearance, and she now survives as a museum ship in London.

The next class ordered after the 'Towns' were the 'Colonies', basically similar to the earlier class except that they were restricted to 8,000 tons (8,130 tonnes) instead of 10,000 tons (10,160 tonnes) because of the London Naval Treaty. Despite this, careful design meant that little of value was lost in the weight saving; the stern was a flat transom instead of the more elegant 'cruiser' stern, mast and funnels were vertical instead of raked, and protection had to be slightly reduced and rearranged. Other than this the first group of the 'Colonies', of which *Jamaica* was one, were similar to the *Southampton* class. The later ships were modified to give better accommodation to radar and light guns, while dispensing from the beginning with 'X' turret, which was also removed from the earlier ships.

The chief disadvantage of the 'Colonies' was that their reduced tonnage as against the 'Towns' meant that accommodation was cramped, and became more so as the men necessary to work the extra light guns and radar had to be added to their complement. Apart from this, they were excellent, well-balanced fighting ships, very much in the British cruiser tradition. The design was modified only slightly in the next class, the *Swiftsure*, only three of which were completed by the end of the war. Another three were kept for several years in a partly-completed state until they were equipped with new automatic weapons, but these ships, the *Tiger* class, take us far beyond the war period.

JAMAICA

Displacement 8,525 tons (8,661 tonnes) standard, 10,350 tons (10,516 tonnes) full load
Length 555 feet 6 inches (169 m 31 cm)
Beam 62 feet (18 m 89 cm)
Draught 16 feet 6 inches (5 m)
Machinery 4-shaft geared turbines, 72,500 shp = 33 knots
Armour belt: 3¼ inches (82 mm). deck: 2 inches (51 mm). turrets: 2 inches (51 mm)
Guns 12 × 6-inch (152-mm), 8 × 4-inch (102-mm) AA, 2 × 4-barrelled 40-mm pom-poms
Torpedo Tubes 6 × 21-inch (530-mm)
Launched 16 November 1940 by Vickers-Armstrong, Barrow

Top: Jamaica, *a 'Colony'-class cruiser, seen off Iceland.* Right: Belfast *after her rebuild*

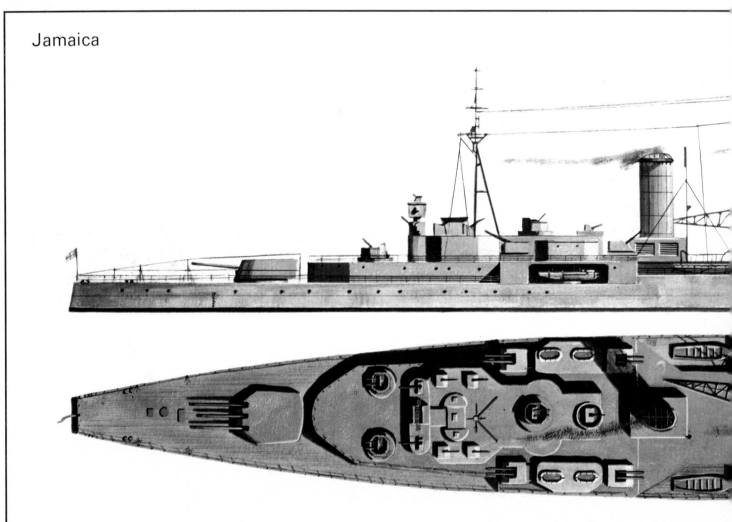

Jamaica

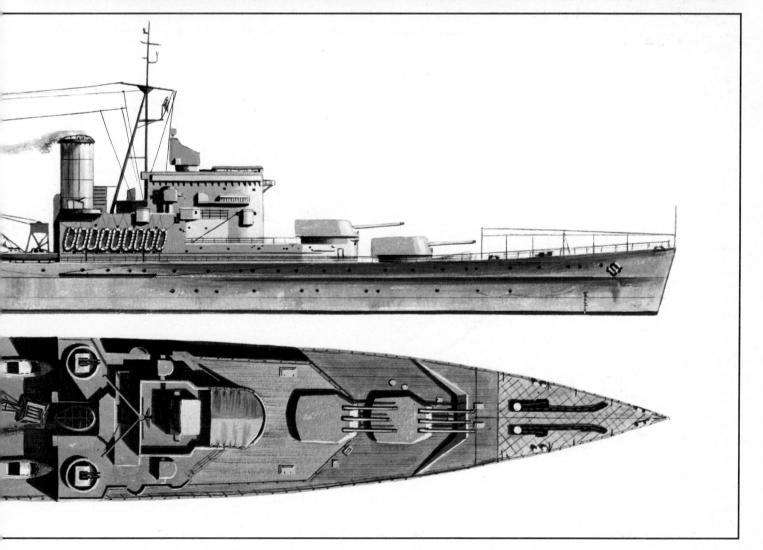

Great Britain: Destroyers

During the First World War the Royal Navy developed what was perhaps the classic destroyer design of all time. Certainly the sturdy 'V & W' class were far and away the best design of their own period; they were equipped with four 4-inch (102-mm) guns (4.7-inch (120-mm) in the later ships of the class) in superimposed mounts, and two multiple torpedo-tubes. They had a good speed, reliable machinery, and were very seaworthy. Many were converted to anti-aircraft ships or long-range escorts, and despite their age they won a great deal of affection from their crews.

The basic formula of the 'V & W' design was copied widely by other navies, and it remained the basis of British destroyer design until just before the Second World War. The 'A' to 'I' classes were all two-funnelled, four-gun vessels (except for the leaders which had five guns) of approximately the same size and performance. They were excellent ships, and they proved to be a match for much larger and better-armed German vessels thanks to their seaworthiness. Their main disadvantage proved to be that they did not have the displacement to accept all the radar and light anti-aircraft guns that the war showed to be necessary for a modern destroyer.

The famous 'Tribal' class were built just before the war because of fears about the increasing size and gunpower of large Japanese, German and French destroyers. They were basically an enlargement of the previous destroyers with twin mountings in place of singles for 4.7-inch (120-mm) guns, and only one set of torpedo tubes. Unfortunately, like the earlier ships, they were deficient in high-angle fire, which was also true of the classes that followed, though stopgaps like replacing one gun or torpedo mounting with an anti-aircraft gun worked reasonably well. The 'Tribals' were in fact probably an uneconomic design; what really mattered in destroyers was numbers, and the next design, the 'J & K' class, gave over twice the number of torpedo tubes with only one less twin 4.7-inch (120-mm) mounting, on a smaller displacement. Weight was saved by using a different system of construction, longitudinal framing, and also by using only two boilers, hence the single funnel that became typical of British destroyers built during the war.

With some alterations in dimensions and the adoption of the simpler and more economical system of having the main armament in four single mounts, the 'J & K' design became the basis of the British standard wartime destroyer design. Towards the end it became apparent that this was no longer large enough, but it was a reliable and sturdy design and did its work well. It was not until the end of the war that the first of the completely new designs began to emerge. These were the large and powerful 'Battle' class, with their main gun armament concentrated forward, and excellent torpedo and light anti-aircraft armament. This class also had better range, being intended primarily for use in the Pacific.

Unlike the Germans and Americans, the British did not go in for high-pressure steam machinery until after the war was over. This was

because of the mishandling of the trials of high-pressure boilers in one of the 'A' class, long before the war; the installation was not given a fair chance to prove itself, so the Royal Navy was saddled with machinery that gave less economy and range than other navies' destroyers. On the other hand this was not all bad, as British machinery was normally very reliable. The Germans' unhappy experience with high-pressure steam machinery demonstrates the dangers of adopting such technical innovations too rapidly.

Top left: The 'K' class destroyer Kashmir *with her famous flotilla leader* Kelly *behind.*
Above: Onslow *in December 1942, showing the damage from 203-mm shells during the Barents Sea action.*
Right: An Independence – *class light fleet carrier leads an* Essex – *class carrier and battleships.*

USA: Aircraft Carriers

Thanks to the work of a few dedicated airminded senior officers the US Navy entered the Second World War with a naval air arm which was second to none. The Japanese had more immediate advantages in their operational experience obtained over China, and in their superlative carrier fighter, the 'Zero'. The Americans, however, were basically stronger, for not only did they have enormous technical and manufacturing resources, they also were ahead of anyone else in the techniques of operating aircraft from carriers. Most of their carrier aircraft types in service in 1941, like the Wildcat and Dauntless, were sound designs, capable with intelligent planning and experience of holding their own against Japanese types. As the war went on the enormous energy, skill and resources of the American aircraft industry meant that planes superior to anything the Japanese could produce at speed or in significant numbers were rushed into service, particularly the Hellcat, Avenger and Corsair. More important still, the Japanese could never replace the

skilled pilots they lost, while the American aircrew-training programme was superbly organized and ever-growing.

While the British tended to regard the design of carriers rather in the light of producing a good ship which also carried aircraft as an incidental, the Americans subordinated everything in their designs to carrying the maximum number of aircraft and getting as many of them in the air as possible as quickly as could be managed. For the British the 'ship' qualities of the carriers took first place; for the Americans it was the aircraft-operating qualities that mattered. Thus it was that the American carriers were often less well protected and designed with less attention to their defensive armament. Both approaches were, of course, valid, particularly given the different strategic, technical and tactical factors affecting each navy. It is interesting, however, as we have already seen in the British carriers, that both nations, as the war went on, tended to adopt more and more of their ally's ideas and methods. One thing that the Americans were certainly

right on was in thinking of the carrier's fighters as being their chief defence against aerial attack. However, with their own excellent fighters they could afford to think this way, particularly after radar had been adapted, with a typically American ability to develop an invention to its full extent, to serving the needs of a carrier force.

The superior nature of American carrier aircraft, their sturdiness and ability to land at higher speeds and steeper angles, also meant that American designers did not need to give much attention to eliminating turbulence in the air over their flight decks. A wartime British report wonderingly remarks that it was almost true to say that American carriers were designed in complete defiance of the science of aerodynamics!

The earliest American carrier was the *Langley*, a converted large fast collier which had an experimental installation for the turbo-electric propulsion later fitted to a number of battleships. She was not a particularly useful vessel, and had been relegated to the task of being an aircraft transport before the war broke out.

Lexington

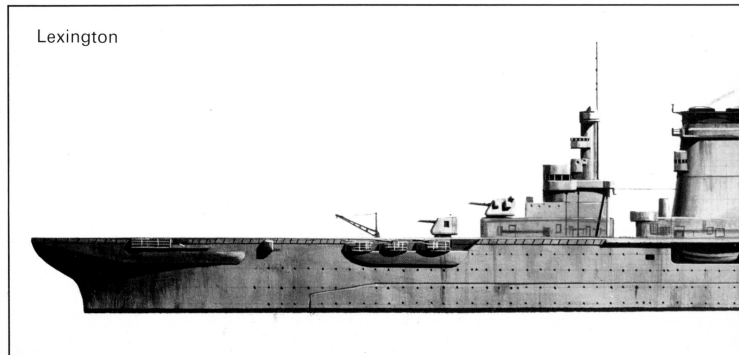

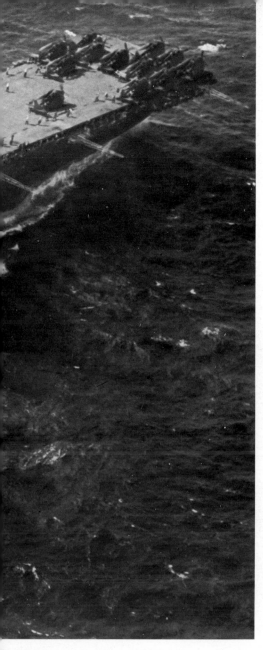

The next two American carriers were very different, and far more effective vessels. It was decided to convert the incomplete hulls of two of the turbo-electric battle-cruisers cancelled as a result of the Washington Naval Treaty to carriers. This was a sensible decision, and the Americans obtained two very large, very fast, and quite well-protected carriers, probably the best of the first generation of this type of ship. Their success makes one wonder whether the British would not have been well advised to have converted the *Hood* to a carrier rather than the job lot of light battle-cruisers and ex-battleships they actually used.

Not every feature of the redesigned *Lexington* and *Saratoga* was justifiable. They were given four twin 8-inch (203-mm) turrets disposed before and abaft the island, a pointless addition as aircraft carriers were far too vulnerable to attempt to 'slug it out' with other warships. These guns were finally removed early in the war, and twin 5-inch (127-mm) turrets substituted. It is sometimes said that *Lexington* was sunk before this could be done to her, but photographs showing her sinking after the Battle of the Coral Sea clearly show the 5-inch (127-mm) mounts.

Gun turrets and the island itself were dwarfed by the most distinctive feature of these ships, a truly enormous funnel. Unlike many later US carriers the bow and the hull were plated up to the level of the flight deck. The plated-in bow was finally readopted by the Americans at the end of the war, but chiefly as a result of the British example.

Because these carriers were not designed as such they could not carry as many planes as they might have done. Even so they managed the impressive total of 90 each. Though the *Lexington* was lost early in the war, the *Saratoga* continued her distinguished career until the end. However, these ships' most important contribution to victory was probably their use in training and exercises in the interwar years, and here their large size and aircraft complement were most important. Smaller ships and fewer aircraft might have meant less satisfactory exercises, less chance to experiment, and less flexibility in trying out new methods.

The first American carrier designed and built as such was the *Ranger*, and in her the American obsession with aircraft capacity was taken to extreme lengths. She only displaced 14,500 tons (14,730 tonnes) when fully laden, yet could carry 86 aircraft, a far greater number than foreign carriers of comparable size, like *Hermes*. Protection, gun armament and speed were adequate but no more, and because of this *Ranger* was usually used for second-line duties during the war. Like most of the later American carriers the hull was not built up to the flight deck. She had the unusual feature of the boiler room being aft of the engine room, and the smoke was emitted through three hinged funnels on each side.

LEXINGTON

Displacement 36,000 tons (36,577 tonnes) standard, 39,000 tons (39,626 tonnes) full load
Length 888 feet (270 m 66 cm)
Beam 130 feet (39 m 62 cm) over flight deck
Draught 24 feet 3 inches (7 m 39 cm)
Machinery 4-shaft steam turbines and electric motors, 184,000 shp = 33¼ knots
Armour belt: 6 inches (152 mm). deck: 1 to 3 inches (25 to 76 mm). turrets 1½ to 3 inches (38 to 76 mm)
Guns 12 × 5-inch (127-mm) AA, 5 × 4-barrelled 1.1-inch (28-mm) AA mountings
Torpedo Tubes none
Aircraft 90 (1 catapult)
Launched 3 October 1925 by Fore River Co., Quincy, Massachusetts

Left: The new Essex-*class carrier* Lexington (CV-16), *part of the famous Task Force 38.*
Below: The original Lexington (CV-2), *with its enormous funnel and the enclosed or 'hurricane' bow, unique to this ship and her sister the* Saratoga (CV-37)

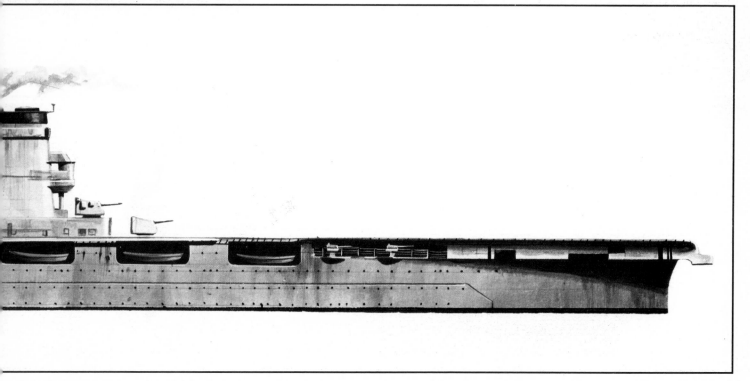

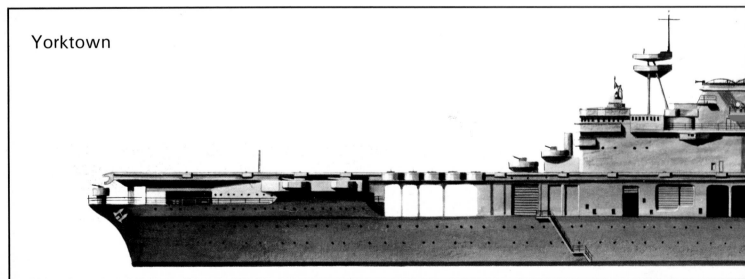

Yorktown

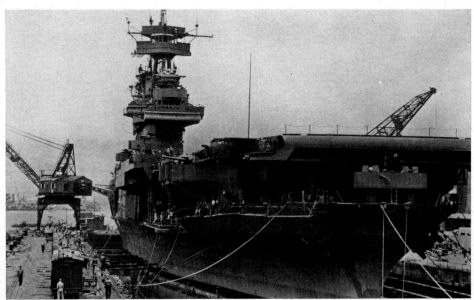

After the not altogether successful experiment in minimum dimensions and fighting qualities of the design of the *Ranger* came the much more balanced *Yorktown* class. All three played a vital part in the desperate fighting of the early days of the war in the Pacific. Two, *Hornet* and *Yorktown*, were lost, and only *Enterprise* survived the war.

Hornet was launched four years after the other two to a slightly modified design, the chief feature of which was an enlarged flight deck, later fitted to the *Enterprise* as well. The basic design of all three was a good well-balanced one; though aircraft capacity was no greater than the *Ranger*'s, on their bigger displacement they could make nearly five knots more speed. Armament, protection and machinery installation were all better. Visually they were distinguished by having a large funnel which was, however, considerably smaller than that of the *Lexington* class.

Like all the earlier American carriers their flight deck was a weak spot, with its wooden planking and complete lack of armour. However, they were sturdily built ships, and both *Hornet* and *Yorktown* took a considerable amount of damage before sinking. Perhaps the most famous individual exploit was the Doolittle Raid on Tokyo. In this a force of twin-engined B-25 army bombers took off from the *Hornet*, larger and heavier aircraft than had ever done so from a carrier before.

YORKTOWN

Displacement 19,800 tons (20,117 tonnes) standard, 25,500 tons (25,909 tonnes) full load
Length 809 feet 6 inches (246 m 73 cm)
Beam 109 feet (33 m 22 cm) (across flight deck)
Draught 21 feet 9 inches (6 m 63 cm)
Machinery 4-shaft geared steam turbines, 120,000 shp = 33 knots
Armour belt: 2½ to 4 inches (63 to 102 mm). deck: 1 to 3 inches (25 to 76 mm)
Guns 8 × 5-inch (127-mm) AA, 4 × 4-barrelled 1.1-inch (28-mm) AA mountings
Aircraft 81 (3 catapults)
Torpedo Tubes none
Launched 4 April 1936 by Newport News Shipbuilding Co.

Top: The original Yorktown (CV-5) *seen during her hectic 48-hour repair which enabled her to surprise the Japanese at Midway. Left: The new* Yorktown (CV-10), *an Essex-class carrier, also served with distinction in the Pacific in operations against the Gilbert Islands, Kwajalein, Truk, Hollandia, the Marianas and Iwo Jima. Below: The first* Yorktown (CV-5)

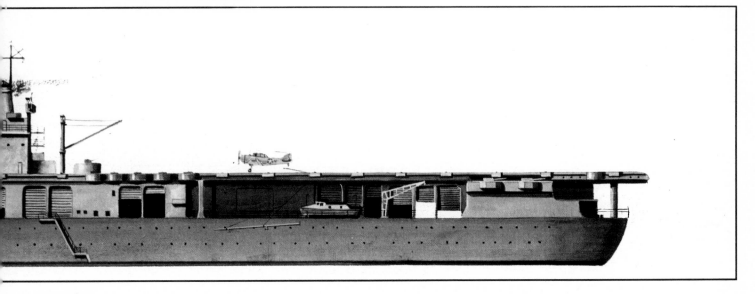

Because of the total carrier tonnage limitations of the Washington Naval Treaty the next American carrier after *Yorktown* and *Enterprise* had to be built to a much reduced tonnage, not much greater than the *Ranger*'s. Like her she suffered from less speed, inferior armament, less protection (though better than the *Ranger*'s), and a smaller operational radius. As one might expect, her aircraft capacity did not suffer, and in one respect, she improved on her predecessors, for she was fitted with the first deck-edge lift. This innovation increased the American lead in the speed and efficiency with which aircraft could be moved from hangar to flight deck and back. However, a deck-edge lift really required the American pattern of open hangar, and would have proved difficult to combine with the British closed armoured box hangars.

Wasp was a little small for full efficiency and the design was not repeated. She was visually quite distinctive, with her tall thin funnel. After proving very useful helping the British ferry fighters to Malta, she was moved to the Pacific where she was lost through submarine attack.

Having tried a range of sizes and types of carriers the Americans very sensibly used their experience to design a standard type of carrier which was built in large numbers throughout the war. This was the excellent *Essex* type, which was not hampered, like the earlier vessels, by treaty limitations. The ships were large, but their increase in size was used to improve their ability to operate larger and heavier aircraft rather than to increase aircraft numbers. There was also an increase in the 'ship' qualities of the class. Armour was fitted to both flight and hangar decks, though the flight deck was still planked and the sides of the hangar were left unarmoured and vulnerable. The heavy anti-aircraft armament of 5-inch (127-mm) guns was strengthened, but was not as well disposed as that in British ships, nor could it engage as many targets as there were only two director towers. Hull protection was good, as these ships were well subdivided.

Improvements and alterations were constantly being made to the basic design, of which 24 ships, excluding cancelled units, were built. The names of the *Yorktown*, *Hornet*, *Wasp* and *Lexington* were preserved by being given to *Essex*-class ships which were on the stocks when

WASP
Displacement 14,700 tons (14,935 tonnes) standard, 21,000 tons (21,337 tonnes) full load
Length 741 feet 3 inches (225 m 93 cm)
Beam 109 feet (33 m 22 cm) across flight deck
Draught 20 feet (6 m 9 cm)
Machinery 4-shaft geared steam turbines, 75,000 shp = $29\frac{1}{2}$ knots
Armour belt: 4 inches (102 mm). deck: $1\frac{1}{2}$ inches (38 mm)
Guns 8 × 5-inch (127-mm) AA, 4 × 4-barrelled 1.1-inch (28-mm) AA mountings
Aircraft 84 (four catapults)
Launched 4 April 1939 by Bethlehem Shipyard, Quincy

Top: The carrier Wasp *(CV-7) ablaze after being hit by a torpedo at Guadalcanal. Right:* Wasp *in 1942, showing her camouflage scheme*

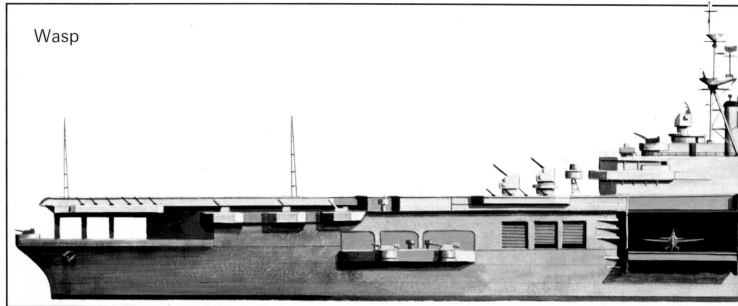

Wasp

the original bearers of the names were sunk.

The *Essex*-class ships were to be the mainstay of the American carrier arm for long after the war, but a class of three much larger ships, named *Midways*, were building at the end of the war, amalgamating much of what was best in British carrier design with American practice.

While the larger ships of the *Essex* class were still being built, a distressingly large proportion of the United States carrier force was sunk in the early months of the Pacific War. There was an urgent need for rapidly produced stopgaps, of finding a way to get extra flight decks into operation as soon as possible. A satisfactory answer was found in converting nine incomplete hulls of *Cleveland*-class light cruisers to *Independence*-class carriers.

To take the comparatively wide flight deck the narrow cruiser hull had to be bulged. Despite the cramped nature of these conversions they performed well in action, and most important of all they were ready when needed. They could only carry half the aircraft complement of other American carriers, but were a vital reinforcement at a critical time, and an intelligent and well-carried-out improvisation.

Although the *Independence* class originally included four 5-inch (127-mm) guns, these were later removed, and like the British vessels the American ships were left with a battery composed entirely of weapons of 40 mm or less.

At the end of the war another two light carriers, the *Saipan* class, were completed. These were based on the design of the *Baltimore*-class heavy cruisers, but the hulls were specially built, not converted, and were of slightly larger dimensions

INDEPENDENCE

Displacement 11,000 tons (11,176 tonnes) standard, 15,100 tons (15,342 tonnes) full load
Length 622 feet 6 inches (207 m 46 cm)
Beam 109 feet 3 inches (36 m 38 cm) over flight deck
Draught 20 feet (6 m 61 cm)
Machinery 4-shaft geared steam turbines, 100,000 shp = 32 knots
Armour belt: 1½ to 5 inches (38 to 127 mm). deck: 2 to 3 inches (51 to 76 mm)
Guns 4 × 5-inch (127-mm) AA, 26 × 40-mm AA, 40 × 20-mm AA
Aircraft 45 (2 catapults)
Launched 22 August 1942 by New York Shipbuilding Co., Camden

Above: An Independence-*class carrier under air attack. Right:* Independence *(CVL-22) in San Francisco Bay in July 1943. The light cruiser hull is clearly visible, with the four short funnels on the starboard side. Although small and cramped, these hurried conversions acted as useful stopgaps until the* Essex *class were available in quantity. Their high speed made them more useful than the escort carriers and so they remained with the fast carrier task forces in the Central Pacific until 1945. The drawing shows the original 5-inch (127-mm) guns forward and aft of the island and funnels; these guns were removed during the war*

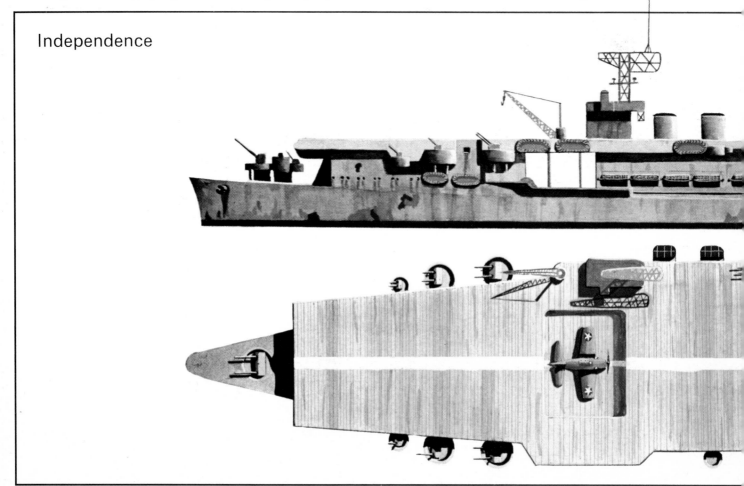

Independence

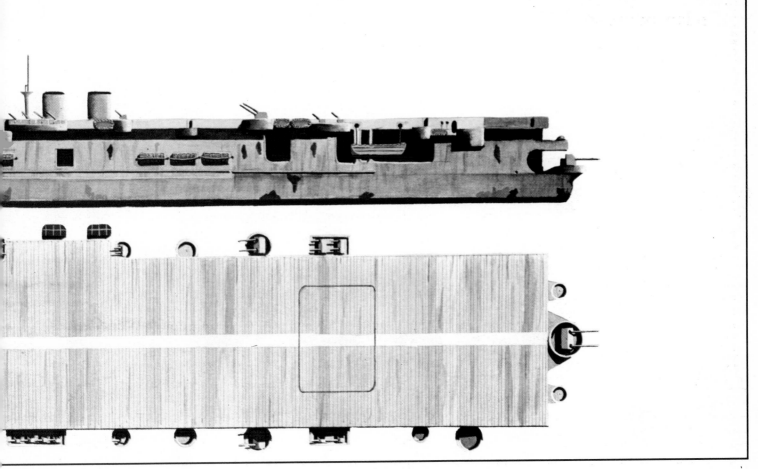

than the *Independence* class. They were not quite as cramped as the *Independence* class, but suffered from the same problems of space.

As we have already seen, the British converted the first escort carrier from a German merchantman. However, it was the Americans who built the vast majority of the large number of vessels of this type which served the Allied cause well. The first to appear from American yards were the six converted merchant ships of the *Long Island* class, one for the US Navy, another used by the USN mainly for training British pilots, and four for the Royal Navy. They were slightly more advanced versions of the *Audacity*, with one major improvement in the form of a lift and a hangar for the aircraft.

The 21 *Bogue*-class vessels were all conversions from merchant ships as well, but unlike the earlier motor vessels were all turbine-powered. They also had bigger hangars and an improved anti-aircraft armament. Ten of these useful vessels were retained by the USN, the other eleven lease-lent to Britain. So far all the conversions had been from dry cargo ships, but the US Navy had acquired four brand-new fast oil tankers which appeared to be suitable for conversion, and these became the *Sangamon* class. They had twin screws powered by geared turbines, and were about 60 feet (15.2 m) longer than the other conversions.

Because of this extra size they were the most impressive of the conversions, having extra aircraft capacity, two lifts and two catapults. Instead of exhausting up a funnel on the deck-edge, the boiler gases escaped through ducts at flight deck level aft. The usual two single 5-inch (127-mm) guns were carried aft, and a standard outfit of 40-mm and 20-mm guns, which grew in numbers as the war drew to its close.

The *Sangamon* class were highly successful, being equal in most respects except speed to the *Independence* class of light carriers. Like many of the other Pacific escort carriers they were used more for providing support to landing forces with bombers and fighters than for escorting convoys or carrying anti-submarine aircraft. The respect given to the *Sangamon* class is indicated by the fact that the last wartime escort carriers, the *Commencement Bay* class, were virtually updated copies, but few were in service before the war ended.

To return to the sequence of escort carrier classes, the first escort carriers built from the keel up, though of similar mercantile-type hulls to the conversions, were the 24 ships of the *Prince William* class, of which all except the name ship were transferred to the Royal Navy. All 50 ships of the *Casablanca* class, which had reciprocating steam engines instead of turbines, were kept by the USN. The numbers in which these ships were turned out are almost unbelievable, as are the building times. The chief yard making them finally got the construction time down to three and a half months.

Before leaving American carriers the two oddest should be mentioned. Very sensibly, much decklanding training was done in the safe environment of the Great Lakes, where the only two paddle aircraft carriers in the world were based. These were the converted sidewheel passenger steamers *Sable* and *Wolverine* and they did much useful work despite their bizarre appearance.

The escort carrier Sangamon *runs her trials before entering service in November 1942. Like other escort carriers she has a small bridge and light anti-aircraft guns in sponsons at the edge of the flight deck. The outline of the original fleet oiler hull can be seen below the flight deck, with the machinery aft. The protruding sponson under the flight deck aft is the starboard 5-inch (127-mm) gun position. The drawing below shows the wooden flight deck with its restricted area for landing, the deck-level ducts used in place of funnels to dispose of exhaust gases, and the two aircraft lifts which made this class particularly suitable for flying operations. This enabled them to be used as fleet carriers when they first entered service*

SANGAMON
Displacement 11,400 tons (11,583 tonnes) standard, 24,275 tons (24,664 tonnes) full load
Length 553 feet (168 m 54 cm)
Beam 114 feet 3 inches (34 m 81 cm) across flight deck
Draught 32 feet (9 m 75 cm) maximum
Machinery 2-shaft geared steam turbines, 13,500 shp = 18 knots
Armour none
Guns 2 × 5-inch (127-mm) AA, 8 × 40-mm AA, 12 × 20-mm AA
Aircraft 30 (2 catapults)
Launched 4 November 1939 (as *Esso Trenton*)

Sangamon

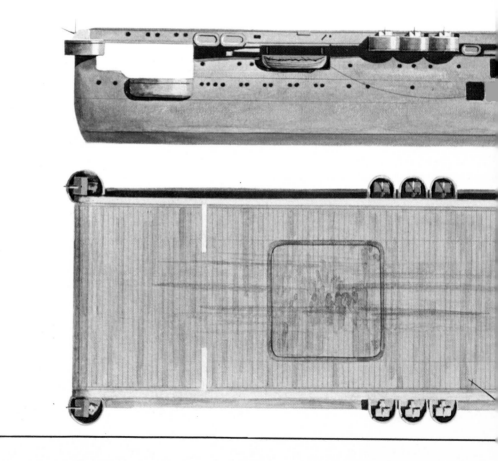

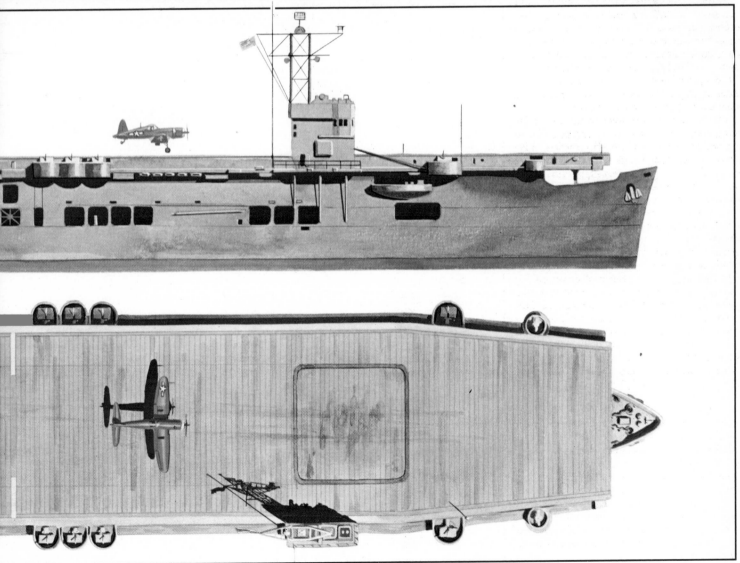

USA: Capital Ships

The Americans, like the British, Italians and Japanese, fought the war with a battleship force partly composed of heavily rebuilt older vessels and partly of new ships. Most of the time the old and the new vessels were used as heavy anti-aircraft escorts for the carriers and as shore-bombardment ships, rather than for their traditional purpose of fighting other ships. The only incident in the Pacific War in which numbers of battleships engaged each other in a surface action was the Battle of Surigao Strait, part of the enormous Battle of Leyte Gulf, and ironically it was the older American battleships which took part, the ones that were meant to stick to the job of shore bombardment. They won an overwhelming victory, mainly because of their use of radar, which had reversed the early Japanese superiority in night fighting.

The oldest American battleships in service during the war were the two ships of the *Wyoming* class. The name ship of the class had been partly disarmed before the war; she was being used as a training ship, like the British *Iron Duke*, and could no longer be considered as a member of the battleship fleet. Her sister, *Arkansas*, retained her twelve 12-inch (305-mm) guns, though she lost her secondary battery of 5-inch (127-mm). Equipped with a new and more powerful anti-aircraft armament of 3-inch (76-mm) and lighter guns, she gave good service throughout the war.

The next class of battleship, consisting of *New York* and *Texas*, were broadly similar to the *Wyoming* except in having ten 14-inch (356-mm) guns. As a result of a quarrel between the Navy Department and the American suppliers of turbines they were unusual in reverting to reciprocating engines for their propulsion. The result of this was that the suppliers lowered their turbine prices to a reasonable standard, and the ships themselves proved to have a reasonable performance despite their old-fashioned machinery. Both were altered like the *Arkansas* during the war, losing their antiquated casemate secondary armament for a better anti-aircraft outfit. The *Arkansas* had the elevation of her 12-inch (305-mm) guns increased for extra range, and similar alterations were made to these two ships' 14-inch (356-mm) turrets.

The US Navy had tended to favour heavy protection for all its battleships, preferring sturdy seaworthy ships with a good armament to faster ships with less armour. With the *Nevada* class (consisting of the name ship and the *Oklahoma*, which latter was sunk at Pearl Harbor) it took a decisive step forward in the technique of warship protection. This was the development of the method of armouring known as 'all or nothing', the logical principle that it was pointless to cover ships with medium or thin armour which could be penetrated by heavy shells, and might do more harm than good. Instead only the most vital points should be protected by armour, and that armour should be as thick as possible. These ships appeared at the beginning of the First World War, and their method of armouring was soon adopted by other powers. Like the previous class both ships had ten 14-inch (356-mm) guns, but these were disposed in two twin and two triple turrets, instead

of the five twin turrets of the earlier ships.

Nevada survived Pearl Harbor but was considerably rebuilt, having all the Second World War modifications of the earlier classes, and a new secondary battery of twin 5-inch (127-mm) dual-purpose guns added.

Of the two ships of the next battleship class, one, USS *Arizona*, was sunk at Pearl Harbor, where her wreck remains, but the other, *Pennsylvania*, had the usual wartime conversion like the *Nevada* with a new 5-inch (127-mm) turreted secondary battery. Basically enlarged versions of the earlier class, the *Pennsylvania* and her sister carried two more 14-inch (356-mm) guns by having all the guns in triple turrets; they also had slightly thicker armour, and improved underwater protection.

The one American battleship illustrated is one of a class of three older battleships less altered by reconstruction during the war, though only because they had been extensively rebuilt earlier. The reason for three ships in the class rather than the more usual two was that the United States Navy had just obtained a windfall of cash by selling off two old non-standard pre-dreadnoughts to the Greeks, the *Mississippi* and *Idaho*. As a result of this sale the two names were transferred to two new ships. The third was named after *New Mexico*, which had just attained statehood. The *New Mexico* class differed from their predecessors in having a clipper instead of a ram bow, increased protection and a new and more powerful mark of 14-inch (356-mm) gun. While the ships were building the casemated 5-inch (127-mm) guns were moved up a deck and placed on the forecastle deck, a much more sensible position as they were less likely to be affected by spray. *New Mexico* herself had an experimental form of machinery, turbo-electric propulsion, but this, though not unsatisfactory, was replaced during her rebuilding.

All three of the class were rebuilt in the early 1930s. The enormous lattice masts, hitherto the trade mark of all American battleships, were removed (most of the other older battleships did not lose theirs until after the beginning of the war). They were also reboilered and had a new and much larger bridge structure fitted. Aircraft catapults were added, and extra anti-aircraft guns.

The lack of a major Second World War modernization for these ships can be explained by their absence from Pearl Harbor when the Japanese struck. However, all three ships had powerful 40-mm and 20-mm anti-aircraft batteries added, *Idaho* being the only one to have her original 5-inch (127-mm) replaced by single turreted mounts. To compensate for the additional weight one of the catapults was removed.

These ships make an interesting contrast with the British *Queen Elizabeth* class, with a larger number of lighter guns, less speed but rather better protection. Though they did not play as spectacular a part in the war as their British equivalents they were still powerful and reliable ships.

The *New Mexico* class were completed towards the end of the First World War, and the first post-war ships were the *California* and *Tennessee*.

They were powered by the same type of turbo-electric installation as had been fitted to the *New Mexico*, and were otherwise like their predecessors, but different in appearance as they had twin funnels. Both were damaged at Pearl Harbor, and after this a major rebuilding changed their appearance completely. The twin funnels became one, and the 14-inch (356-mm) guns were the only part of the armament which was not changed.

The *Tennessee* class were followed by the four ships of the *Colorado* class, in which twin 16-inch (406-mm) turrets were substituted for the triple 14-inch (356-mm) of the earlier ships. One ship of the class was never completed because of the Washington Naval Treaty; the other three were rebuilt to a varying extent during the Second World War.

The Washington Treaty caused an entire class of six 16-inch (406-mm)-gunned battleships to be cancelled and scrapped on the slipways. Another class of six ships was also never completed, America's first and last attempt to

MISSISSIPPI

Displacement 33,000 tons (33,529 tonnes) standard, 35,100 tons (35,743 tonnes) full load
Length 624 feet (190 m 19 cm)
Beam 106 feet 3 inches (35 m 38 cm) (over bulges)
Draught 29 feet 3 inches (8 m 91 cm)
Machinery 4-shaft geared steam turbines, 40,000 shp = 21½ knots
Armour belt: 8 to 14 inches (203 to 356 mm). deck: 4 to 6 inches (102 to 152 mm). turrets: 8 to 18 inches (203 to 456 mm)
Guns 12 × 14-inch (356-mm), 12 × 5-inch (127-mm), 8 × 5-inch (127-mm) AA, 3 × 4-barrelled 1.1-inch (28-mm) AA mountings
Torpedo Tubes none
Launched 25 January 1917 by Newport News Shipbuilding Co.

Mississippi (BB-41) *in 1934, just after modernization; she has catapults on 'X' turret and on the stern*

Mississippi

build battle-cruisers. This aberration was fortunately brought to an end by the treaty, though two of the hulls were put to a more sensible use, and became the aircraft carriers *Lexington* and *Saratoga*.

By the time America launched her next class of two battleships, the *North Carolina* group, the Second World War had broken out, though America was not yet involved. They were not quite as fast as most of their foreign contemporaries, but their 28 knots was a great advance on the 21 knots of their predecessors. Their protection was sound, while the main armament of the three triple 16-inch (406-mm) turrets and secondary dual-purpose twin 5-inch (127-mm) turrets were impressive. It was a pity that the Americans' choice for a light anti-aircraft weapon was the unreliable 1.1-inch (30-mm) gun, but fortunately by the time of Pearl Harbor these weapons were already being replaced by license-built Bofors and Oerlikons.

The four ships of the *South Dakota* class followed the *North Carolinas*, of which they were

shorter and broader versions. They were excellent vessels with particularly good underwater protection. Because of their extra beam they needed more power to reach the same speed, but all in all they epitomized the virtues of the American approach to battleship design, and justified their promise in action.

After the dumpy, pyramidical single-funnelled *South Dakota* class came the handsome and impressive *Iowa* class with their two large funnels. Six ships were ordered but only four were completed by 1945. With the British *Vanguard* they represent the last generation of battleships. Yet compared with both the British ship and preceeding American classes they seem to be rather poor bargains. Their armament, except in light anti-aircraft guns, was no better than the *South Dakotas*'. To obtain the extremely high theoretical speed of 33 knots they had to devote an enormous amount of space to machinery, and also had to be nearly 200 feet (60.9 m) longer than the *South Dakota* ships. Yet in bad weather the smaller British *Vanguard*, theoretically con-

Above: The massive foremast and control top of a battleship blaze at Pearl Harbor.

siderably slower, could easily keep pace with the American giants at a speed of 29.5 knots because of her more seaworthy hull. The British ship had thicker armour, particularly on the decks, where it was most needed, than any American capital ship, and this protection was at least as well disposed. Because of the *Iowa* ships' length their protection was worse than that of the *South Dakota* class and much thinner than most published figures indicate. The story that a greatly improved type of armour was used was just an attempt to conceal this comparative weakness. This is not to say that these American ships were poor designs; they were useful and formidable fighting ships, and certainly a better executed design than that of the *Yamato* class, but they do not compare in technical excellence to the *Vanguard* or the *South Dakota* vessels, despite the first ship's old guns or the latters' lack of speed.

USA: Submarines

Few realize that the American submarine arm waged the only completely successful submarine offensive – that US submarines succeeded where the U-boats failed – in completely strangling the lifelines of a maritime nation. If the atomic bomb had never been dropped, Japan was already doomed to defeat because the ships which brought essential supplies had nearly all been sunk. Though aircraft, surface ships, mines (many laid by American submarines) and British and Dutch submarines had all played their part, the lion's share of sunken Japanese tonnage was claimed by US submarines.

Much of this success was due to the incredible failure of Japan for most of the war to take adequate precautions to defend her commerce. This was a blunder only matched by an equally unbelievable failure to use the large and well-equipped Japanese submarine force against American and Allied shipping, which provided the essential logistic support for the war in the Pacific. Much of the success, however, was due to the high quality of American submarines and submariners; despite the Japanese doctrine of concentrating their submarines on the task of sinking enemy warships, it was the Americans who achieved a much higher total of enemy ships sunk by submarines. The American success in undersea warfare is even more creditable when it is realized that American submarine torpedoes (like German) had a shocking record of malfunctions in the early months of the war. It took nearly a year of the Pacific war before the Americans had an adequately lethal and reliable weapon for their boats.

Even more than the carriers and destroyers the American wartime standard submarine

design is an example of the process of producing a wide variety of small experimental classes or 'one-off' designs in peacetime, trying them thoroughly over a long period of time, and then combining all the best features in a standard design which can be mass-produced in a hurry.

At the outbreak of the war America had a number of submarines built during or just after the previous conflict. These were the 'O', 'R' and 'S' classes, which were not much use for anything except training; some of the 'R' and 'S' classes were transferred to the Royal Navy for this purpose. One of their chief disadvantages was that they had a totally inadequate range for the Pacific, and it is not surprising that the Americans were so impressed by the large German 'U-cruisers' of the First World War and that they proceeded to adapt the basic design to their own purposes. As the Japanese did exactly the same, it is interesting to see the differences and similarities between the submarines evolved by both nations from this common starting point.

Although the earlier interwar American submarines were initially given numbers prefixed by the letter 'V' it is simpler to refer to them by the fish names they later received. The *Barracuda* and her two sisters were, like most of their successors, large boats, concentrating on range and surface speed rather than the fast diving and underwater performance which was beginning to assume greater importance for most European submarines.

The next submarine built in America was the ·huge *Argonaut*, fitted with two 6-inch (152-mm) guns and designed as a minelayer. She was followed by two similar boats which were not, however, fitted for minelaying, and carried more

torpedo tubes instead. These, like all the early big American submarines, were powered by the same type of German diesel that had been used by the U-cruisers. Next came the *Dolphin*, a not entirely successful attempt to achieve the best qualities of these big boats on a smaller displacement. The following boats, the *Cachalot* class, reduced size still further, but were rather more successful. Their hulls were welded, a technique of construction in which the Americans were well in the lead, and which gave stronger hulls for less weight.

This class had been a little small but had still shown that 1,500-ton (1,524-tonne) submarines could operate successfully in the Pacific. Their successors, the *Porpoise* class, were slightly larger and introduced one of the most vital components of the future standard wartime submarine. This was a good, reliable, light and powerful home-produced diesel. In fact, as the result of a naval design competition, no fewer than four firms developed successful engines of this kind.

The *Salmon* and *Sargo* classes slightly in-

RAY
Displacement 1,526 tons (1,550 tonnes) surfaced, 2,424 tons (2,462 tonnes) submerged
Length 311 feet 9 inches (95 m)
Beam 27 feet 3 inches (8 m 32 cm)
Draught 15 feet 3 inches (4 m 66 cm)
Machinery surfaced: 2-shaft diesel-electric, 5,400 bhp = 20¼ knots; submerged: 2-shaft electric, 2,740 shp = 8¾ knots
Guns 1 × 3-inch (76-mm) AA, 1 × 40-mm AA
Torpedo Tubes 10 × 21-inch (530-mm)
Launched 28 February 1943 by Manitowoc Shipbuilding Co.

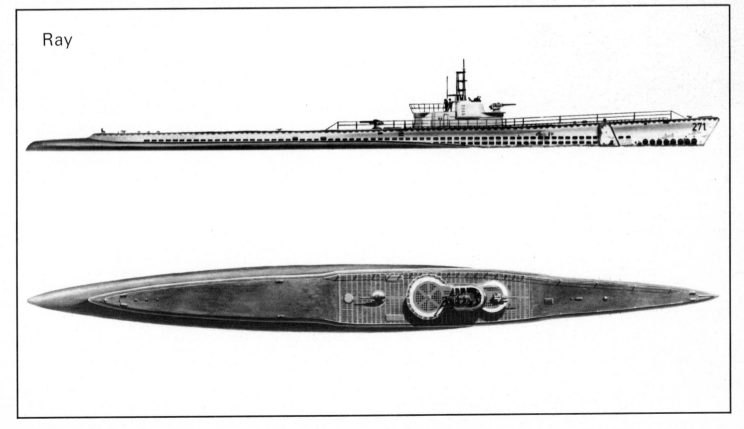

Ray

creased surface speed and torpedo outfit, and had a somewhat complex drive arrangement on the surface, using both geared diesel and diesel-electric drive, except for four which had diesel electric drive. In contrast the next group of classes, the *Tambor* and *Gar* vessels, used direct drive, but these were an aberration from the main line of American submarine development.

The *Gato* class, of which *Ray* was one, had been designed, and the first boats ordered, before America joined the war. The design was adopted as standard, and over 200 were finally ordered. These had the welded hulls, excellent diesels and large torpedo armaments developed in preceeding classes, with the range and high surface speed essential for success in the Pacific. They also had more attention paid to habitability and crew comfort than the submarines of any other nation. This was, admittedly, not saying much, as all submarines, until the advent of nuclear boats well after the end of the war, were notoriously cramped and uncomfortable. None-

theless the greater comfort of American crews did pay dividends by permitting longer patrols. These big boats did not dive as fast or manoeuvre as well underwater as the smaller German or British boats, but they had less need of these evasive tactics. Japanese anti-submarine forces were not as numerous or technically sophisticated as those of the Germans or the Italians (who had quite a good record in anti-submarine operations).

Gun armament varied quite considerably.

The main weapon varied between 3-inch (76-mm), 4-inch (102-mm), or 5-inch (127-mm) calibre, although the latter was the most common type. One or more 20-mm guns were often supplemented by 40-mm ones. Radar gradually became one of the most important parts of the submarine's equipment, and a large proportion of 'kills' were obtained by intelligent use of this device. The later units of the class, from the *Balao* on, were given thicker hulls to enable them to dive deeper, while a new class, the *Tench* group, still changed the basic design very little, as there was no need to alter a type which had proved so ideal for its purpose. After the war new ideas about submarine design came into favour, and many ships of these classes were altered to the new 'Guppy' formula, streamlined for underwater speed and with more powerful electric motors and more battery power. However, the submarines of the *Gato* and *Tench* classes had already done their basic job, the defeat of Japan, very adequately.

Many older submarines and less successful experimental types were used in the humble but essential job of training the enormous numbers of men required for the wartime submarine programmes. Although built in 1933, the Cuttlefish *(SS-171) and her sister* Cachalot *(SS-170) were soon relegated to training duties.* Cuttlefish *is armed with a 3-inch (76-mm) gun abaft the conning tower and a 20-mm anti-aircraft gun, whereas her sister carried the 3-inch gun forward*

USA: Destroyers

Johnston

American destroyers had two great advantages. One was their standard gun armament which consisted of the superb 5-inch (127-mm) weapon. This was the best destroyer gun of the war, equally effective in low-angle and high-angle fire; it fired a respectable weight of shell at a good rate, and was easy to man. The second advantage was that by the time America entered the Second World War she had developed a reliable high-pressure steam plant, which gave economy and performance without the frequent breakdowns that German ships suffered. As a result the standard wartime destroyers were probably the best large destroyers in the world, besides being the most numerous. Thanks to the excellent fleet train, the Americans could rely on refuelling at sea rather than excessively large bunkers to cope with the immense distances of the Pacific, but even so their ships had an impressive radius of action.

Part of this excellence was possibly due to the fact that the Americans started their interwar destroyer development with an inadequate design, and built a whole range of types in the 1930s which gave them a chance to experiment with different arrangements of size and characteristics. Once war came they could standardize on one excellent type and mass-produce it. This was in direct contrast to the British, who had begun with excellent design and had by and large stuck to it in the interwar years, but then did far more chopping and changing of their standard design during the war.

For years after the First World War the Americans built no destroyers. They had over-produced enormous numbers of their standard 'four stacker' design, which compared unfavourably with the contemporary British 'V & W' classes. The disposition of their gun armament, and more especially of their torpedo tubes, was very clumsy and they were exceedingly narrow. Their best features were their good speed and their flush-decked hull, a structurally sounder arrangement than the raised forecastle deck of most other destroyers. Despite their disadvantages the USN had many of these destroyers left at a time when want of fast escort ships was the most pressing need, and both the fifty 'least-lent' to the Royal Navy and those retained by the USN performed valuable work. They underwent many conversions, to long-range escorts, fast transports, destroyer minesweepers, and seaplane tenders.

It was not until 1932 that America laid down any more destroyers, the *Farragut* class, which were not unlike the British interwar flotilla leaders, with five 5-inch (127-mm) guns and a raised forecastle, but possessing slightly greater size and bunker capacity. Like their British contemporaries these vessels appeared a little small to deal with the super-destroyers being built by France and Italy, and more especially the influential Japanese *Fubuki* class. Like the British 'Tribals' which were also inspired by those Japanese ships, the *Porter* class of flotilla leaders had eight guns in twin turrets, but their anti-aircraft and torpedo armaments were both heavier than the British ships, and as a result these vessels were somewhat overloaded.

The *Mahan* class reverted to the *Farragut* type, except in having three sets of torpedo tubes, the after ones of which were mounted abreast of each other, not an ideal arrangement as each set could only be fired on one side. These destroyers had their guns in a combination of shielded and open mounts, but a modified version of the class mounted the prototype single 5-inch (127-mm) enclosed turret which was to prove such a success. Standard wartime modifications to all ships included the removal of the fifth, mid-ships-mounted 5-inch (127-mm) and the substitution of light anti-aircraft weapons.

The *Gridley* and *Benham* classes increased the torpedo armament further by having two pairs of quadruple tubes. They only carried four 5-inch (127-mm) guns, and were notable for their single funnels. The *Porter* class of flotilla leaders were followed by the five ships of the *Somers* and *Sampson* classes. These had one less twin turret than their predecessors, but carried an extra set of torpedo tubes, and also had a rather ugly single funnel.

With the *Sims* class the USN reverted to a torpedo armament of two sets of quadruple tubes; originally three were to have been fitted, but stability was not adequate. Unlike the earlier classes the aftermost gun as well as the forward ones had a turret, but the other gun aft was still in an open mount.

The next two classes, *Benson* and *Livermore*, returned to two funnels, as they had adopted 'unit' machinery with alternate engine and boiler rooms, which increased the length slightly but made for a better chance of surviving major machinery damage as all the boilers were unlikely to be put out of action at the same time. The large *Bristol* group ordered in 1940 were very similar, except in having four instead of five 5-inch (127-mm) guns, and extra light anti-aircraft guns instead. All the gun mounts were turreted.

JOHNSTON

Displacement 2,050 tons (2,082 tonnes) standard, 2,940 tons (2,987 tonnes) full load
Length 376 feet (114 m 60 cm)
Beam 39 feet 9 inches (12 m 11 cm)
Draught 13 feet 9 inches (4 m 19 cm)
Machinery 2-shaft geared steam turbines, 60,000 shp = 37 knots
Armour none
Guns 5 × 5-inch (127-mm) DP, 10 × 40-mm AA 7 × 20-mm AA
Torpedo Tubes 10 × 21-inch (530-mm)
Launched 25 March 1943 by Seattle-Tacoma Shipbuilding Co.

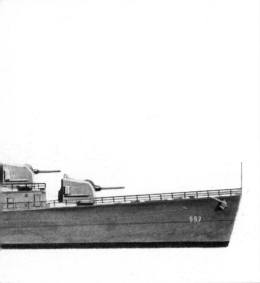

Above left: A typical 'flush-decker' destroyer, Crowninshield (DD-134), a survivor from World War I which went to the Royal Navy as HMS Chelsea in 1940 and to the Soviet Navy as Derzki in 1944. Left: The illustration shows the Fletcher-class destroyer Johnston (DD-557), which was sunk at the Battle of Leyte Gulf gallantly defending escort carriers from attack by Japanese battleships. These destroyers were built in large numbers as the standard US Navy design of the war, and they proved highly successful

Allen M Sumner

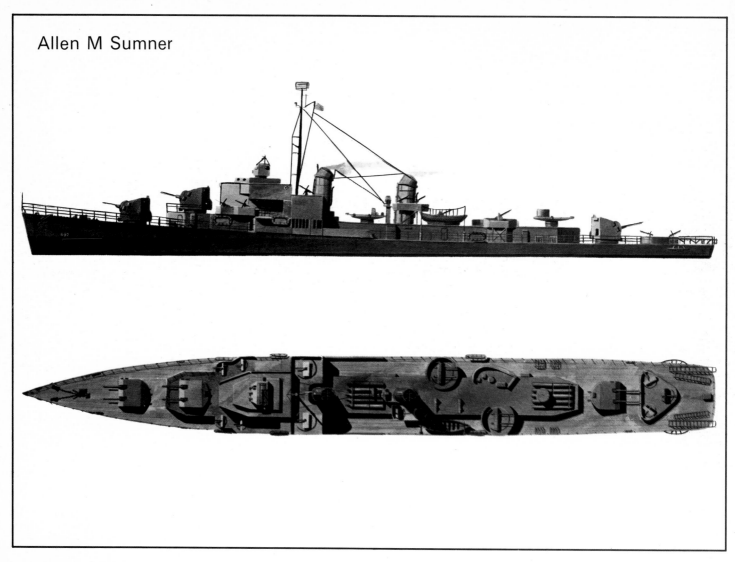

The standard wartime destroyer design was the *Fletcher* class, of which 24 had been ordered before Pearl Harbor; immediately after that another hundred were contracted for, though not all were completed. This excellent design was an enlarged *Bristol* to take extra anti-aircraft weapons, while carrying five 5-inch (127-mm) guns and ten torpedo tubes. The basic difference from the *Fletcher* class's predecessors was that the hulls were flush-decked, a throwback to the best feature of the 'four stackers'; they also introduced double-reduction geared turbines to give extra economy.

Johnston was one of these fine ships. It will be noticed from her drawing how the American designers were not afraid to place the torpedo tubes high in the ship. They made use of bottom ballast when necessary to counterbalance such high-mounted weights, a step which was anathema to most foreign naval architects and avoided whenever possible. Perhaps the best feature of these ships as compared to the British standard destroyers before the 'Battle' class was that they were large enough to carry an impressive battery of 20-mm and 40-mm guns, very necessary in the Pacific and other theatres of war. Once again the Americans had produced a workmanlike design which did not exaggerate any one characteristic at the expense of others, but instead was a well-balanced and battleworthy type of destroyer.

Three of the class had the extraordinary installation of an aircraft catapult and seaplane in place of the torpedo tubes and one turret. This idea was a bit of a non-starter, as destroyers were too small to operate an aircraft adequately, and in any case there were enough spotting aircraft available in other more suitable vessels.

The *Allen M Sumner* class were adaptations of the *Fletcher* class to take three twin turrets. This turret had already proved its usefulness in larger ships, and the only major alteration necessary to these destroyers was a slight increase in beam. Both torpedo tubes and the anti-aircraft guns had to be redistributed, but otherwise these ships retained the pattern of their predecessors, powerful and well-equipped fighting ships. The only major differences within the class was that one group were built as fast minelayers, with all the torpedo tubes removed and an extra quadruple 40-mm mounting added. A later modification to many of the other members of the class was the substitution of similar 40-mm Bofors mounts for the after bank of torpedo tubes. Like their predecessors the ships of this class were built in large numbers, as were those of the final wartime destroyer class. This was the *Gearing* group, whose only new feature was an extra 14 foot (4.3 m)-long section inserted in the hull.

Both *Gearing* and *Sumner* ships were to be the mainstay of the destroyer force of the USN for

Above: The Allen M. Sumner (DD-692) *was the first of an improved* Fletcher *design put in hand in 1942. The only important differences were a longer hull to allow more fuel and twin 5-inch (127-mm) guns in place of the single mountings. The* Sumner *class were a mainstay of the US Navy's postwar destroyer force*

ALLEN M SUMNER

Displacement 2,200 tons (2,235 tonnes) standard, 3,515 tons (3,571 tonnes) full load
Length 376 feet 6 inches (114 m 75 cm)
Beam 40 feet (12 m 19 cm)
Draught 15 feet 9 inches (4 m 80 cm)
Machinery 2-shaft geared steam turbines, 60,000 shp = 34 knots
Armour none
Guns 6 × 5-inch (127-mm) DP, 12 × 40-mm AA, 8 × 20-mm AA
Torpedo Tubes 10 × 21-inch (530-mm)
Launched 15 December 1943 by Federal Shipbuilding Co., Kearny

many years after the war. Eventually some of them were modernized and rebuilt, with helicopter facilities in some cases, and with new weapons and electronic equipment. Only now are they finally going out of service. having served long and valiantly in various guises, just as their four-funnelled First World War predecessors.